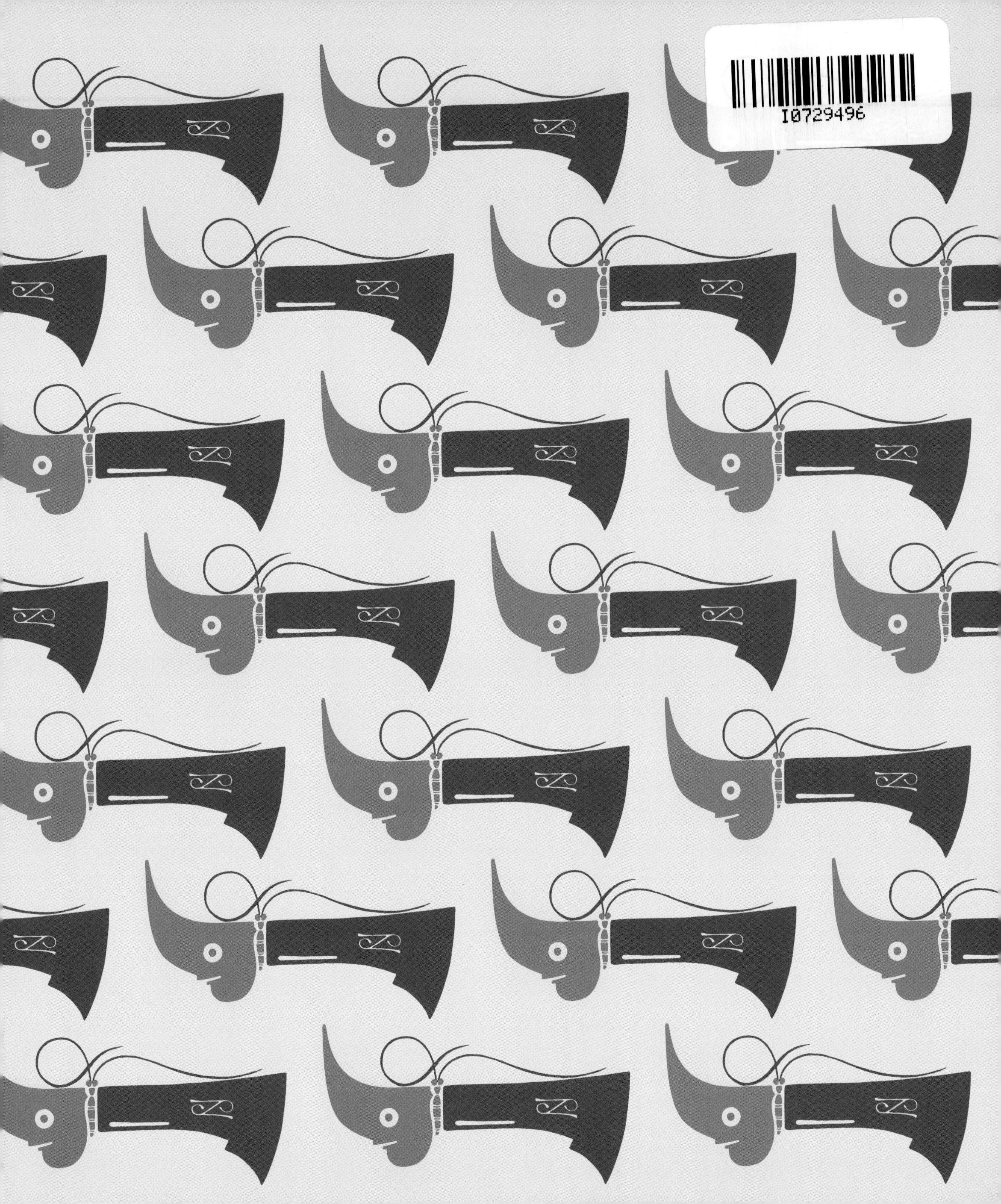

INNER
PORTRAITS

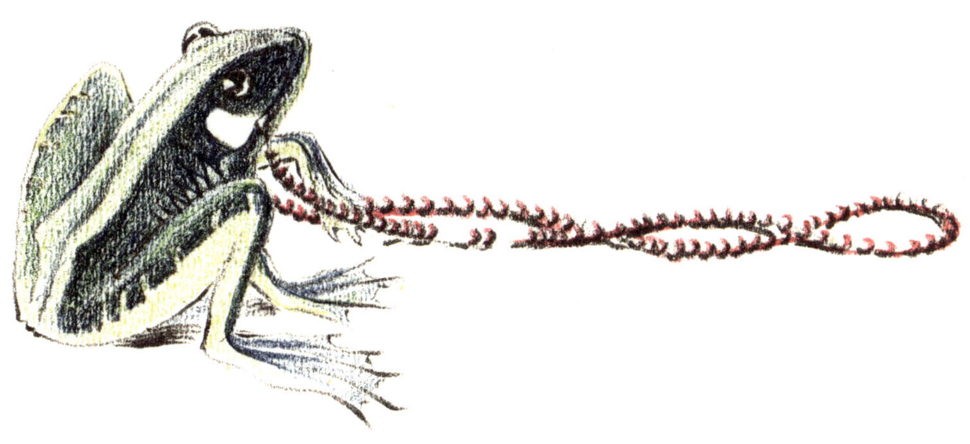

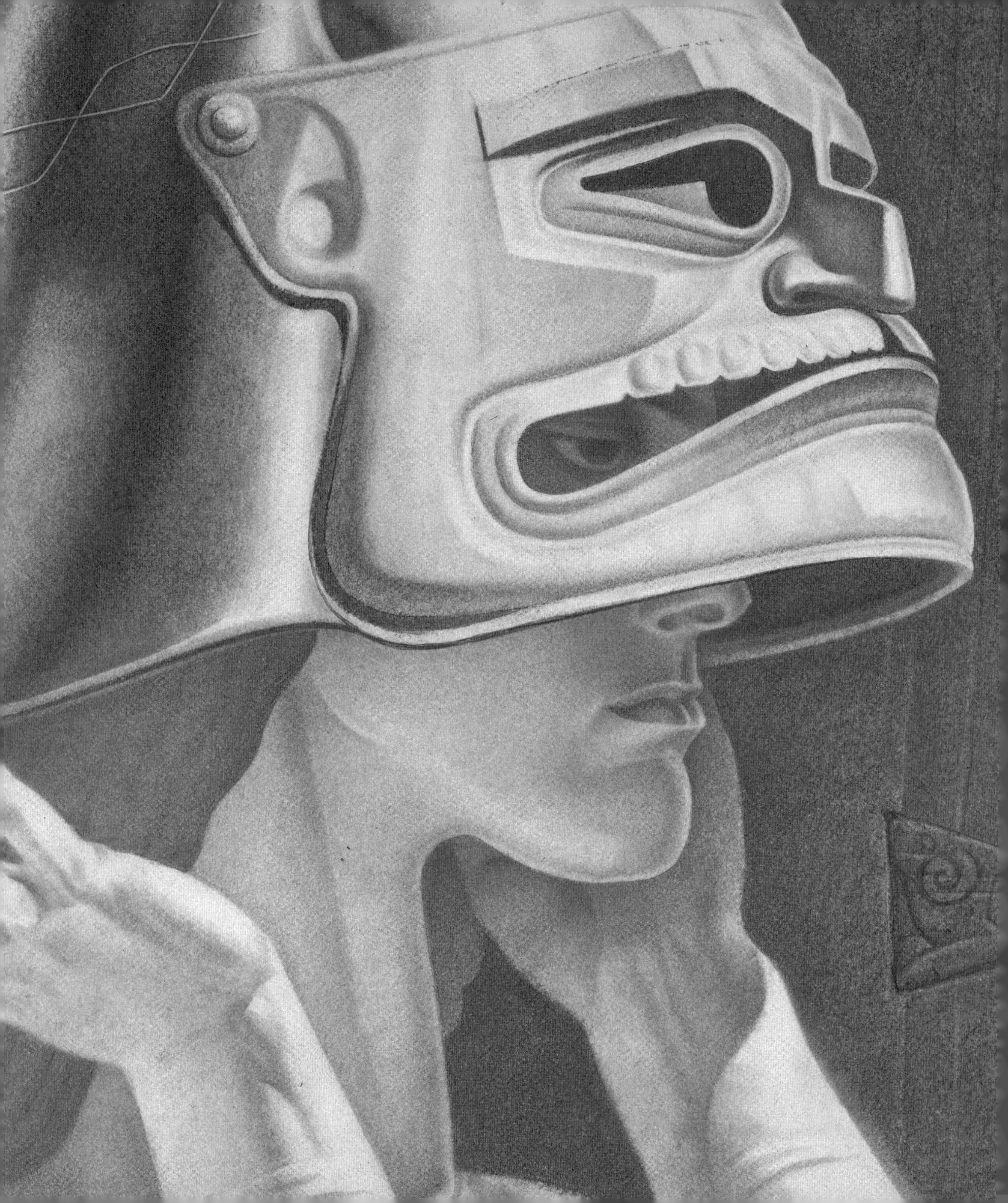

INNER PORTRAITS by SZUKALSKI

LAST GASP

SAN FRANCISCO

Last Gasp, 777 Florida Street, San Francisco, CA 94110 | *www.lastgasp.com*

Cover and Book Design by Piet Schreuders, Amsterdam
Edited by Glenn Bray and Lena Zwalve
Scans by Glenn Bray
Special thanks to photographers Bill Debley and Nick Springett

Third edition, newly revised and expanded. Second printing.
ISBN 13: 978-0-86719-879-9

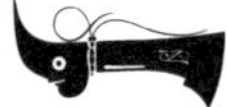 **WHIM-AXE** – On the endpapers is the composite pictogram of a butterfly and an axe – the butterfly for the restlessly fluttering, fleeting intangible quality of thoughtful Inspiration, and the axe for the bringing of Inspiration down to earth to the eaters of bread through shaping into touchable form which we call Art.

Official online source of all things Szukalski:
Archives Szukalski | *szukalski.com*

Art prints by Szukalski:
Varnish Fine Art Shop | *varnishfineartshop.bigcartel.com*

Szukalski bronzes foundry:
Decker Studios Fine Arts Foundry
Sanford Decker: *sdfinearts@gmail.com*

PRINTED IN SOUTH KOREA

Preface

When I came to see Szukalski's work for the first time, in 1989, it was a revelation to me. The imagination of light and shadow in the works seems to invoke the third dimension in order to then surpass it, thus revealing the symbolic formulation of what we call character and type.

This, by the power of his genius, makes Szukalski's work (not only his portraits) stand up overwhelmingly next to that of the greatest masters of *all* styles and cultures.

To know that the old master's hand has come to this planet, into this desolate humanity, once again makes an artist glad who had studied the great works of the masters of the past and strives to match their trace.

Szukalski's work should be celebrated, his philosophy studied—his lesson has to be received, especially by the new generation, in order to set the vague visions they sometimes have, on a solid rock of eternal information.

This book shall serve as a guide to the depth of Szukalski's message.

– Prof. Ernst Fuchs

Vienna, Austria, July 30, 1999

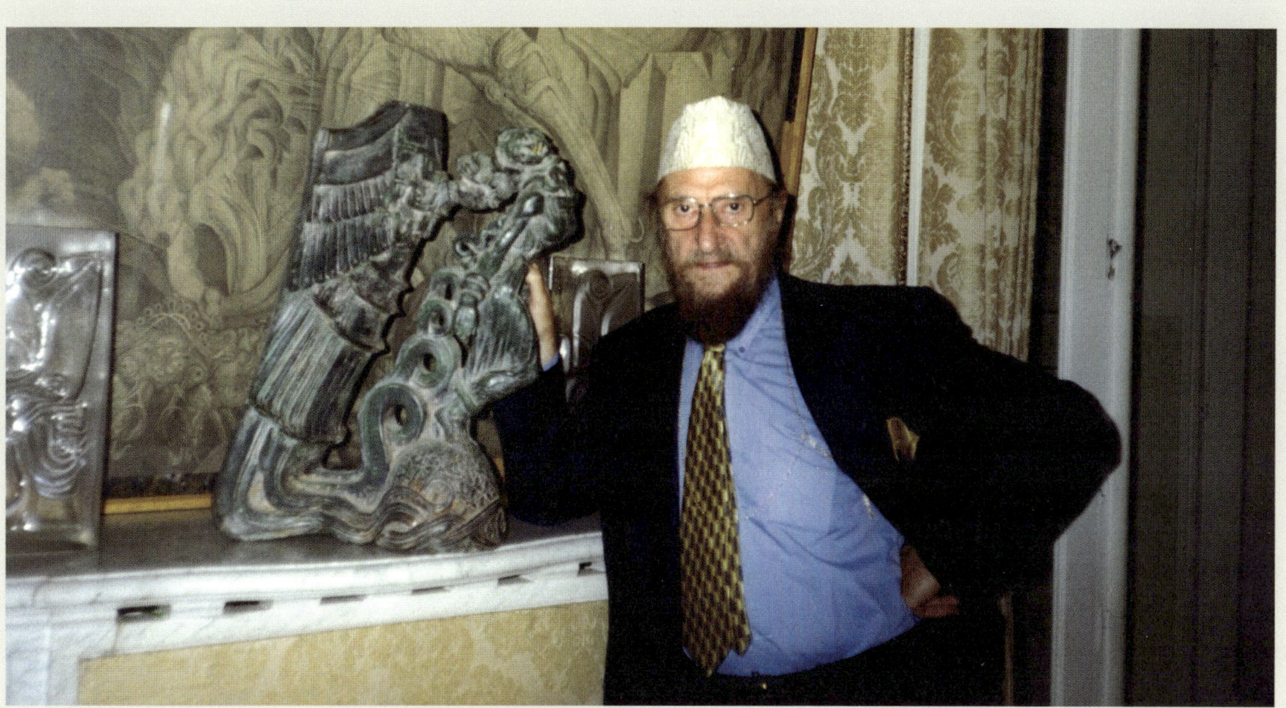

ERNST FUCHS WITH SZUKALSKI'S "MARIANNE" STATUE
1999

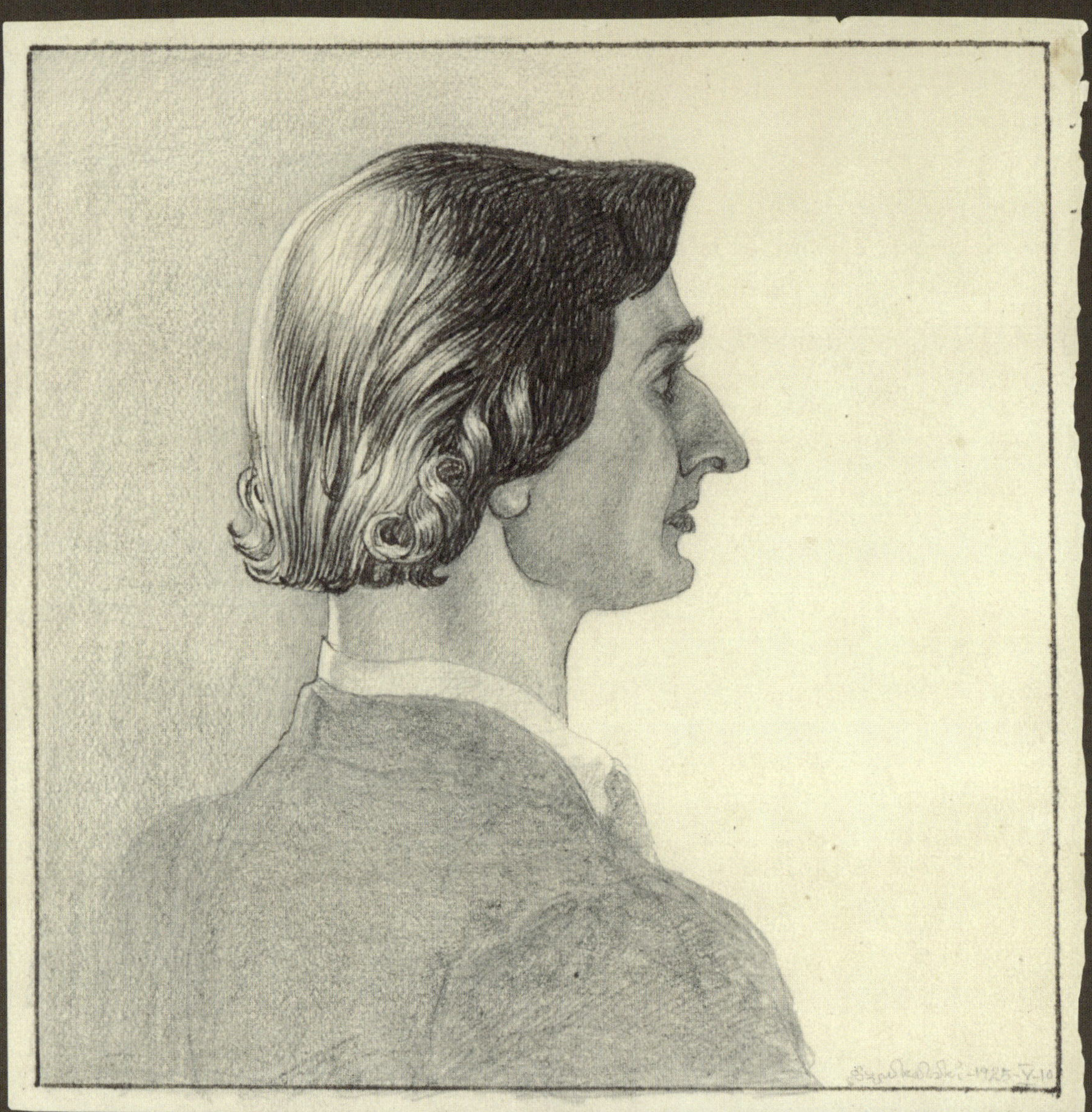

SELF-PORTRAIT
1925

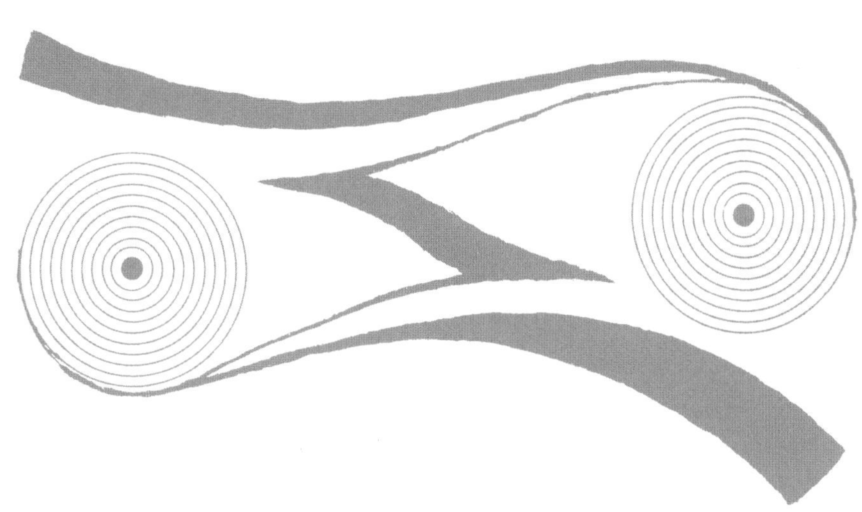

Deceive or Reveal

■ ■ ■

Napoleon, who came from the Isle of Corsica, was a little man and, like many Italian people, inclined to dimply chubbiness. No doubt, he suffered from an inferiority complex, which is indicated in the fact that at an early age he entered the army, so to gain some masculinity.

From the beginning as a leader of the French Revolution, till becoming Emperor, Bonaparte told painters, like the master David, that great heroes should never be painted as they are, but greatly idealized, for after their death no one would know their likeness anyway, so why not make them demi-gods, and the world would believe only the paintings, not handed-down verbal descriptions.

For the opposite reason we have political cartoons, so to sharply focus our observations and show the essence of a personality. A politician is basically a parasite who, by deception, aims to get to the top of possibilities. The layman cannot fathom the hidden personality behind the silken speech and honeyed voice, but the finely trained eye of the artist cannot only interpret the likeness but, by means of stylized physiognomy, intensify the real personality.

Each person has facial lines, left there from frequent resorting to them. These are the lines of laughter, of anger, of cynicism, wistfulness, greed, generosity, and many mixed expressions. The most recurrent mood leaves the deepest marks. Portraits painted or sculpted just like the person, are bad Art. They are merely examples of photographic taxidermy that should be repro-

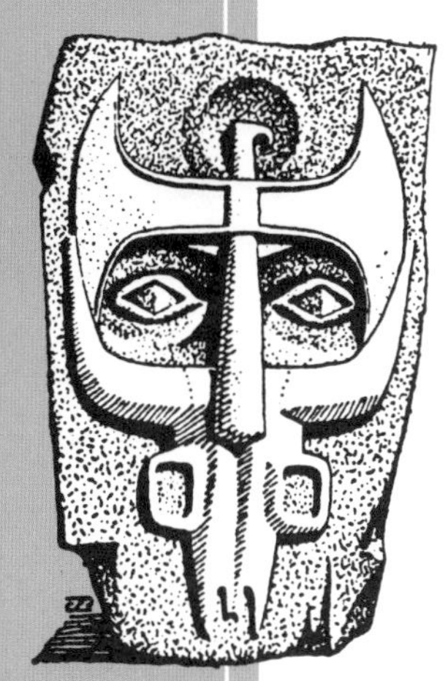

duced in the Sears Catalog. We do not make portraits of people for their contemporaries, but for their descendants, and they ought to be INTERPRETED, that is, certain marks should be omitted to bring out other, more delicate marks that reveal the inner person, not misrepresent him or her. The portrait of a Pope by Titian is a testimony for truthful revelation in Art. By "reading" the Pope's hyena carcassgleaning eyes, the painter penetrated the hypocritical politician who owned most of the whorehouses in Rome.

In the portraits I make, I attempt to bring forth the two most contradictory but dominant features I "see," despite the obvious put-on garnishings of amiability. Although I exaggerate the facial proportions, the likeness nevertheless makes it… legitimate. It is the intangible that is the likeness of the SPIRIT of the person immortalized. The best moment in canvas or clay, is when the sitter is caught lost in thought, all to himself, oblivious to the artist. That is precisely the moment of TRUTH, as if undressing alone before you go to sleep, when besides the clothes you shed, you undress to the marrow of your shinbones; you are even without your personal shadow since the candle has been blown out. Now! There is your likeness, undeniable, but you cannot be seen.

Stanislav Szukalski
(1893–1987)

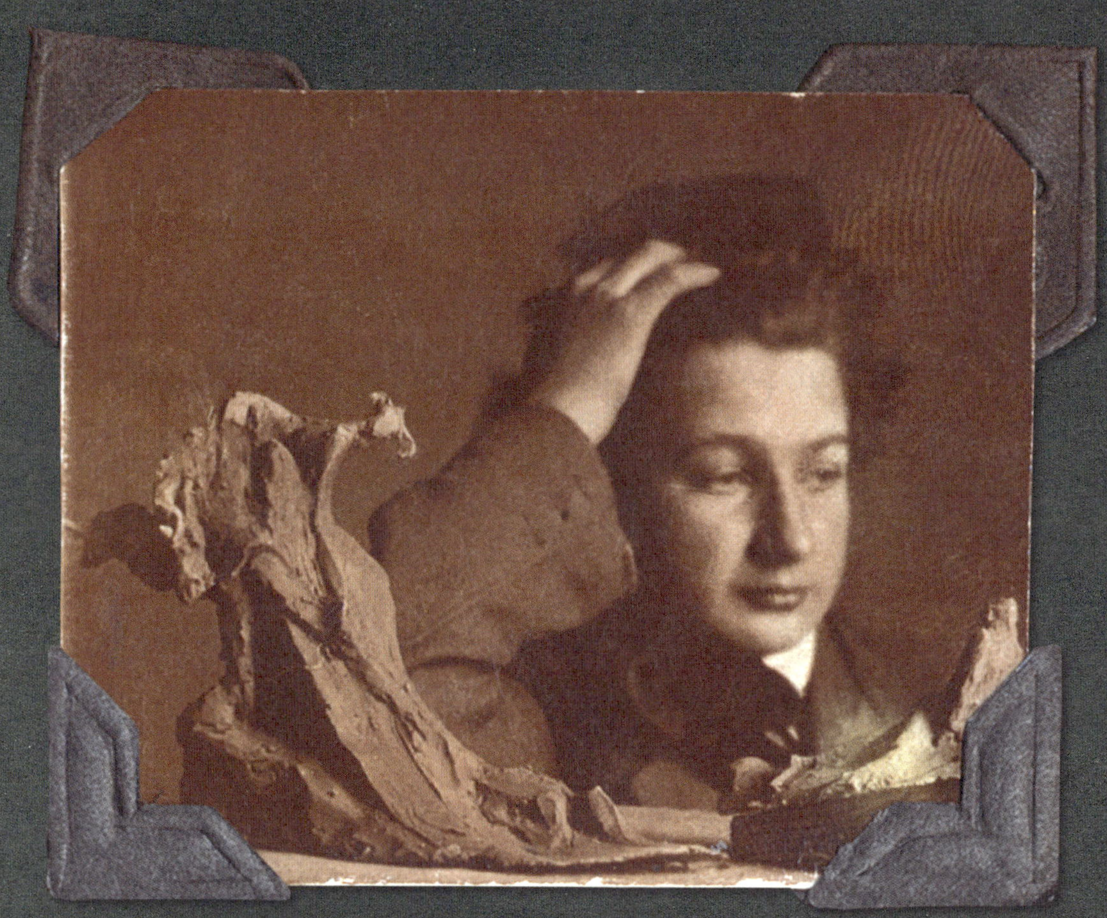

YOUNG STASIU
Circa 1905

Self-Portrait

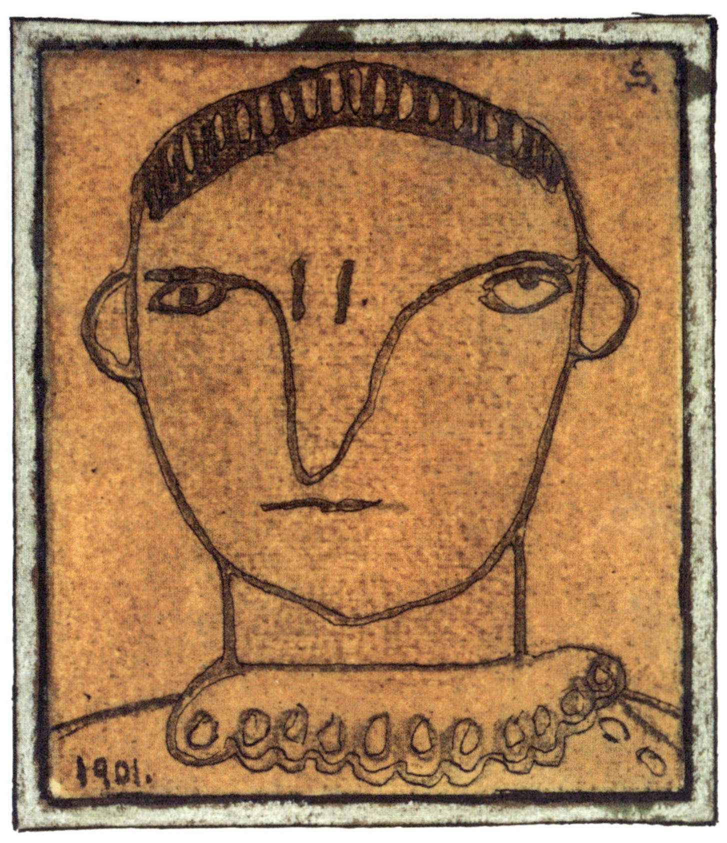

Drawing (actual size 3″ high)

Woman Without Eyes

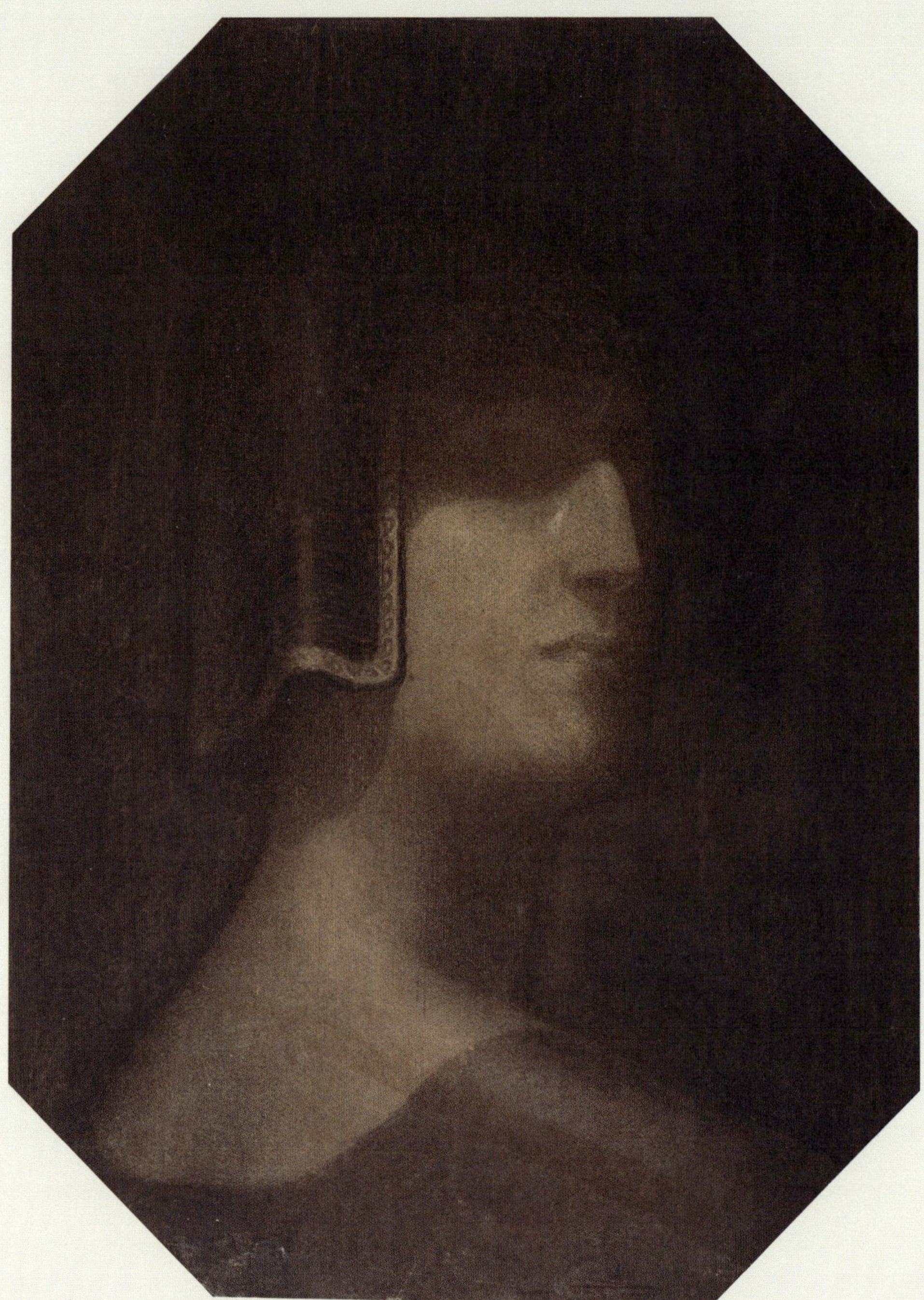

12

Head of an Old Man

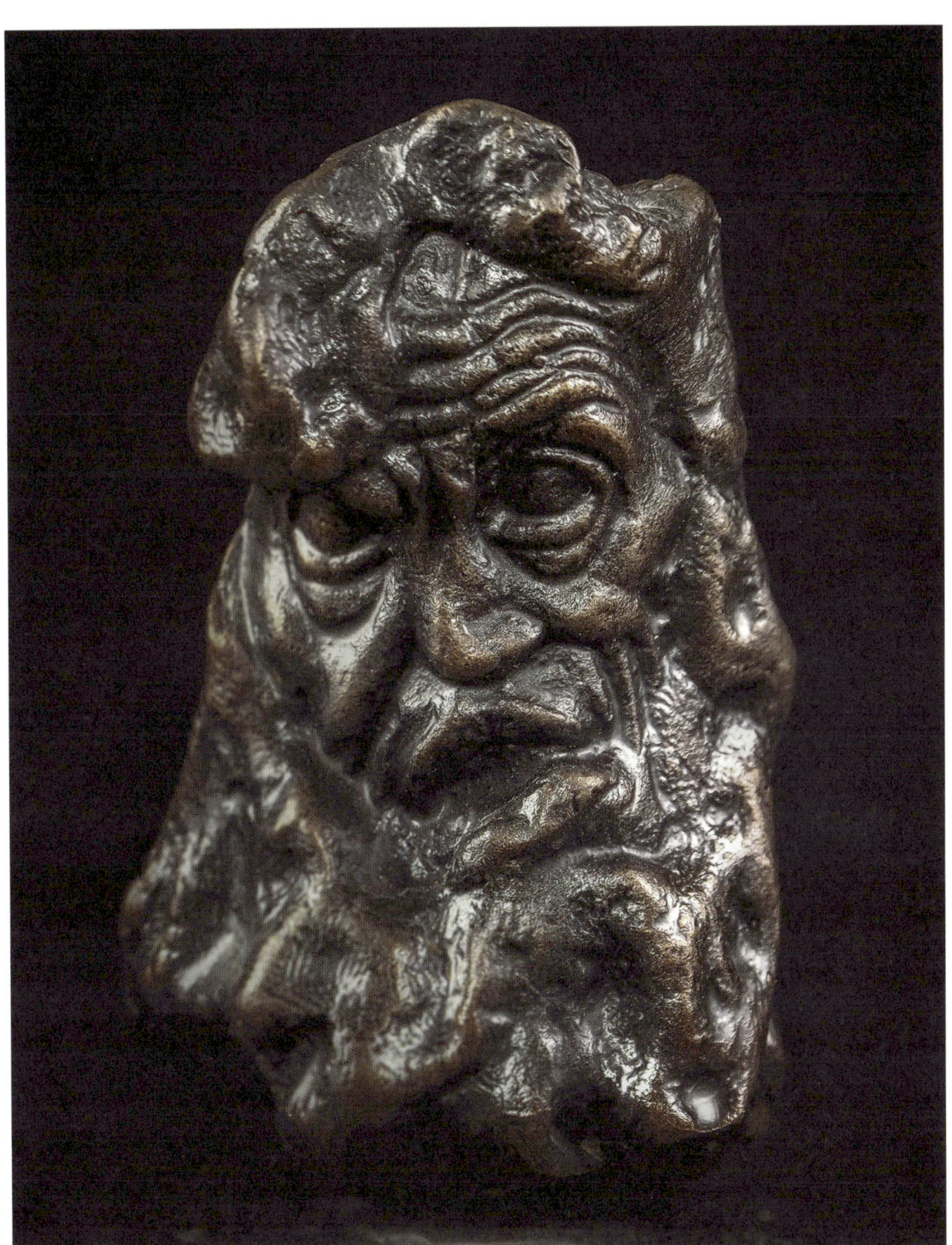

Carved in a 3″ tall rock, around age 16.

13

Self-Portrait

Since infancy I have been robust; I have never even had children's diseases. When walking with my father, I tried to match his steps, thus got into the habit of making long strides, and when mature, I never met a man who could equal them. This was due to a trick I evolved while walking. It consists, till this day, of directing the feet straight forward, as the Indians do, and in the very last instant of placing the front foot on the ground, pushing myself forward without an upward bounce, effortlessly. It was Ben Hecht who first noticed this "floating in the air" as if I were ballet-trained.

Prior to marriage, I walked, even when I had not had any food for a few days at a time, swiftly though seemingly not taking any huge steps. Since marriage I have not walked, because Americans never walk. They must have automobiles to go to the bathroom. They will eventually be born legless, for they do not find pleasure in normal physical effort.

Though I never exercise, people are astounded at the steel-hard muscles I have at my late years. When I strike my abdomen with stiff fingertips, you can hear the two hard objects meet across the room. My neck is 16⅓″ though my total height is 5′7¾″. Recently I discovered why my shirt-collars have to be excessively wide: every creature, while sleeping, must turn every so many minutes. Cows turn every 40 minutes. When I turn from sleeping on one shoulder to the other, I arch my body between my heels and the tip of my head. Thus I exercise my neck, unknowingly, lifting some 150 pounds each time.

Though you may regard me as a fine technician now, I once had to devise my own way of attaining perspective in drawings without making the usual hundreds of straight lines coming to one point, by not sketching carelessly.

I believe sketching is bad for an accomplished artist, for it re-introduces the sloppy workmanship of his student time. It would be as if a fine surgeon, after acquiring his great skill, would restart dissecting again while operating on a brain or eye.

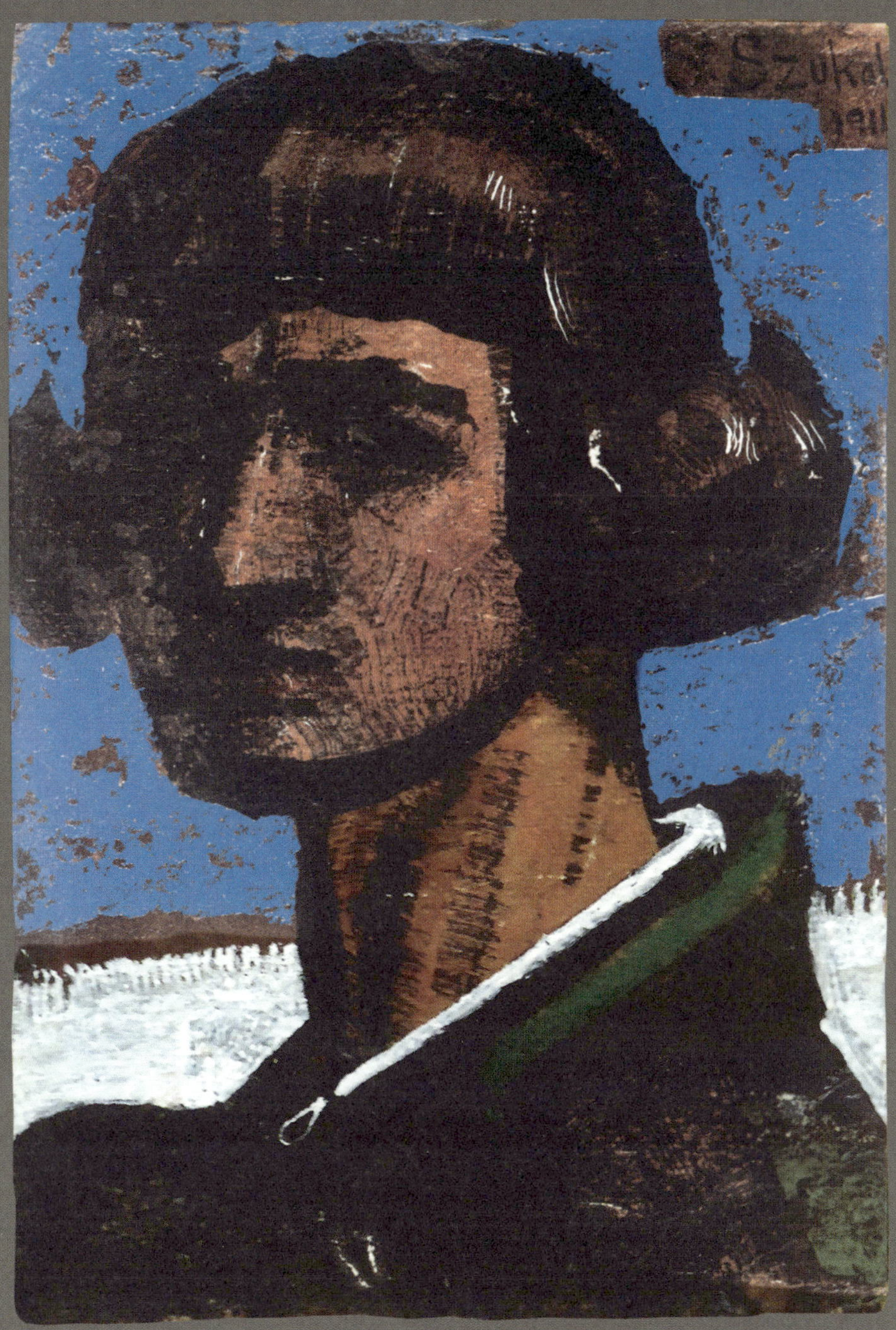
Szuka
1911

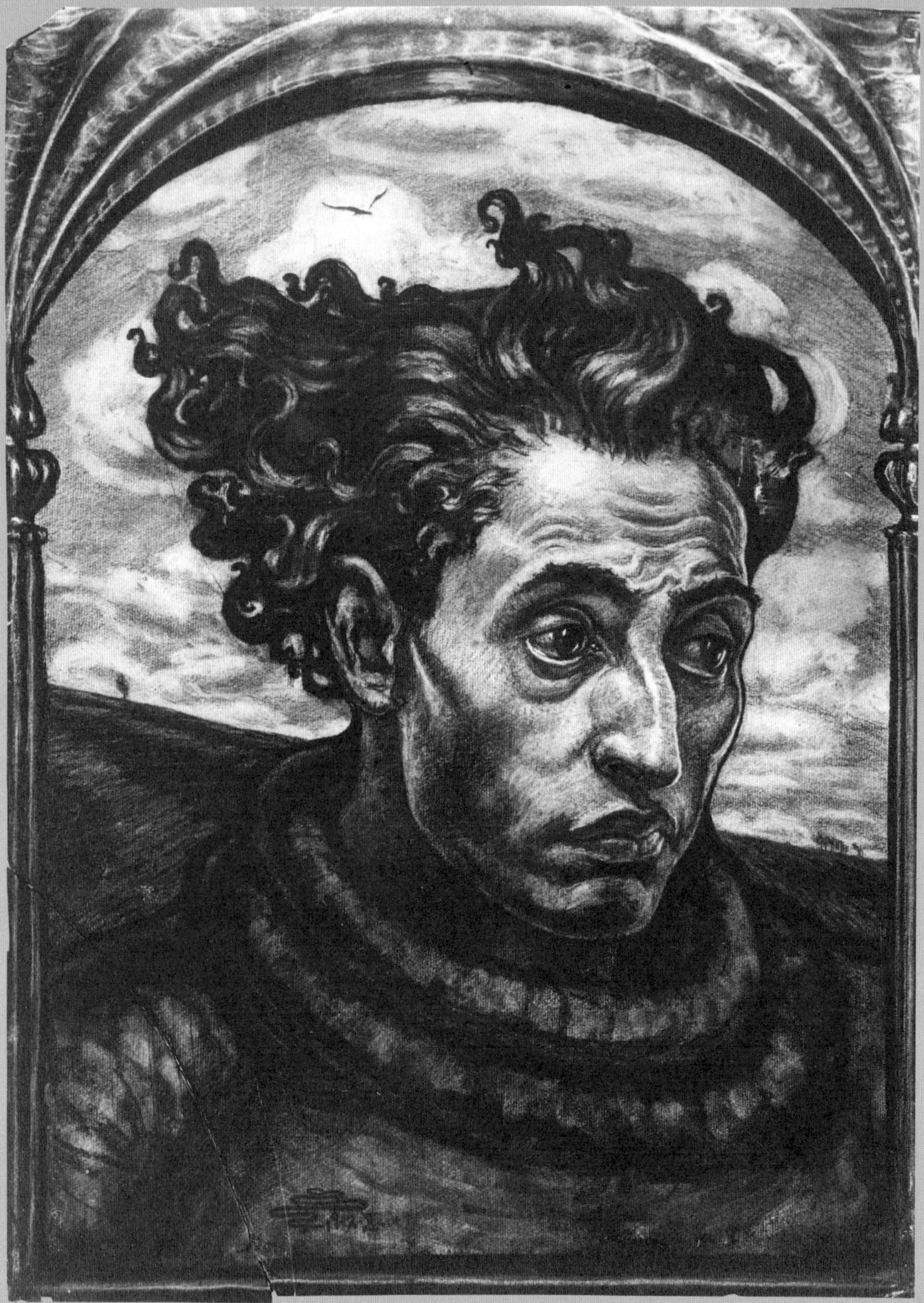

Merezowicz

He was an Armenian from Lwów (City of the Lions) who studied at the Academy of Art in Kraków, in the class of Professor Axentowicz, also a Polish Armenian. He was very popular with the ladies, although indiscriminately attracted by any skirt.

Because he was afflicted with epilepsy, he had difficulty finding someone who would share his room and rent. So I invited him, primarily because I was so eager to study convulsions. Soon, at night, when there were no lights to be switched on, I would hear him moan, while his head would pound the hard bed. I would walk across the room in the dark and, crawling onto his bed, hold his arms down and kneel on his thighs and hold him immobile till the attack had passed, that he would not scratch my eyes out.

This drawing I made of him is carelessly unfinished, since as yet I had not discovered that Poles of the intellectual kind can not work diligently. It was a little while before I realized their failing and began to tighten my drawings by completing them. At the same time I got in conflict with my professor, who insisted that I study from models, which I refused, preferring to work from memory.

Merezowicz never became a good artist. Finally seeing that he had not brought with his birth a spark that would develop into Light, he, like all my colleagues from the Academy, aped French Modernism. Thus, he became one of a million-and-six failures of all nationalities who were born without the Common Sense to solely DEPEND upon THEMSELVES, instead of on posing models.

Drawing of a Beggar

■ 1912 ■

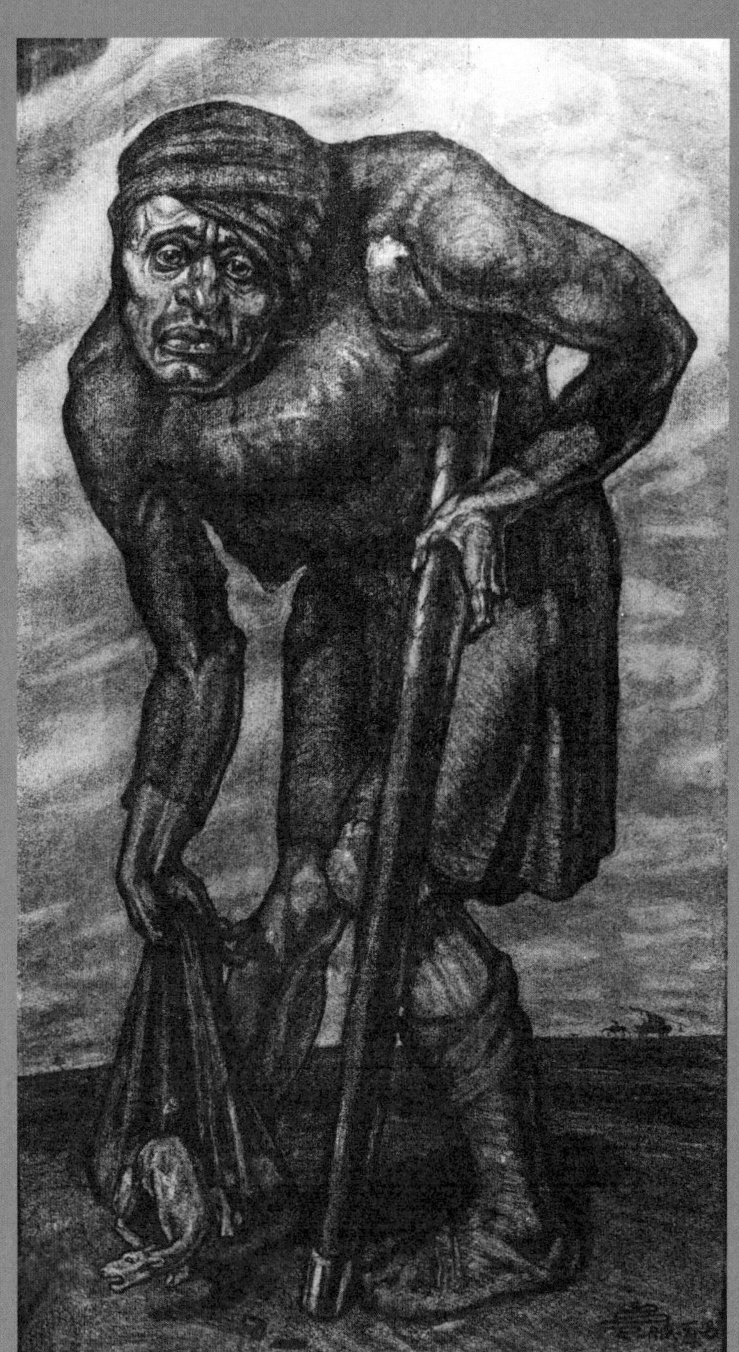

A Blind Beggar

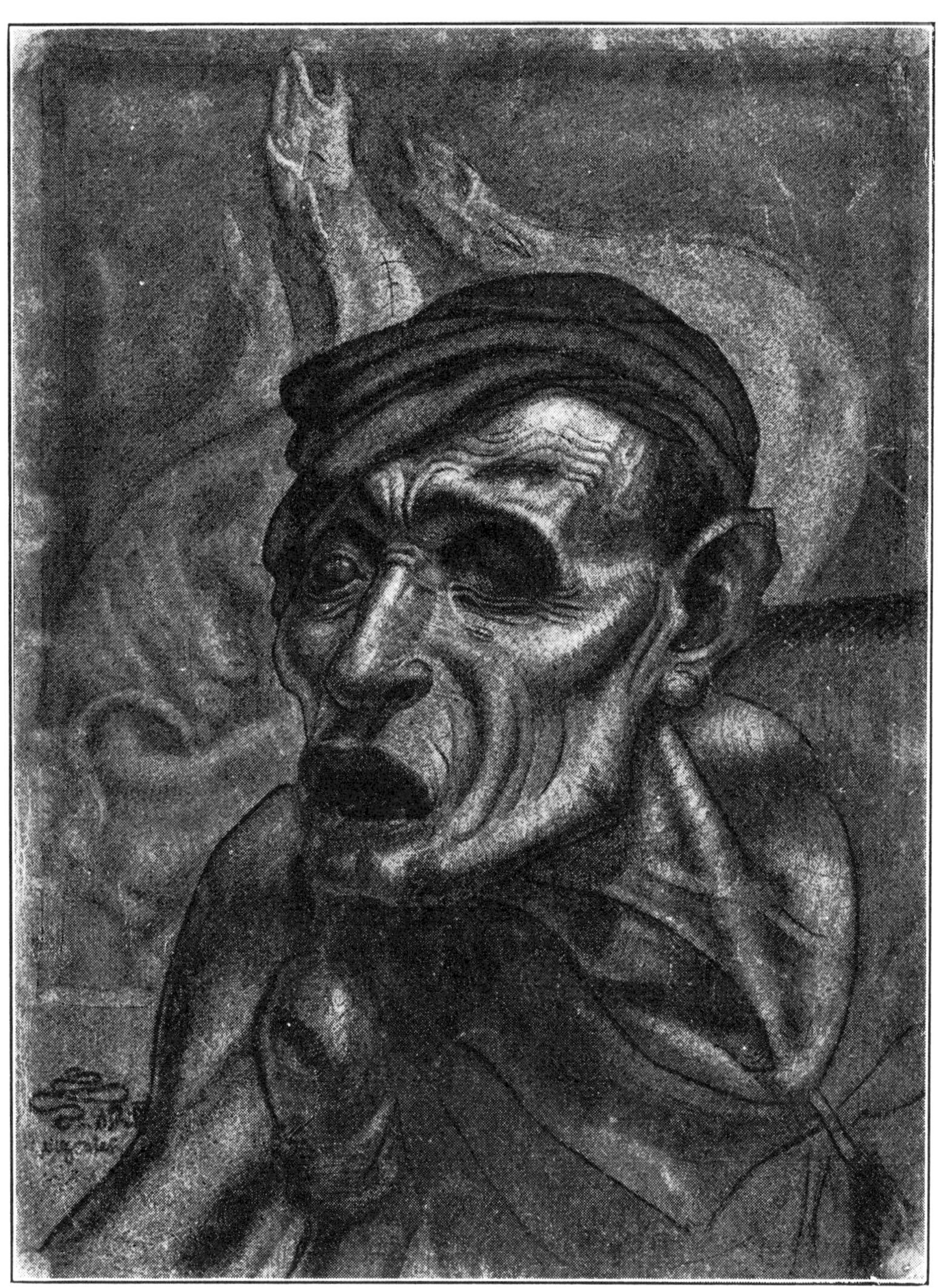

When in my teens, I made it a point NOT to read books. I organized the Chicago *Vagabond Club* which was attended by Chicago's brightest intellectuals to discuss all matters with the speaker of the evening. I began to notice that our author-speakers were usually people who did nothing with their hands and had no professions. An exception was Louis Sullivan, who introduced Frank Lloyd Wright to architecture and wrote a book titled *Architecture and Democracy*. I was rather contemptuous of authors and their books, feeling that reading other people's thoughts might alter my own course of thinking and limit my own capacity, and that memorizing what others had already thought, was parasitic. Only in arriving at my own conclusions would I be able to contribute something worthy.

So instead, I wrote down notes and definitions of things, in English, to express my thoughts simply and economically. Some of the early samples would be: "Platonic love is licking sugar through a plate of glass" or "Those who study, rat-pack other people's thinking. Those who do things, Create!"

At age 19, I drew this woman's head, marking the vertical asymmetry of faces and bodies caused by the fact that our heart is on the left side of the body, causing that side to tire faster if we do our work with the left arm. So most people use the right arm more habitually, in order that the heart be less abused by bodily shocks. Thus the right side of the face is wider, and the body and shoulder on that side are more massive.

My education was my own prevailing INTEREST. Following my saying "Learn! Don't be taught!" I was to learn by PARTICIPATION. In study, one leans back, parasitically, and takes it ready-made, effortlessly. It is the effort that MAKES talent. This was my adolescent, but independent effort to Understand.

Vagabond Club Formed.

Douglas G. Dixon, vagabond chieftain, gathered his adventurers in Jerome Blum's studio at 616 South Michigan avenue last night and formed the Vagabond club. Members were chosen from those with adventurous minds, idealists, and people who appreciate freedom.

"With Chicago as a center we intend to organize chains of vagabond clubs around the world," said the vagabond chieftain. "The first club was formed in London twenty-five years ago and there are more than 3,000 members. The purpose is to teach the vagabond spirit of Francis Villon, Robert Louis Stevenson, De Quincy, and all the other illustrious ones who rebelled against convention."

Some of the vagabonds danced with their coats off, others sat on the floor and talked to each other without the formality of an introduction. The guests were artists, painters, singers, dancers, and littérateurs.

The Zancigs were there, as were Mr. and Mrs. Jerome Blum, painters; Mrs. Seymour Edgerton, poet; Miss Winifred Taylor, Miss Viola Cole, Mr. and Mrs. Maurice Brown, Dr. Maurice Aisen, chemist, and Stanli Szukalski, the boy sculptor.

* *

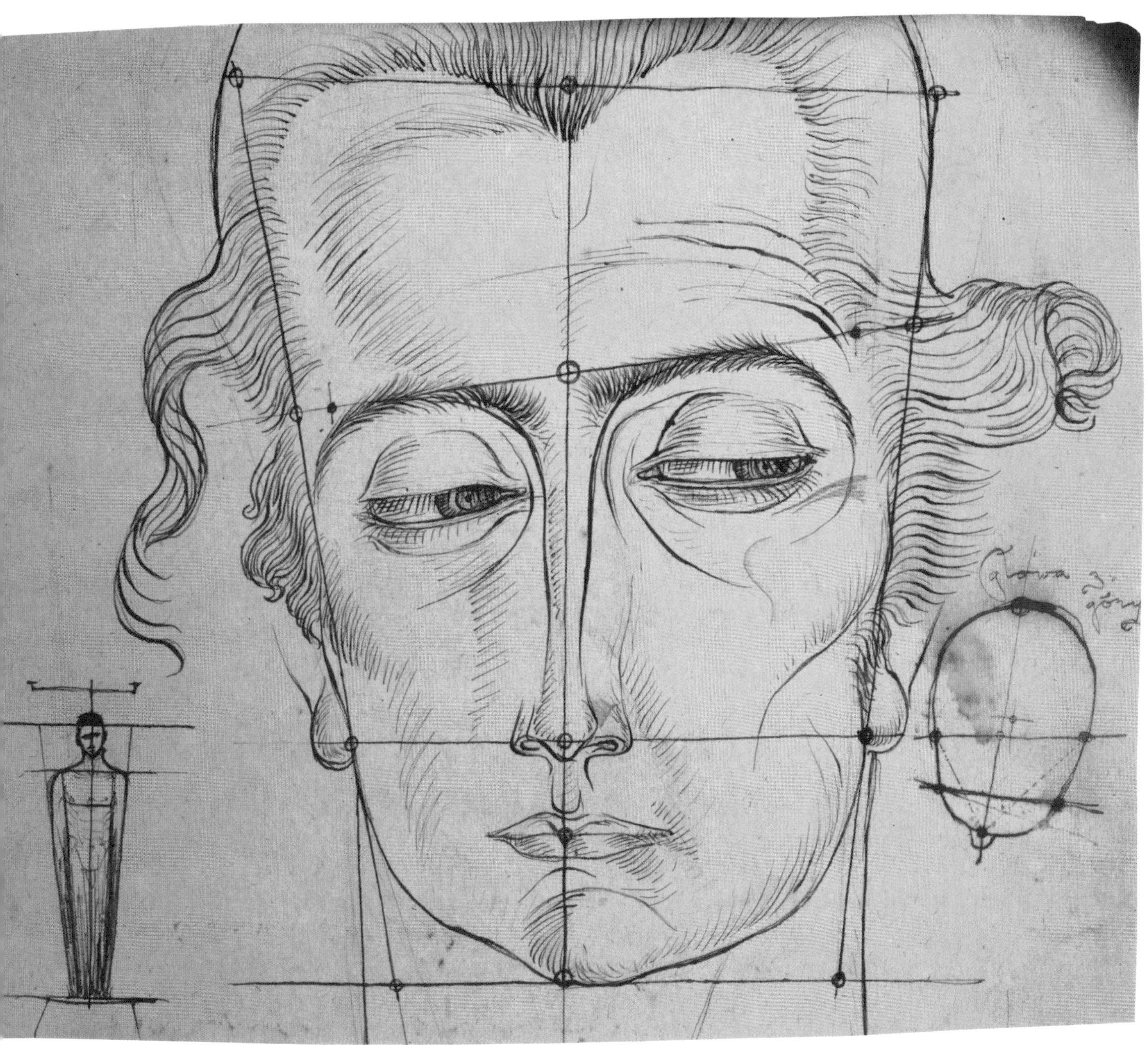

Głowa z góry

Differentness is Not Originality

Greed produced Modernist aRT (with a small "a"). With the event of the invention of the locomotive and the steamship, began the venturing of provincials from Russia, Poland, the United States, towards Culture which had always been the exclusive possession of a few other nations. Backwoods man began to rise off his four feet and attempt to walk on his hind legs whereby, thought he, he might acquire CULTURE, something he intrinsically did not possess.

So, onto France, whose Revolution had made a tremendous splash of which the delayed echoes, between the pages of recently printed books, were released upon the stagnant provincial eddies whose primitivism was just dying out. In the beginning, only the wealthy could send their sons to Paris, so that out of pigs' ears purses could be wriggled. And even though they may have returned merely more arrogant, they at least learned to speak "French," which produced the desired "differentness," while they remained *glombs* among other *glombs* (Polish for a "cabbage head stripped of its leaves").

Though France benefitted financially from the mass migration of "arty" foreigners, it has been severely undermined by these hicks. They, being merely of the quantitative type, were able to mass-deprave Art by weight-imposing their anti-creative trends. Thus, these tricksters obliterated the native French artists who might have been, had they been free of this foreign pestilence, the sterile Locust, that describes itself as "Modernist," while depraving the host nation with subversive Cosmopolitanism (pronounce: anti-Patriotism).

One cannot "choose" to make Art universally cherished, since it is not any particular type of Art that becomes such, but its expressive quality. Therefore, it is not Cosmopolitanism that makes Art universally appealing, but its greatness, humanity-serving persuasiveness, hence, spiritual Nobility. In fact, from what I have observed, it is the opposite of cosmopolitan spiritlessness, the intrinsic National Character, that makes Art universal. The talentless hordes of the democratized failures, liberated by Public Education, not capable of producing original works of inspiration, are forced to "experiment," in the dismal hope that accidentally some of them may discover a trick that would make their nondescript work "different" from the worthless avalanche of modernist doodlings.

When I was just out of my teens, I made this drawing with a diagonally sliced piece off the rough edge of a board. It produced an interesting "trick" that would make me a "different" artist among the Parisian multitudes of foreign failures. But any "differentness" can instantly be copied. A real, creative artist disdains such cheap tricks as unworthy appetizers. Spreading honey on sawdust bread cannot make it more palatable. If anything, it is ELOQUENCE that the artist should seek, not odd spellings of words. I made only four or five drawings with a piece of wood, then dismissed the new trick as unworthy of me.

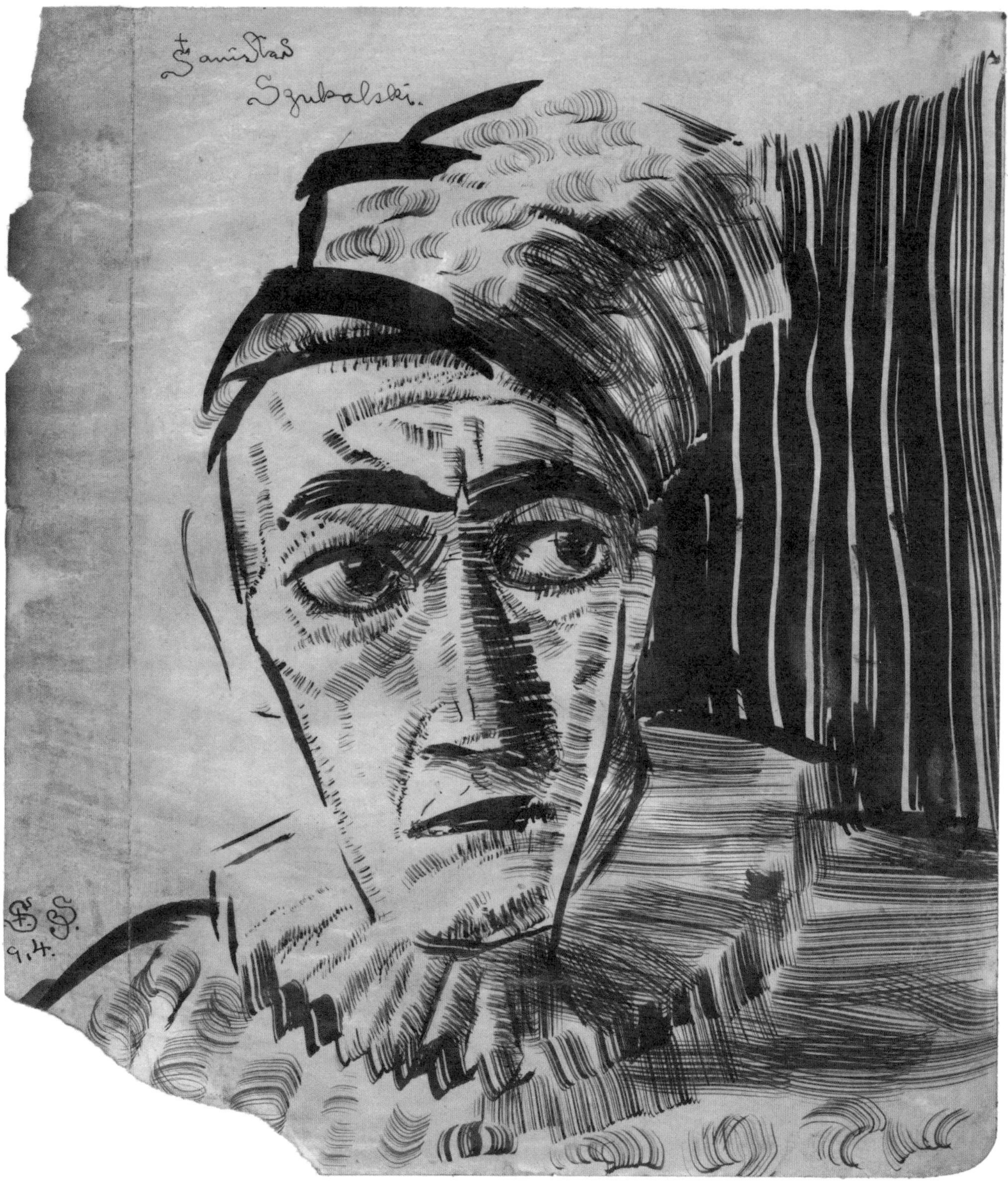

Stanislav
Szukalski.

An Experiment

After leaving the Krakóvian Academy in Poland for the United States in 1913, I made a few "sketches" with pen and ink. They were not careless doodles, but premeditated, decorative alignments where I paid careful attention to the flow of lines into one another. Improvisation did not please me, having brought myself up in such discipline that had no room for carelessness and irresponsibility. Such forms I regard as experiments.

Any pattern created by the Laws of Nature, such as those of viscosity, crystalogy, etc., is invariably beautiful. When tar glides down a cement slope, it ALWAYS is aesthetic; a trunk of a cypress stripped of its branches could serve as a column for an architectural structure; if glass, melted, spills on the floor of the glass factory, its forms are ever beautiful. But when man makes a drawing or pattern, it is always ugly, unless he dares use his talent for Art.

I actually believe that everyone has a Talent, but few are bold enough to start in areas where they may excell because their minds rarely co-operate with their innate inclination. Outside of the daring few who develop Talents, only the insane can produce unintentionally beautiful drawings, for they serve their illogical impulses, hence are the expressionists of twisted minds prompted by the Natural Law of Pathology.

Though the adjacent drawing is meaningless, it has a certain "beauty" that was not intentionally gained, but is, since I bent the lines and thickened them where I desired, subject to a certain anatomically-related Law which governed me to make them. There was no attempt at being philosophical or theoretical. Even if you turn this drawing upside down, it retains a certain beauty, as that of the line system in a tree or stone. The point to be made here is that no matter what you do in sculpture or painting, even if you know nothing of anatomy or proportions, do it slowly, compassionately, …as if you were a brain surgeon, and the carefully done thing will be beautiful.

If your child were dying, and you were carried by despair to run to God's Mother to speak ungrammatically, and you touched her cheek with a muddy hand from falling, is the mark you leave on her face… dirty? Or is it the mark of your heart-break? You need not apologize when you speak in tears!

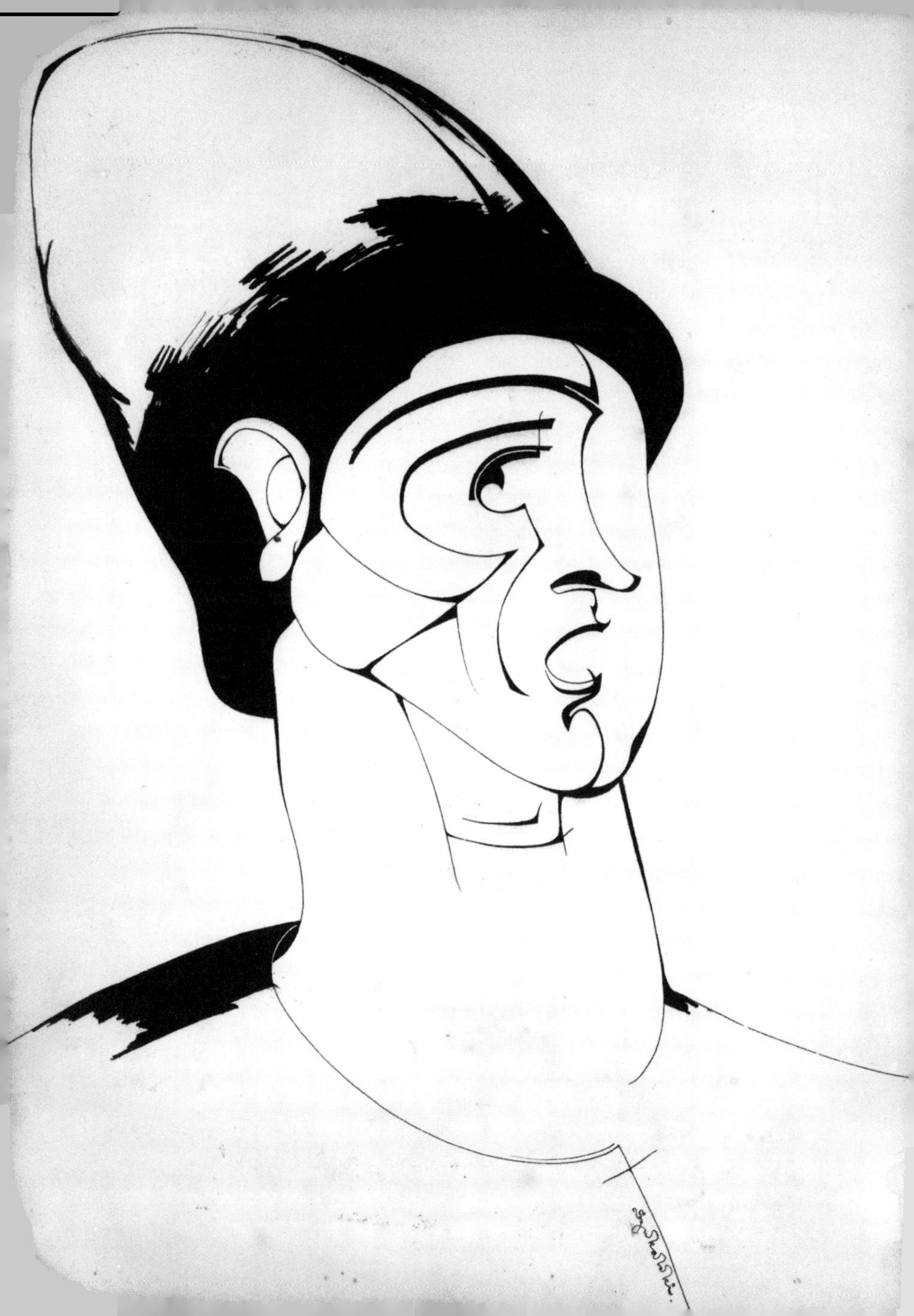

Self-Portrait

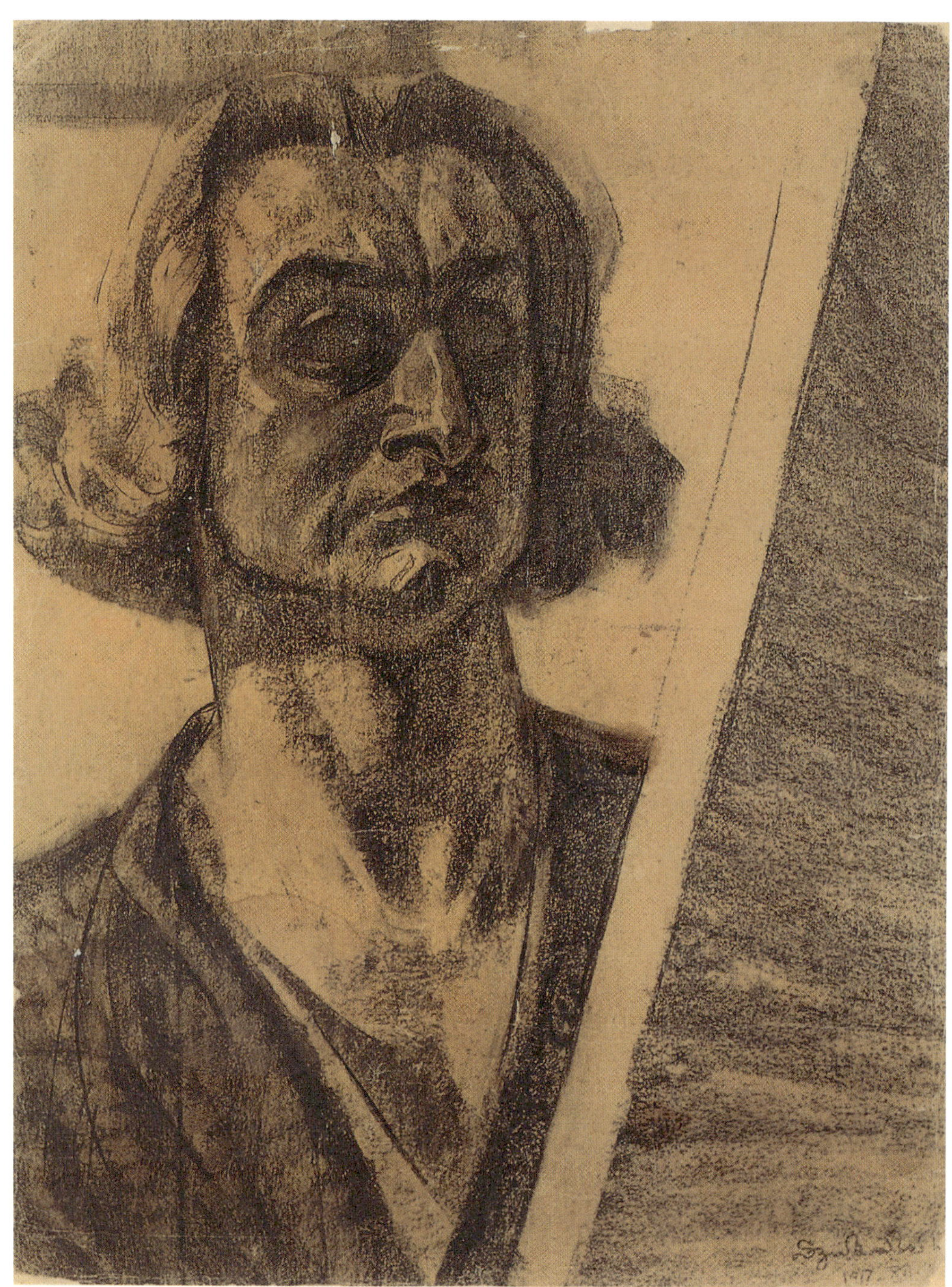

26

Portrait of a Man

■ 1914 ■

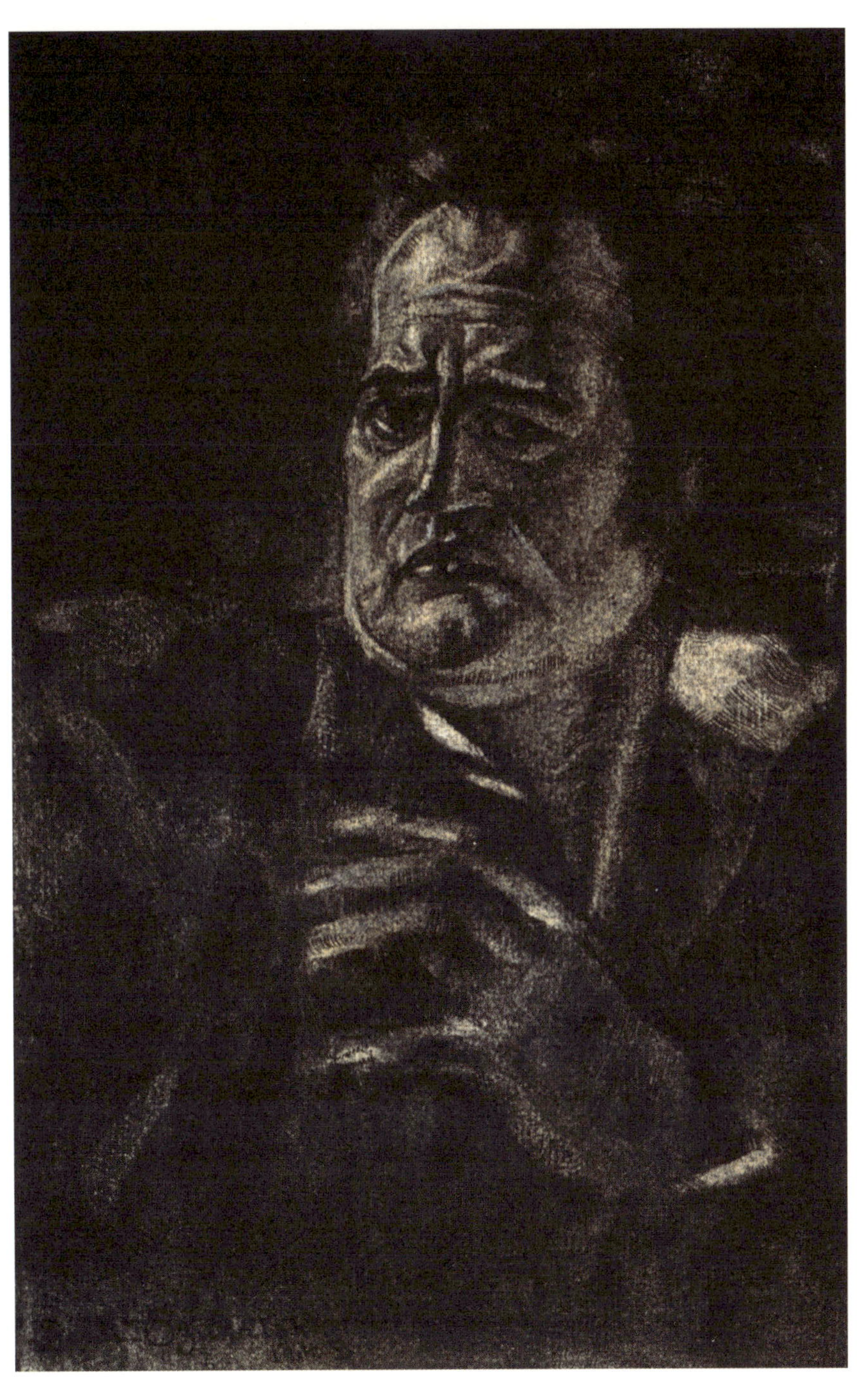

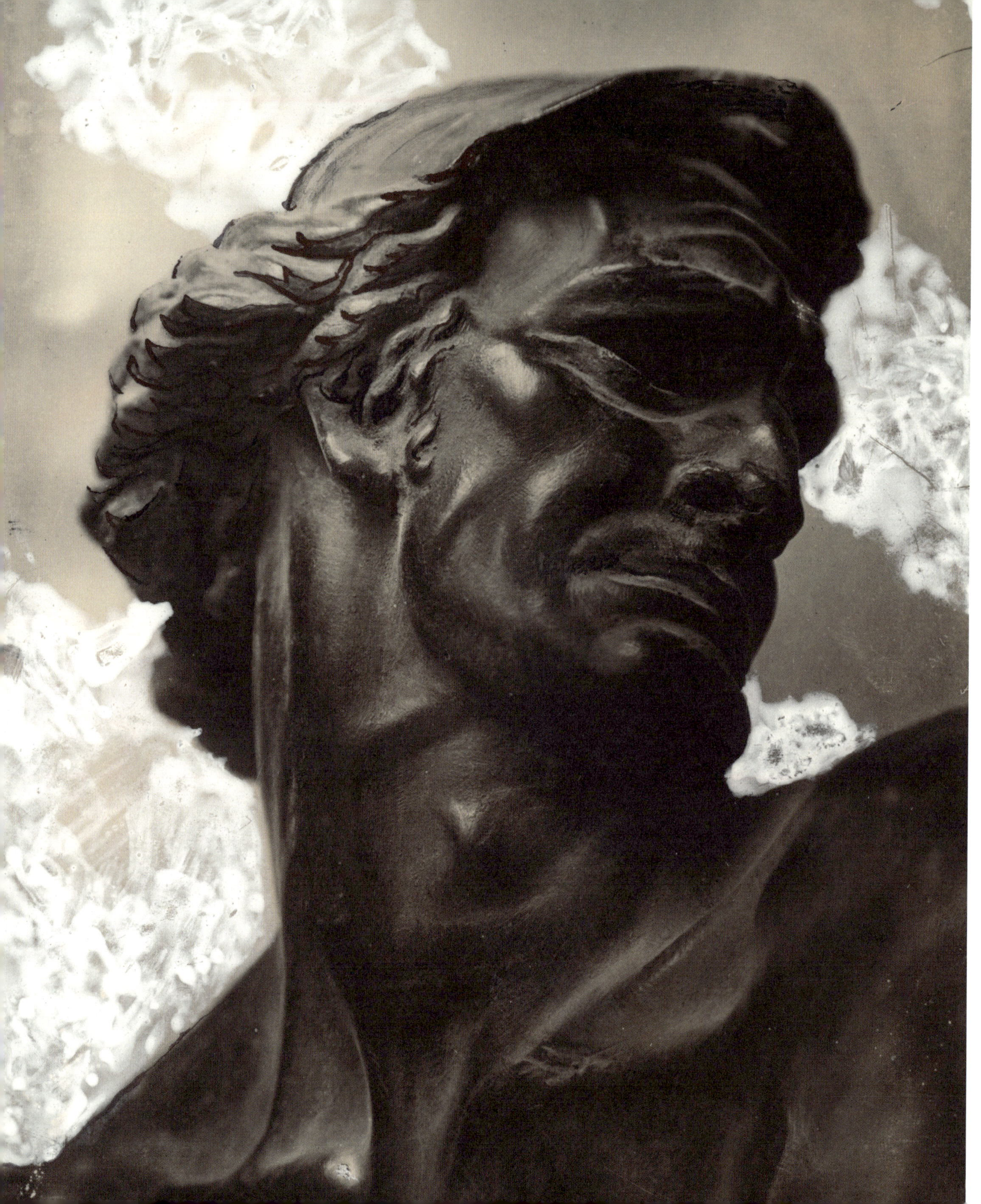

David

For centuries, reading the Bible was all but forbid-
den by the Church, which preferred to keep the
faithful in ignorance. There had been many authors
of the Bible and the Church had no need for constant arguments on the correctness of interpreting
the inconsistencies, thus blocking the possibility of
turning Credo's cleavages into sects and usurpato-
ry "churches."

Being rather indifferent to the Bible
anyway when a very young sculptor, noting mainly an edition with Doré's woodcuts, I had not retained the Bible stories in which David was a
fledgling teenage boy, and made him a man of some
thirty years. The work was completed when I was
20, while I was still overcoming the boyish tendency to "finish" work as soon as possible. The hands
and feet were left unfinished. The nostril is jagged.
There are holes at the base of the neck. After *David*,
I became obedient to my own advice and turned
into a full-fledged sculptor, just as the little girls of
Gidle had so generously insisted I was. However,
not before I made my *Stuttering Philosopher* was I
at last capable of holding my horse and not be carried away by Tedium out of the saddle and onto the
ground.

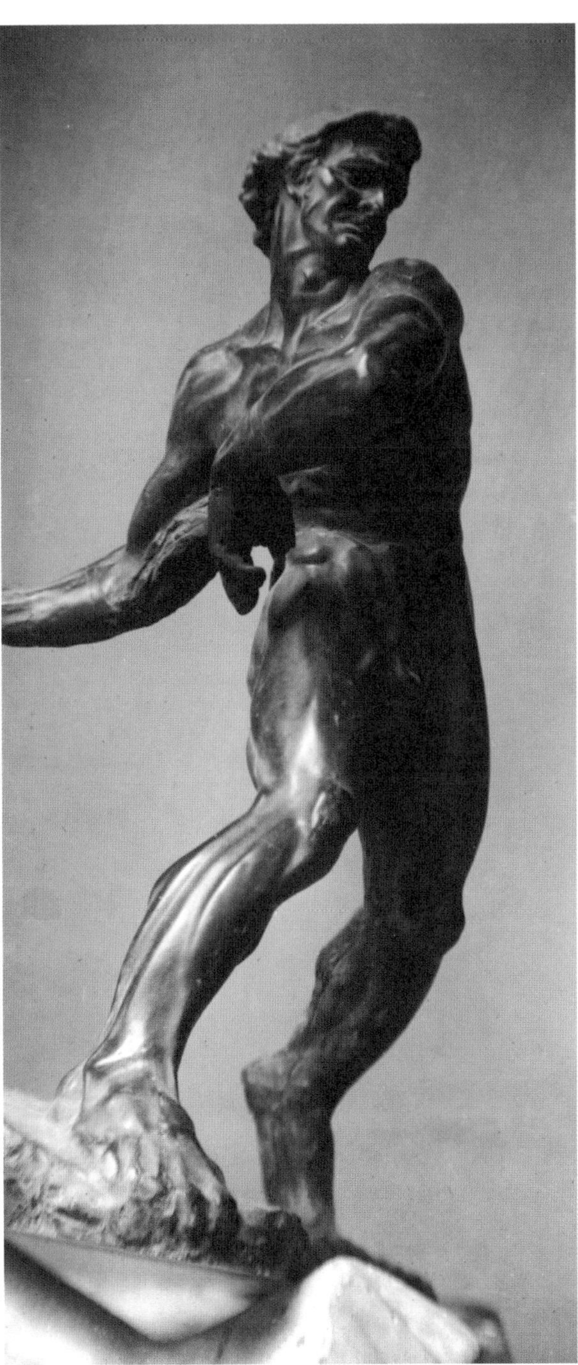

29

A Cynic

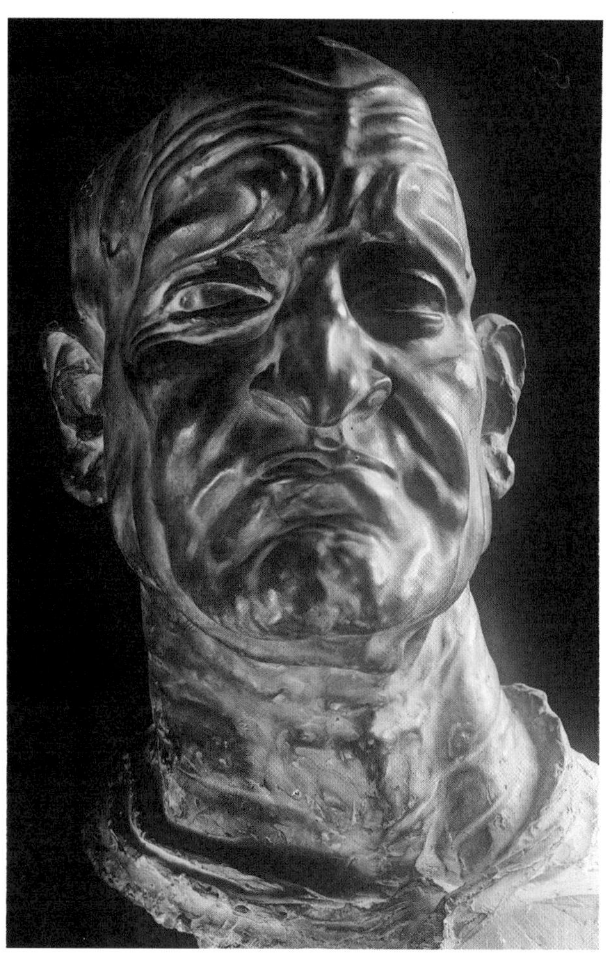

I made this head, nearly twice life-size, when I was just twenty years old. I was not too familiar with cynicism, but I knew enough not to merely make this man a sneering cynic who attempts to undermine everyone's enthusiasm by being sour and envious. I attempted to show that this man, with the face like a tree twisted by the blow of night winds and a remnant smack of bitterness, might possibly know both sides of the dilemma. The expression is like a bruise caused by never-slackening adversities; calamities which never look back to see if their victims remained crawling on all fours or resignedly awaited the coming of their last breath.

This is the only sculpture (besides *Bolesław the Bold*) that Poland *ever* bought from me. The bronze cast is presently in the Bytom Museum. However, the original plaster sculpture for the casting was stolen from the Katowice government building where my works were stored by the Ministry of Art and Culture.

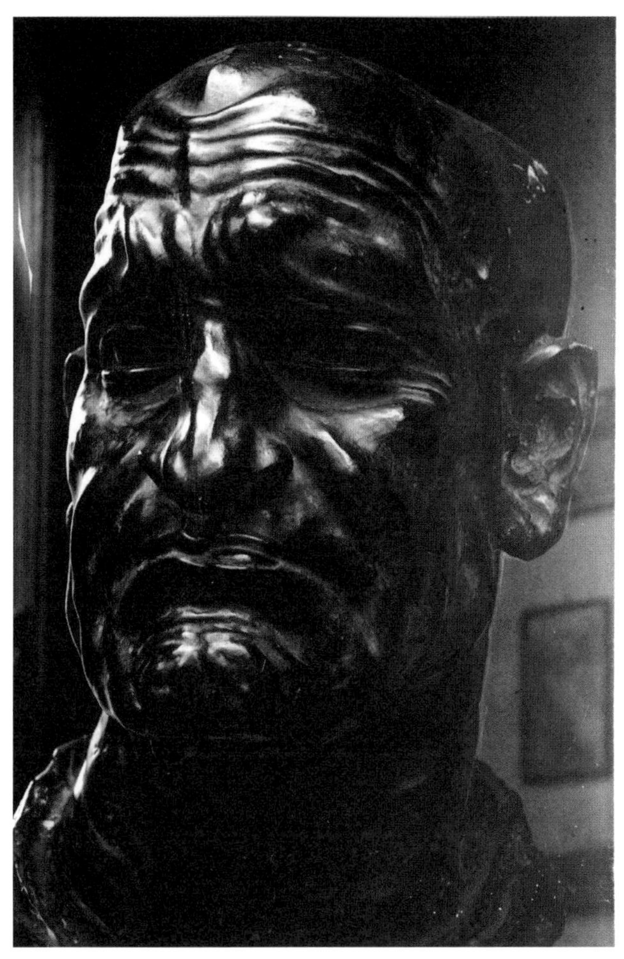

◼ A comment should be made here about the basic difference between sculpture and painting. While the painter has many elements with which to convey his message to the canvas, like a darkly tainted moment of gloom, or the brightly joyous mood of Youth, the entire prism of emotional shadings, and tremendous distances by means of perspective, the sculptor is limited only to the three-dimensional form. While the painter may use various brush-strokes that belong to effectiveness, even suspend some strokes in the air, the sculptor must keep his form neat and sequently joined with surrounding forms in mathematically logical continuity. Under no circumstance can he use painters' tricks, effects and appetizers, for that would outright… disqualify him as a sculptor. He, compared to the painter's freedom of any means of expressing thought, adheres to the same enforced condition as the gestures of the mute.

But, there is *justice* for the sculptor which compensates him for his professional limits. While the painting has its mood petrified forever, and can be reproduced faithfully in only *one* phase of presentability, the sculpture, though monochromatic, can be photographed in a MILLION different ways, from a million directions all around. It can also be photographed and seen in different lighting creating MILLIONS of effects. The change in direction or color of light COMPLETELY alters sculpture, while the greatest masterpiece in painting can be photographed only once. Thus while the painter has the whole gamut of tricks to work with, the sculptor has one additional element, which is *time*. His masterpiece, even centuries from now, can be seen in still another light and then another multiplication of directions. Look at the adjacent photographs of the same sculpture, and note that you have two distinctly DIFFERENT sculptures. In fact, it would be possible to erect an entire museum dedicated to a million differently lighted photographs of the *Winged Victory of Samotrace* and behold 1,000,000 victories.

This element of multiplicity of sculpture has not been commented upon before. Therefore, I am the first to bestow upon the sculptors the new, honorific title of the "professional who constantly multiplies his works, even after his death." ◼

Portrait of Cho Yo

One day while working at the Chicago Art Institute on my sculpture *The Orator*, a small man with long white hair and a beard came into the room and introduced himself as Professor Cho Yo. He was Chinese, though his hair and beard were wavy. He admired my work and showed genuine appreciation of aesthetics, revealing great knowledge of Oriental Art. He had almost as much interest in every detail of my sculpture as if he were the sculptor himself.

Professor Cho Yo came to visit me practically every day bestowing his gentle friendship. I learned that when the World's Columbian Exposition was being prepared in 1893, he had been delegated by China and Japan to supervise and lecture on Oriental Arts. He remained in Chicago for the rest of his life and became an honored member of the Press and University Clubs. He was said to have written a book on the mathematical laws of chance recurrences, based on the principle of the numeral 9.

Cho Yo owned a large collection of Chinese and Japanese Art, including thousands of the finest woodblock prints and paintings on kakemonos. Having been absorbed in his scientific pursuits, his income was very limited. Frank Lloyd Wright met him eagerly, for it was through him that eventually his Imperial Hotel in Japan was erected. Wright, the worldrenowned architect, was unappreciated in the U.S. His ways of being, his thinking shocked the Americans, who at that time were very unworldly. The Japanese government was the first to offer him a commission to erect the now famed Imperial Hotel. Whenever Cho Yo·needed a few dollars, he practically gave Wright one of his pieces from his collection. Thus, Wright acquired a great number of bronzes, carvings, prints and archaic bells for little money. Professor Cho Yo, being an Oriental of high breeding and great culture, was extremely gracious and generous to the architect on whom his finesse of manner was futily lost.

I didn't know the professor for very long, for eventually he stopped coming to the Institute, since I was too young to be an equal companion to a man of his learning and age.

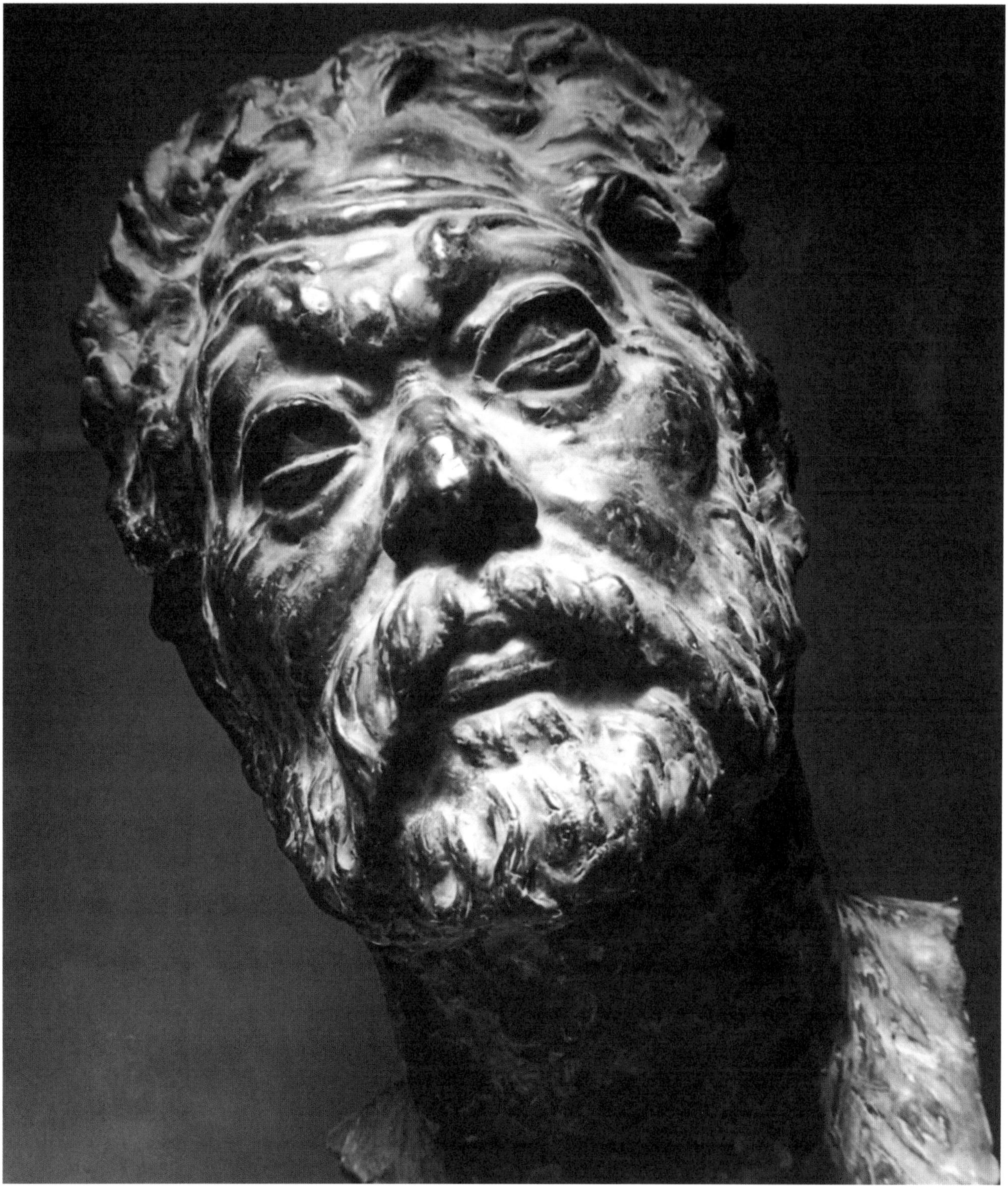

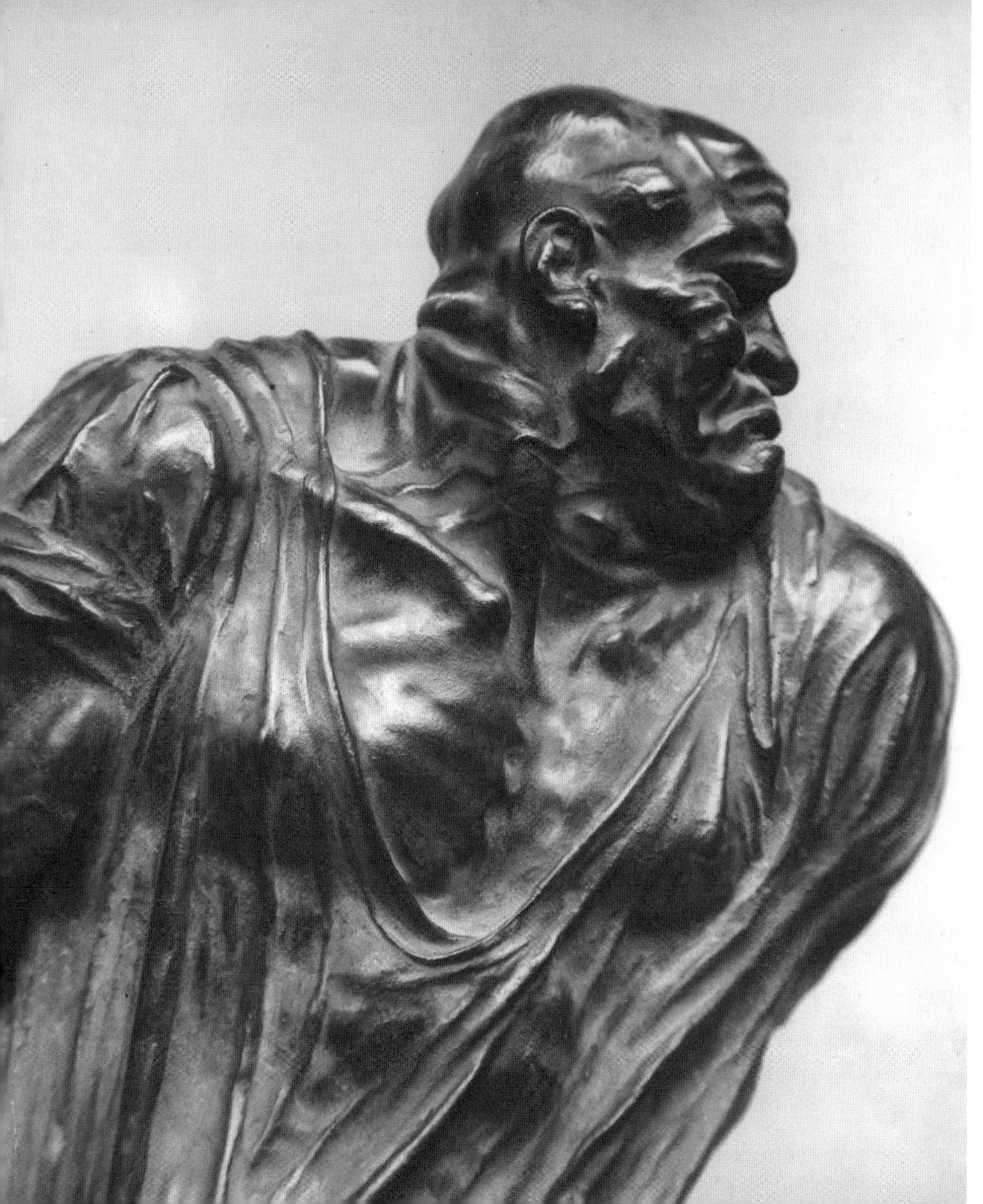

One-Armed Man in the Wind

The invention of ideas is dependent on the ability to express them. As we improve our skill to convey, our concepts grow more complex and diverse. Thus we start out with the trite and banal in order to evolve to the more dramatic, poetic and philosophical.

This was the second sculpture I made at the Chicago Art Institute after leaving the Krakóvian Academy. I was barely 20 and my blacksmith father could not afford to rent a separate place for me to work. I was given a work area in a classroom of Mulligan, whom I regarded as an untalented sculptor. He began to resent me after student friends started visiting the class to see how I progressed. He ordered me to become one of his students or lose my place of work.

As I look at this sculpture, I am greatly impressed. In recent years, through my research for my 39 volumes on anthropology with some 11,000 pen drawings, I became aware of the various types of bodies, and I automatically had known this as a teenager. The elbow of the One-Armed Man is far above the waistline, which means he has the "Russian arm" (like Molotov): the upper arm is too short and the torso is too long. These features ALWAYS combine with the pug-nose and short legs of – what I now call – a Yetin-syn (Son of the Yeti).

A layman may not suspect that sculpturing or painting draped fabrics from memory is far more difficult than remembering the anatomic details of the human body. This was the second time I tackled draperies and folds. I finished part of the sculpture, but still missed the necessary patience and neglectfully left the lower part of the figure and the shoes unfinished. However, I marvel at my ability at that age to convey the facial expression. I used no model, but made the grimace of tightening muscles around the eyes, to guard them against the wind, from memory.

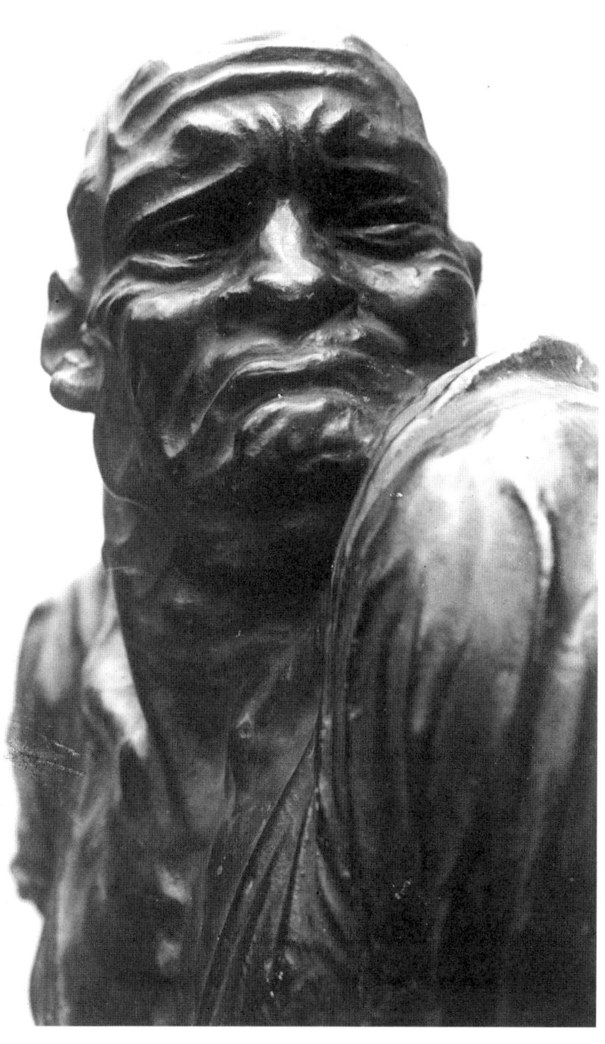

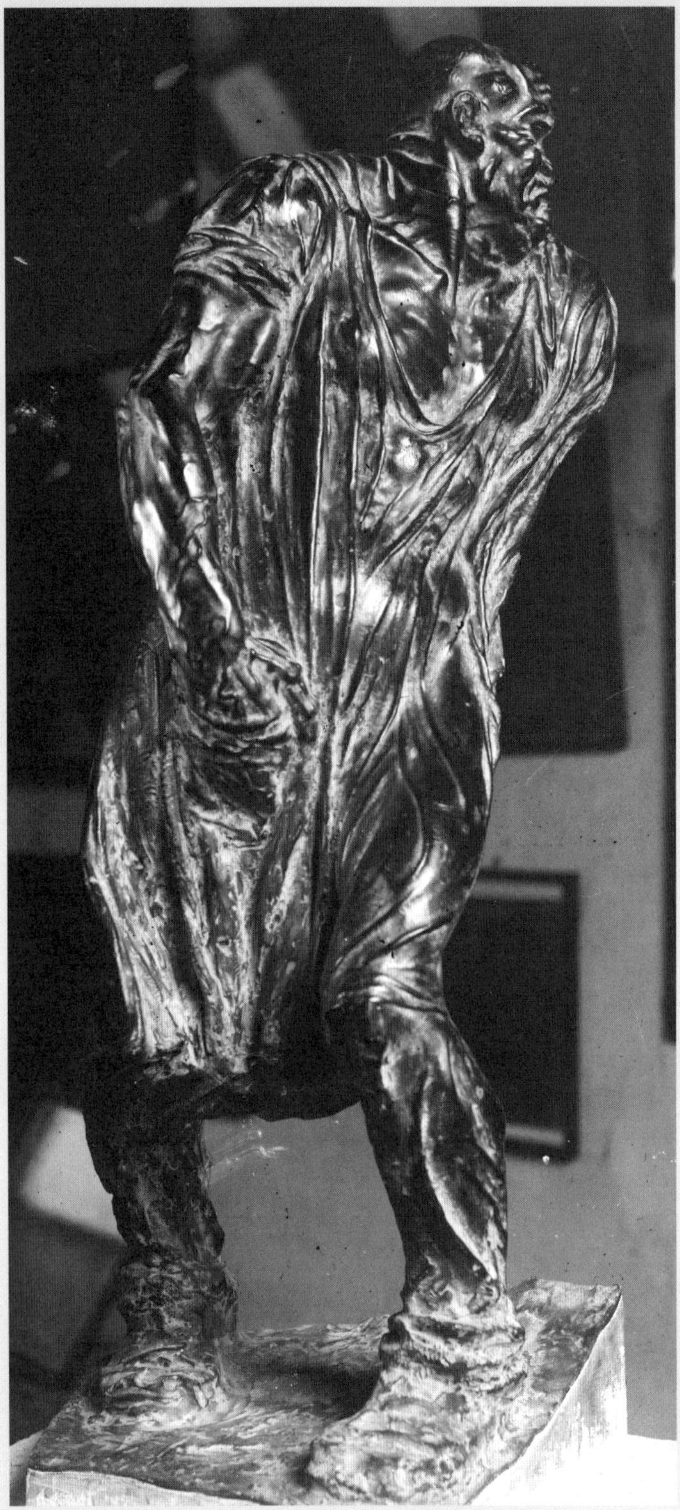

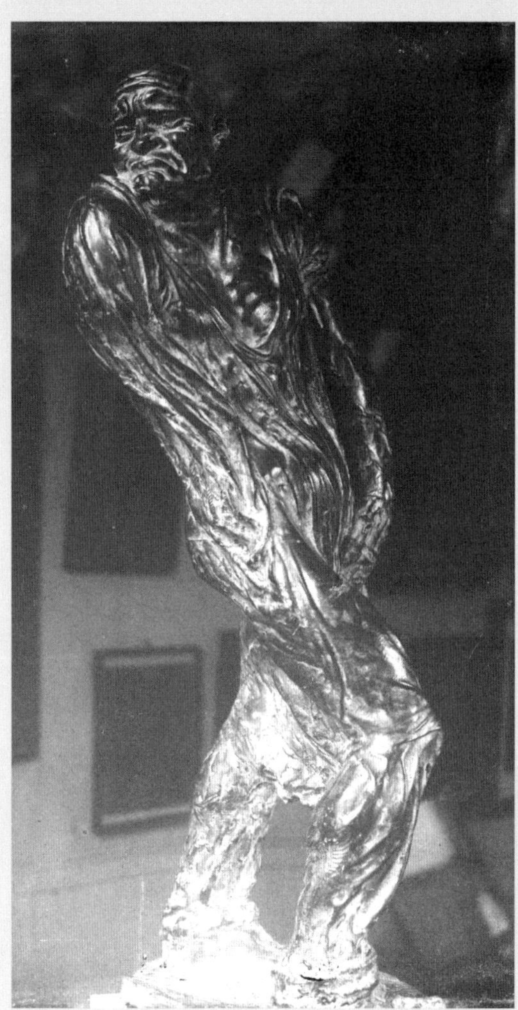

ONE-ARMED MAN IN THE WIND
1914

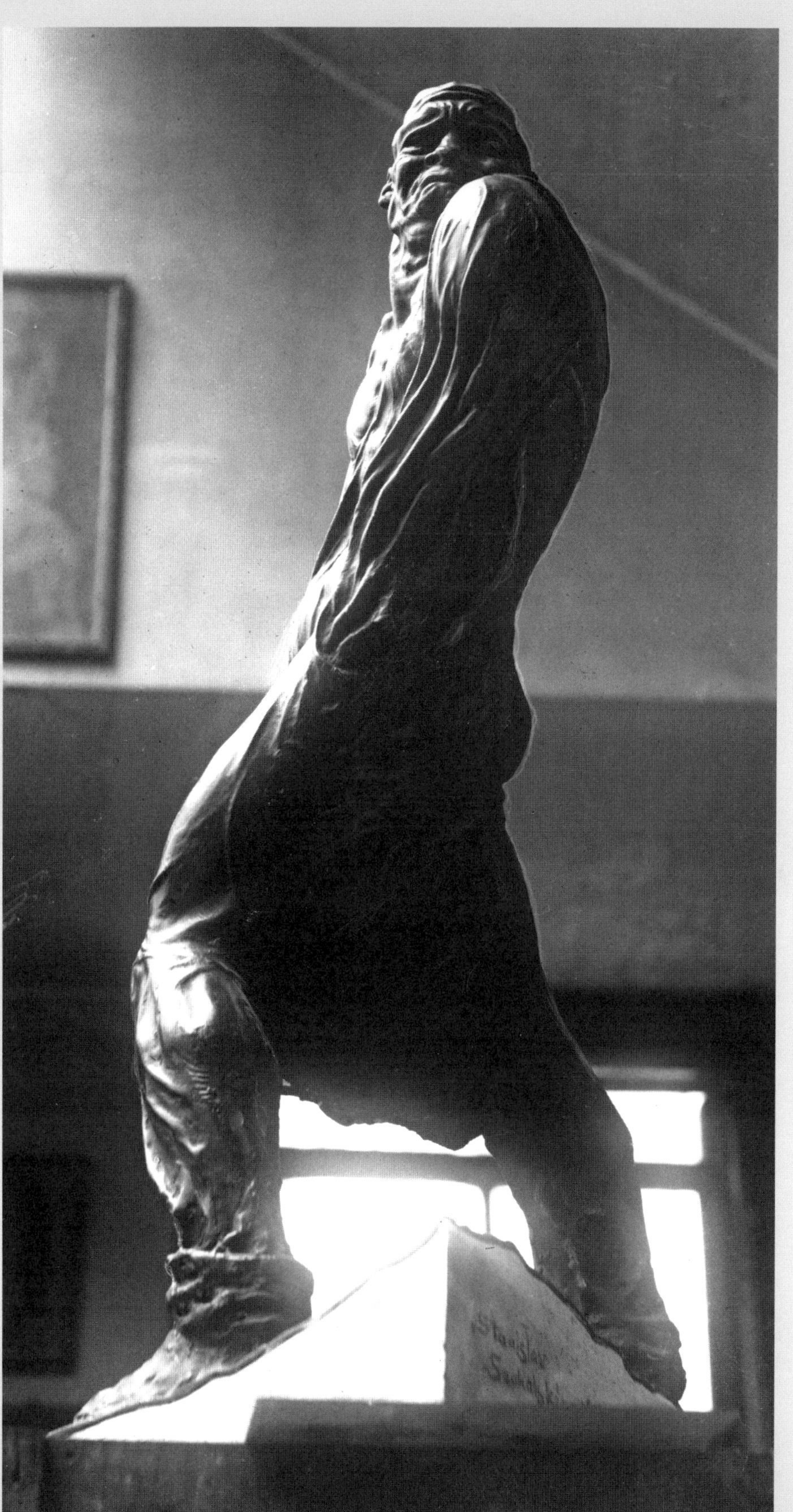

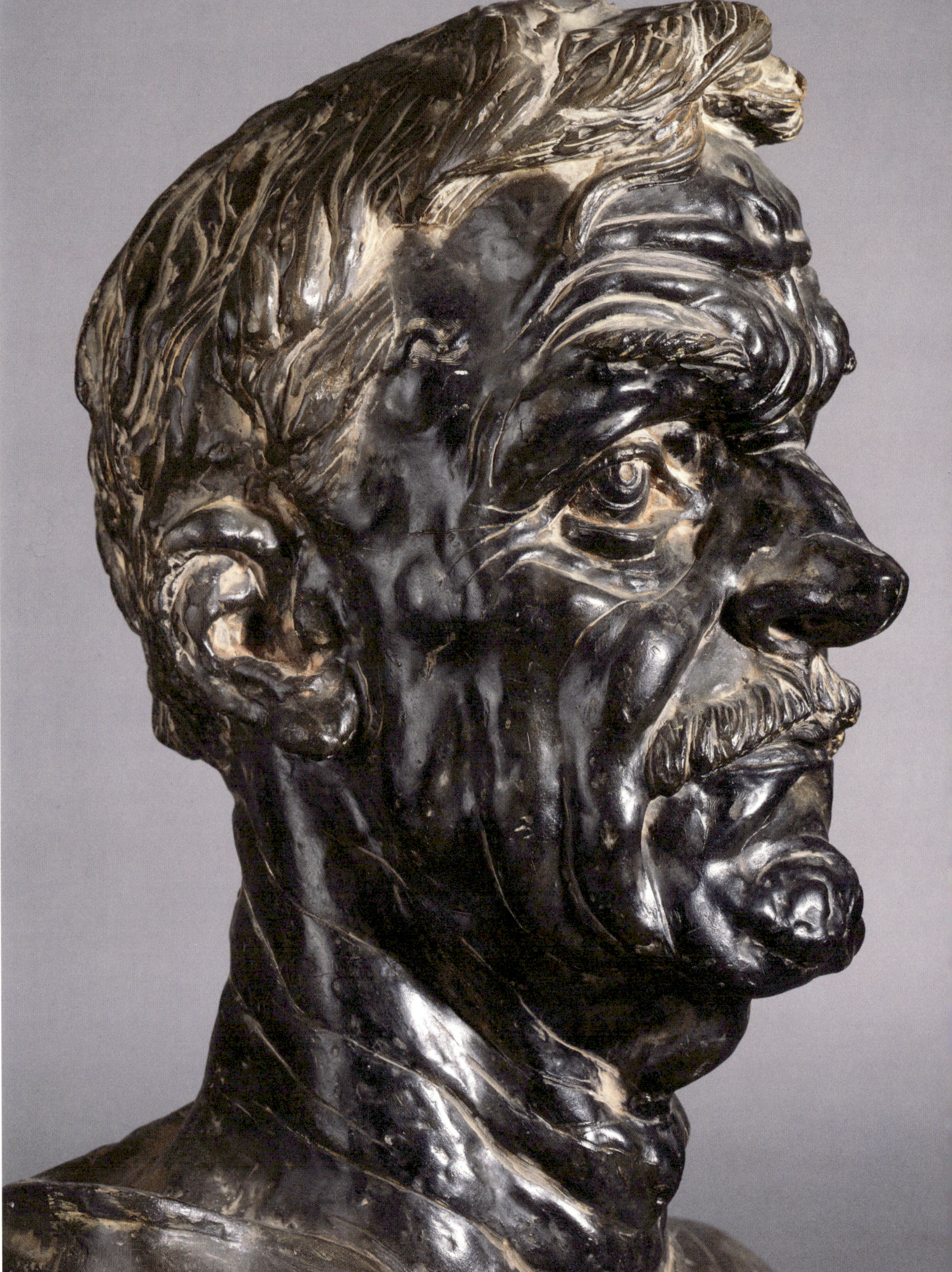

An Irishman

Right after finishing the *One-Armed Man*, I started the portrait of a man who had never spoken to me, who was rather shy and appeared to be in a perpetual daze. He regularly visited Mulligan's class just to see how I was progressing with my sculpture.

He was short and had shorter legs than what was proper for his body. While walking, his arms hung stiffly downward without swinging, somewhat zombie-like, and no light was shining from within him. He gave the impression that he had borrowed the skin that hung on his head, from a larger man; it was not well fitted to his bland personality. Paradoxically, his complexion was ruddy and his hair red, which, despite the lividness of his total withdrawal, gave the semblance of health. I attempted to draw him out of his shell in discussion, but he usually responded in monosyllables. He posed for me on two afternoons and, feeling a rather heavy mood in the room whenever he came in, I decided to finish the overlarge-sized sculpture without his presence. When he saw it finished and cast, he looked as if he did not see it, so that there was not even a ripple of a response from him. I then thought that perhaps he was an Englishman, not Irish as the others at the Art Institute had informed me. He was a painter, but I could not tell if he was a delayed student or an accomplished artist.

It would be an interesting experiment to arrange a portrait of a person who would not speak to me, would never even let me hear his voice; whose name, social status, national background and education I would not know a thing about – then finish the portrait, using as many sittings as I would need to make the absolute best portrait I ever did. Then, on showing the model the finished masterpiece, to be introduced to him, hear his voice, hear of his past, his profession, national origin and philosophical attitude towards life.

After this total acquaintanceship and new friendship, I would do another portrait of him, again having him pose as long as need be to finish as perfectly as the first portrait, and then see the difference between the two portraits: one made of erroneous impressions and suspicions as to his personality, the second of a now intimate friend who I know on both sides of the page. I am positive that the two portraits would be as unlike each other as if they were made of two antonymic beings.

We must remember that, exactly copied photographically from nature, a portrait is never a good "likeness." I have seen numerous photographs of the same person where I would swear they were numerous different people. The *real* "likeness" comes from the intangible relationship of lines and shades coming together in interplay with our own interpretation through our association with the disposition of a particular man.

Similarly, while I made this portrait of the Irishman, I was only guessing at him, very likely misrepresenting his personality, and such sculpture – though it may be a fine piece of art – would NOT BE a portrait of that person.

Face in the Light

40

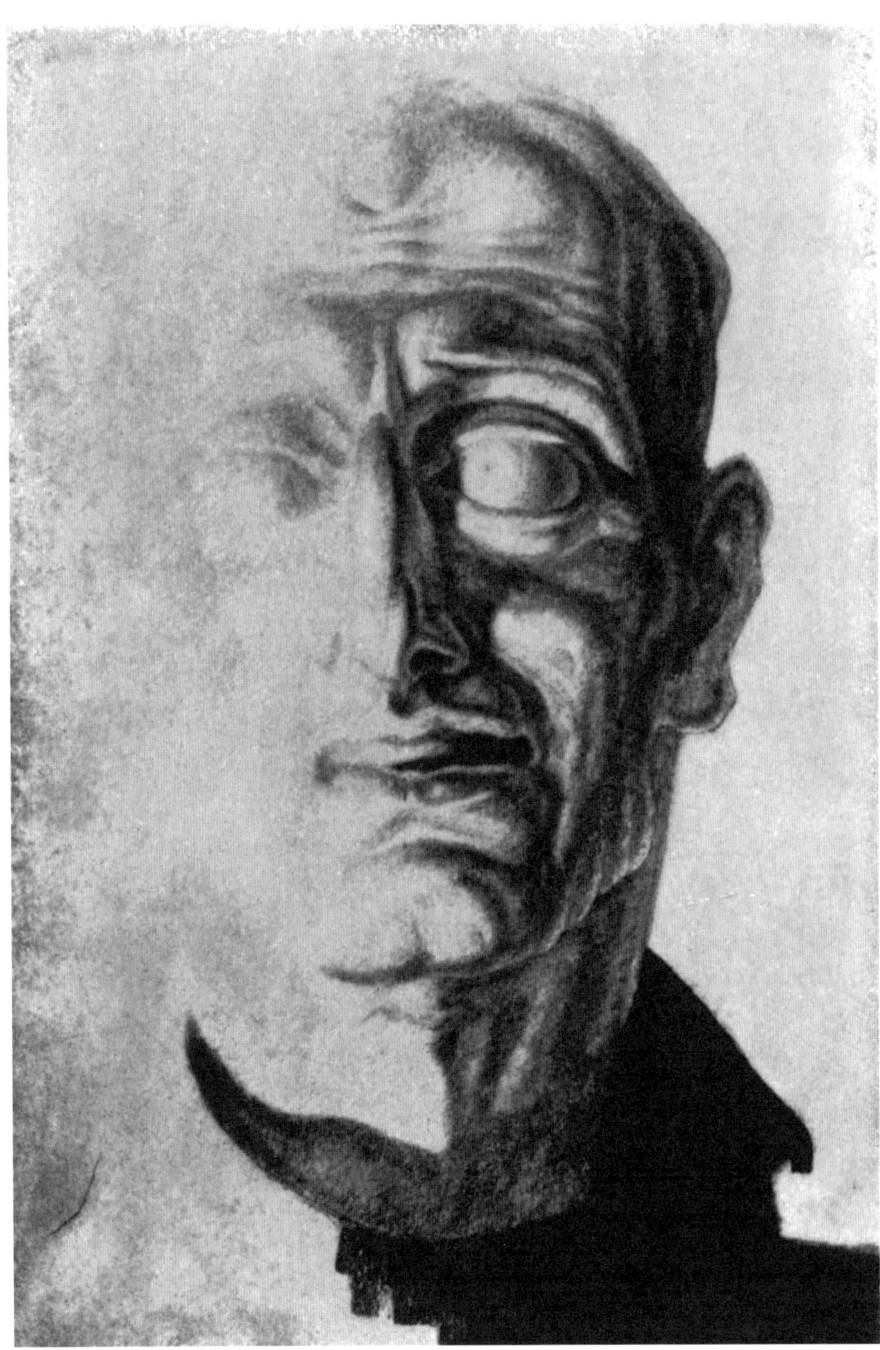

A Hunchbacked Clown

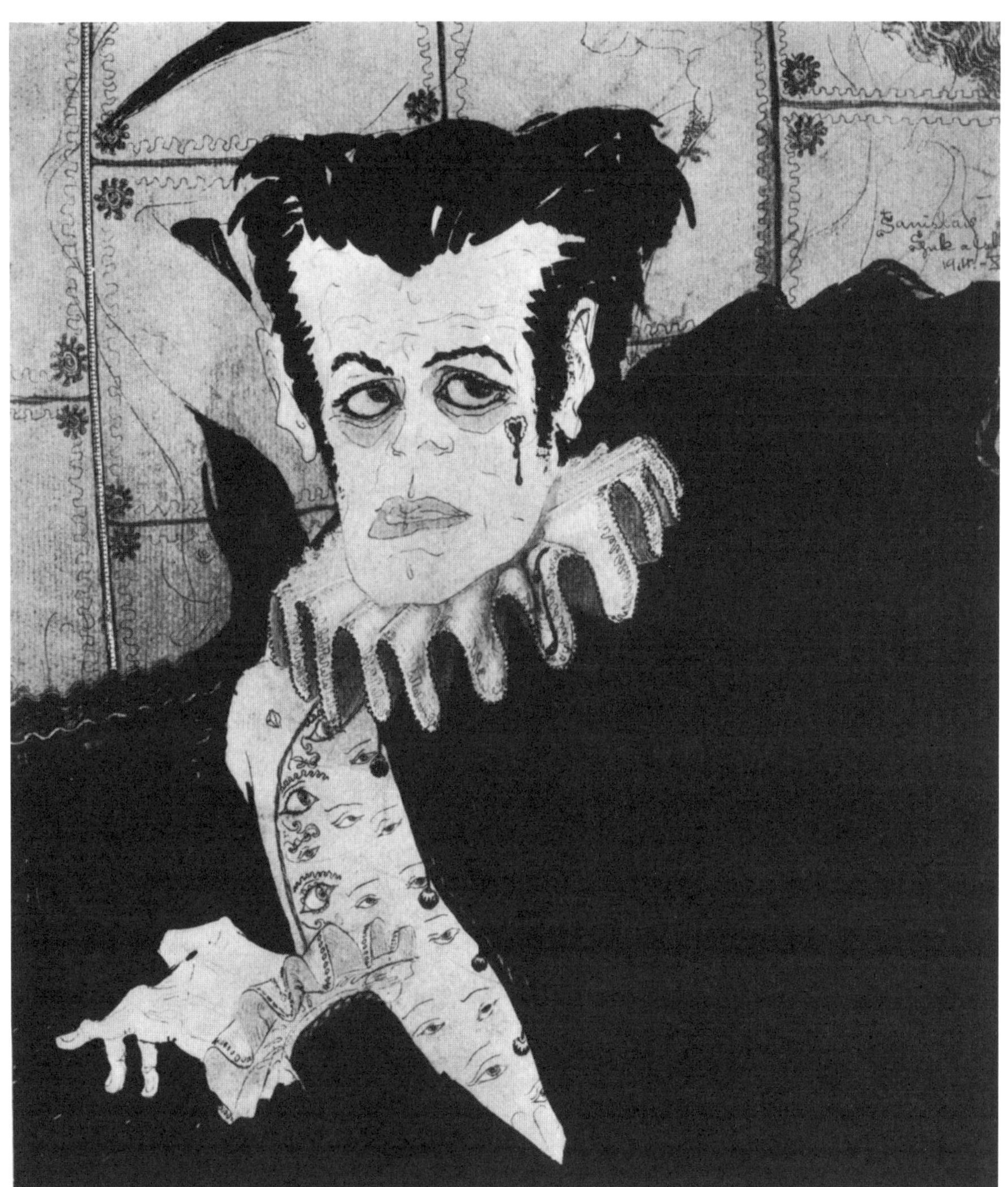

A Stuttering Philosopher

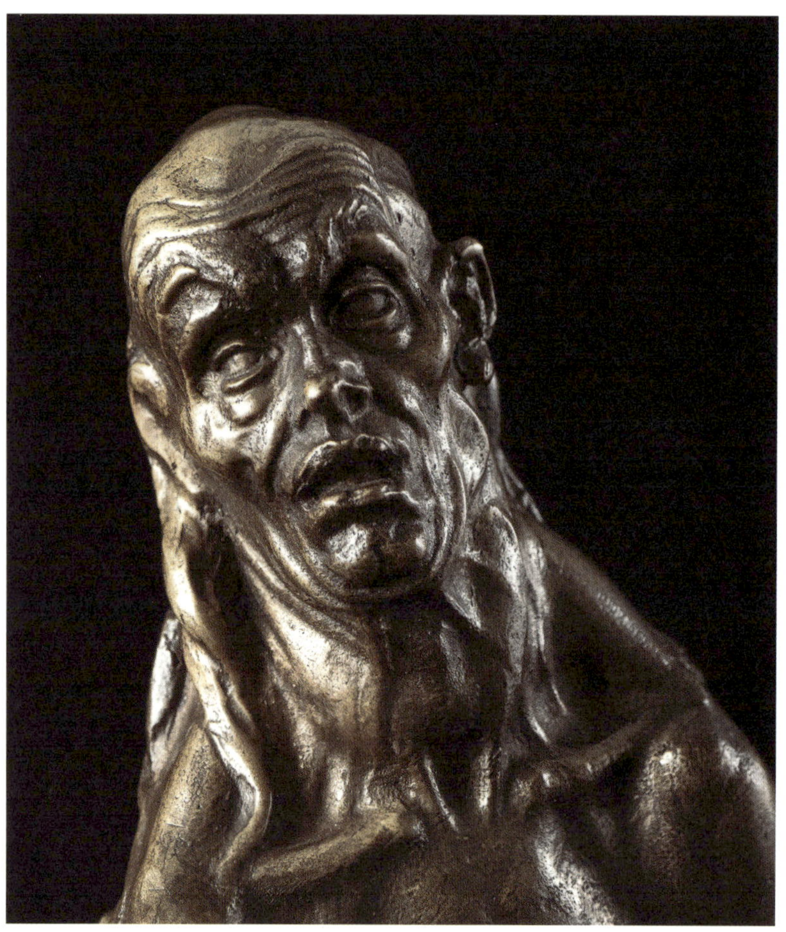

While at the Academy of Kraków, I made only one very large study from a model to learn the structure of the human body. After a disagreement with the professor over my total dismissal of studies from models, I made only two drawings from a female model; one of her torso, another one of her arm.

After starting to work all alone, while living above Bryden's Gallery on Wabash Avenue in Chicago, I made this figure of the *Stuttering Philo-sopher* who gesticulates with fingers and toes. His neck is thick of the muscular effort he must make in order to speak through the blockage caused by his convulsing brain. He has particularly powerful abdomen muscles, typical of stutterers who so laboriously convey their frightened thoughts, thoughts which are tragically damned within and for which they need a very long breath.

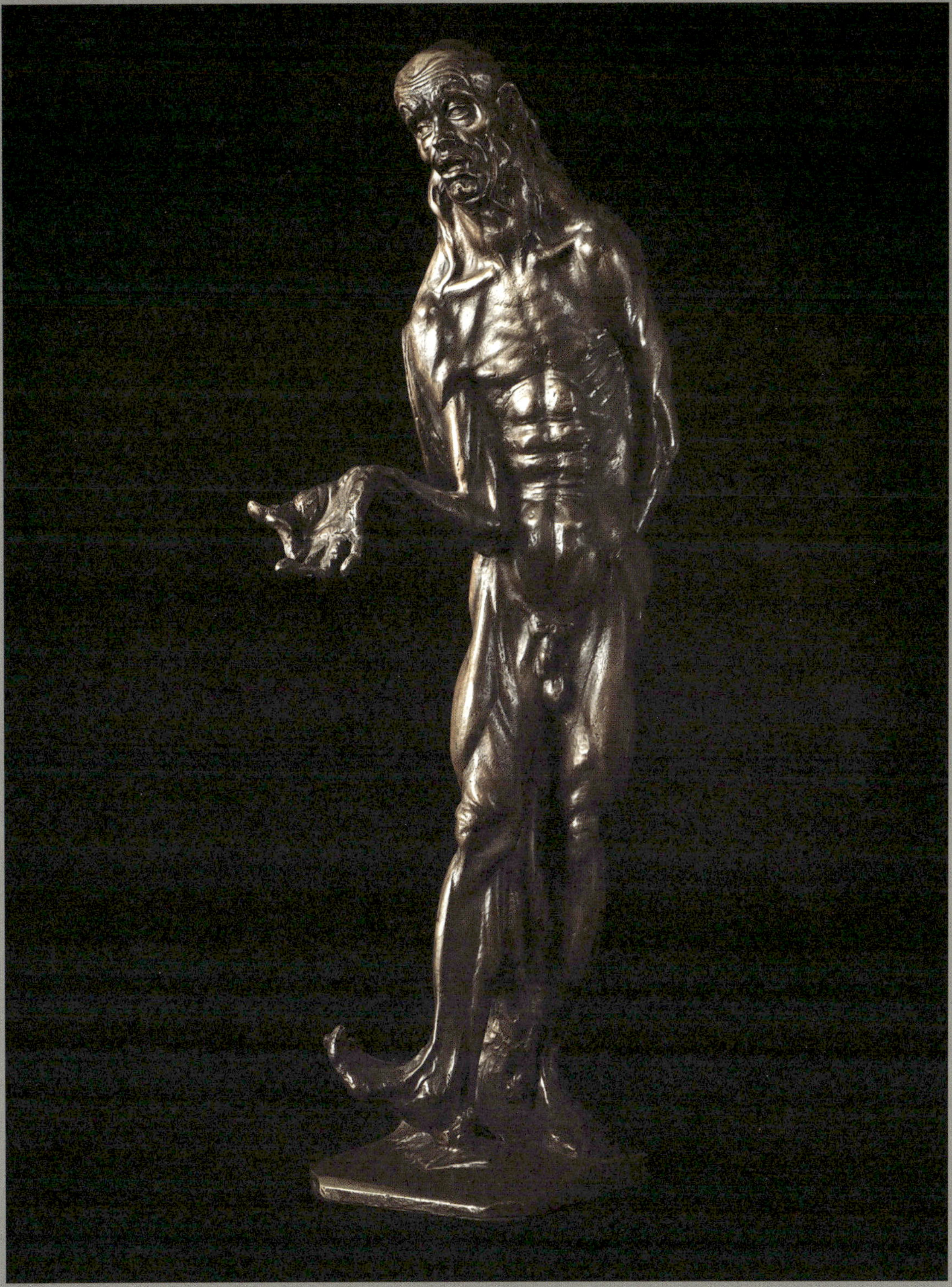

My Father Dyonizy Szukalski

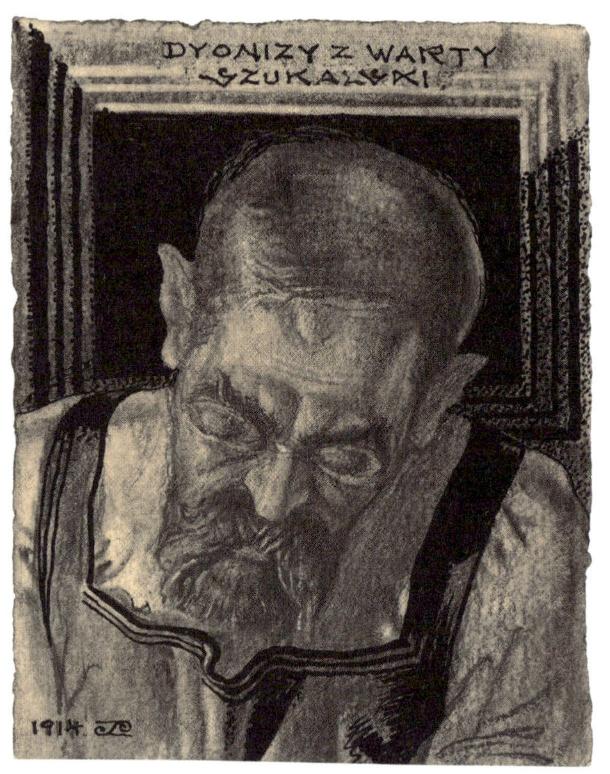

DYONIZY Z WARTY SZUKALSKI
Drawing, 1914

Grandfather had nineteen children, with a tiny wife. Some people were astonished at his masculinity, saying in the Anglo-way "What a man!" But I must correct them by informing them that he was not much of a man, for that was all he could do, since he only had nineteen erections in his life. Surely, the hog would have had twenty-six children had he been able to have a few more ambitious moments to his manly credit. I never learned from my family how many boys and girls were there.

Though I knew my father much less than my mother Konstancja, since he was in Africa fighting in the Boer War against the English, I adored him and never found any points of disagreement. His patriotism aroused mine to the utmost capacities in the desire to serve Poland, though the same feelings in recent years have turned me against the cultural Parasitism of Poland as a society, where the intellectual Poles have looted everything I ever created, keeping silent on the matter, awaiting my death.

I made this portrait of my father when I was twenty-one, in a studio loaned to me by sculptor Mario Korbel, when he had to go to Paris. It was in the Fine Arts building of Chicago on Michigan Ave., near the Art Institute.

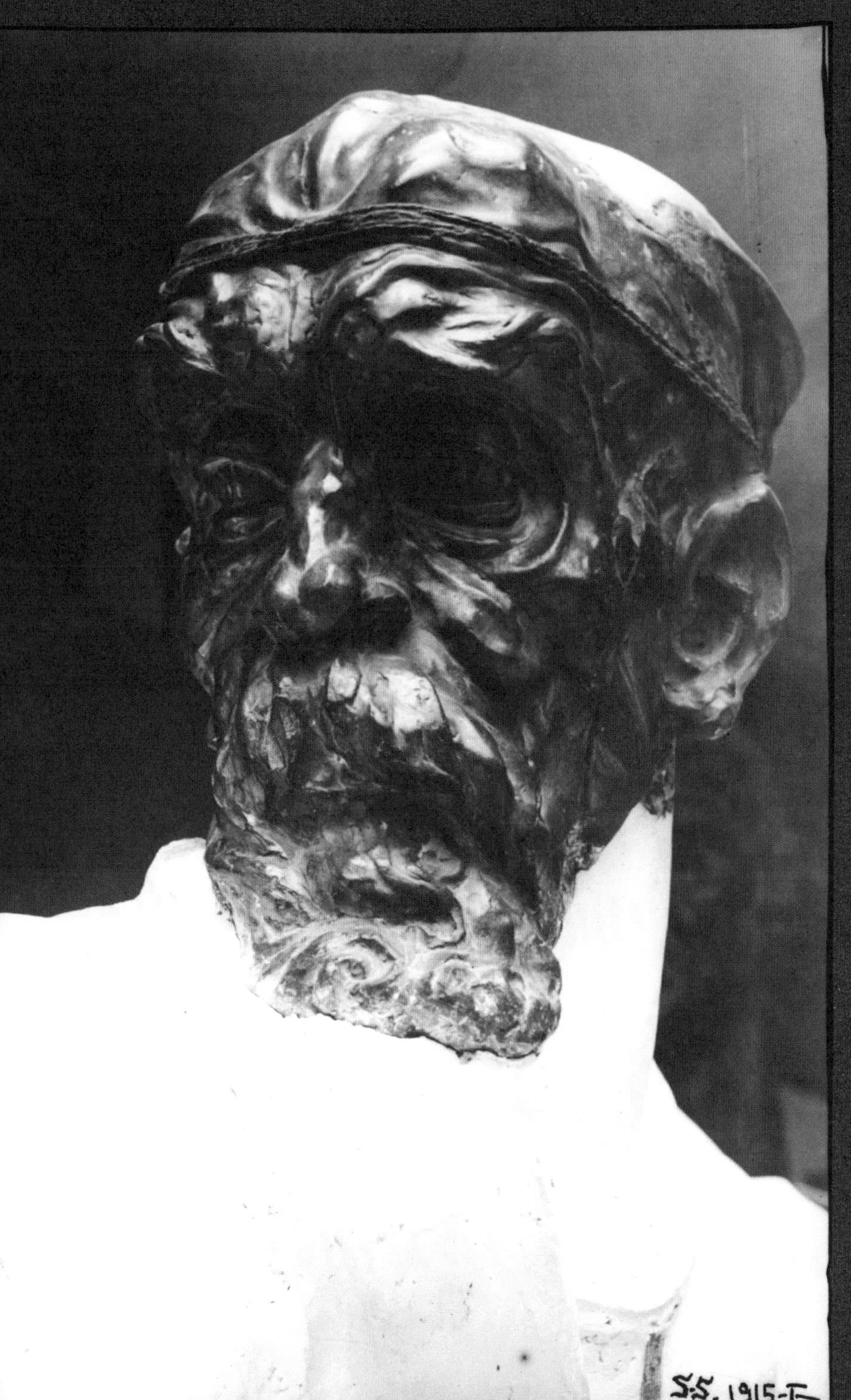
S.S. 1915-I
S.S. 1915-I

Mr. Bosworth

My studio in the old Kimball Building on Wabash
and Jefferson Street in downtown Chicago was
adjacent to another studio, where two young lady
painters practiced their profession. One of them,
Miss Bosworth, a most feminine, charming girl,
greatly interested me and after a few meetings I was
invited to her home to meet her family in Elgin, Illinois. Her father was a handsome patriarchal American with a beard. Eventually, he visited me in my
studio where this portrait was done in just one sitting. As usual, after talking with him for about an
hour and a half, I finished the work from memory,
exaggerating his individual traits of physiognomy.
The bust is much over life-size.

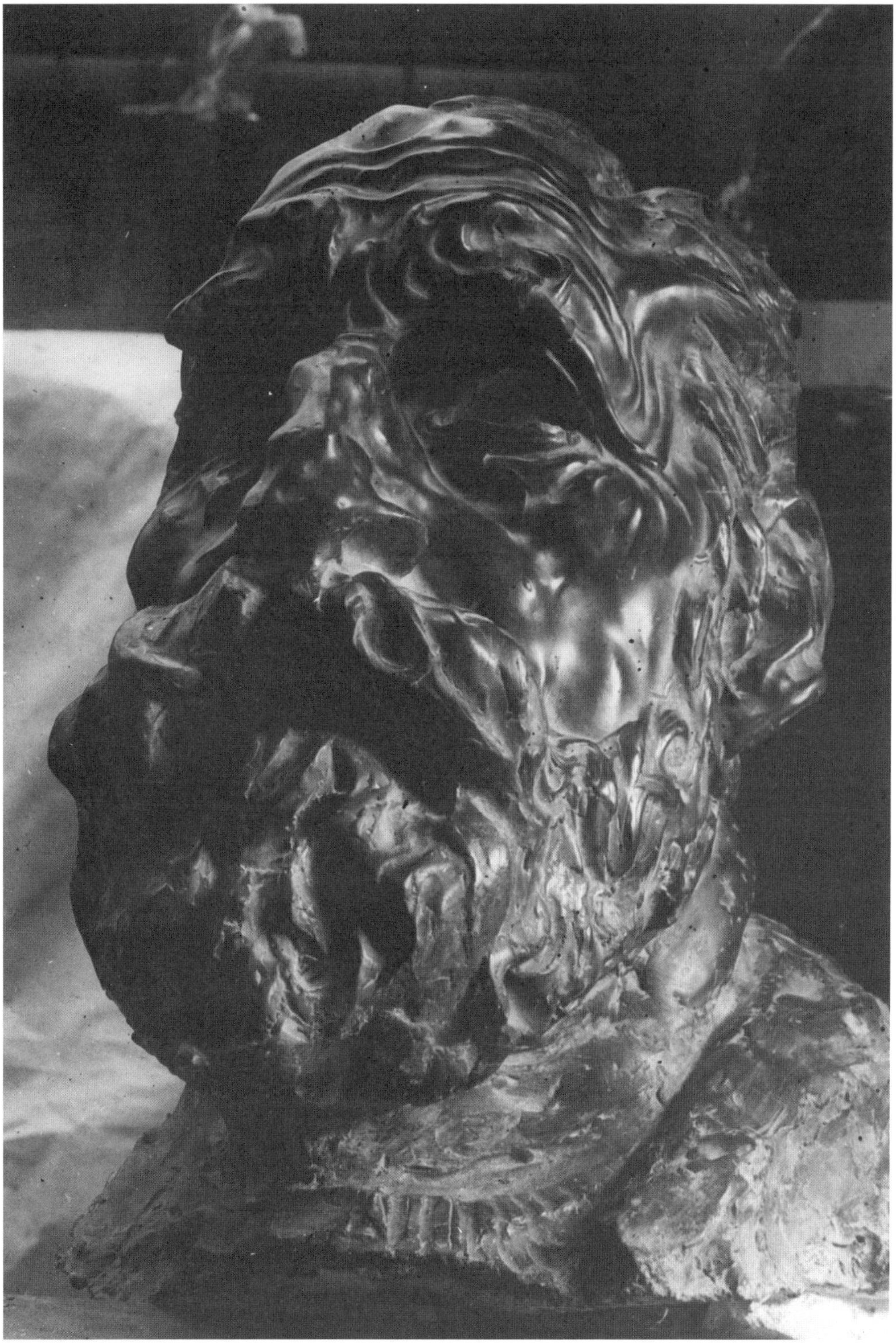

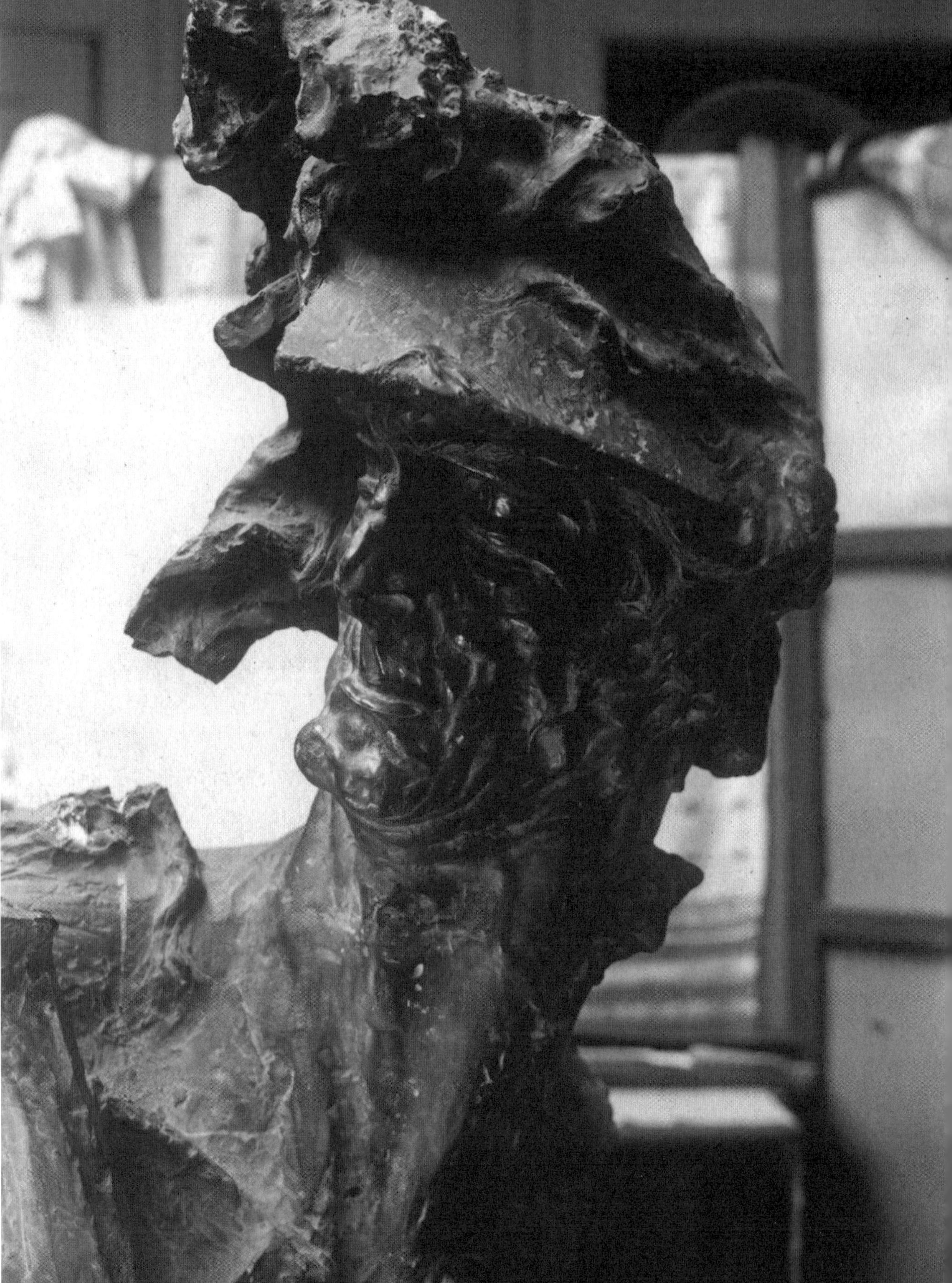

48

A *Warrior*

In 1915 I had to move from Kimball Hall, which was being dismantled and replaced by a greater structure. On Wabash Street, close to Adams, was Bryden's Gallery. It was probably the oldest building in Chicago having remained from the very first architectural splurge. It was massively built, chased with frivolous ornamentation in stone that, throughout the decades, had been thickly painted over in black-green. I made my new studio here, on the third floor.

Having no way to heat my new refuge, it was so cold and mausoleum-like, I termed it the "Dragon's Lair." That winter I greatly suffered from the Chicago cold. One morning I found my newly-begun sculpture, an over-lifesize bust of a warrior in a helmet amidst swirling flags, literally frozen to pieces. The clay so froze that the water in it gathered in crackled geometrics, separating each small fragment as if by glass. Parts of the sculpture fell to the floor. Since I work very rapidly, having no use for models and therefore knowing in advance what is to be done, the *Warrior* was well progressed in expression, if not in form. I rushed out and brought back a sack of plaster. Immediately I covered the frozen clay with a plaster cast before the ice began to melt from the daylight's warmth. Thus the sculpture was saved, though I was never thoroughly satisfied with it, since it is the very last days, the very last minutes of finishing touches, that make the difference between a good and a bad work of Art.

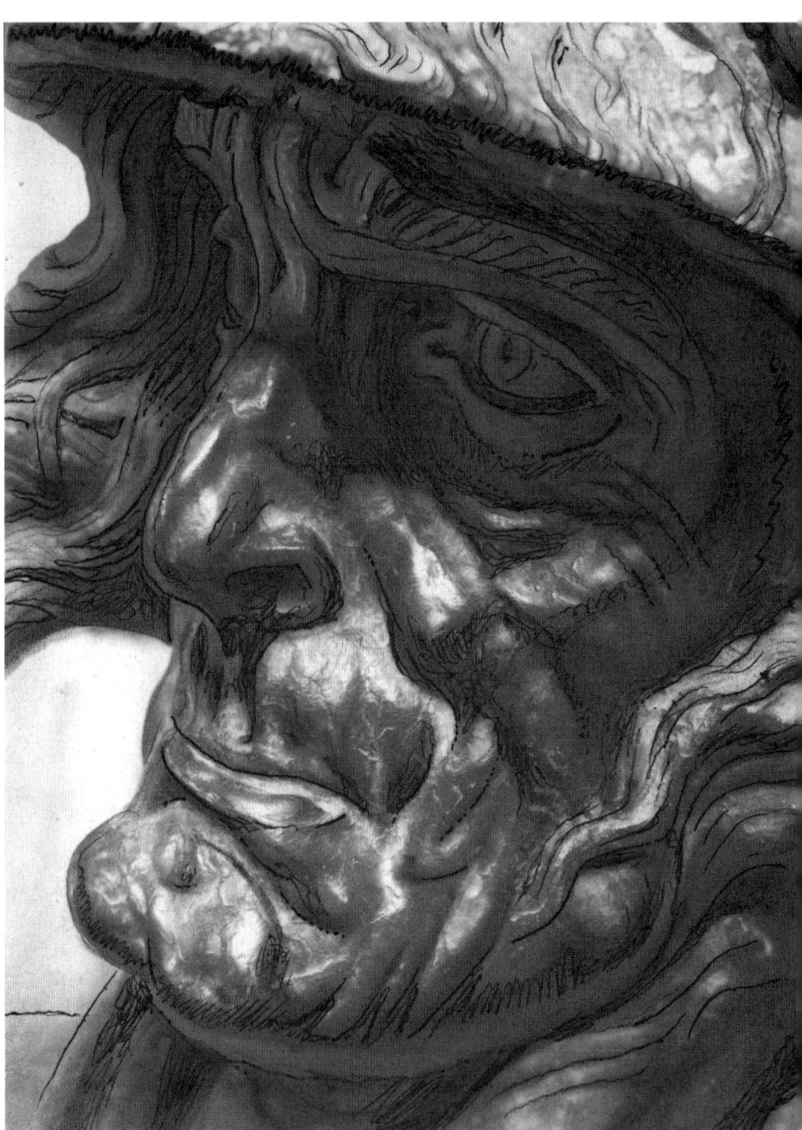

A Portrait of My Grandfather

Reconstructed from Childhood Memories

A Jew

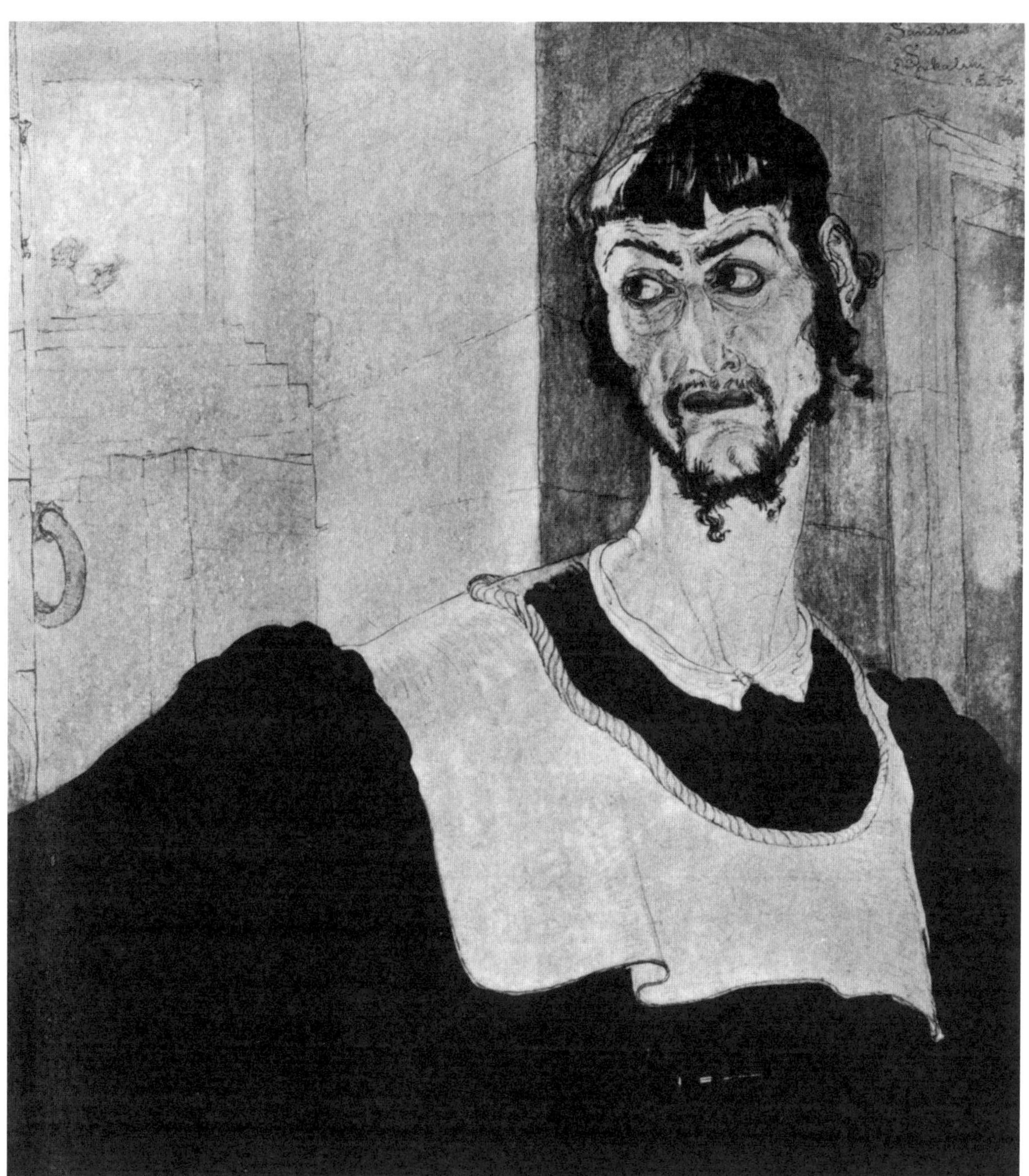

A Grain Merchant

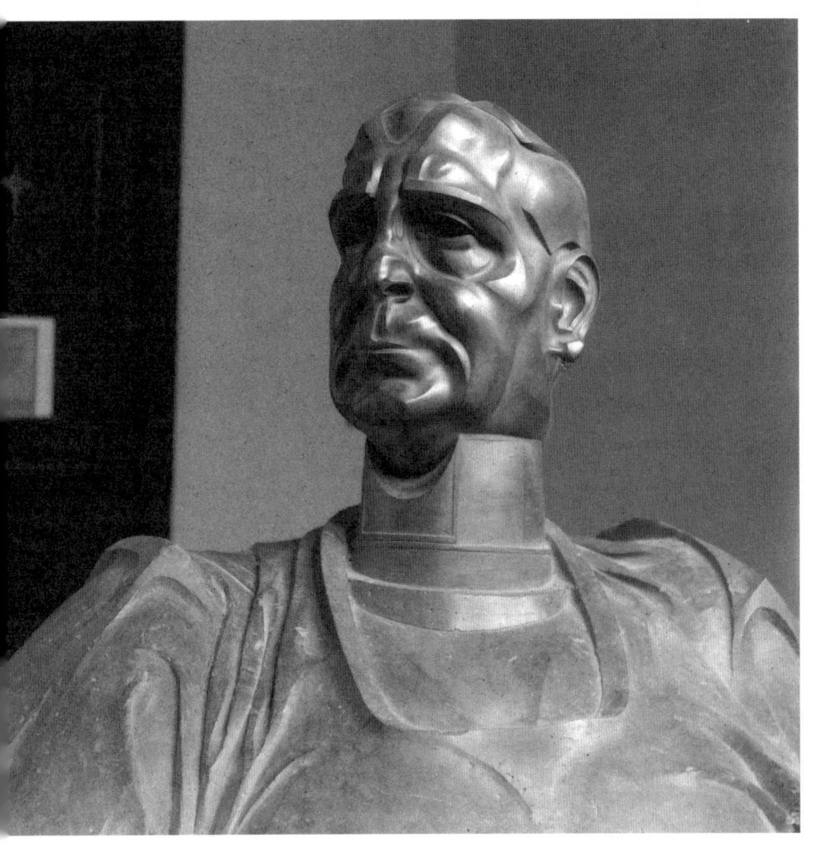

velous Civilization as Americanized "foreigners," have something happen to their mouths. Their lips completely alter so that, when closed, the mouth looks like a mousetrap that just caught a mouse and either has to free it, or will be obliged to swallow it. Apart from this, they get folds in their cheeks on each side of the mousetrap.

When I first came to America as a twelve year old, I noticed these traits on the face of my beautiful teacher. She had these sharp wrinkles an inch away from the corners of her mouth. Even then I could not make up my mind if it was the pronunciation of English words causing this, or the tensions of daily life in this Civilization.

Had the Grain Merchant been a labor leader, he could have made a Dictator, for the roll of fat in the back of his neck classes him, in my system of thinking, with the Yetinsyny (the sons of the Yeti), the world's Empire builders.

He looked formidable with his tin-can American lips, his high collar, and shiphulk shoulders, bringing to my mind the "silly" notion to liken him to a grain silo. So I made this clay portrait much larger than life-size, altering his profile where the pinched nose-skin folded.

He was a friend of Maximilian Kramm, the once renowned European pianist who was now teaching nondescript pupils. It was Kramm who proposed to the merchant that they visit me and commission me to make a portrait. He stood posing for me for about an hour, dressed in a suit "fit to kill." With rimless glasses pinched on his nose, he was elegance personified.

The lips are typically American. Nowhere will you see a mouth so thin as on older Americans. Even Italians, Poles, living in this mar-

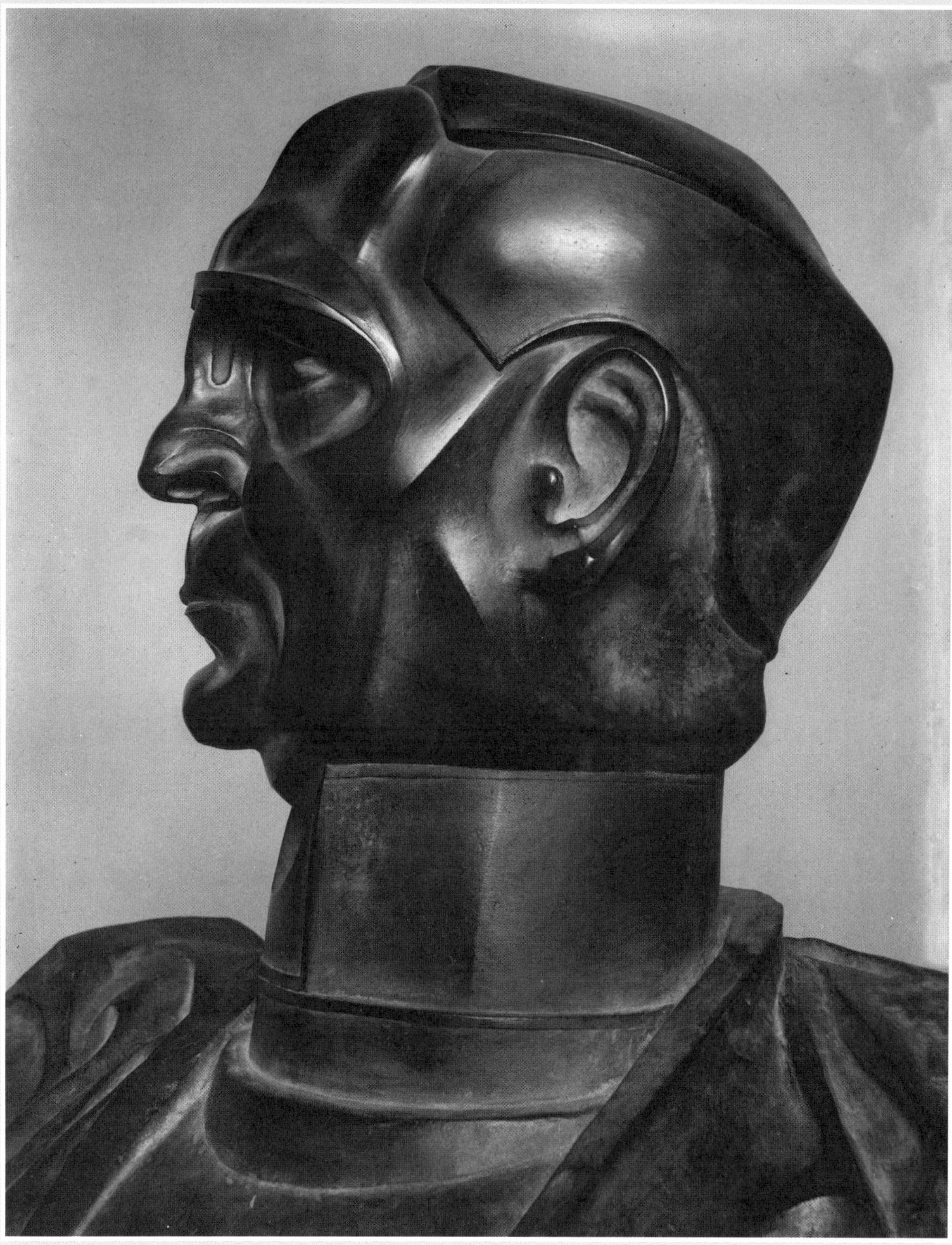

Laughter

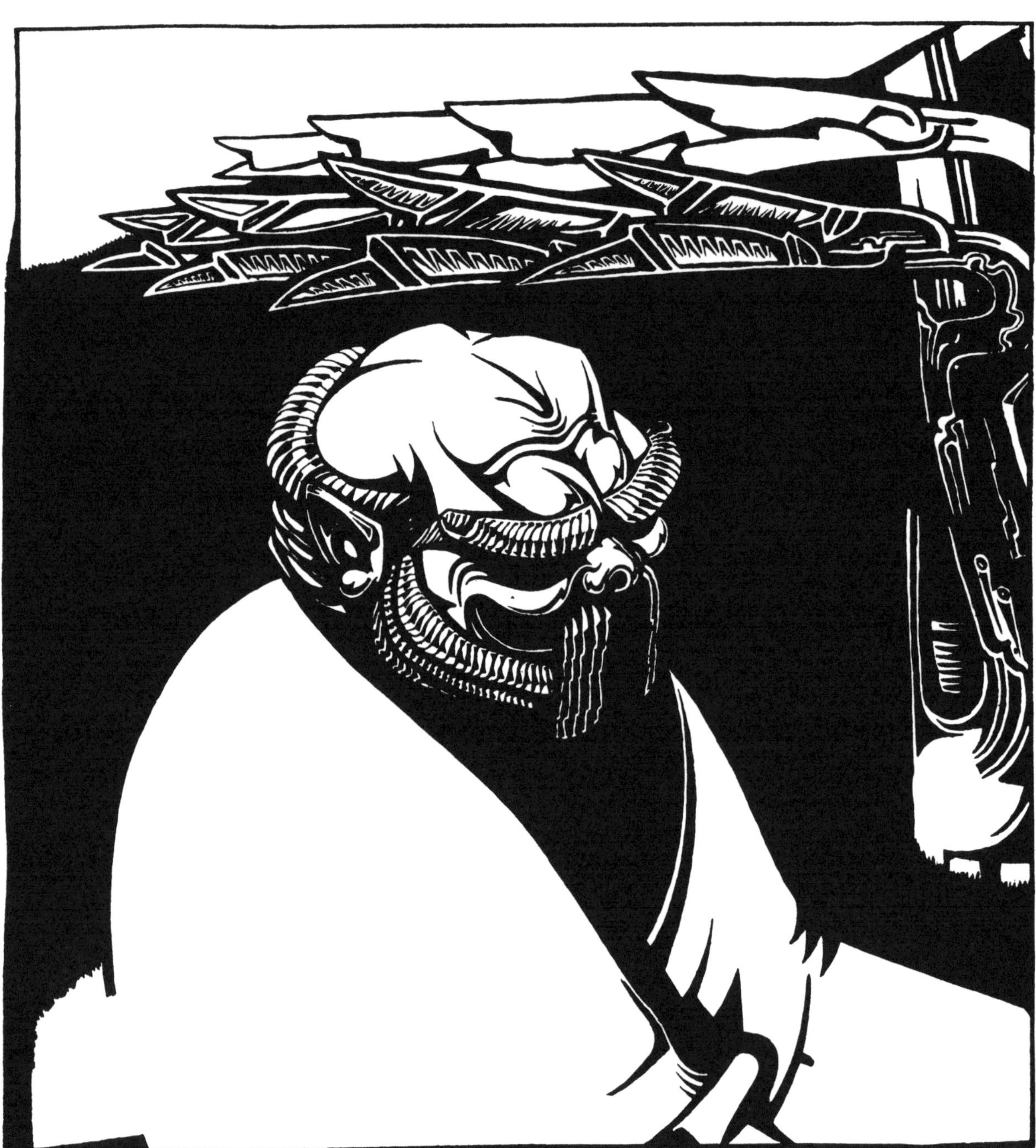

54

A Prisoner of Conviction

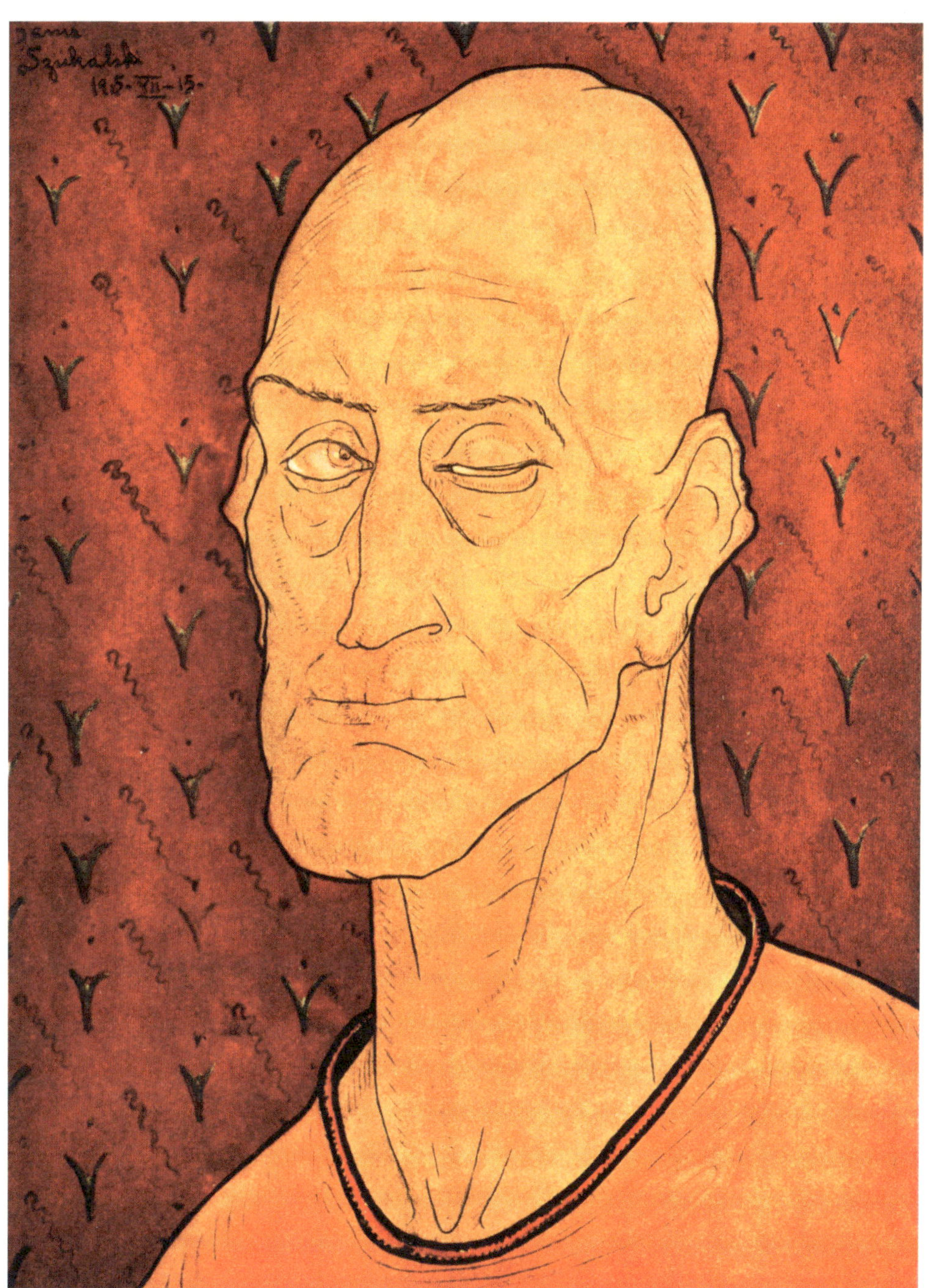

Envy Street

All the photographs of my sculptures in my first two monographies, published in Chicago, were made by me with a very old, small Volklander camera. At that time, there were no flexible films, but glass negative plates. Some of the plates were spoiled by having been accidentally exposed to light.

Such plates I did not throw away, but used them for making more drawings. I improvised directly on the filmy side of the plate, using a sharp-pointed pin at the end of a stick or my pocket knife for larger (black) areas. The plates were large (about 5″ × 7″) and I made a number of drawings, later intentionally exposing them. I made prints of them in my darkroom, but all but a few have survived. The bulk of them have been stolen by Poland.

The subject of this drawing on the glass plate is *Envy Street*. The Hero, a "doer," is returning home from an expedition with his faithful horse, being jeered at by the Polish intellectual riff-raff that always "knows" everything better without ever DOING anything in their life. It is they who cultivate the Mildew of Bondage, so that the virile neighbors enslave Poland repeatedly. They blame the invaders, or Providence, or God… but never themselves for the barbaric inhumanity suffered. They do not know my saying, that "History is but a symptom of the intrinsic WORTH of a given nation." When a nation becomes Glorious, it is due to the fact that they cherish men of INSPIRATION. When a nation is pitiful, it is because such Inspirers are jeered and hounded to death. When nations are led by the MESSENGERS of national biology, they sit on God's lap, purring and free. When they are left to their uncharted meanderings, they are misled by sterile intellectuals.

No wonder many turn to prayers and employ the Virgin of Czestochowa to protect the nation from Yetinsyn Predators as did the Tibetans of Lhasa, whirring their prayer-wheels in frantic delusion that doing nothing brings the unearned Nirvana.

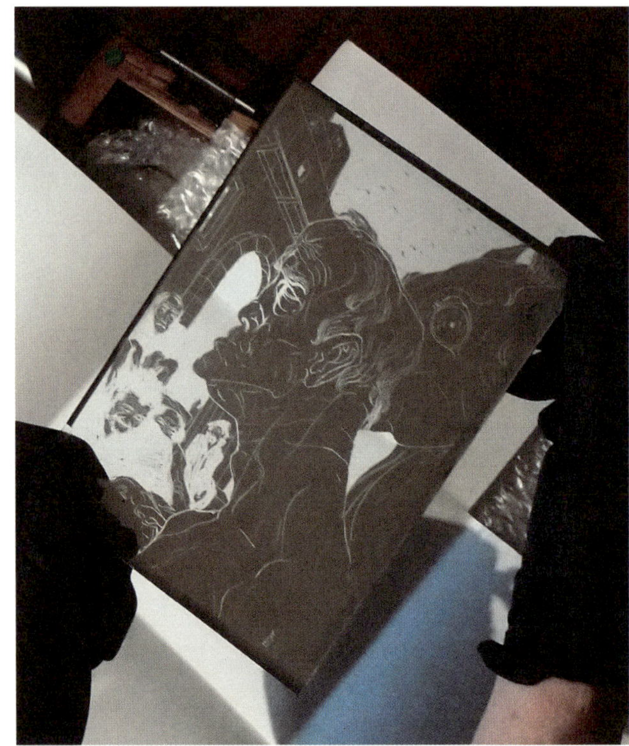

The glass negative.

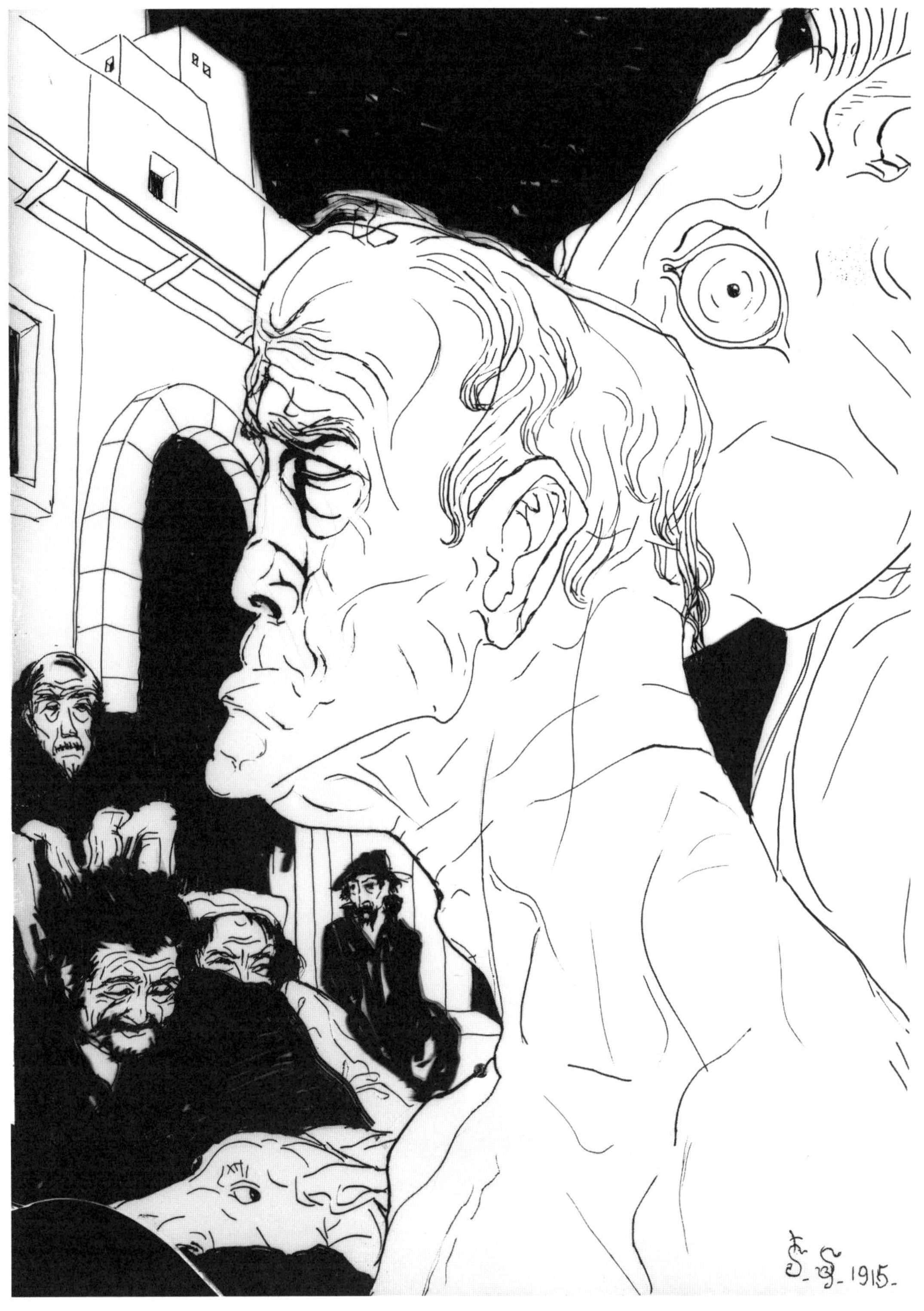

Back Portrait

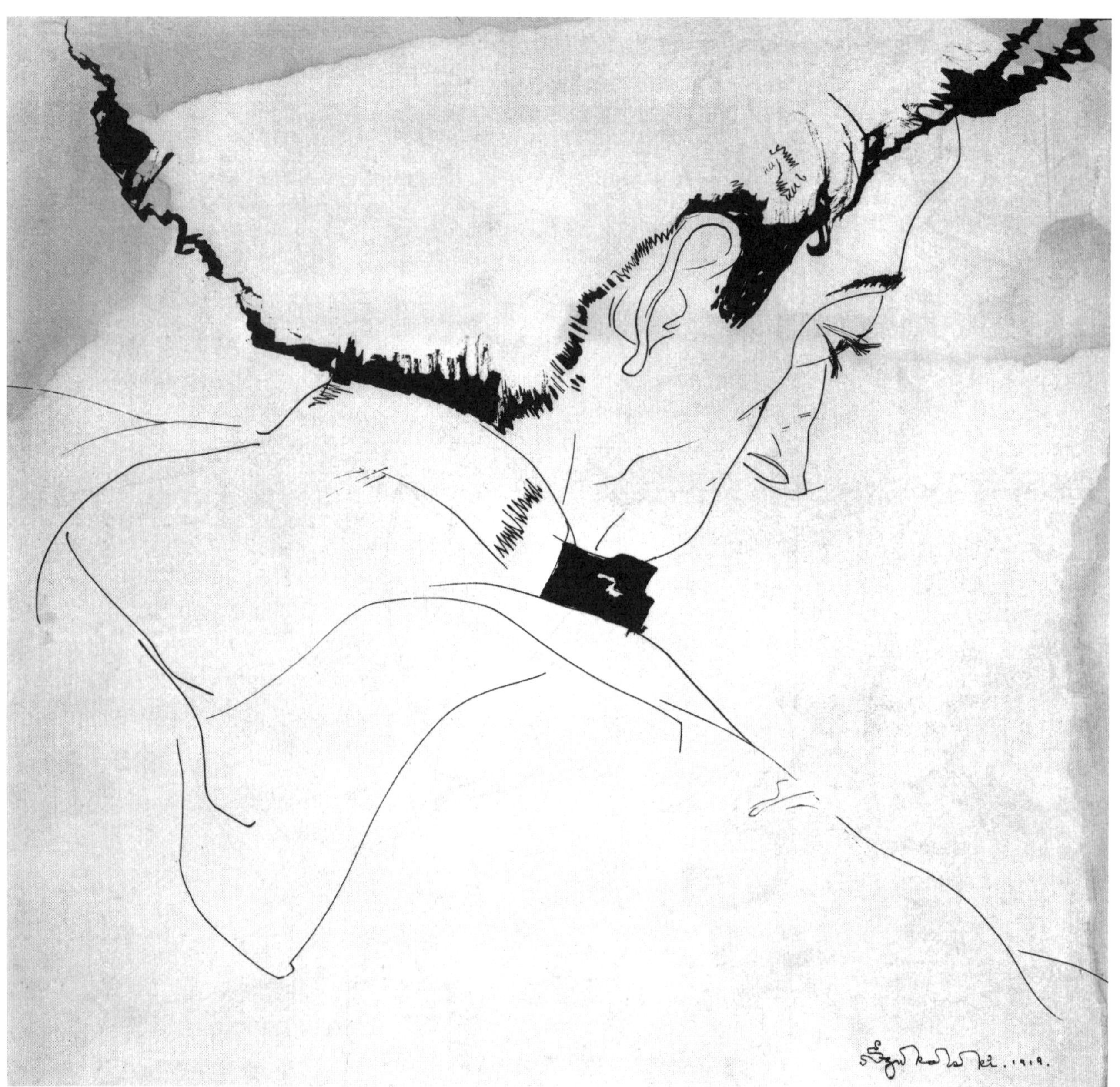

Profile Portrait

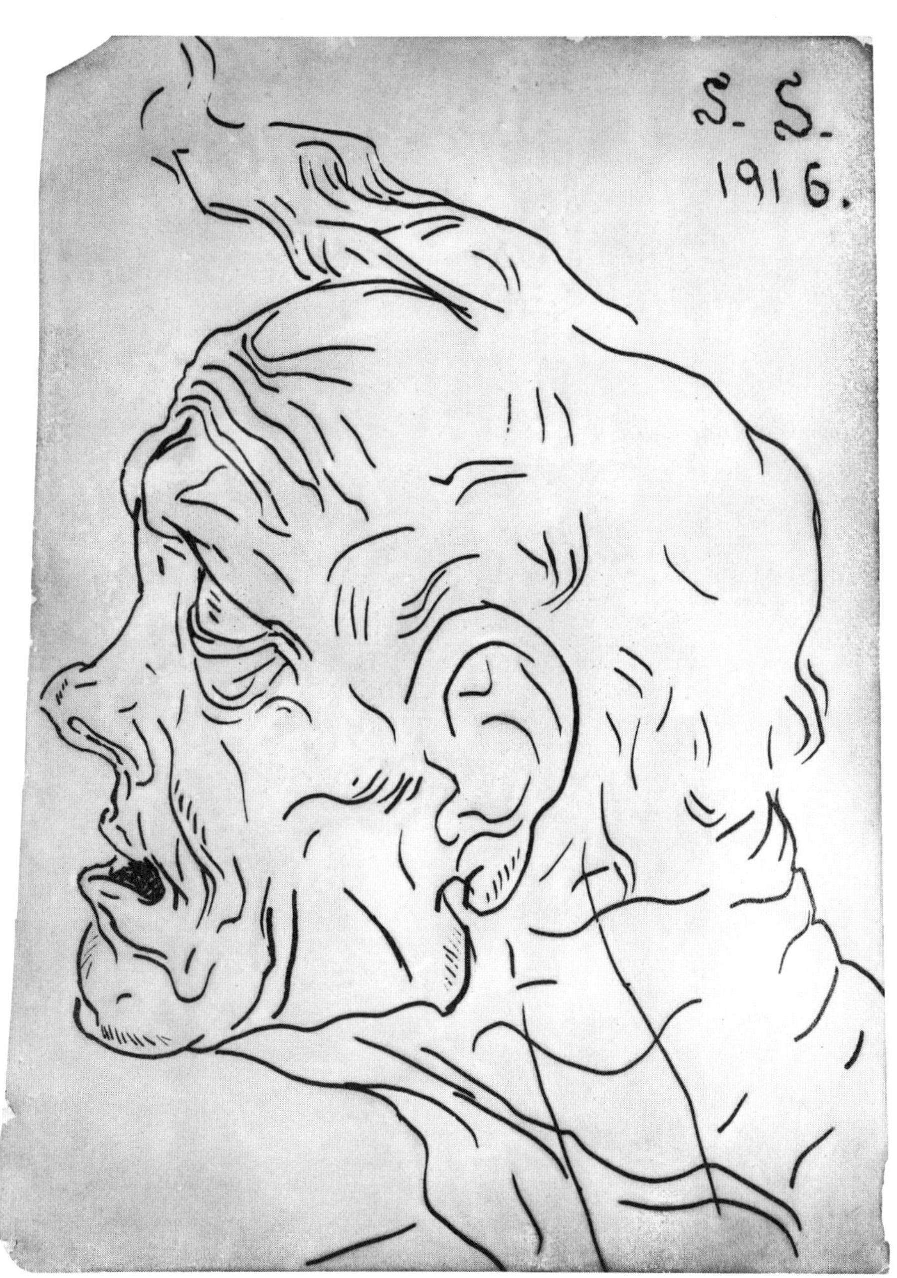

State

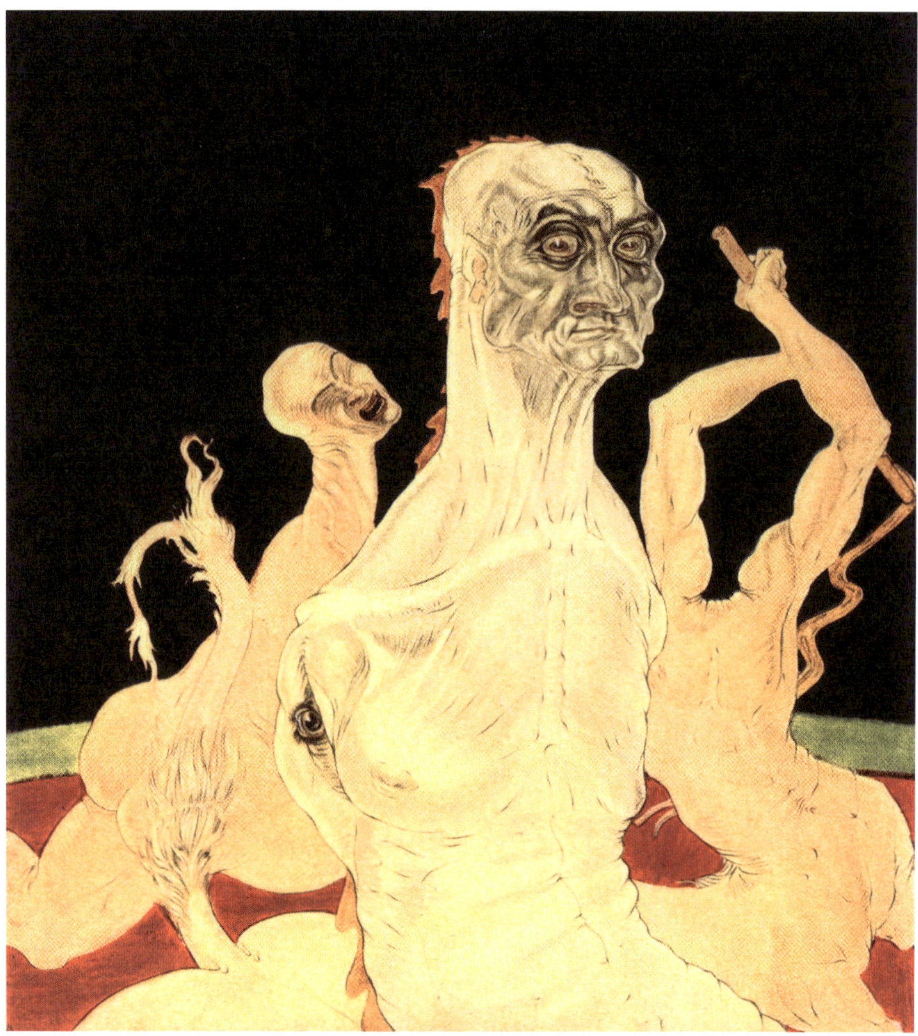

In the foreground is the willpower of State. It is armless because its potent will renders arms unnecessary. It has a rooster's comb on its head as well as the aggressiveness of that fowl. It rides on an old horse of tradition whose tail is moulting. To the right rear is the executive element of State. It is headless, it obediently swings a brass whip, driving the third character of this play to trample the green soil into a bleeding mass. The figure symbolizing the populace is eyeless and earless; it sees not what it does and hears not the protesting outcry emerging from under its colossal feet. Still it is evolved enough to suffer its own pains. It perceives all commandments through the brass whip which lashes it around the arena.

Man and His Conscience

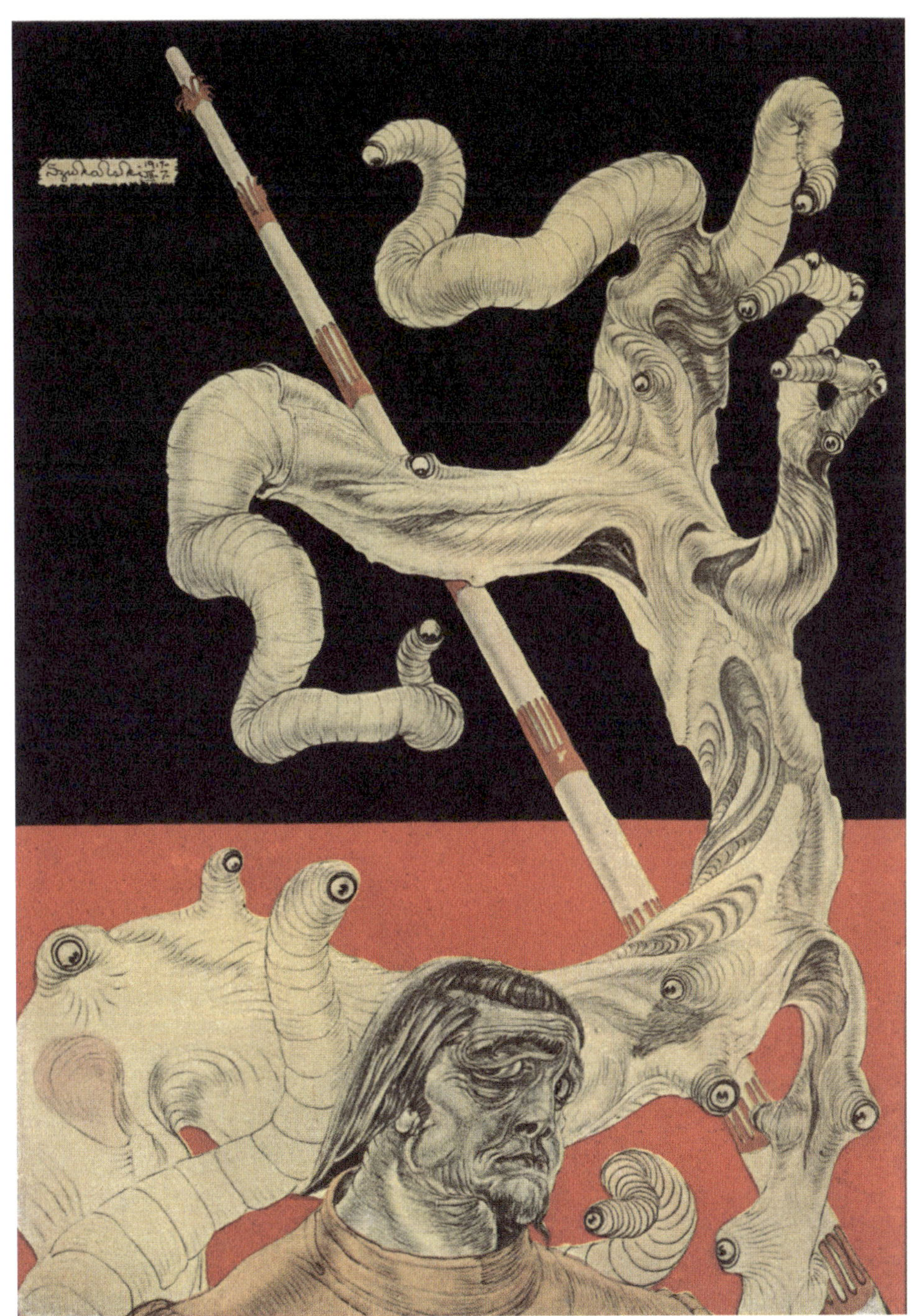

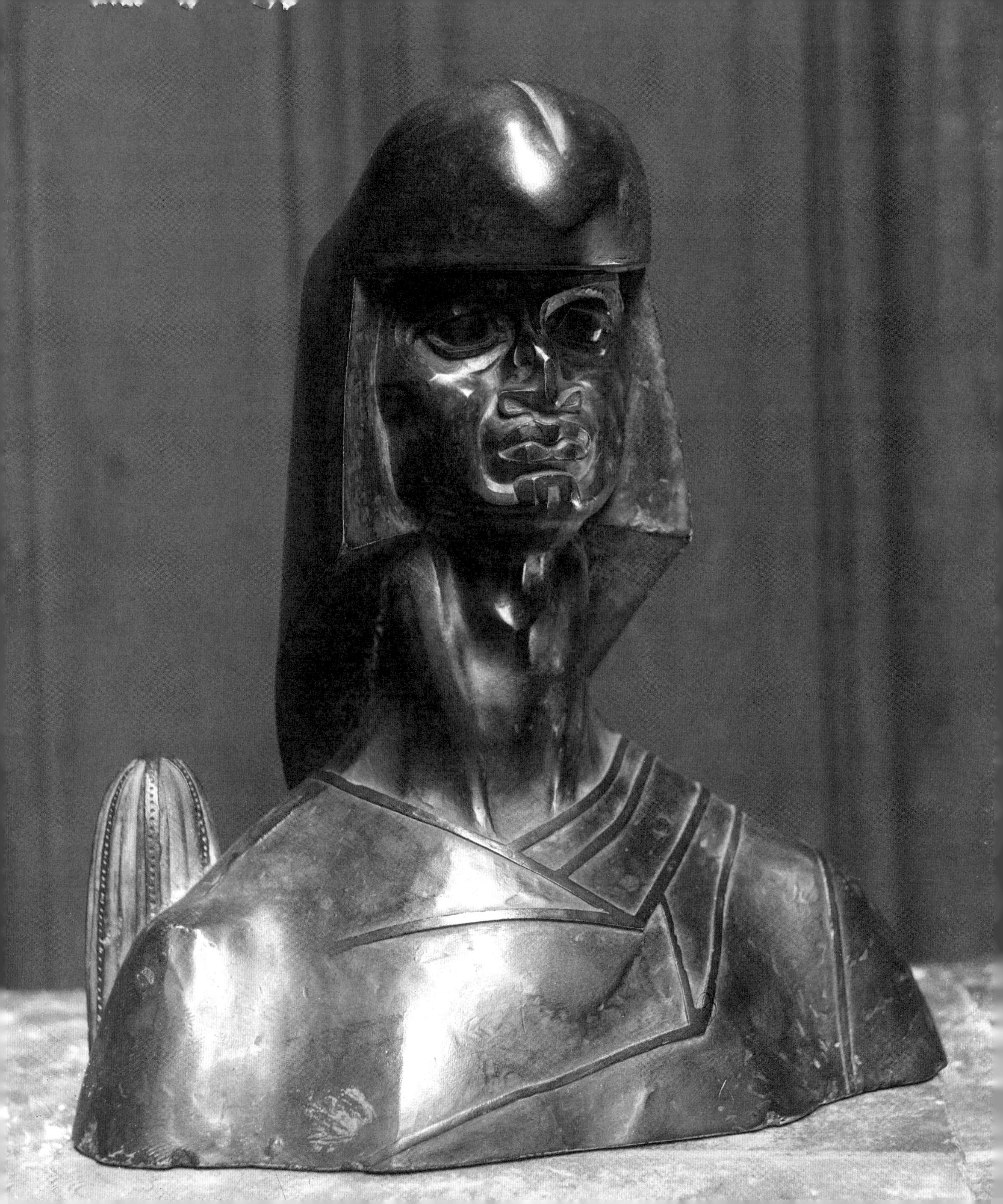

A Hopi Indian

Some of the captions with these sculptures are remote, because I wish to smuggle into the reader's mind that ART is far simpler than the pseudo-profound orations of contemporary intellectuals imply.

In many cases among the finest examples of Art, the creators were simple-minded people who expounded no theories about their profession, but merely followed their instinctive judgments like regular workers. I shall approach you as possible youths who long to create with impatient hands, but may have become paralyzed by self-doubt because this epoch has built so many sterile notions. From my long life as a sculptor, I can tell you the REAL TRUTH, since my superfluous skills qualify me to call my opinions VALUABLE.

Art is SIMPLE. You need no qualifications (like slim fingers, soulful looks, or a murmuring stomach that the person next to you could suspect as being the voice of God). Simply proceed without training, for Art Schools will give you sterile advice that will prove that you have no Talents at all. Start your first work and continue to work without asking anyone's opinions, until you are trapped in it and unable to stop. That being "caught" by what you do is the signal that you have serious potentials.

The fact that you are drawn into that first work proves that you have CHARACTER. Having character is a TALENT, a superior quality. And it is your patience that may shape a lump of clay into an "interesting" object. Art must be INTERESTING, but only to YOU, not to your professor, father or priest. You are the FINAL JUDGE, because it is YOU who is doing the daring.

Now indeed, every lump of clay is given a chance to become a masterpiece, born under the palm of your hand and cherishing gaze of your eyes. It is not the concept (for in the beginning all concepts are worthless) that makes it eloquent, but the surfacing of your biologic potentials. It is your belief in yourself that will make everything you do an eventual masterpiece.

This piece was a means for me to begin to apply sharp edges and stylized forms. I have never been among the Hopi Indians, and at the time I made this work, did not know how they looked. At the age of 23 I was not interested in anthropology and mistakenly gave the sculpture negroid lips. But I finished that mistake… carefully. In fact, it is the mistakes that give "style" to Art. A work without flaws is without style. A cast made from a human body is anti-Art. What Norman Rockwell did with his art was mere taxidermy, composed anecdotally. If you are a beginner, make your mistakes BEAUTIFULLY and they will be Art. Beyond all! Do not fear to undertake the next work and do not stop until it is done COMPLETELY, then… sit back and admire… YOURSELF.

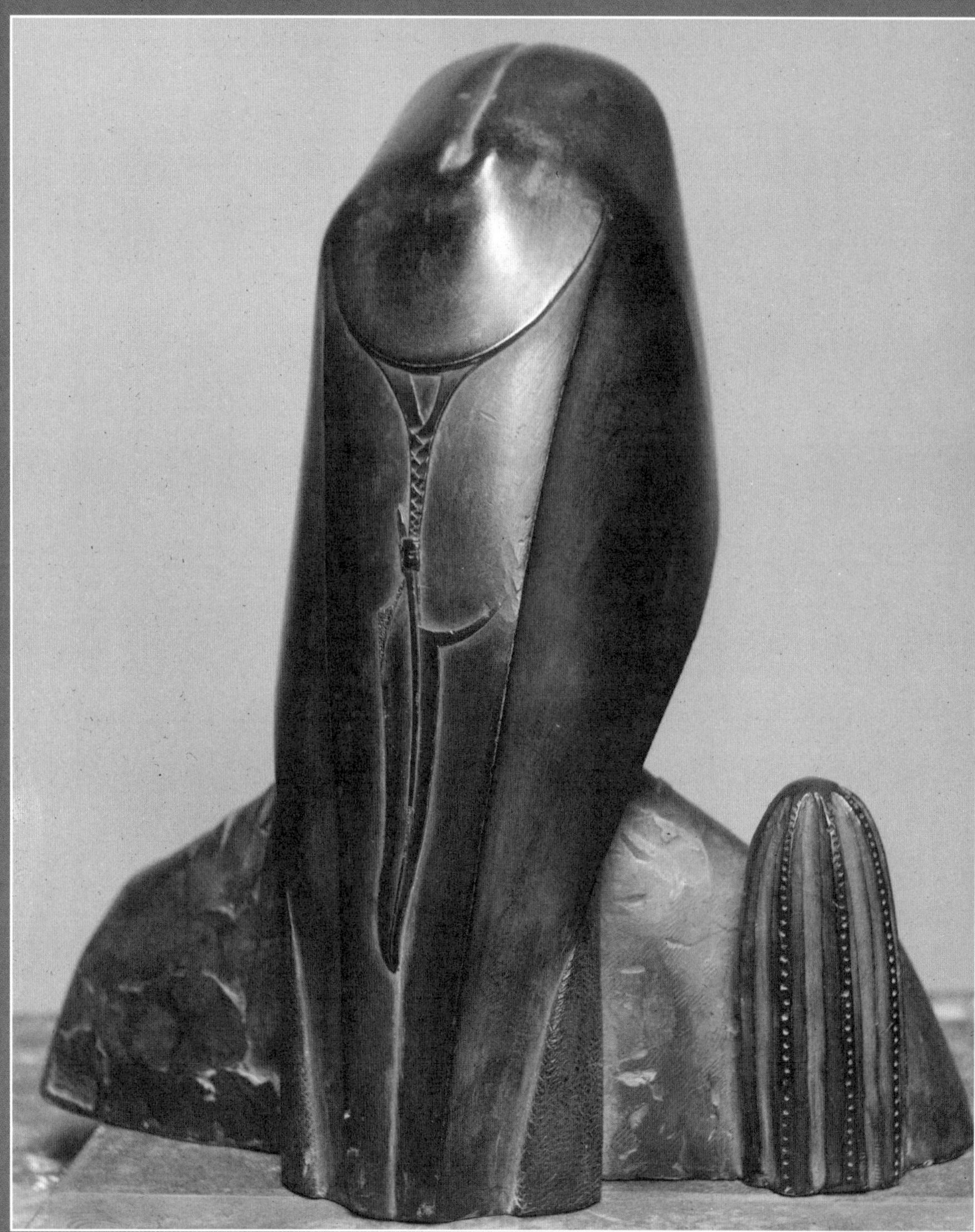

A HOPI INDIAN
Back

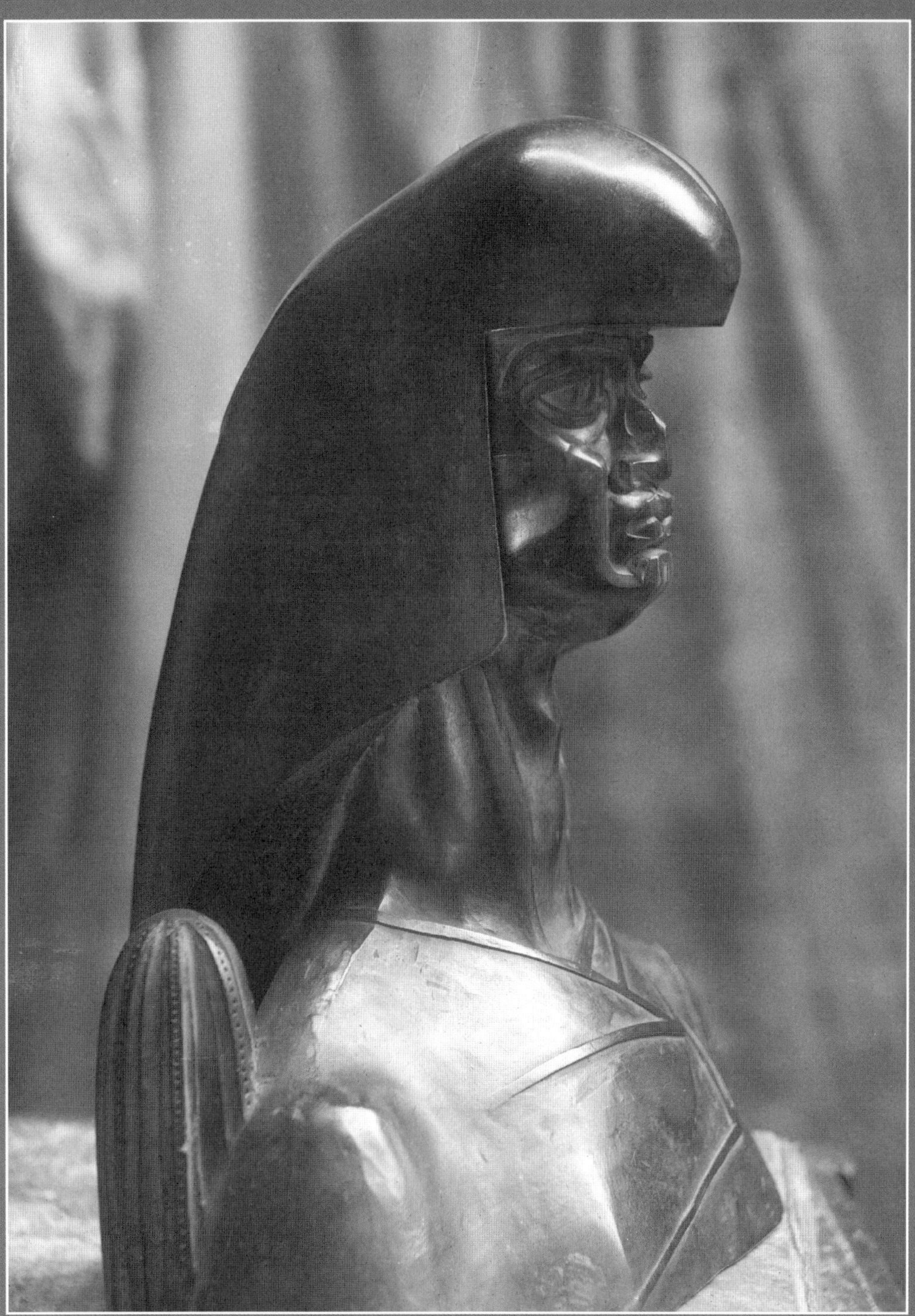

A HOPI INDIAN
Side view

A Limping Hypocryte

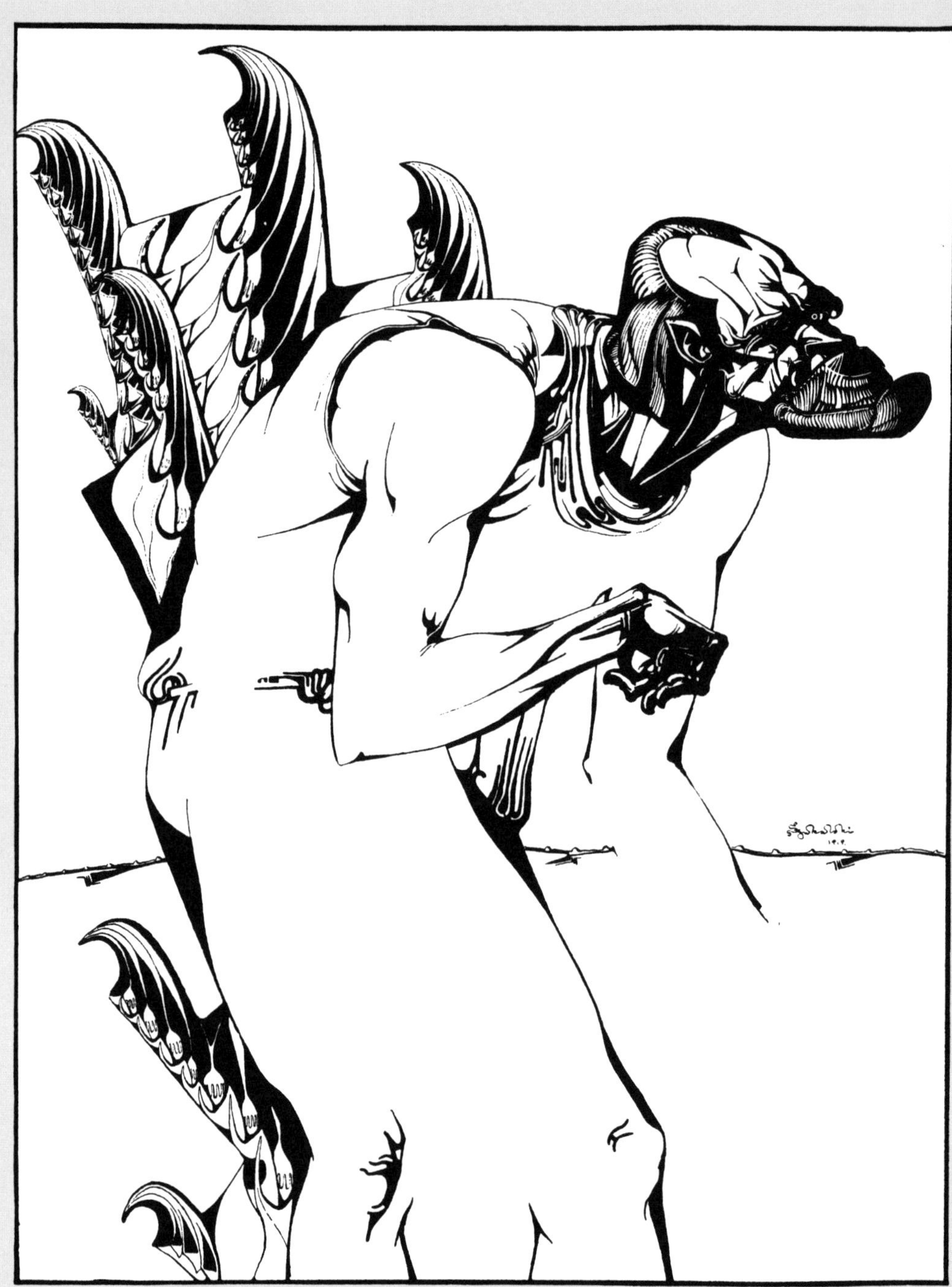

Dollar-a-Year Man

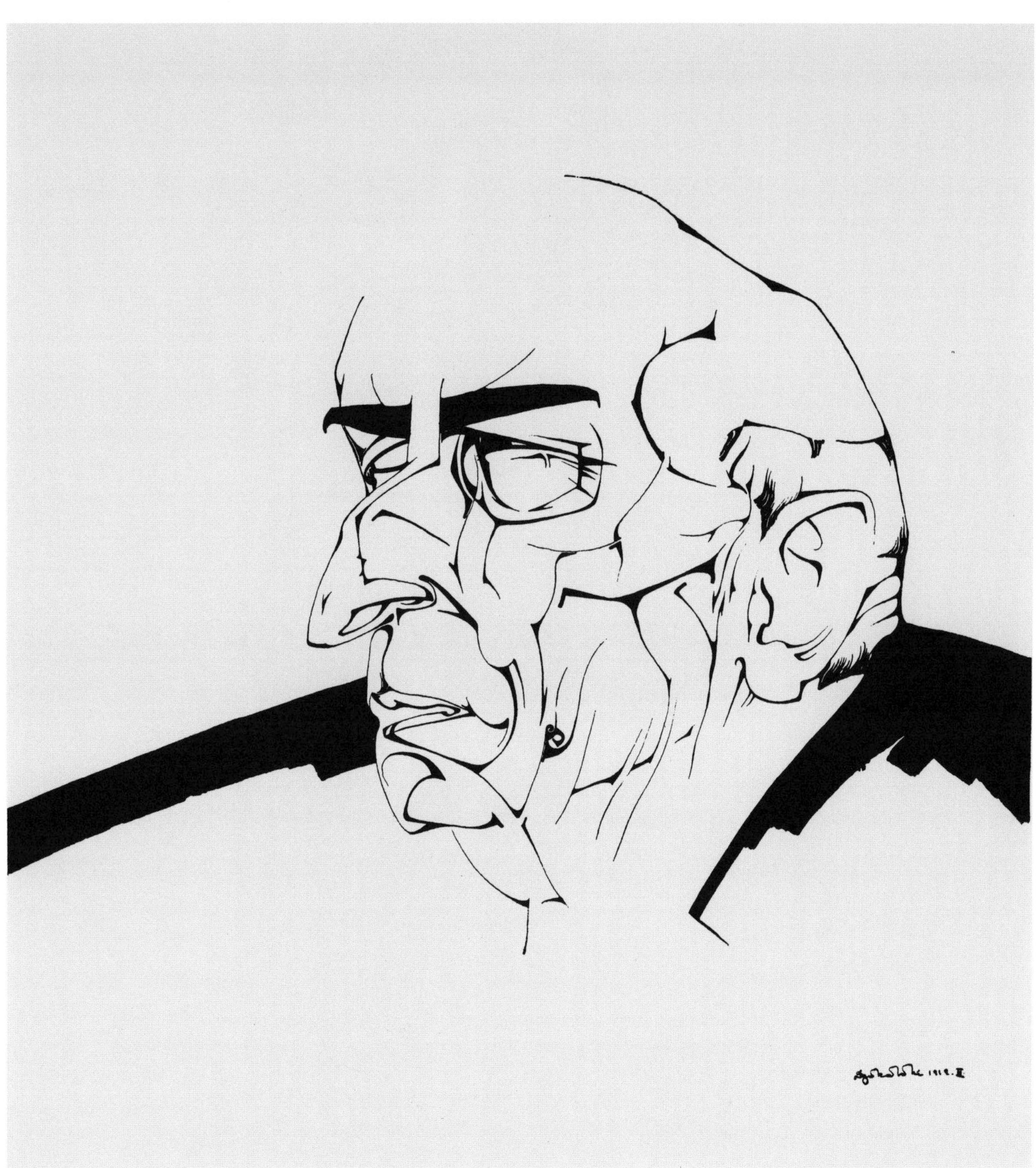

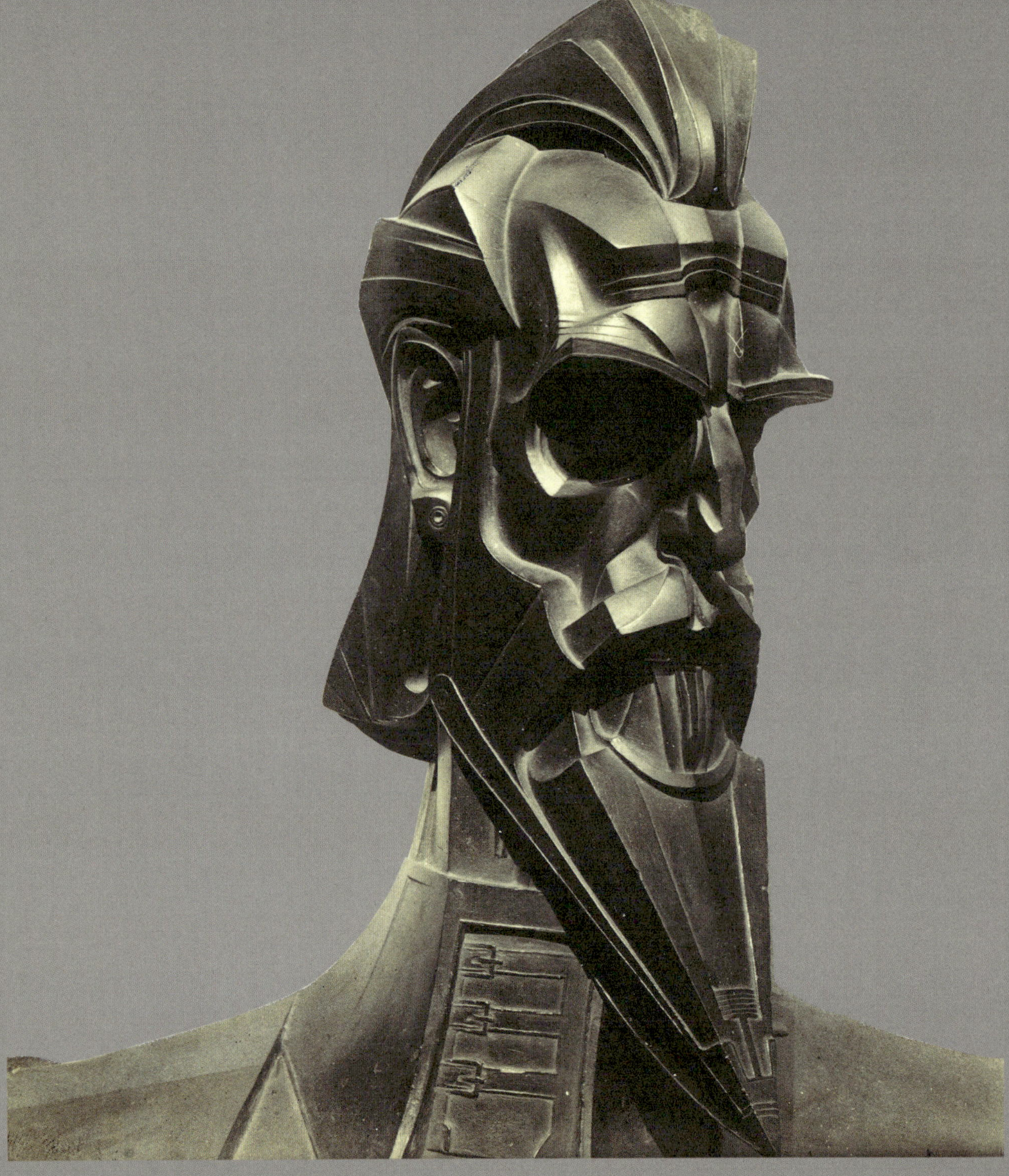

A Portrait of Van den Bergen

This portrait was one of three sculptures I advised myself to do – always having been a father and pedagogue to myself – when in my twenties. I had to break away for awhile from my anatomically inquisitive modeling in which, instead of avoiding the details of anatomy, I made almost vivisection-correct bodies, all from memory, without ever looking at models. In these few pieces I attempted to reduce forms to three dimensions.

Occasionally, while I worked, a white-haired man with the Hollandese name of Van den Bergen, who lived in a suburb of Chicago, visited my studio.

He was a former sculptor of exceptional abilities, but as I, he was impractical, so that he fared worse and worse in this superpractical America. After passing through the meat grinder of American misapplication of great men, he ended doing plaster heads for oculists' windows, on which the latest in glasses were pinched.

He was the noblest being I ever met, a highly cultivated man of considerable erudition. He must have been about seventy, while I was still in my twenties. He and I walked erectly, as a father and his son, and were most congenial in our views on the world and cultural matters. He posed for me while we were discussing with other visitors.

In this portrait I attempted to commemorate his stalwartness and spiritual rectitude. Not academically tracing his features, I percolated the essence of his personality out of his less obvious presence in this ignoble world. To me he always seemed to resemble a Gothic church tower, and here I conveyed my admiration for him.

Head of Politvarus (Piłsudski)

The ancient totem or coat-of-arms of Lithuania is *Pogon* or "Chase," a horseman in pursuit. This, in turn, was derived from a misunderstood archaic pictograph, showing the Dawn God riding his White Horse. Since I have dedicated these last 38 years to anthropology, I discovered the most ancient of all human languages (older than Pali, Pankrit or Sanskrit), out of which ALL ancient languages and savage dialects branched. I named it PROTONG. *Genesis* reports that "There was only one language and one speech in the world." That language I have… rediscovered.

Everything on this globe that has a human-devised name, regardless of its time of naming or place on continents or islands, was compounded of my Protong and I can resegment and translate these names, thus providing the history of this globe far-far beyond prehistorians' imaginings.

Thus, the word "centaur" was made of "Dzen Da Ur," which tells us that the ancient Greeks invented this creature to picture his ability to bring the Light, the description phrase meaning "He (to the) Day Gives Birth."

The bewinged Horse of Pegasus was named "Bega Z Us" in a compressed Protong phrase, which means "He Runs (out) From mortally-Asleep," i.e. the dead one, which is the now-submerged – showing only the top of its forehead – but at one time tallest of all lavaic mountains in the Pacific, *Mataweri* ("Mother of Worship"), erroneously named by the discovering Hollanders… Easter Island.

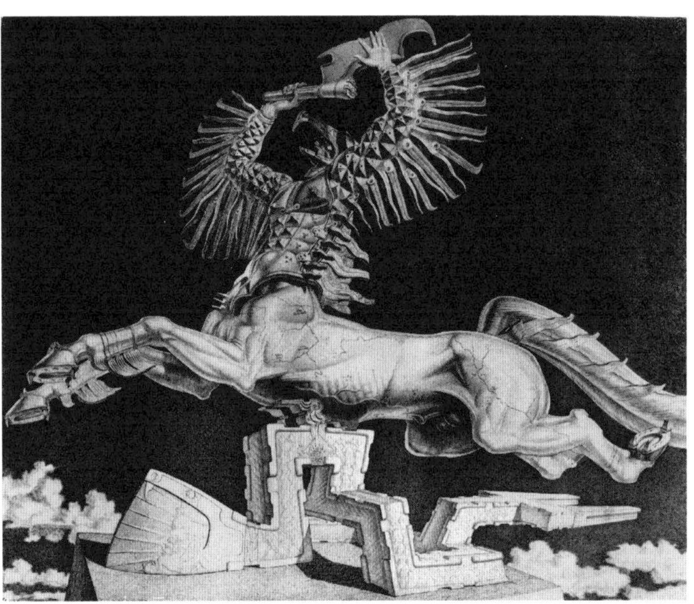

POLITVARUS is like the bewinged Pegasus, born out of Gorgon's volcanic head.

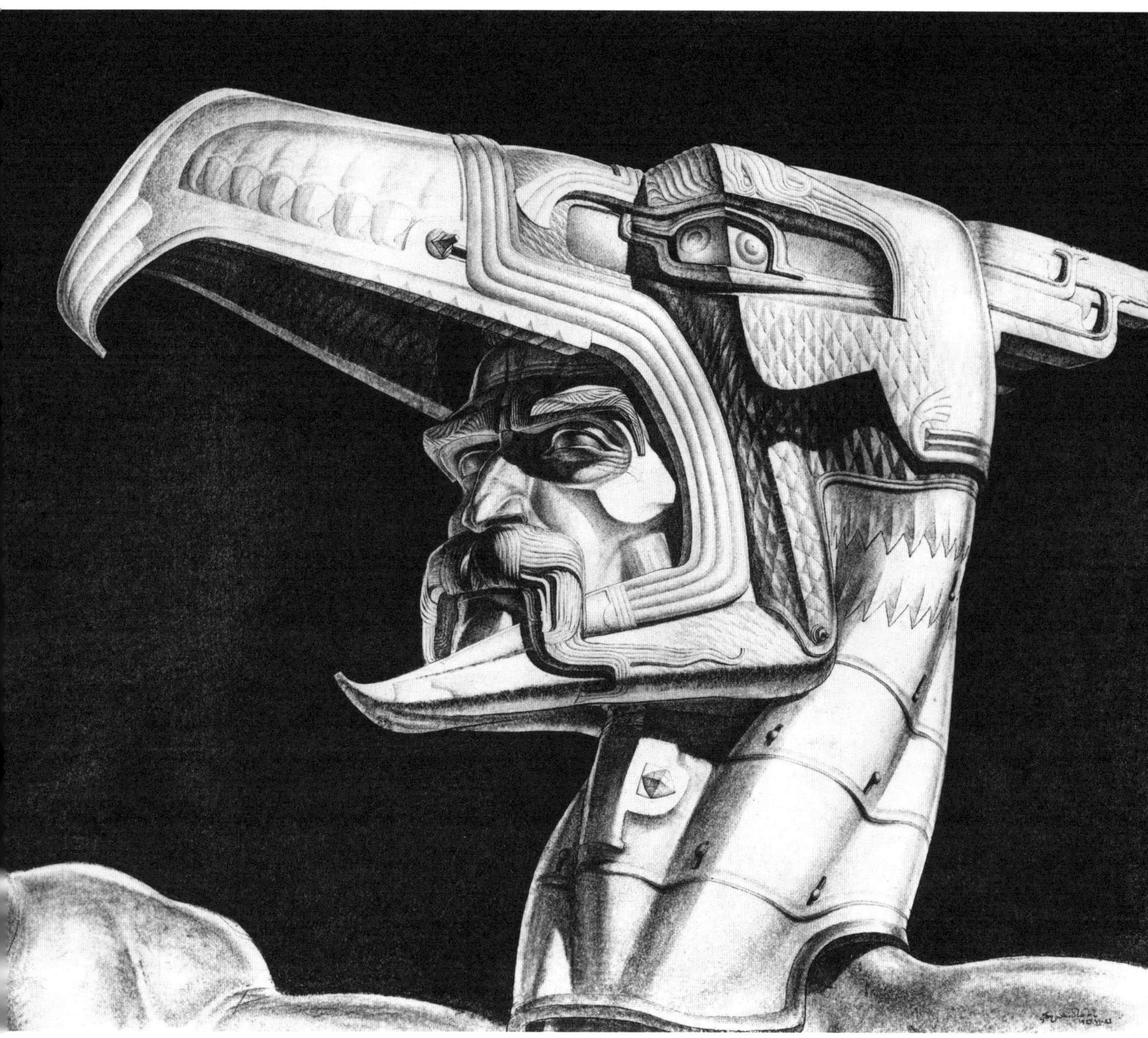

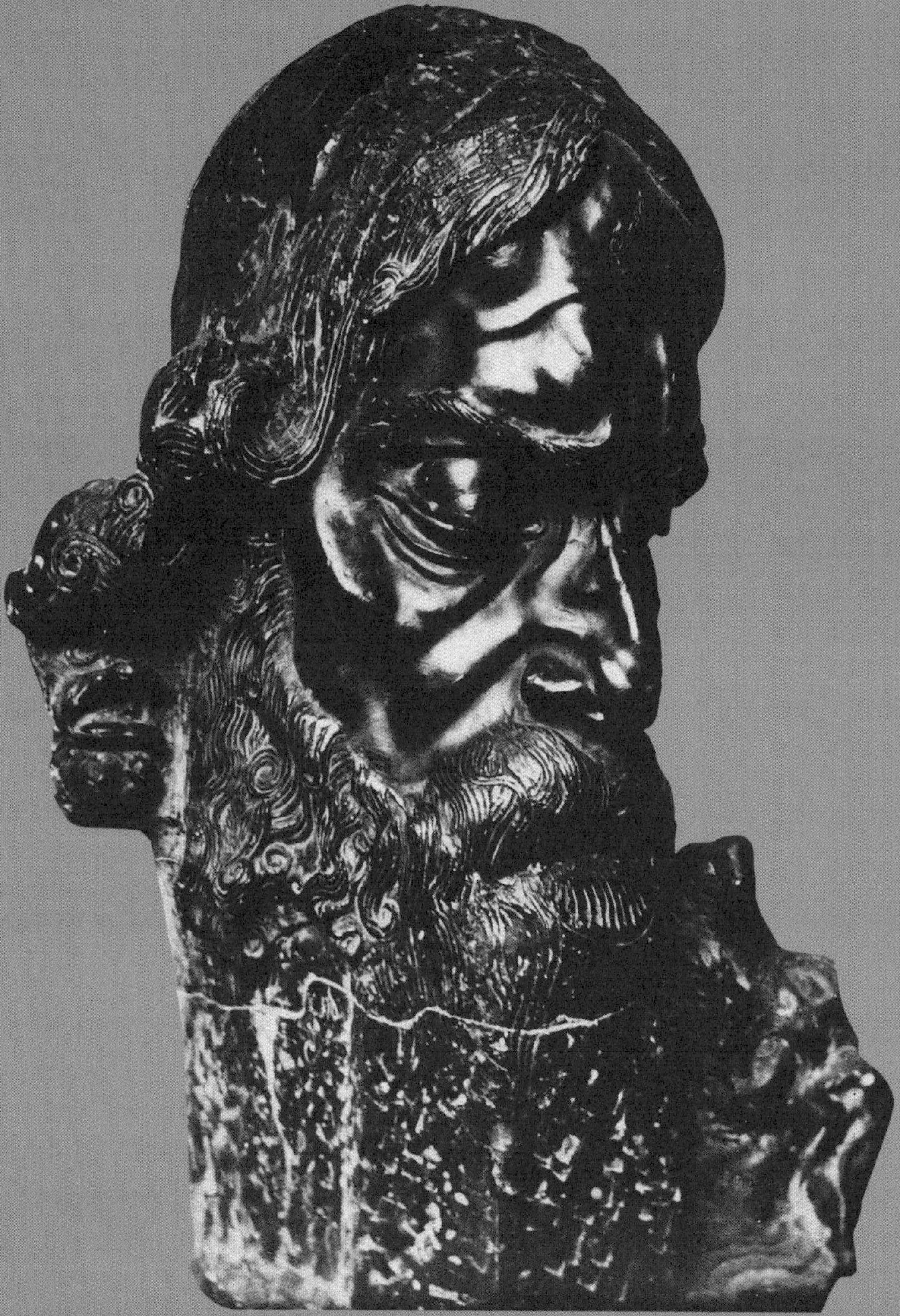

Rabindranath Tagore

When I was twenty-two years old, living close to the University of Chicago, on 57th Street and Jackson Park, I received a letter from Mrs. Moody, the widow of the founder of the Moody Institute of Bible Interpretations. I was startled, since theological matters were a sphere of speculation I refrained from being involved with, having been brought up in Poland where religiosity stifles the very breath of Polonism, which for me took the place of any other concern whatsoever.

Receiving my affirmation to her question if I knew who Tagore was, she informed me that he was eager to meet me, and would I therefore come to dinner on a certain evening? I eagerly accepted the invitation.

Rabindranath Tagore, being the richest man in his native Calcutta, had presented it with his Santiniketan, a vast university which included polytechnical, medical, agricultural and cultural institutes. As the most spiritual poet of India, he had received a Nobel Award and, in Britain, elevation into knighthood.

He was a white-haired, elderly man with a soft voice that he, like many Hindus, used in a rather high pitch (which I thought was due to weak larynx muscles, spending days in silent meditation). One of the purposes of his trip, besides lecturing, was to raise funds for the building of a hospital for the victims of elephantiasis, for which purpose the Moody house was temporarily his. After the first visit, I was invited many times to see him.

In his company was

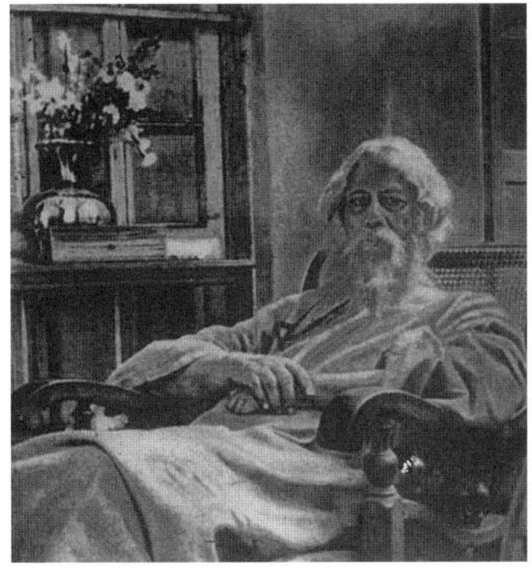

Rabindranath Tagore

also a student of Santiniketan, Mukul Chandra Dey, a youth slightly younger than I. He showed me some of his small drawings, with which I was singularly impressed. The older gentleman was rather displeased that Mukul insisted on going to Paris to "finish his study." Though I had never been to Paris at the time, I held views uncomplimentary to that "center of Art." Those were the years of brainwashing of the public of every nation, from Russia via Italy to the USA, into artificial ecstasy about the droolings of Kandinsky and Picasso, which I, while still a student at the Krakóvian Academy, recognized as the veiled intent to DESTROY our Culture. (Much later I read that Lenin had indeed commanded his "ideological" underlings that "In order to control the society of every nation, we must first CONTROL Art, everywhere!" Thus, the press was coerced into raving about everything in Art that depraved it and thereby… nullified it.) In Paris,

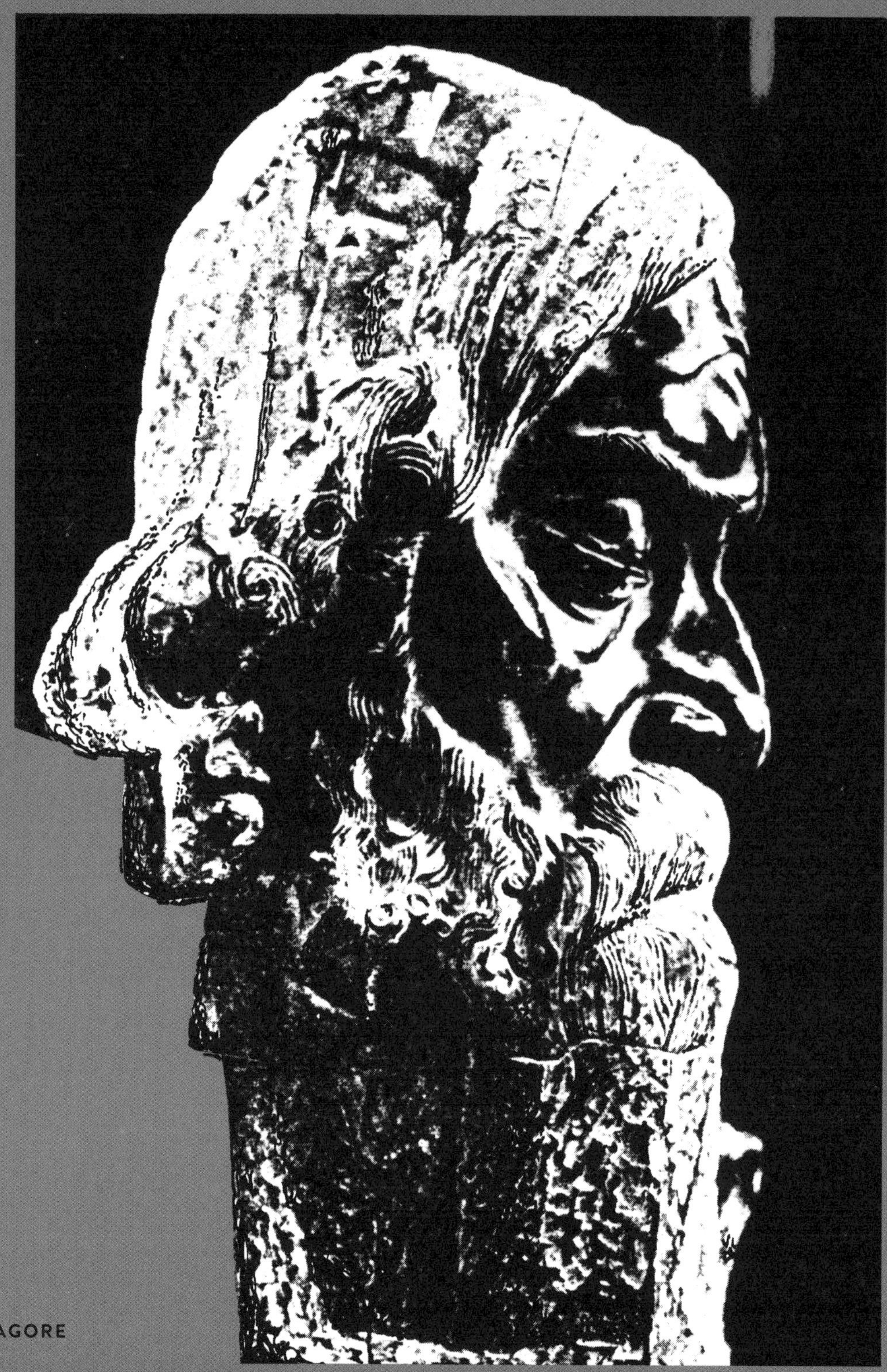

RABINDRANATH TAGORE
Retouched photograph

the Art Schools had introduced a new manner of accepting students. Instead of being subjected to examinations, all candidates were accepted, as long as they could afford the tuition. Thus, it happened that all the worthless human misfits, after having failed in their own countries, found their haven in the French metropolis, eventually to cosmopolitize it out of existence as world leader.

Mukul had fought off Tagore's attempts at dissuading him from going to the Mecca of all failures, finally being allowed to accompany him to America, on his way to France. At that time I did not know of Tagore's attempts, but advised Mukul to return to Calcutta, develop his own Art as a HINDU to a higher degree and first become renowned as an artist of India. "You are already a fine artist, but with your silly anticipation of finding miraculous Culture in Europe, you will swallow as a new religion any pseudo-movement, any Ism of the misfits who abuse painting and sculpture with combs, forks and brushes stuck in their noses to give an easy semblance of individuality. Later come to Europe, with enough belief in yourself to look upon European Decadence with CONTEMPT and the ability to select really worthy examples of Art from all ages and Cultures."

My arguments persuaded Mukul to return to Santiniketan. Tagore, overwhelmed with pleasure, called me to see him as soon as I would. Through the weeks of our numerous meetings, he knew of my attitude towards Art pedagogy, my contemptuous view of Art critics, whom I regarded as the carriers of the Modernist Plague, and my unorthodox definitions of all established views.

Almost immediately after I entered the room where several friends of Tagore had assembled, he said: "I am convinced that you indeed are a natural pedagogue, and because of your intrinsic interest in the development of my pupil into a great artist, I decided that you should reorganize my Santiniketan. My nephew, Abanindranath, the greatest artist of India, will assist you. Will you agree to come to Calcutta?" Without a moment's hesitation, I agreed and he embraced me. This was an unprecedented honor bestowed by the great poet. I had associated with Hindus for some time and always longed to visit their Civilization of ages past. The dream was not to be fulfilled, however. The British Consulate had heard about my Vagabond Club, where the most brilliant intellectuals of Chicago assembled and exchanged views. I was always contemptuous of nations that amassed vast Empires on which to parasite and, though the Hindu Culture interested me, I recoiled from its out-of-outer-world introspections and constant meditations. Consequently my reputation as a "Wonder Youth" with shocking views had preceded me to the British Consulate and it refused me the granting of a visa.

If I had kept my inconvenient opinions to myself, the Council would not have heard of me. But then, I might have been less popular and I might not have been invited to the suppers I otherwise rarely ate, and my thunderous thinking might have been mistaken for the grumblings of my forlorn stomach, and people would have shunned away from me.

On one of his visits to my small apartment, I made this much-over-life-size portrait of Tagore and offered it to him as a gift. Later he had it copied by a sculptor in Calcutta, and presently it is a permanent monument to him inside the Santiniketan.

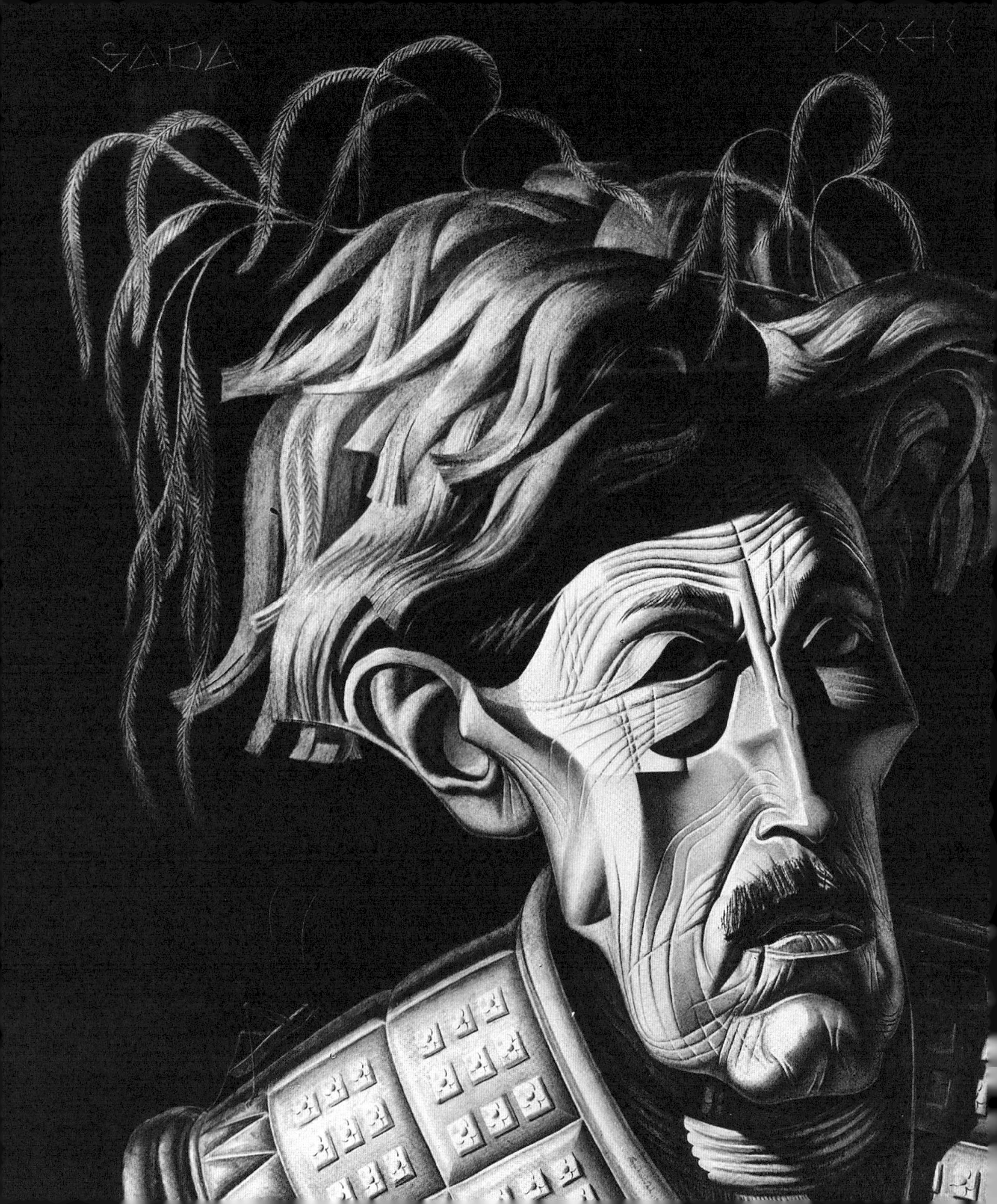
SADA

Sadakichi Hartmann

He was a ballet dancer, professional or not I never learned. For years I had heard of him; then one day when I was living in Hollywood, he knocked on the door and introduced himself. It was from him that I learned of his former association with ballet, for I knew him as a poet and writer, emulating Albert Hubbard's *Little Journeys to the Homes of Great Men*. He was not a thinker, but a rehasher of other writers' opinions, mostly a libertine and floater. Being neither Japanese nor German in upbringing, he had none of his parents' backgrounds.

His extraordinarily narrow face and lack of jaw mark him as the tail-end of a biologically spent strain of a family. He is the absolute opposite to my type of build. I, being of round face, am never hesitant in my choices, persistent to the point of obsession, sexually inexhaustive, and never alter my views on vital things once they are started.

I am convinced that individuals with round or square faces are endowed with extraordinary vitality, from which springs all CREATIVITY. Narrow faces indicate speculative, calculative skills. They are non-creative, but make good lawyers or interior decorators. They make the worst possible lovers as they are NEVER overcome by Passion.

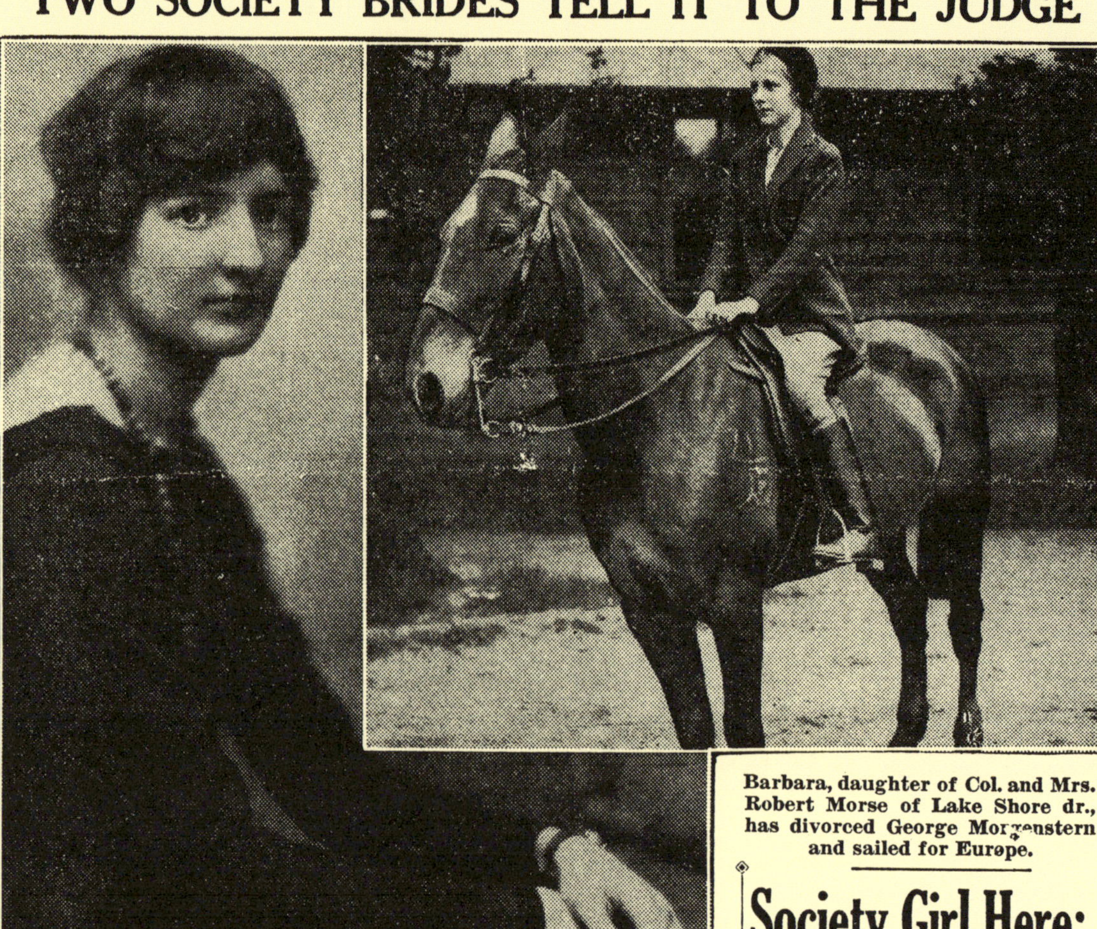

TWO SOCIETY BRIDES TELL IT TO THE JUDGE

Barbara, daughter of Col. and Mrs. Robert Morse of Lake Shore dr., has divorced George Morgenstern and sailed for Europe.

Society Girl Here; Plans to Divorce

Mrs. Stanislaus Szukalski, the former Helen Walker.

Helen Walker

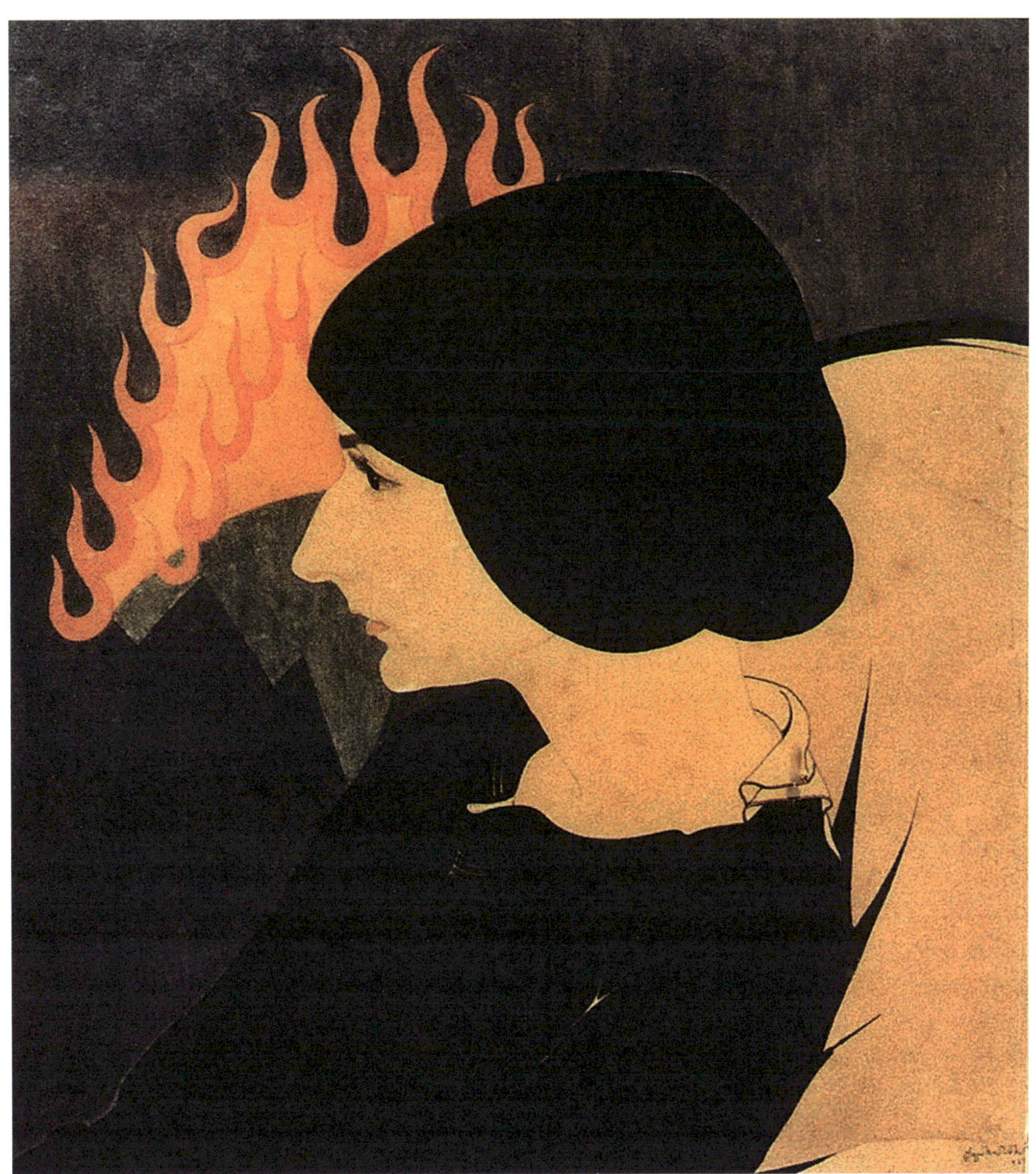

Eddy Kaminski

We met in Hollywood, but he hailed from Milwaukee, where he learned to paint. Though he was thick-skinned, he had surprisingly many friends, because he was gregarious and talkative as all Poles. We met again in Paris where he studied with a very successful Polish painter of great skill, who painted with the palette knife. He startled his teacher by leaving many paintings unfinished when, under his tutelage, they traveled the picturesque places of France. He learned the specific technique of the palette knife, however, which can be effectively used to dazzle the onlooker, even if the painter has no knowledge of painting or Art.

When he had twenty canvases "finished," he suddenly had to leave his teacher, returning to Paris. I met him there as he was arranging an exhibition of "his" paintings. The day before the opening, a French Art critic came to him with a ready article about the greatness of his Talent, the length of which took a few pages. "I am so profoundly impressed by your paintings," said the man, "that 1 wrote this long article. However, printing of it will take $900, for the publisher has to omit another critic's article about another artist." My new acquaintance was so pleased, that he wired for the money from the United States, and paid.

Back in Hollywood, the rave about the NEW GENIUS discovered in France reached me and numerous other people. With such evident success, he gained enough patronage to buy exclusive property in Westwood, where in his home he received many other Culture Vultures eager to associate with Genius.

So far, I had never seen any of his paintings. When I did, I was incredulous how, with bluff and a vocabulary of a truck driver, he had been able to fool people so readily. His charming wife was an asset, however, so that with her, his crudity mixed with jovial insincerity and his uncritical friendliness to one and all, seemed merely put-on.

One day I said to him: "Eddy, why don't you join three students I have and learn how to draw, by discovering the secrets of Light and Shadow?" To this he agreed and the next day he was in my studio on Cahuenga, way up on its concrete stilts, overlooking Hollywood. Months later, I learned that the very next day he had gone to the Art Center School, telling the director, Mr. Adams, that he had evolved a new method of teaching Art, explaining the principles I had just revealed to him. He got a teaching job, which position he retained for a few years. He worked with me for awhile, but gave that up soon, feeling he was too busy teaching, which he had not told me about.

A few years later, he published a book about "his Method." His written discourse began with the egg, with which I always begin my talk on Light and Shadow. When "his" book came out, he stopped seeing me. He had not developed any Talent in spite of my Method, for, being a Pole with pretensions to Culture, he was incapable of sitting down to WORK. He was like a Shaman priest or a politician, bluffing his way to easy living and a set of admirers of his "art" who never even saw what he did. Two years after his book came out, he died, unbemoaned and unnoticed.

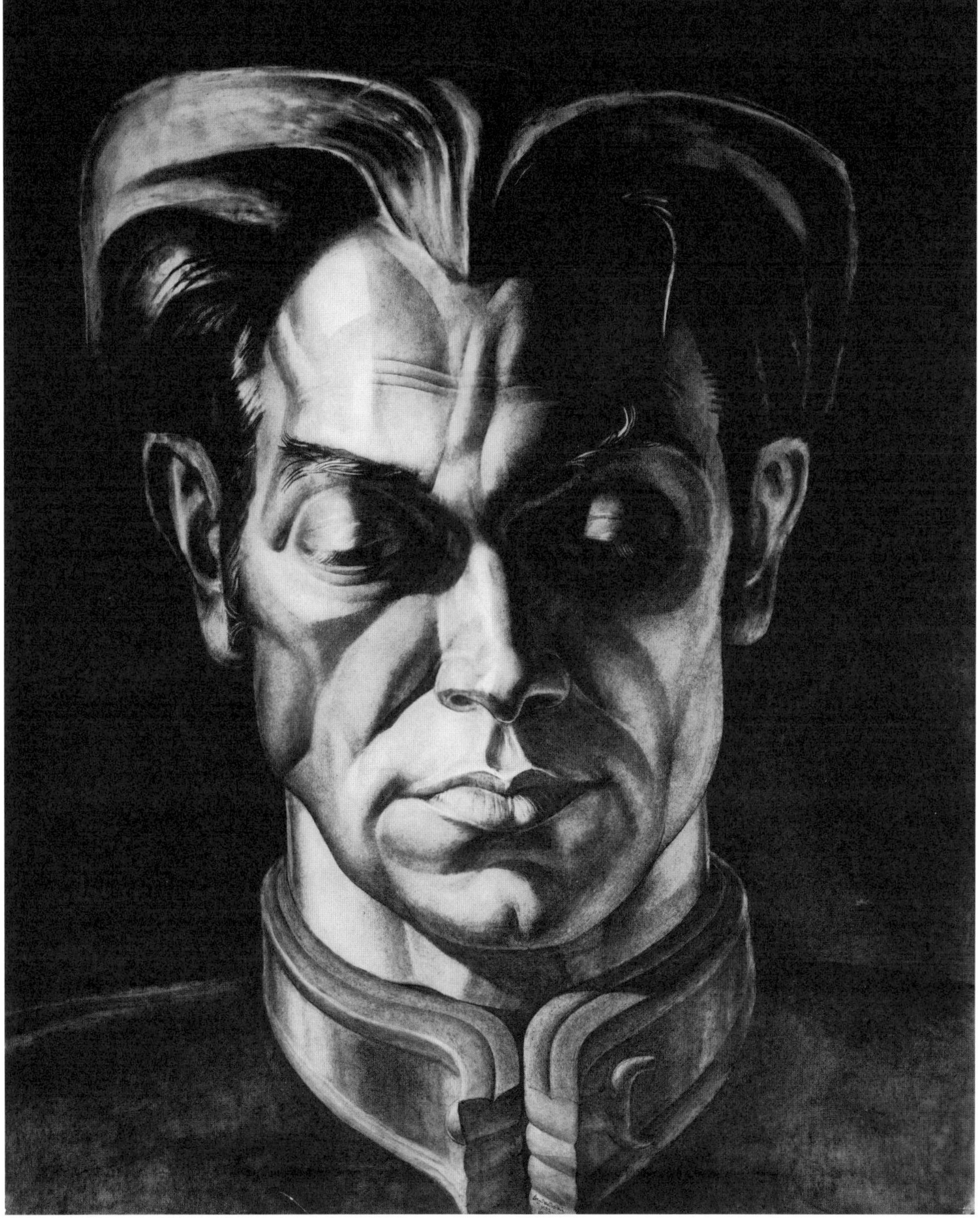

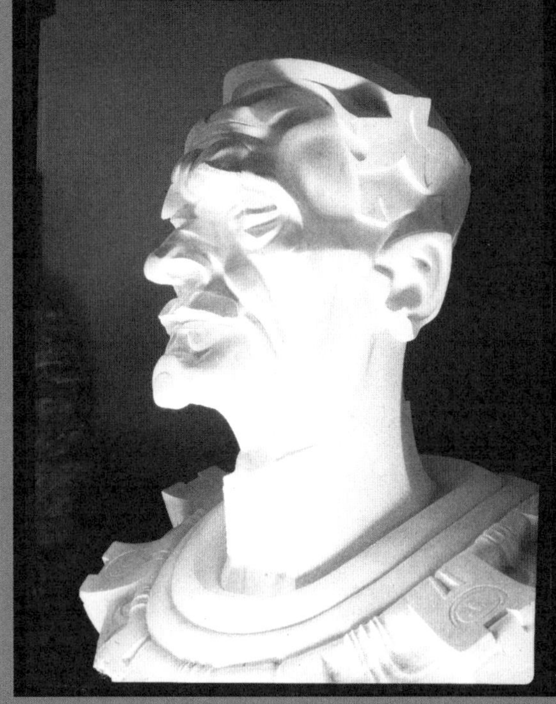
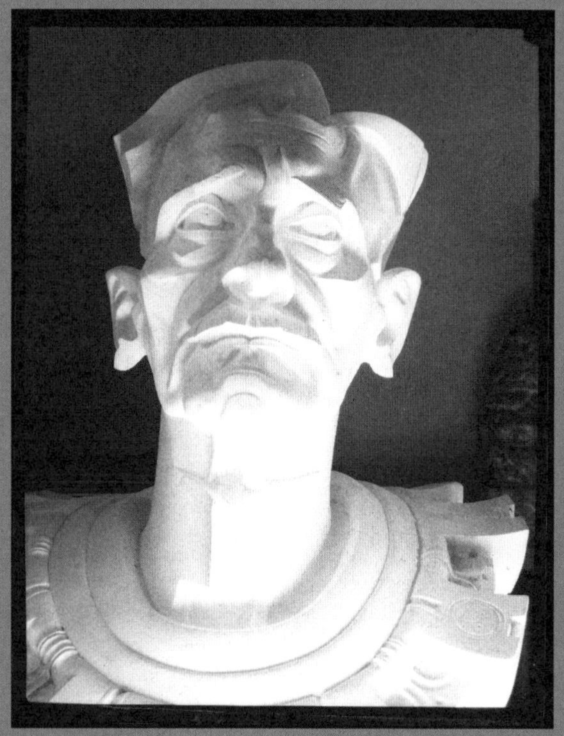

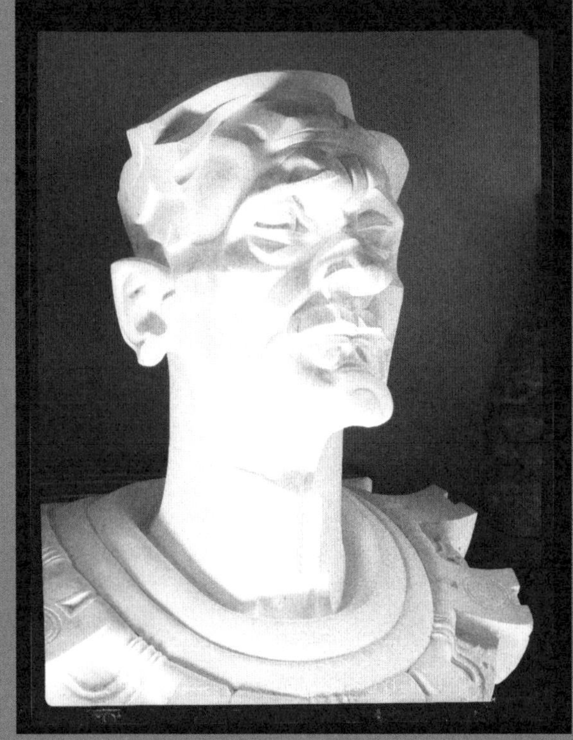
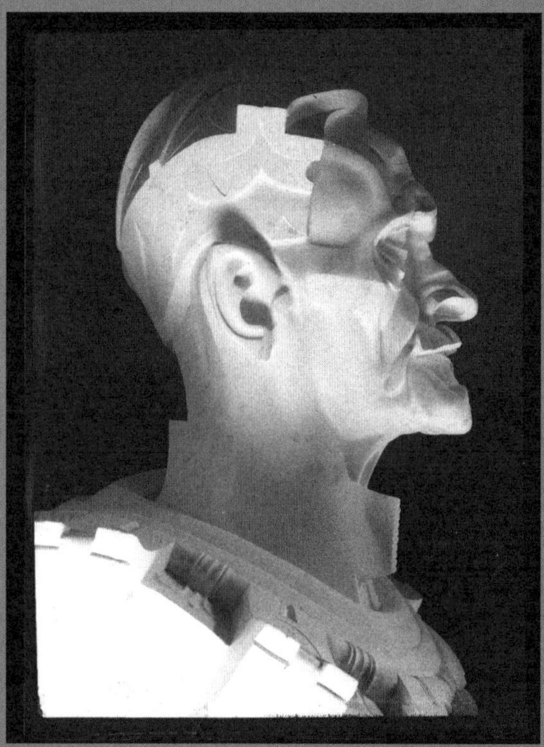

Dr. Albert Michelson, the Physicist

■ 1932 ■

Michelson's family and that of my first wife, Helen Walker, were close friends in Lake Forest, Illinois. While living in Hollywood, California, we were invited to a lunch at his house, together with Dr. Einstein, his wife and their daughter. While we were eating and conversing, suddenly Dr. Michelson rose up above his dish and, raising his voice to a shout, directed long pent-up anger to Dr. Einstein who sat next to him: "I resent your insolence! For years you have been living off my ideas, writing books about my theories without mentioning it was I who first thought about them. You are a parasite and I have had enough of you… Out of my house! I will not take your insolence anymore! Out! Out! Out with you!"

Einstein meekly left the table, calling his wife and daughter to come with him. They left immediately, and through the window I could see how Mrs. Einstein took her husband by the hand so that he would know when to cross the street. The great mathematician was so absent-minded that he often buttoned his pants to the buttonholes in his overcoat.

Some days later, I made this sculpture of Michelson in ordinary room light, which is the most untoward direction of light to do any modeling. He stood for me for about an hour, which sufficed for me to get the vital information about the construction of his head and his physiognomy. The sculpture is twice natural size.

While talking to him to find out more about his personality, I asked if it would be possible for me to get a few photographs at Mount Wilson Observatory of the eclipses of the sun, since I had some theories on the subject of the "corona" of the shaded sun. He was annoyed at such a request and said rather peevishly: "It is annoying to us scientists when laymen try to solve dilemmas with which the scientific world has wrestled for centuries! No, I don't think they would have such photographs to make presents of to non-astronomers."

Yet it has been 80% "ignoramuses" like me, who made the most basic discoveries in medicine. As a six-year-old, I pinned a little celluloid-framed mirror on my shirt, facing the sun, so that the little reflected spot fell on the shady side of the white-washed peasant house and I could see my and my chums' different, greatly enlarged pulsings of our heartbeat. When in Chicago in my early twenties, I met Dr. Dass, a physicist from India, and told him about my childhood experiment. Years later this physicist, after experimenting on my principle with an electronically devised apparatus, received the Nobel Award for measuring the tremblings of pin-pricked carrots and the limpid tremblings of a "tired" steel girder of a dismantled skyscraper.

Around Michelson's neck I made numerous mirrors reflecting the sun. His epoch-making device was the Interferometer, a miraculously mirrored prismatic prodding to measure the speed of light, for which he was awarded the Nobel Prize.

■ As an aside, I must point out that the only photographs I have of this portrait-sculpture are most unfortunate. Sculptures should never be photographed while in white plaster, since in that material only the shadows come out. All white (lighted) planes are without depth, since they are not highlighted. Thus, in photographs of plaster scultures, we view them at great disadvantage, for only half of their form is shown.

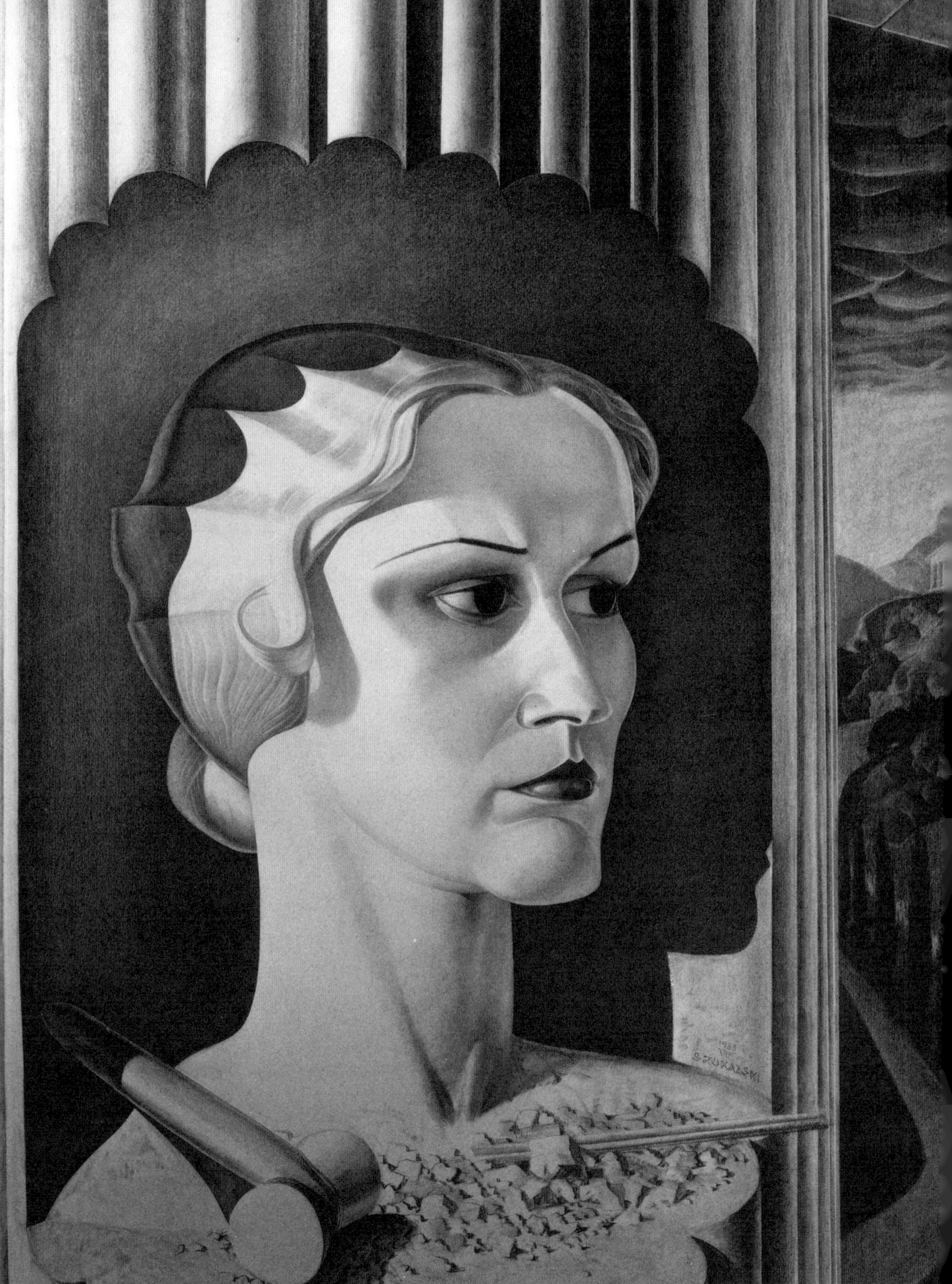

Arianne

Among the ladies I have known was this girl of cultivated manners and classic looks. When she relaxed
from her social amenities and returned to her private
self, she unknowingly revealed monumental steadi-
ness. Here, from the inside of a classic column, she
watches, watches unemotionally heroic.

Incidentally,
as a hint of beauty: ladies should never pluck their
eyebrows so thin as to appear nonexistent from
twenty feet away. If you knew as much as I about
eyes, you would, dear ladies, never alter the original
shape your parents gave you.

Not many people know
this, even among fine artists; no one has ever told me
and I have never found such astounding information
in books, authored by the educated counterfeits of
naturally wise men. Precisely because I was uneducated, I learned everything myself, thus discovering
that it is the eyebrows, not the eyes, that make the
expressive face.

The eyes themselves are merely
shining buttons stuck in the hollows of the skull, pro-
tected against falling out by the eyelids. When you
stand before the mirror and cover your eyebrows
with your hand, you can make all sorts of grimac-
es: ridiculous, dramatic, brazen, coquettish, but the
eyes will remain the same MEANINGLESS glass
buttons, because you cannot see the behavior of the
eyebrows. The eyes are not capable of expressing
anything whatever; it is the most subtle, multiduplic-
itously emotional eyebrows that account for more
expressiveness than the entire body and the rest of
the head together.

Zbyszko, the Wrestler

■ 1934 ■

He and his older brother, also a world champion
wrestler, came from Kraków, Poland. The older
brother had been educated at Jagiellon University
to become a lawyer. Their name was Cyganiewicz,
meaning "of the Gypsies."

This portrait was in-
tended to be mine, since it was not a commissioned
work. I left it at a shop to be framed and was to
pick it up the following day, but Zbyszko had gone
two hours earlier, saying I was unable to come, and
stole my work.

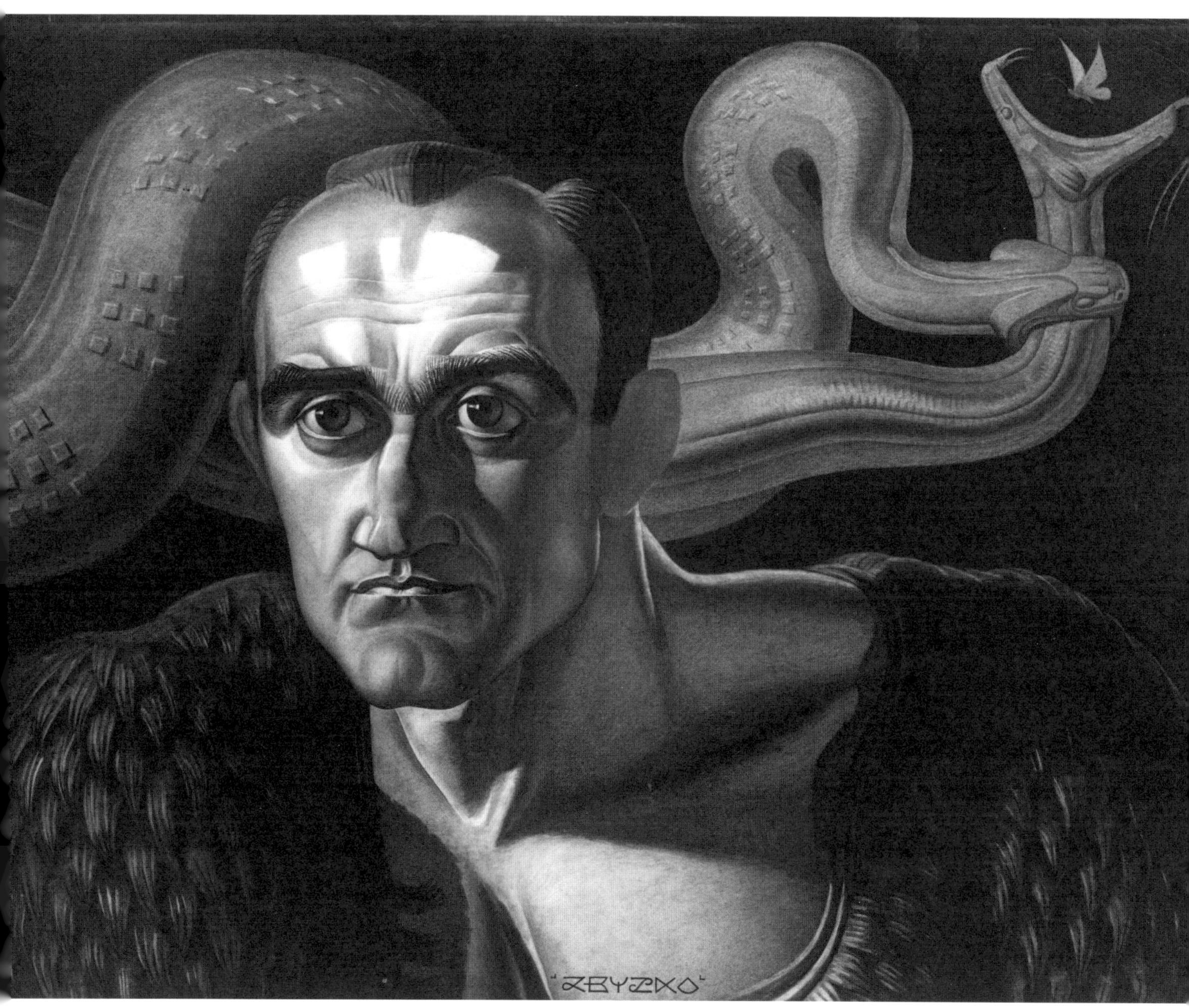

"ZBYZKO"

Svend Lassen

An exemplary Dane, a biochemist, who is presently settled in Santa Barbara, dedicating his later years to research in finding new sources of FOOD for un-naturally multiplying mankind.

My wife, Joan Donovan of Cape Cod, I and the Lassens have been friends for many years, while living in California. I have always admired Svend's face, firstly because I was drawn to its type, secondly because, as an artist, I recognize it as a "passport" to the personality. Faces are the "introduction" to personalities. But my portraits are not mere likenesses. I bring out the unphotographic traits, revealing the hidden self, the spiritual Ego.

I have used Svend's face in my volume on *The Anthropolitical Motivations* to illustrate the Human Type, in contrast to the a-Human, Yetinsyn features of Karl Marx, Lenin, Hitler, Khrushchev, John L. Lewis, Hoffa and other such descendants of the human rape victims of local species of the Abominable Manapes.

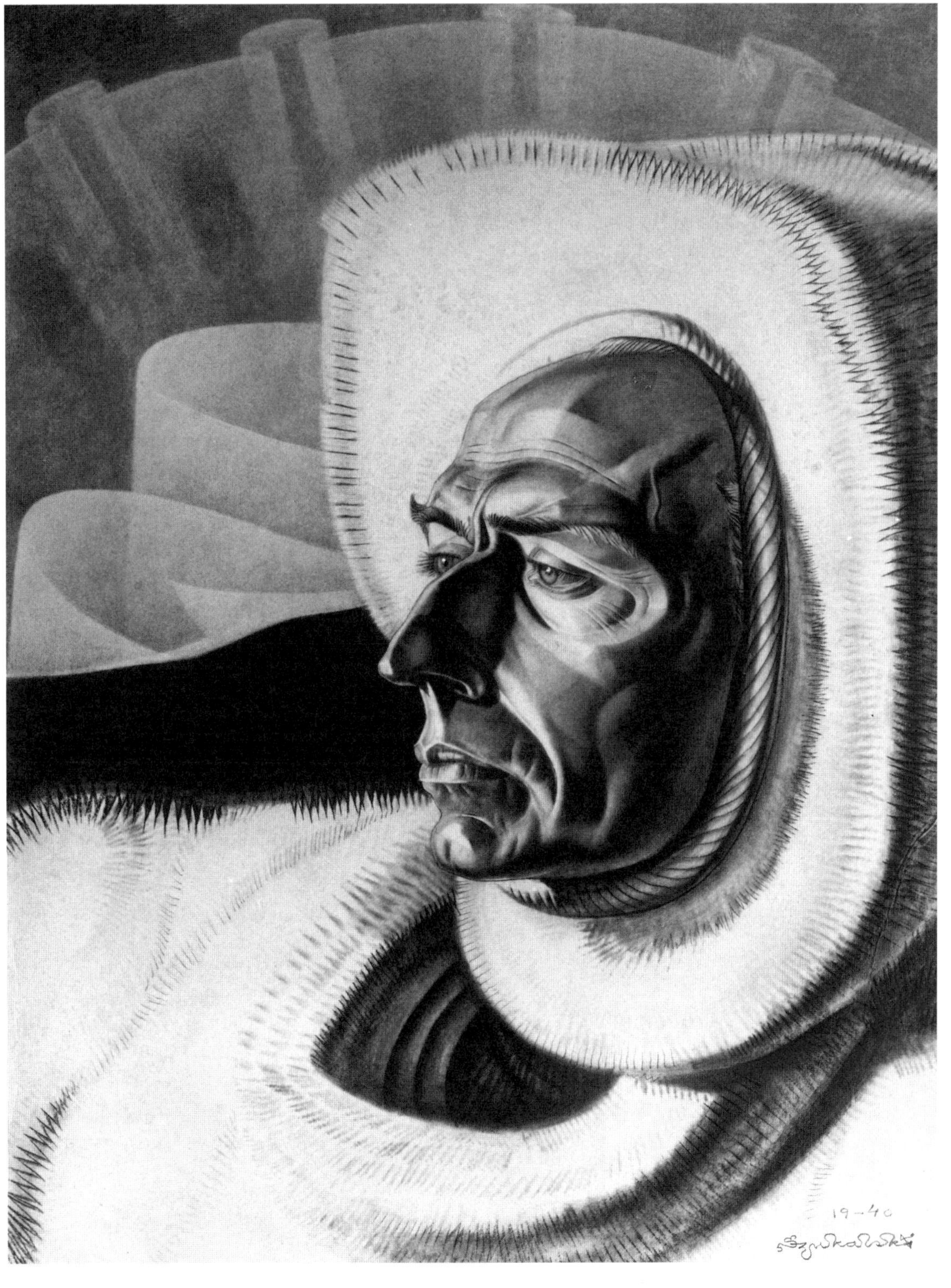
19-40
Szukalski

Remussolini

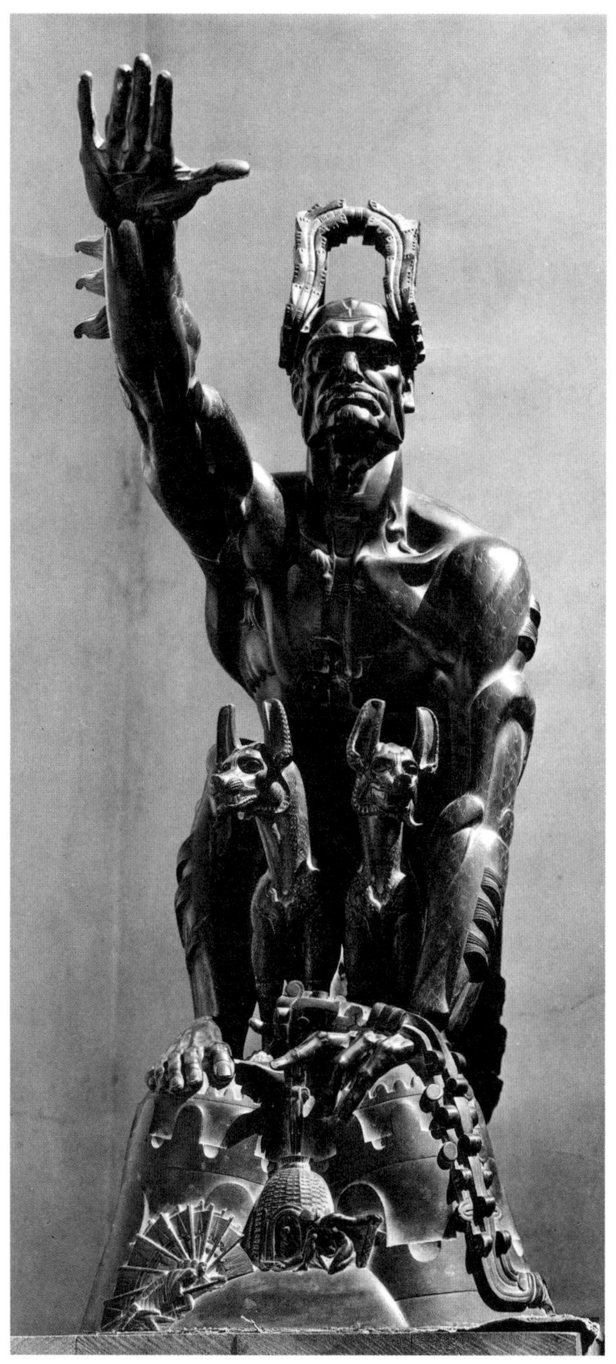

When Communism almost overtook Italy, the nation rose from its historic *siesta* and marched onto Rome to squelch the traitorous conspirators and freed their nation from the first paroxysm of the oncoming nightmare of the possible enslavement by the Yetinsyny of Moscovy.

The then-Europe's hero, Mussolini, was world-acclaimed as the Saviour of Italy. Many books were written and in America motion pictures were made, extolling him. I, on my part, made this sculptured project for the monument of this providential man (without looking at photographs of him).

The famed *Lupita* (She-wolf), nursing the twin infant boys, Romulus and Remus, was created by an Etruscan sculptor. Romulus was the mythic founder of Rome. The second of the twins has not distinguished himself and is remembered only for being the brother of the other twin. Therefore, I made a composition that brought to life Remus as the reviver of the hibernating nation, paraphrasing Lupita and the twins by making Remussolini training young twin wolves. The sculpture was made in Hollywood and was an almost life-size project for this monument.

Though I greatly admired his patriotism, I felt that he really was not as great as the political circumstances carried him up to. Despite the ecstatic expression of total adoration by the Italian populace for the *Duce*, I suspected that he would not match the greatness anticipated of him. Why such doubt? Because of his eagerness to appear super-heroic, ever strutting, so to convince

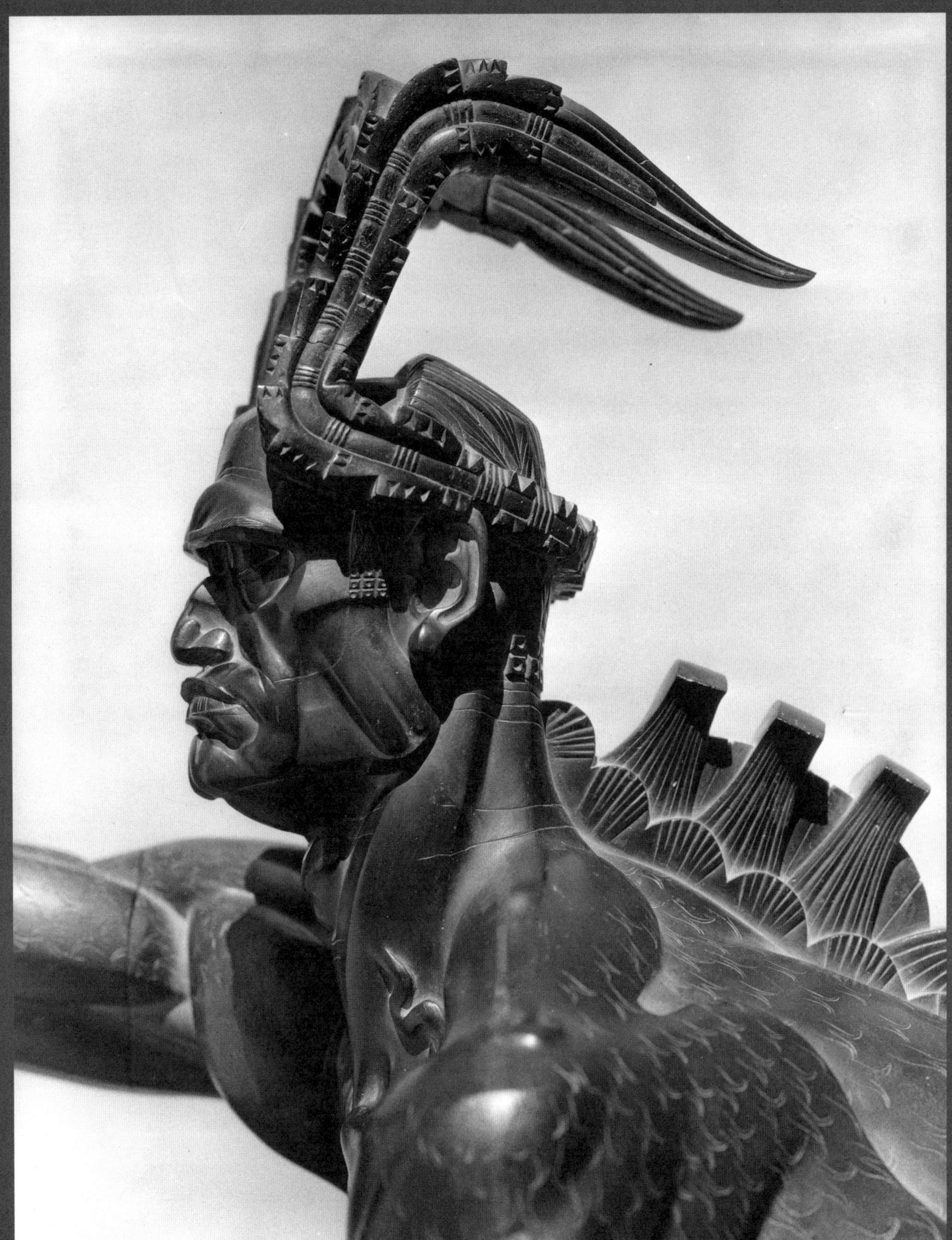

himself that he really was a hero, not a former socialist, a conspiring punk with a crushing inferiority complex.

A man with a singular mind to fulfill the mission, does not strut before his nation. His passionate acceptance by the monolithic multitudes should have sufficed to assure him that he was a hero. It was an ill-chosen time for his histrionics, when his nation in orgiastic ecstasy unanimously proclaimed him "Duce! Duce! Duce!," a semi-divinity. His play-acting was out of place. He would not live up to his people's anticipations.

To smuggle my hidden and anticipated disappointment in this Hero, I gave his image in the future monument an over-sized laurel for his head. It had to be double-arched upwards above his forehead, so not to fall onto his shoulders.

Monuments are erected to the memory of Great Men. Who are the "Great?" All those who CHANGE the world and its HISTORY, be they Good or Evil. They may have been beings through whom one or many nations benefitted, or they may have been pug-nosed, monstrously criminal exterminators of Humanity, thus causing either the Liberation or Enslavement of one or many nations, which altered the fate of Mankind. The likeness of such men must be preserved, so that future generations will recognize their ilk and not again be misled into frantic acceptance of similar misleaders. Are we not glad we have the portrait of Nero? He should not be condemned for failing to be great, but the gullible nation for choosing pompous midgets eagerly play-acting the role of a providential superman, when there was no other substitute on the bouncing Roman horizon of seven hills.

92

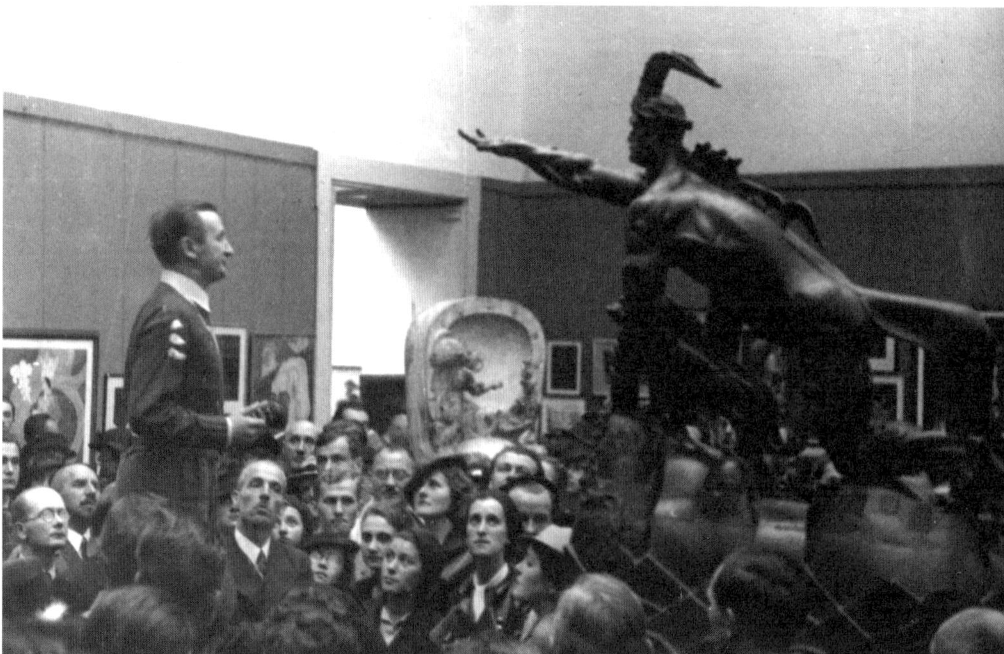

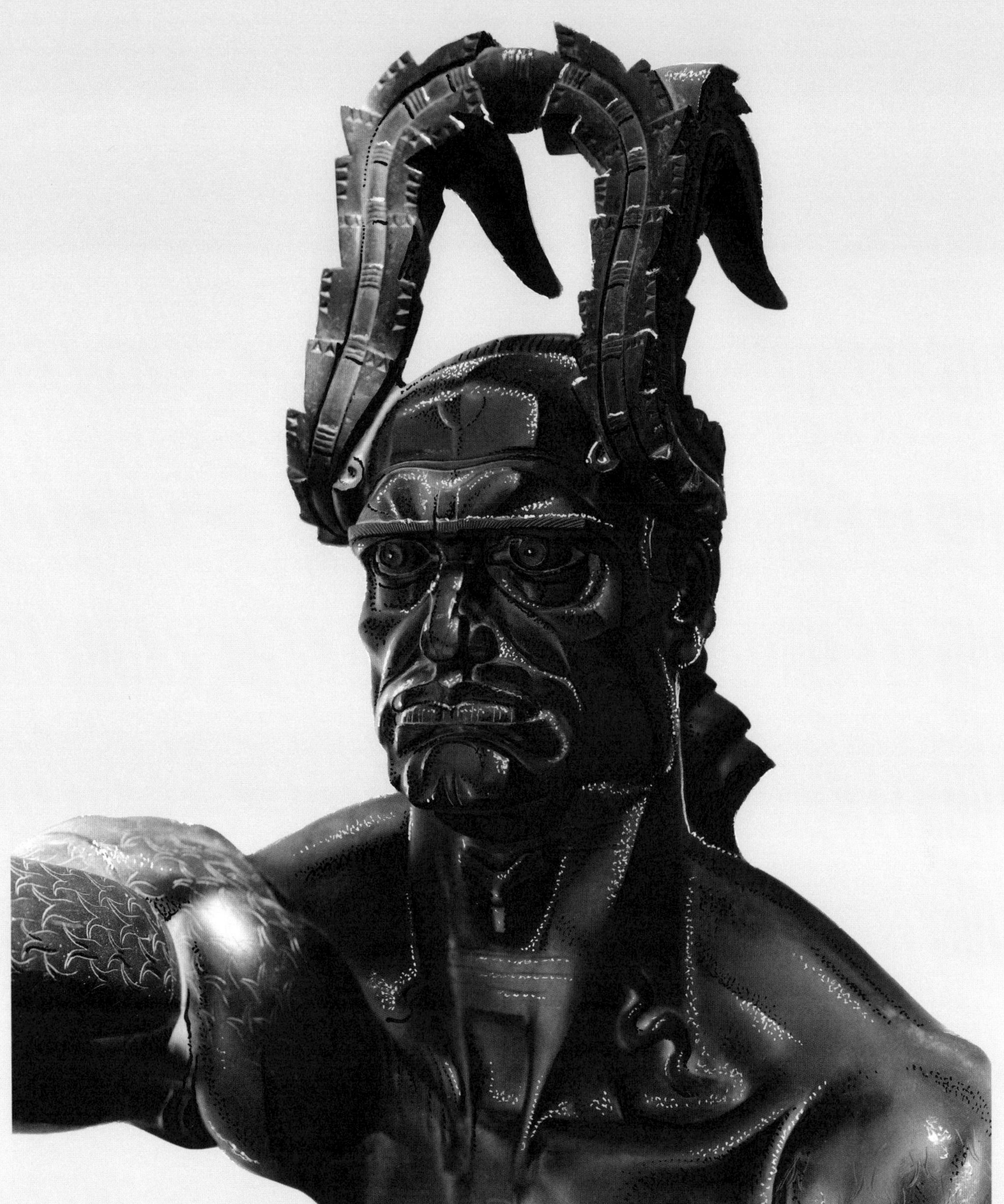

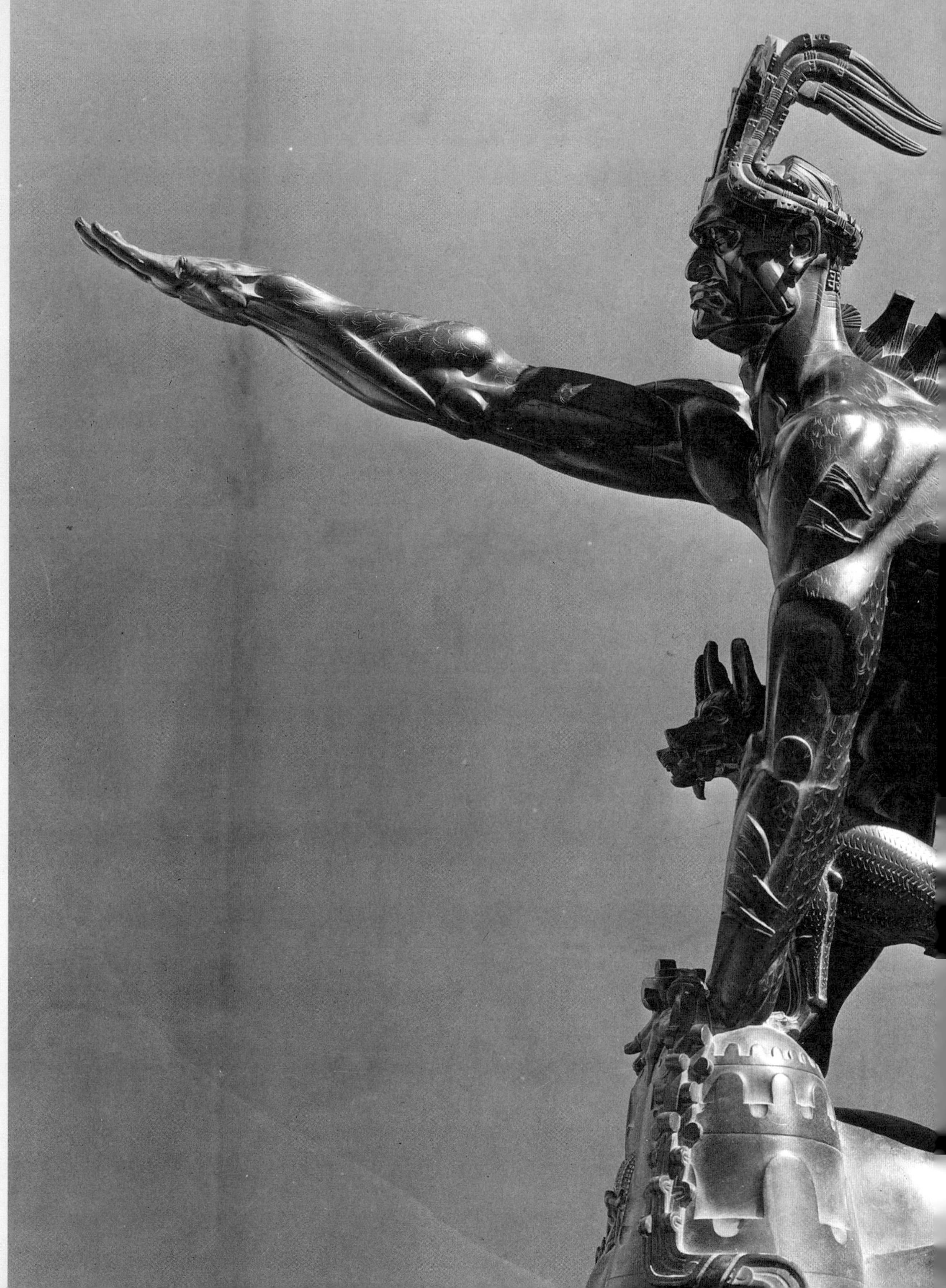

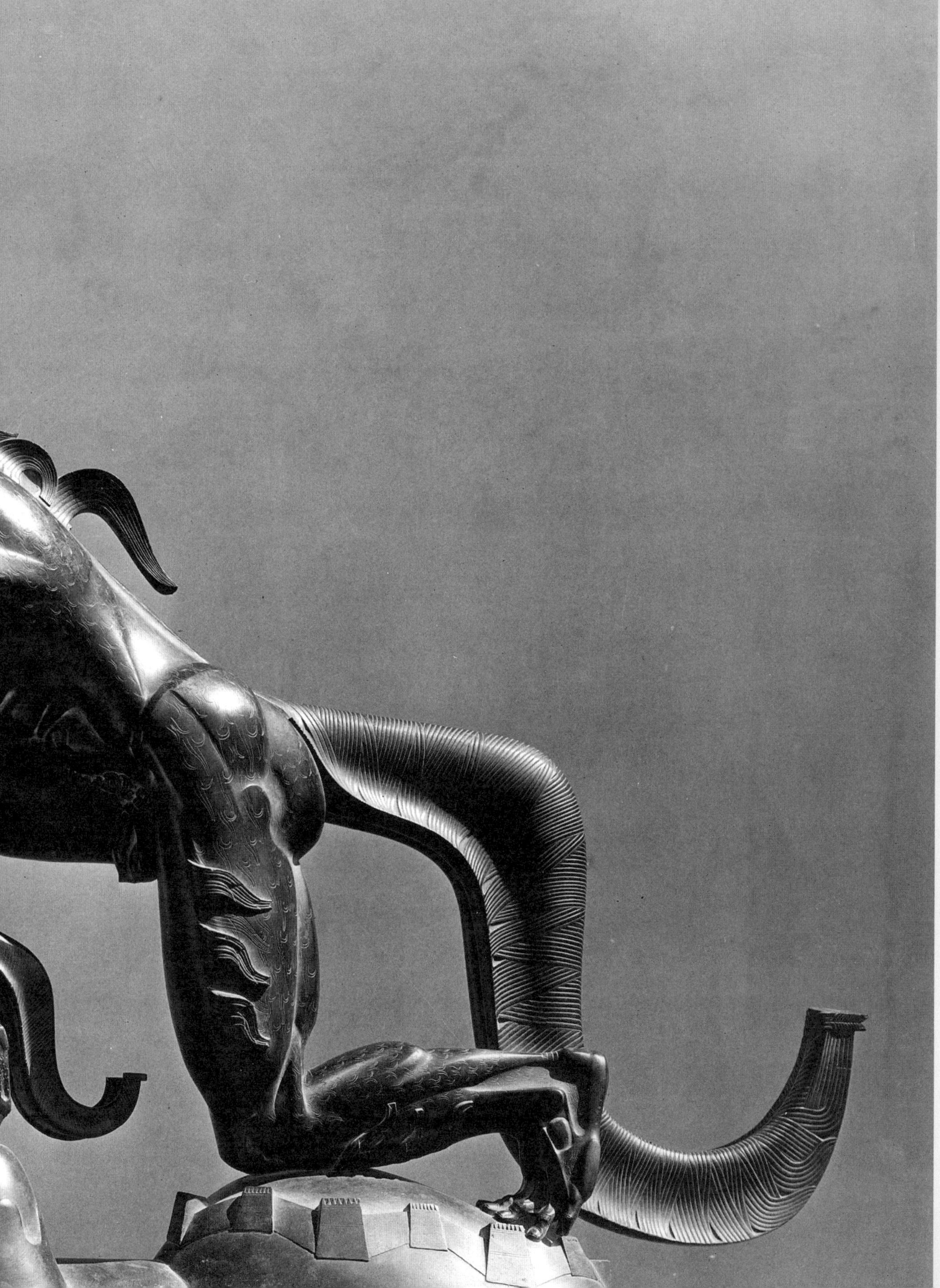

Józef Klemens Piłsudski (1867–1935) came from beyond the parentheses of currently known Poland, born with the Mission to enter Revolutionary work without wasting a year of hesitation. At his maturing, a select few within the greater Russian Empire had begun to get together. The springboard for their concerted action to free their people was triggered from within the Socialist-Revolutionary parties that sprung both in Russia and Poland.

Piłsudski became the head of the Polish Socialist Party, which on a vast plan first would portion to the Poles their national territories. Among their activities was robbing banks to provide the Revolutionary organization with money. For safety, and to confuse the Moscovian police, Lenin and Trotsky occasionally lived in Kraków where with Piłsudski, using the pseudonym of *Dziadek* ("Granddaddy"), they would meet in Michalik's Café, just a few strides away from my art academy. There, they discussed the plans for the overthrow of the Czarist tyranny.

But the difference between them, unforeseen at first, began to percolate. The Pole was of a different species, for he belonged to the hard-working, soil-tilling race, while Lenin was of the nomadic, predatory ilk. In the devious ways of his species that is born out of the dusts of sterile prairies, Lenin began to encroach beyond the line of demarcation of his "people's" activities, to which instantly Piłsudski stood up and let him know in a thundering, passionate voice:

"You leave Poland to me! I will not tolerate
Russian hands where my people die!"

The Polish Liberator had understood the character of these sub-human Yetinsyny and had foreseen that sooner or later, he would have to deal with a race of psychotic killers, and the Russians dared not again mention any schemes to mix the two Causes as mutual concern.

He now had a far greater task before him, for, while the Moscovian leaders had the gigantic Russian Empire to dethrone, he alone had two other Empires (German and Austrian) to unseat before his Poland could be freed. Piłsudski became a World Hero who is viewed as the father of the Second Polish Republic re-established in 1918, 123 years after the 1795 Partitions of Poland by Austria, Prussia and Russia. And when again the Bolsheviks invaded Poland in 1919, now as a Communist Power, he defeated them with his skinny legion and imposed the harshly exacting Riga Peace, under which the predator had to regurgitate all the stolen territories including parts of Belarus and Ukraine.

Always remember, it was Piłsudski who not only to Poland Freedom gave, but to Europe and America. If the Bolsheviks had not been stopped in Poland, they would have overtaken the rest of Europe, where supremely civilized nations would have become slave-laborers, so underpaid by Russia that all industrial competition would be wiped out by her underpriced exports and America would be reduced to a mere agriculture.

I placed over Piłsudski's head a crown of straw, supported there by two angels, as peasant artists would have honored him.

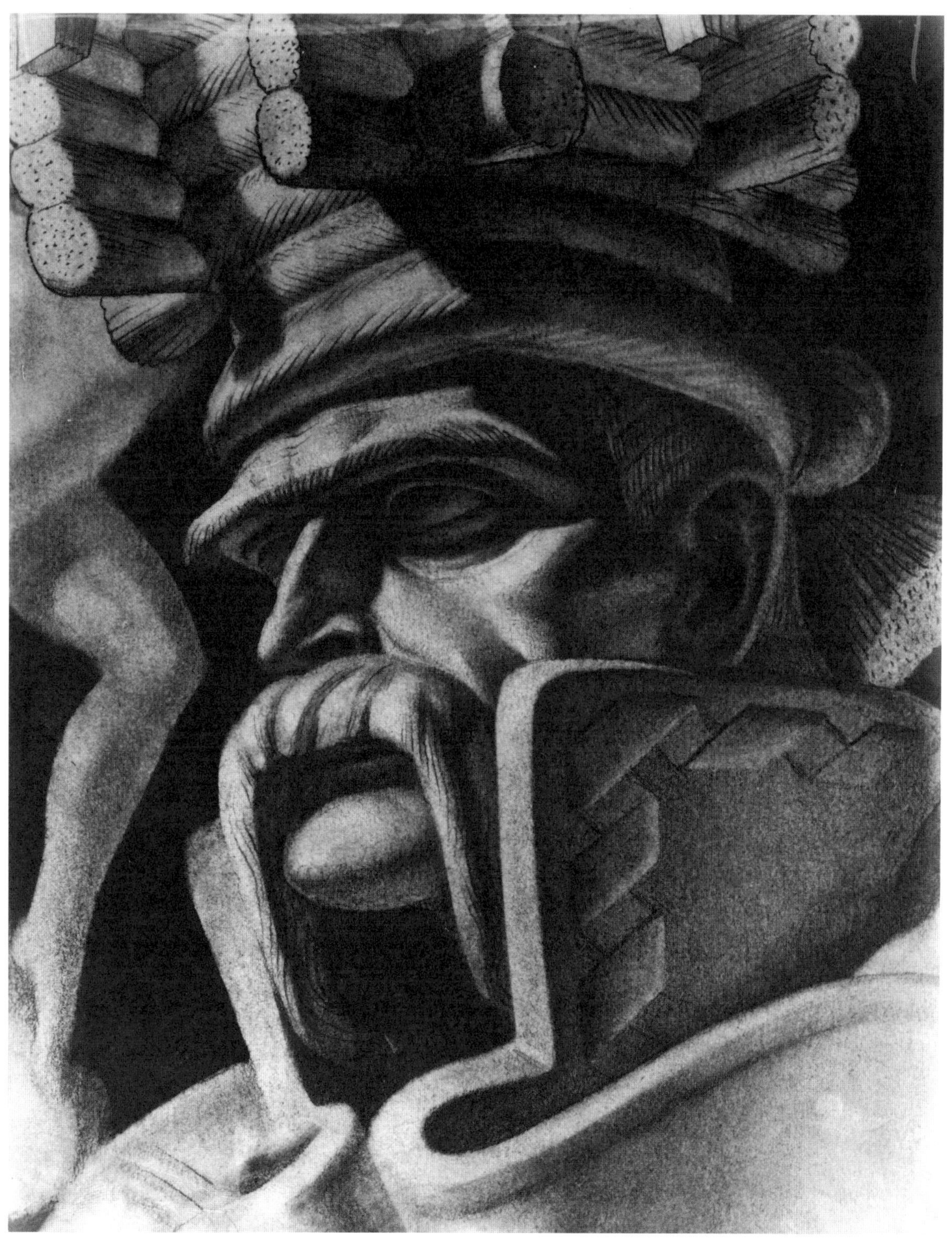

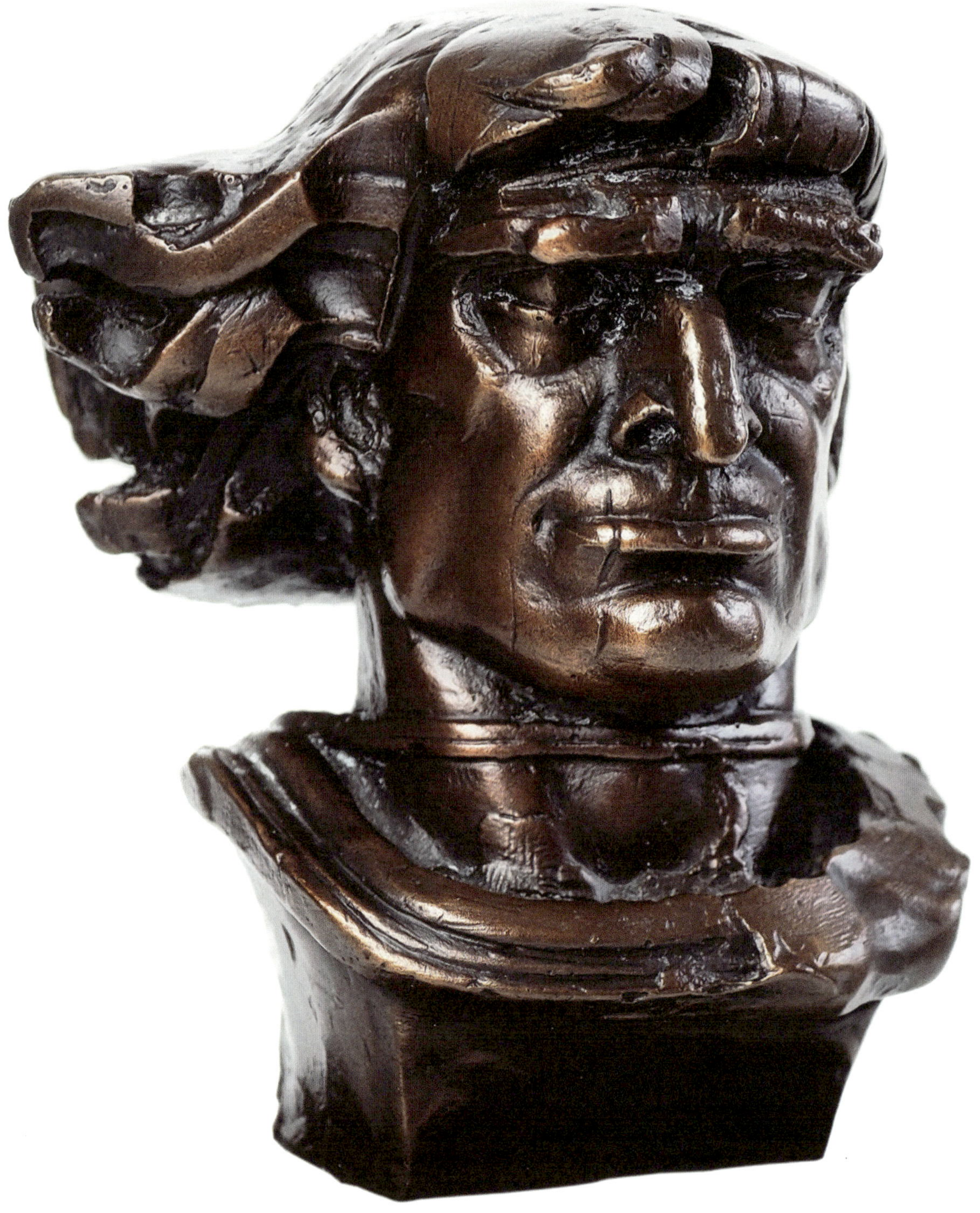

Bronze, 4″ tall

Bolesław Chrobry

The most renowned foe of the Christianizing Germans who, like Russia today with her new religion, Communism, were using the pretext of Christendom to exterminate Humanity that would not be conquered by their ideological bait; a method always used by the world-parasites for the entrapment of unwary nations.

Chrobry was the ruler of a powerful Poland, whose port city Wolin – according to early German chroniclers – was the greatest metropolis of Europe.

He was an uncle of Kanut the Great, who conquered Britain. His sister married Gorm the Old of Denmark and was so nobly wise that the grateful Danes sainted her, calling her their *Danebot*, the "Civilizer of Danes."

She had three sons, Kanut, Harold Bluetooth and Pentatoki. Bluetooth Christianized Norway and Denmark and repeatedly attempted to take Europe's th-century metropolis, Wolin. He finally succeeded and renamed it Yomsborg which, after resegmentation of the name, reads "Jo (m) Z Borg" or "I'm From the City" in Polish. Soon he lost the city to the Poles. When he regained it later, Bluetooth ordered it completely destroyed and even the foundations dismounted and thrown into the sea. Like a true Christianizer, as the later Spaniards did to the Aztecs in ancient Mexico and the Incas in Peru, he came to destroy the most ancient city and Civilization.

Naturally, no portraits of the heroic Bolesław Chrobry exist. But on one of his talisman coins I found a crude presentation of his likeness. So, taking a hint as to the type of man he was, I improvised his portrait in this sculpture. To make it seem more authentic, I gave him a sword cut across his chin and mouth. The horizontal strap under his chin holds his helmet, which rests on his back.

Though Governor Grażyński, who in an armed uprising had taken Poland's old territory back from Germany, commissioned me to do this monument for Katowice, I had to go elsewhere to find a hall large enough to make the three-and-a-half stories high sculpture. At last I found one in the Warsaw Polytechnic. However, the animosity of the Polish intellectuals – because I was an "American Pole" with greater talents than any artist in my former Motherland – was so virulent that, after secretly being informed that I would not be able to finish the work there, I rented a former brick factory, where the colossal statue was erected in clay on a steel rail armature, with the assistance of two Italian enlargers, which was kept secret from the hostile compatriots.

When the Germans besieged Warsaw, a bomb shattered this building, the ceiling fell on the clay statue and I was trapped under the debris. Fortunately, the girders held the weight diagonally and I was unharmed, though the dust of crushed bricks nearly suffocated me. I remained under the rubble for some forty hours, before investigating people freed me.

The model sculpture is hidden away in Poland, awaiting my death, when it will be brought to light to show the foreign visitors how Cultured the Polish parasites are.

Stanisław Gliwa

■ 1938 ■

One of the earliest members of my Horned Heart Tribe, he was one of a cluster of youths to leave the School of Applied Arts and the Academy of Fine Arts in Kraków, Poland, to become so.

I, myself, had come to the Academy on the spur of the moment, while walking from the railway station, fresh from America to finish my secondary education in Poland. I was accepted into the Academy as a fourteen year old youngster, without the necessary entrance examinations given to the older graduates of other Art Schools. I spent three-and-a-half years there, not making the obligatory studies from models, but nonetheless receiving the highest awards for my "invented" works. In the last two years I filled more than one room at the Palace of Art with my drawings, paintings and sculptures, while my more mature friends never had exhibited any works at all.

After my second return from America, though, where I had fully developed my creative abilities, I could not get an exhibition anywhere in Kraków, for the professors of the Academy and its former students blocked my chances of being known to Poland.

Thus, I started the war on the Academic Method as destructive to innate Talents. Soon the youths of the above mentioned institutions sent their delegations to see me in the National Gallery (*Sukiennice*). More and more youths gathered about me and we began meeting every third day at Michalik's Café to discuss the formation of the Horned Heart Tribe. Each time, in the simplest words, I explained the principle of my createlier (*tworcownia*) pedagogy, of working from memory, never from models. After two weeks of meetings, I departed for the United States. Within one year, with Stanislaw Gliwa (pron. glee-vah) as an important member, the Tribe became the most renowned group of exclusively creative, inventive artists.

Some of them were executed by the Nazi Yetinsyny, one, Jewish tribesman, Strassberg, committed suicide in faraway Tiflis, while dying from hunger. The remaining few recently had, for the first time since the war, an exhibition in Communiststrangled Poland. Had the Tribe of the Horned Heart been organized anywhere but in Poland, it would have fared better, but in the barbaric society of Polish pseudo-intellectuals, my students were boycotted, prevented from having joined exhibitions, yet they survived, none of them a failure, for my Method developed their Talents.

Gliwa, while defending Poland, became a war prisoner for two years. Then, he was able to join the 2nd Army formed by General Anders in Iran to move into Italy to fight the German Yetinsyny. Where various national armies had failed at Montecassino, the Poles finally succeeded in obliterating the vast complex of the ancient fortification and its invaders. The large cemetery attests to the vast number of Poles who died there. Gliwa was the main photographer and illustrator to record the Battle of Montecassino. His moving, striking work was combined with author Melchior Wankowicz's account and later published in three volumes.

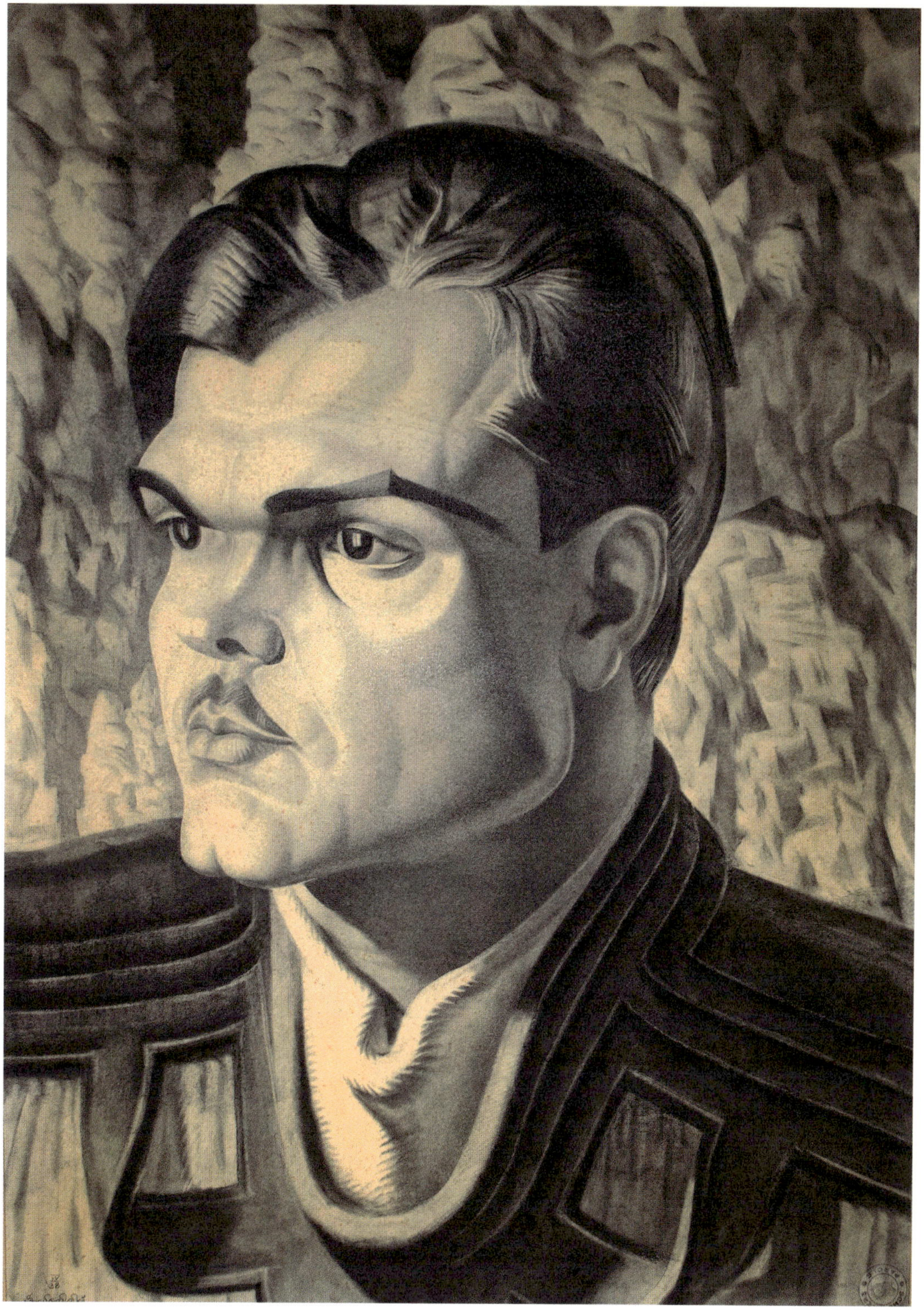

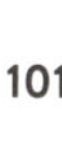

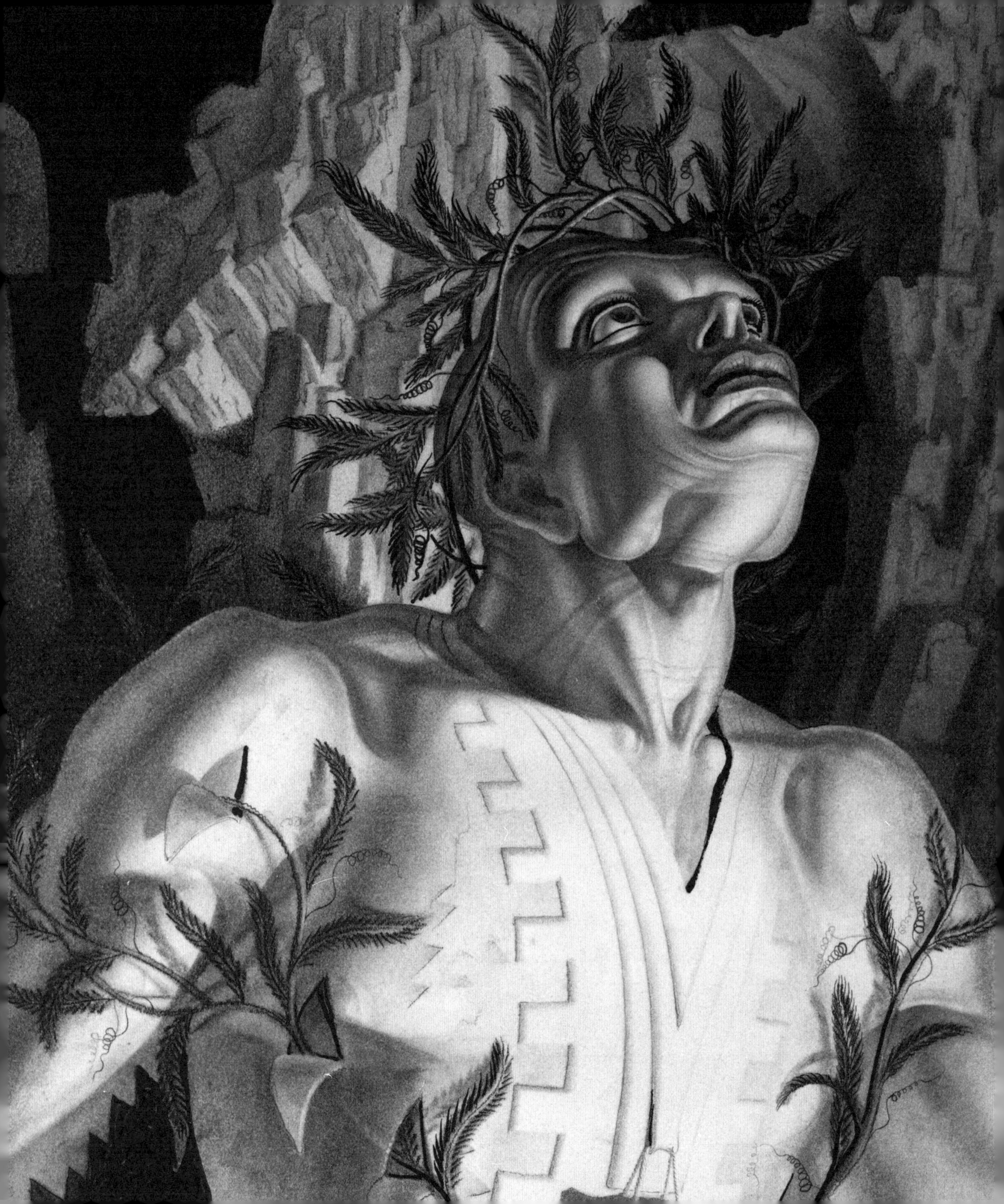

Bybyots

He is the Legend-teller, green-complexioned and immortal, but only as long as there are new and newer stories founded on new heroic deeds. Bybyots and the frog Rege-Rege, the Mythic Nurse of the ancient Poles, are constant companions. He is an old man but very youthful. He has no eyebrows with which to scowl or get angry, yet he never laughs.

He was, like all the other characters in the tragedy *Rege! Rege!*, invented by me. I invented all the events of this legend in order that Bybyots may have good reason not to die for lack of stories to tell.

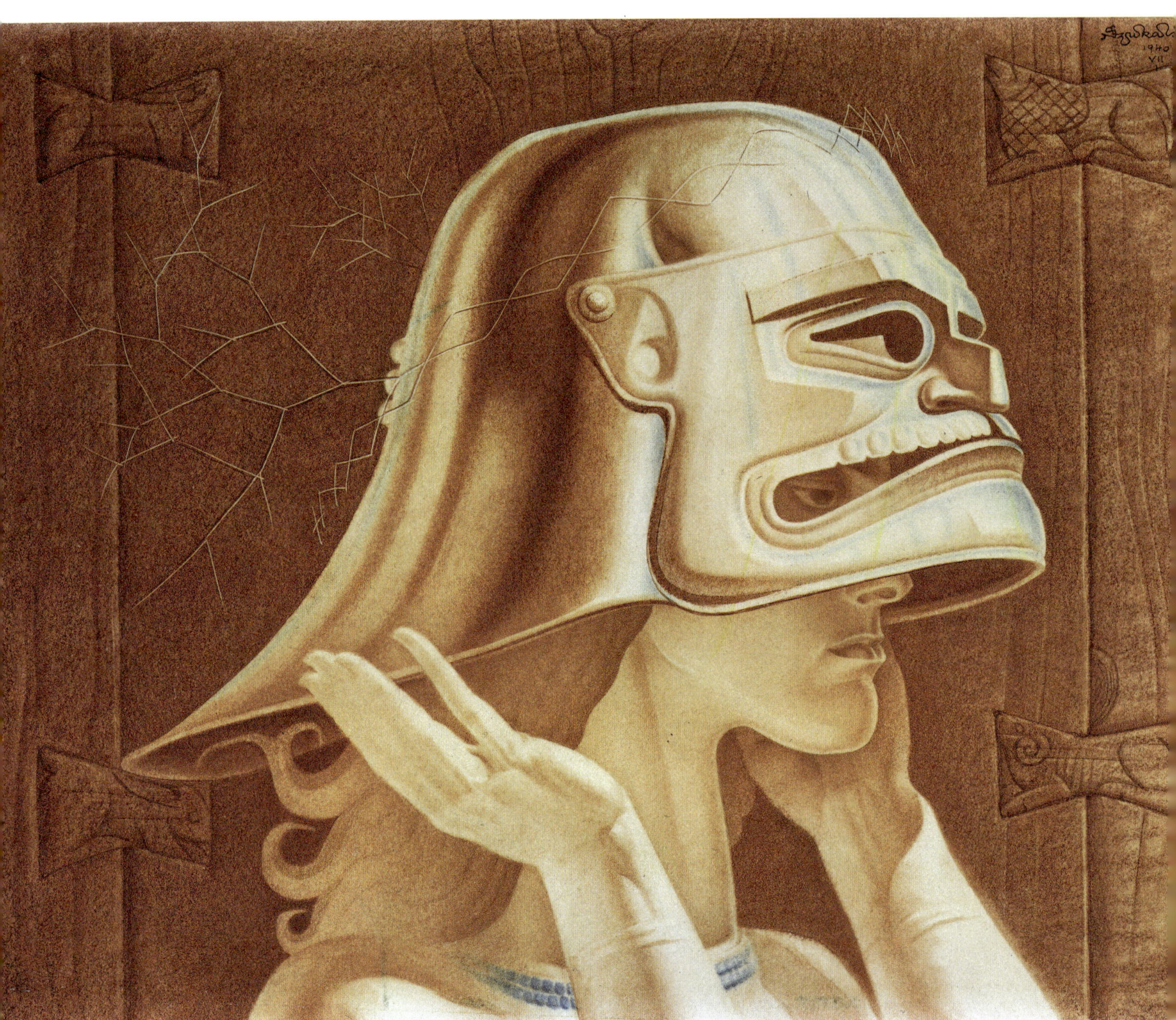

The Ancestral Helmet

Just another careful "silly notion" that gave me an excuse to do my best. Get in the habit to work with utmost concentration, and you will be THE BEST. We scream piercingly when born, yet may become dumb mutes from never making an effort to COM-MUNICATE. It is the effort that gives us the ver-tical posture and creative thinking. Crawl on your knees in an effort to walk your own paths and you will become a thinking person who will be able to bring original values, never perceived before, for within each one of us there is a separate universe of yet uncreated Gifts.

Those who are well-edu-cated may well be mere apes that have learned the ways of Humans, but who cannot think; misled simpletons bedressed with other birds' feathers. To think is to be ORIGINAL. Those who follow their own council, lead themselves upward, for their thinking is bewinged.

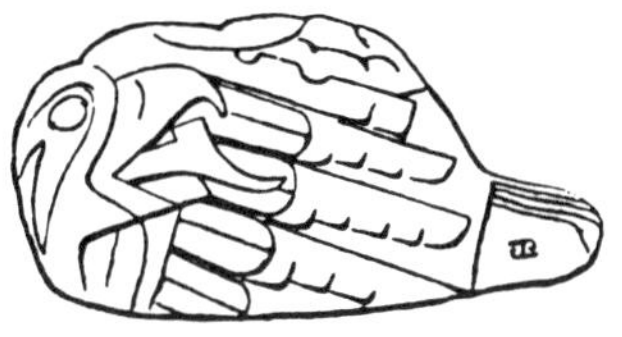

Faces in a Column Pillar

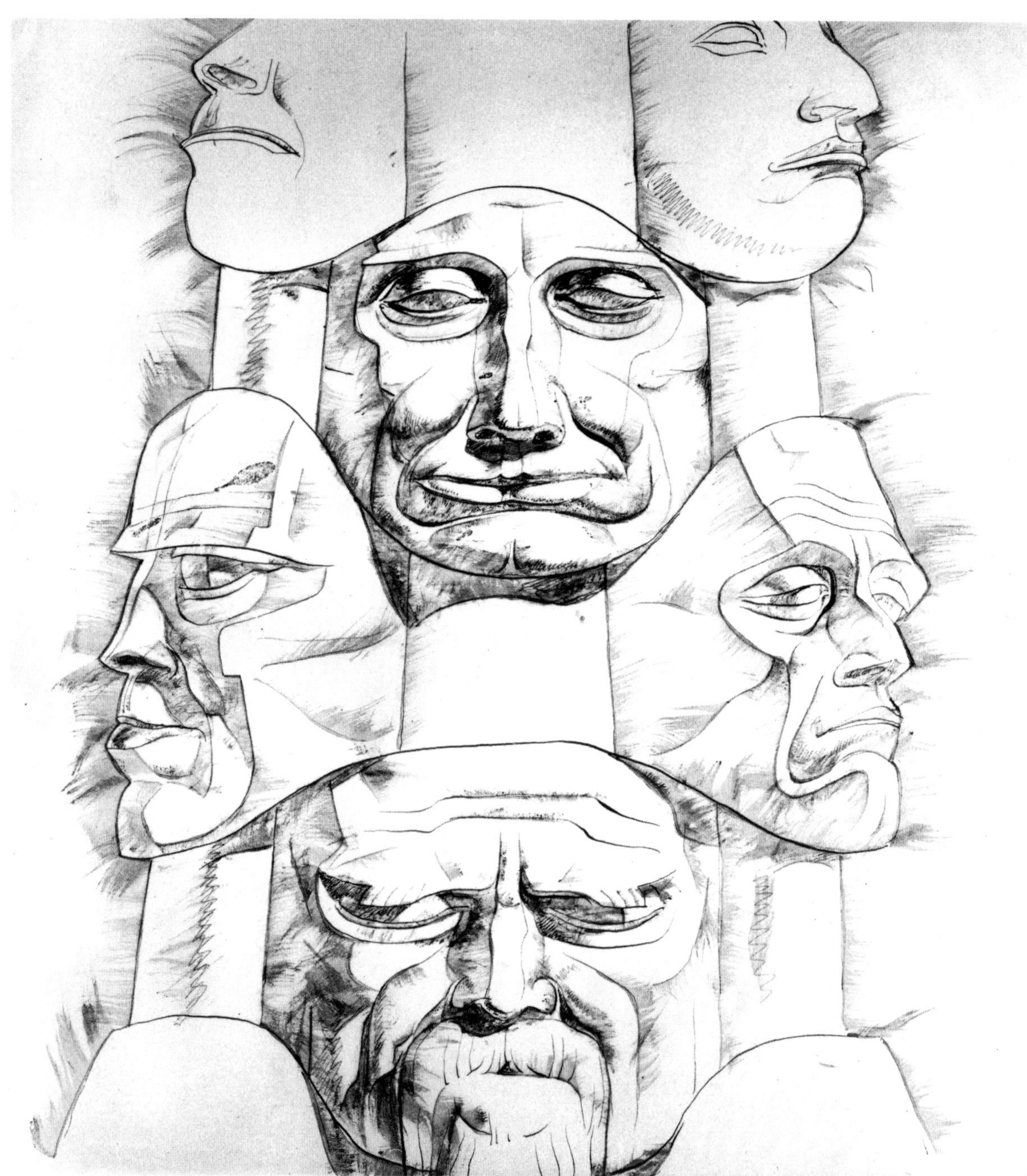

Winston Churchill

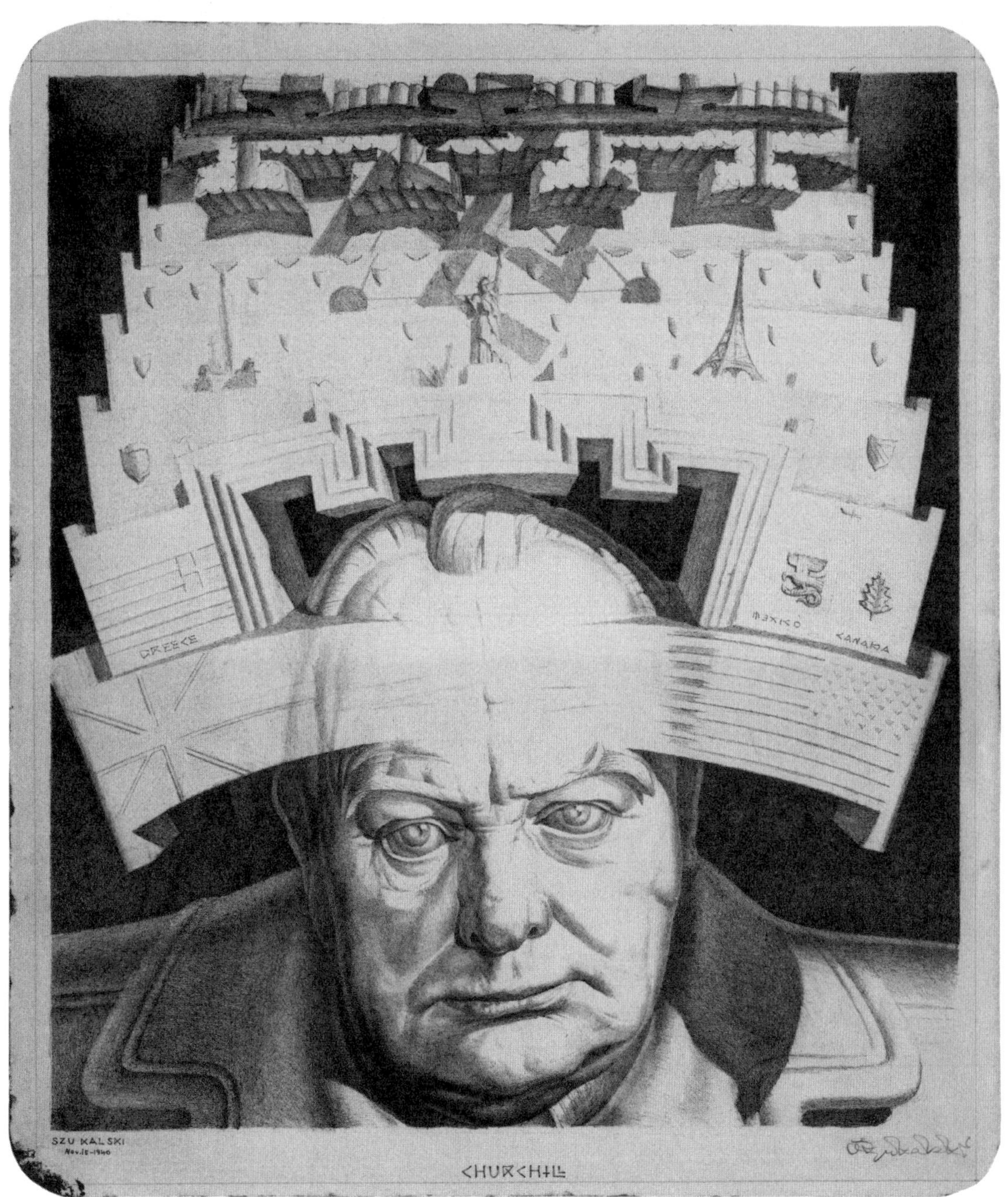

Influential English statesman during WWII

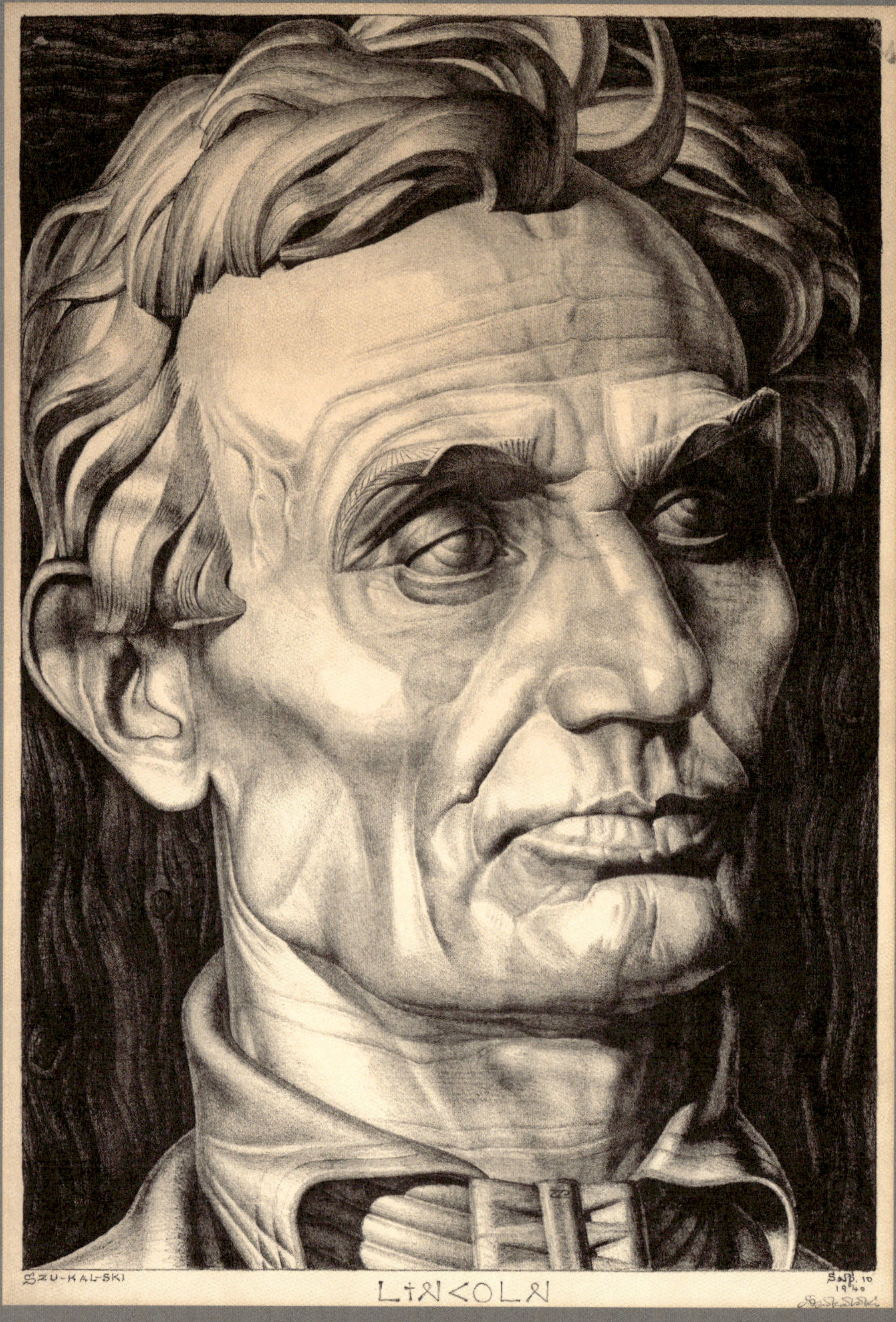

SZU-KAL-SKI
LINCOLN

Abraham Lincoln

Being raised from boyhood to maturity in Chicago, I was ever conscious of the historic figure of Abraham Lincoln. This was brought about by my inordinate interest in animals. My father, Dyonizy, used to take me to the zoo in Lincoln Park from our Polish neighborhood, instead of going to church as most of the peasant immigrants did. It was there that I became acquainted with the splendid monument to Lincoln by the very fine Irish sculptor, Augustus Saint-Gaudens.

Apropos monuments erected to Lincoln, I regard this one as the most supreme of any in the United States. The one carved in marble by Daniel Chester French, sitting in the shrine in Washington, is academically correct, but without the spirit which ought to animate it. One should feel as if in the PRESENCE of a living hero set in a particular gesture, not before a stuffed skin. When looking at Gaudens' sculpture, I feel humble, but not when dwarfed by the one in Washington.

Having known very many people, including every variety of radical, I developed a deep scorn for the latter, whose chief motivation for thinking is a hidden grudge, not provoked personally, but preordained. I was acquainted with, among other Chicago literati, Carl Sandburg, and we took a few walks together through Washington Park. Despite his later writing of the biography of Lincoln, I have always looked down on him, even in my youth, because although already in his thirties, he still was a Socialist. A man adhering to Socialism in his maturity, which he should have abandoned at the time of coming to late puberty, must have stuck like a scratched Victrola record, intellectually, if without embarrassment he could still claim he was anti-Capitalism. Without great wealth and the GENEROSITY of some millionaires there can be no scientific, nor cultural, progress. Only non-motivated simpletons could crave the equal division of prosperity, the well-deserved rewards of those who work hard using their intelligence. Only misfits would murder a class of people with initiative and set themselves in their place to form the Dictatorship of the Slow-wit Proletariat.

I have always admired Lincoln most of all for his high degree of Common Sense, which by the way is so UNCOMMON, that to those few who possess it, mankind eventually erects monuments.

I made this lithograph from one of the authentic photographs taken during his life, but I drew him as if in sculpture. I would rather have carved his likeness, but my American circumstance did not permit me to have a studio with a skylight which is so utterly indispensable in making precise sculpture.

The lithographic plate of this portrait, along with a few others, was stolen by its German printer who claimed he did not know what happened to them when he moved to La Jolla from Pasadena.

Ludola, Father of Krak

■ 1940 ■

Legends depend on the articulateness of a given Folk. If they were too primitive, any cataclysm would barely be recalled. In degree, how short a story of the folklore is, the more primordial it is. The trees and rocks, apes and Sasquatches left no fairy tales, because they were not observant, because they had no words with which to make comments. Legends begin with folk GOSSIPS, comments on significant incidents. At first they are crudely inarticulate, just as the bare mention in the Bible of what actually took millions of years: that "God created the world in six days." Legends from which Mythologies were elaborately created, as in ancient Greece and India, reveal, besides the tragedies themselves, in what degree these peoples were affected by them. It is the Mythologies of the people that motivate them to create their Civilizations. Therefore, people who do not comment, compliment, discuss, extol, or differentiate between the Great and the Worthless, are dead people who do not matter. It is the REACTABILITY of people that makes them PRESENT in the world.

This is another illustration from my tragedy *Rege! Rege!* (the sound a Polish frog makes). Ludola is the mute blacksmith whose tongue was torn out to prevent him from teaching the ancient *Po Gan* ("After-the diluvial-Exile") beliefs.

Ludola's function was to forge the souls for the newly born on his anvil and to repair the rusted, long-unused ones of the elderly. Thus, he learns all about the misfortunes of his nation, but is unable to convey what he learns, for he cannot talk. However, his son Krak presses his ear to his father's chest and learns what passes over the anvil. This inspires Krak to alter matters accordingly.

The name Ludola, developed from ancient Protong "Lud Dola," means "People's Fate." Although this little man is an invention of mine, he has the likeness of a typical, shy, hardworking father, the guardian of all in the village. He is pictured here in one of the caves of Ojcow, located near Kraków, pumping his bellow, adding more urgency to his heart's flame.

The entire myth about Krak, the legendary founder of Kraków, is of my invention.

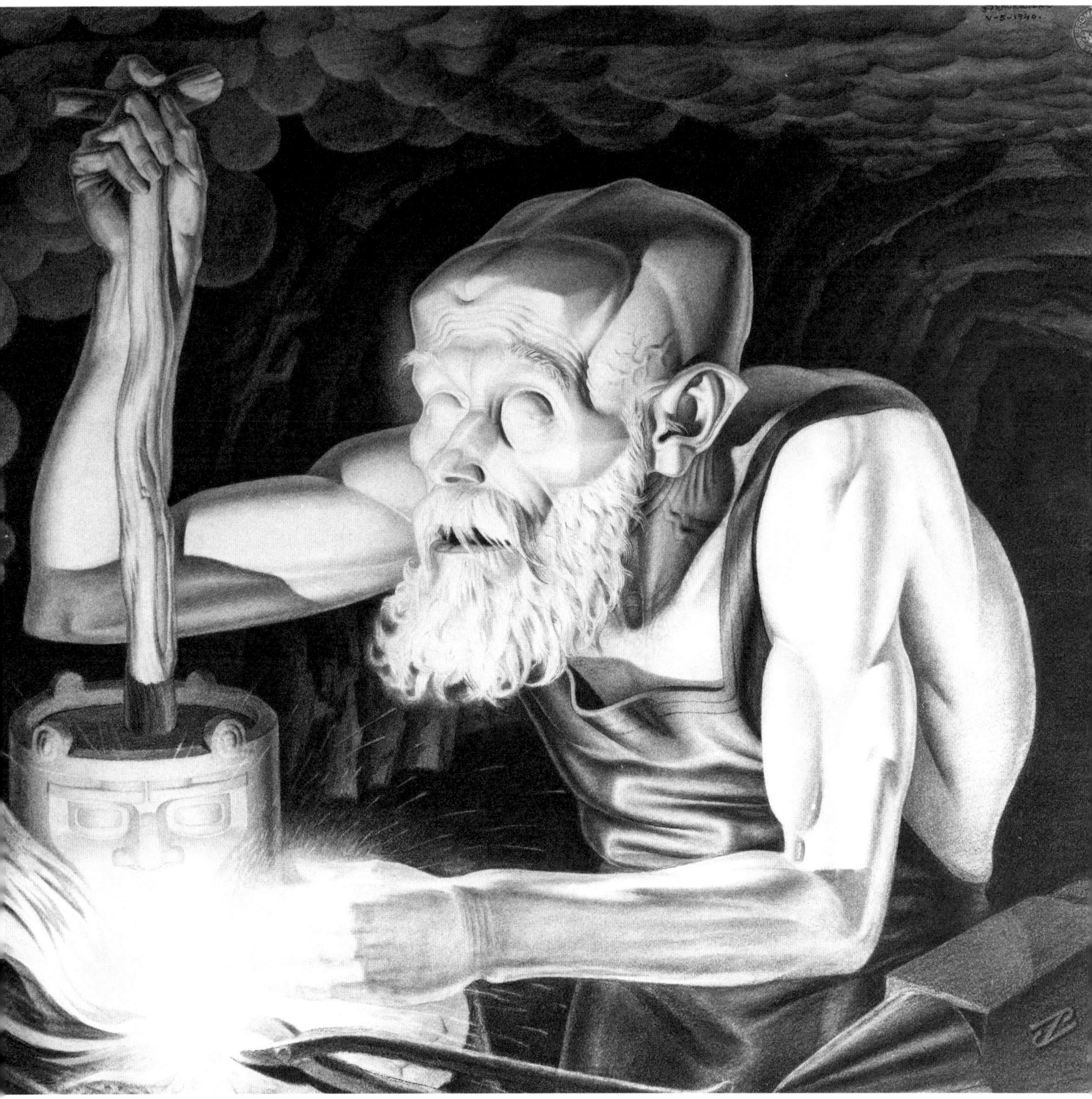

Aviator's Oath

I made this lithograph in California, at the time of World War II, to honor the Polish aviators who escaped from the German Predators and were gathered by the British government to defend Scotland, exclusively. There were 18,000 of them in Scotland. It has been observed by many people, besides me, that there is some unexplainable affinity between the Scottish and Polish peoples, to such an extent that there were startingly many marriages of Scottish lassies to the Polish aviators.

Years ago, I contrived the EAGLEAXE emblem, intentionally linking ancient Crete's Double-bladed Axe – the holiest of symbols, each triangle being pictographic of one of the twin continents from where our ancestors escaped from the Deluge – with the Polish Eagle, which harkens back to astral ages. Presently, the Eagleaxe became the emblem of Neuropa.

I raised it above a *hata* (Polish for hut). The ancient Hittites called themselves "Hata," being the first ones to introduce single-room huts. Little huts were often depicted in Aztec and Inca Art, to symbolize Homeland, Country. Here it is covered with the traditional thatch of straw, with smoke from the hearth seeping out at the sides of the roof. Instead of cross-beams at the corners, I made human hands that hold-on-and-on to themselves. The night skies are crossed by the planes the United States sent to Britain to fight against the Nazi-Yetinsyny.

I sent the lithograph to the Poles in Britain, proposing they use it for a poster to raise some funds. But crocodiles, sharks and "intellectual" Poles do not answer letters, nor show any graciousness (the Polish language does not even have an equivalent for this word). Whoever of them received the lithograph, stole it and kept silent, as the Poles have done for the last fifty years after looting everything I ever created.

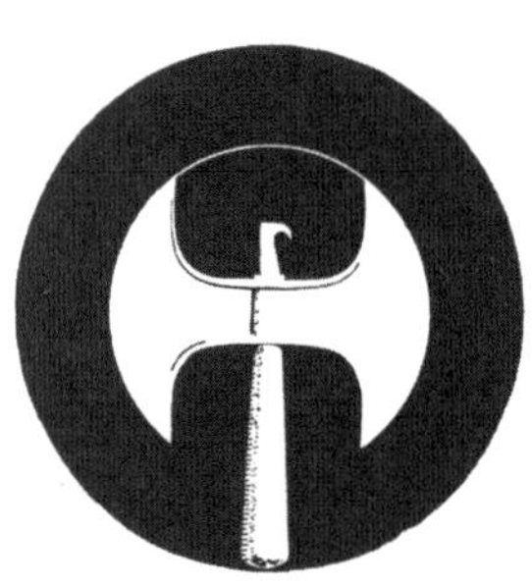

"EAGLEAXE" EMBLEM
From *Atak Kraka*, 1939

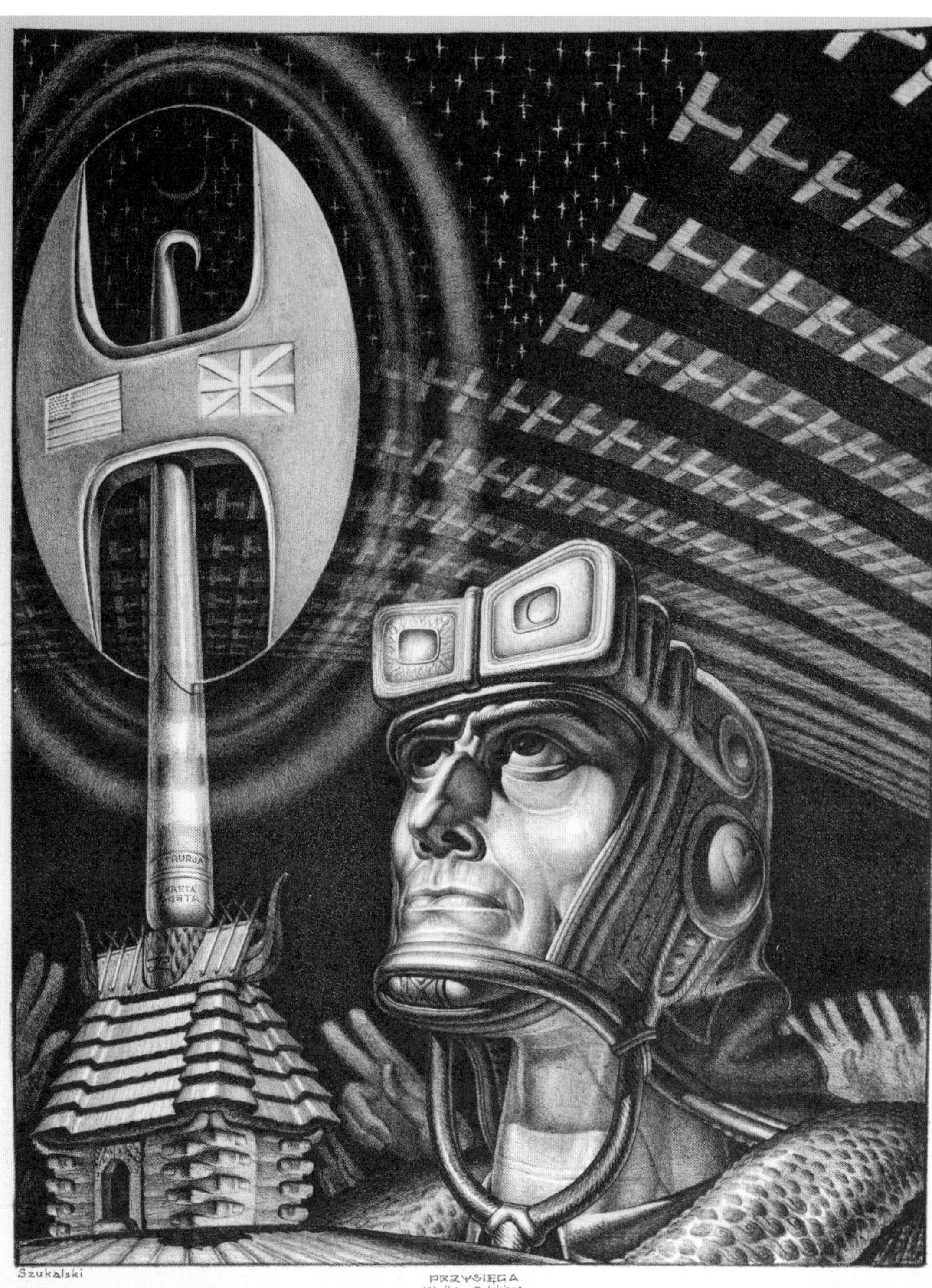

Szukalski
PRZYSIĘGA
Lotnika Polskiego
na
ŚWIĘTOPORZA

114

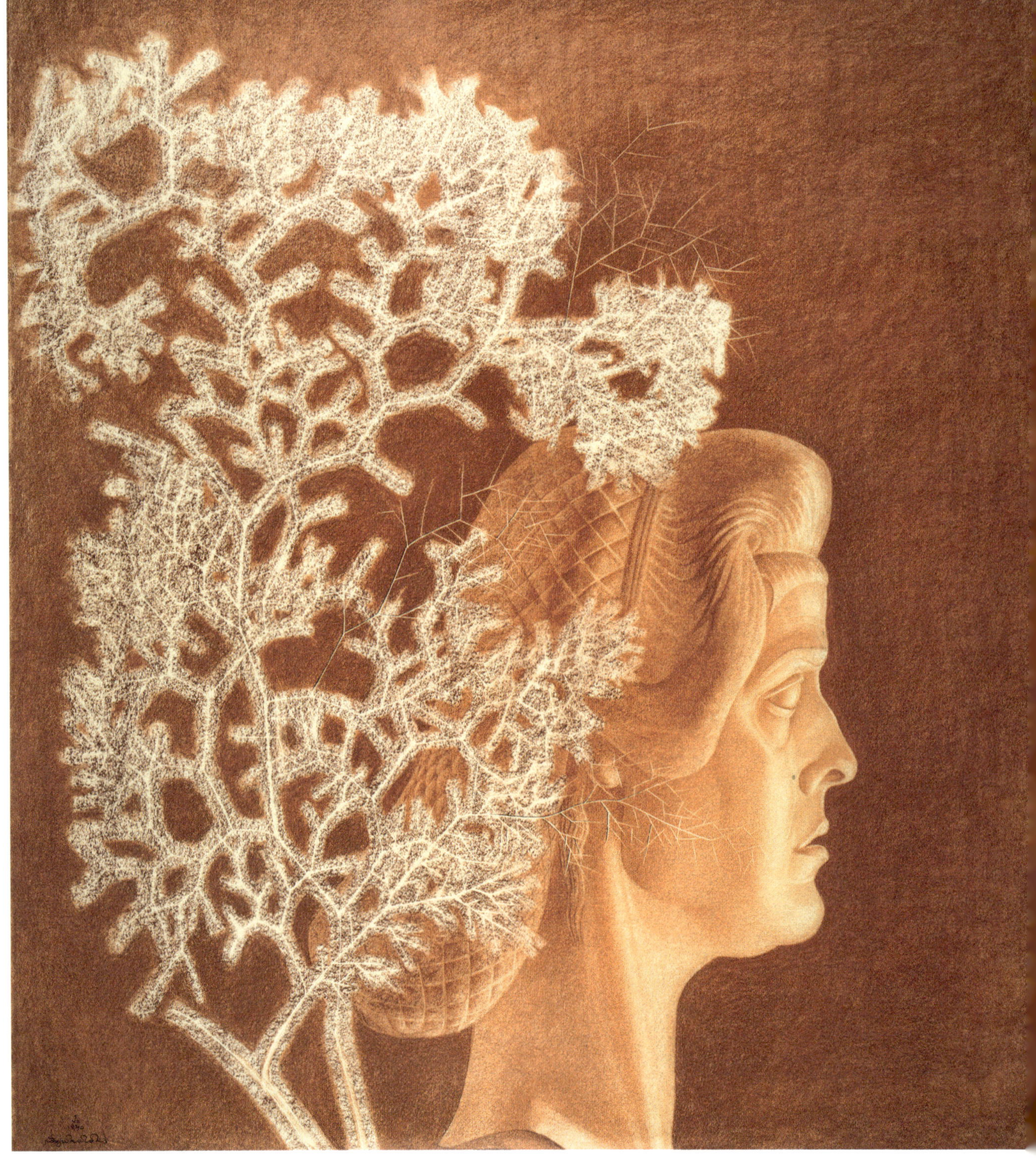

Portrait of Joan

While putting this volume together, my most beloved Joan Lee Donovan Szukalski, my constant "patron saint" and ever-loving and adored wife died (in tragic circumstances of which I will write in the second volume of *Troughful of Pearls*).

Once, in an outburst of utter despair over the remorseless finality of my love's departure, howling out my grief like a speared animal, I caught myself in a mirror and was struck by what had become of my face. I am sure that the face of the biblical Job was as much a frightening mass of "hashed" meat contained only by its skin. In my youth I was quite handsome, but my perpetual grief over the inhumanity of the pseudo-intellectual Poles has finally, irreversibly done its hateful duty in altering me into a "face" in the crowd.

Newspaper item, 1934

Lotus

Returning to California, escaping the siege of Warsaw, I found an apartment in Westwood, California with by beloved second wife, Joan. One of our immediate neighbors was this classic looking Japanese girl, named Lotus. She generously sat for me to draw her in carbon pencil. This drawing is much over life-size. It still intrigues me that I rarely see beautiful Chinese ladies, yet I very often meet with the beauty of Japanese ladies. I have found no answer for this, though I am inclined to think that the Chinese race evolved in greater hardships and heartbreaks than the Japanese. I am positive that heartbreaks destroy our good looks.

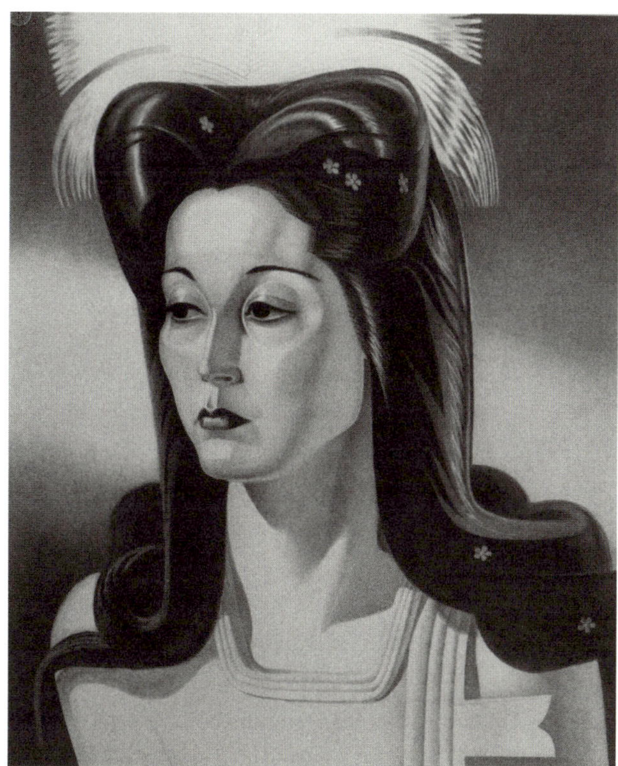

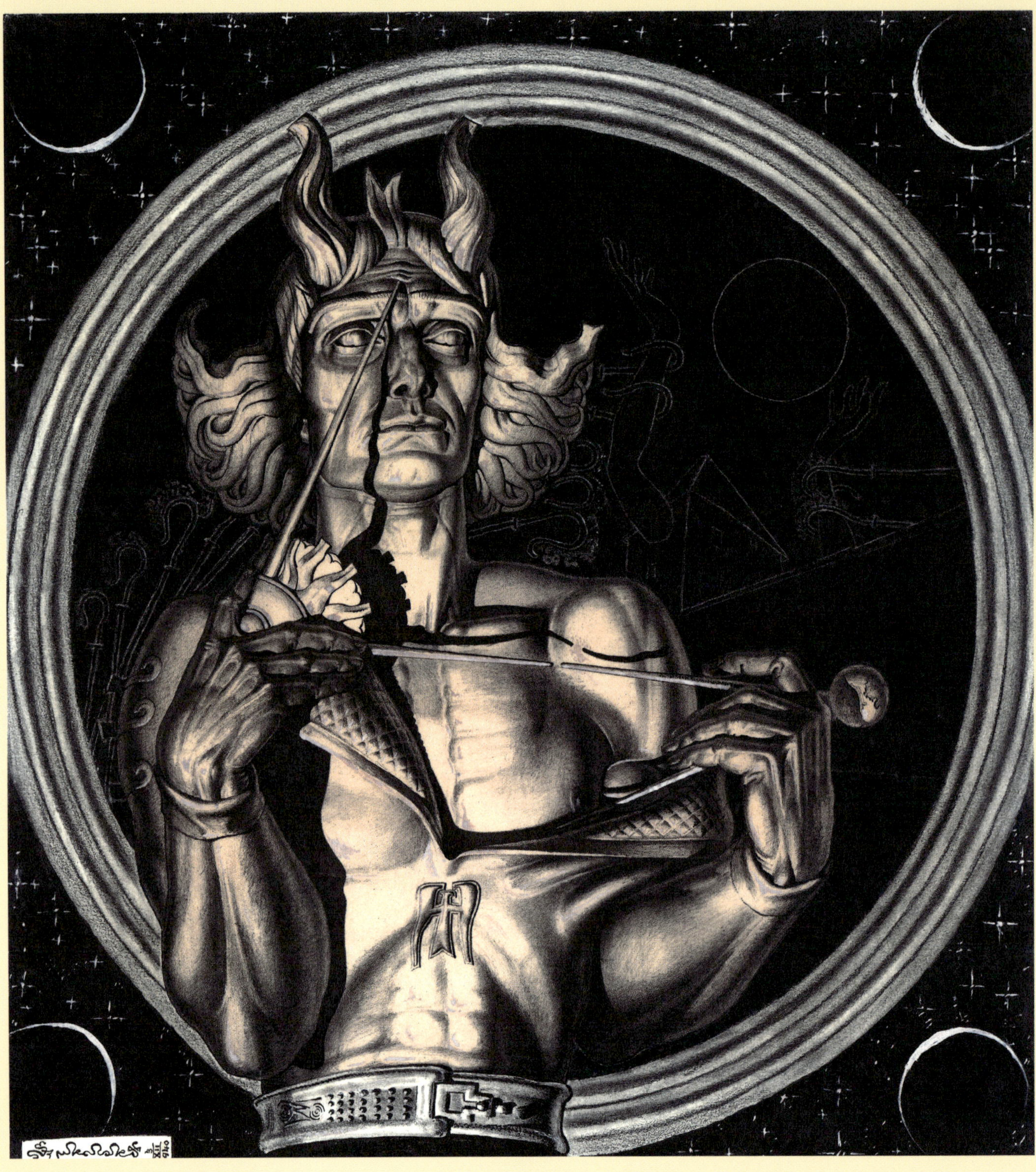

Copernicus, the Astronomer

Mikołaj Kopernik's family hailed from the Polish village Koperniki, where prospered many families that cultivated and harvested dill, so indispensable in the pickling of cucumbers. The German-English "dill" is called in Polish *koper*, therefore the name of Kopernik means "a diller."

From the attic of his provincial confinement to oblivion he boldly dismissed the whole motley crowd of good and evil demons that so confounded our mutual ancestors, thus freeing pure Science from the tyranny of shamanic anti-reason. Then he correlated the brilliance of man's Mind with the radiance of the all-causing Sun. At the same time, he recognized the affinity between his Heart and the heartbreak World, thus sperming an aimless Universe with the divinely human purpose.

Though a mere earthling, he rearranged the then-existing interplanetary chaos according to his own logos. Single-handedly, he stopped the idle wanderings of the errandless Sun by hitching it to the immovable post of Rationalist Consistency and by... demoting the self-obsessed Earth to mere spinning around it, despite the promised eternal damnation.

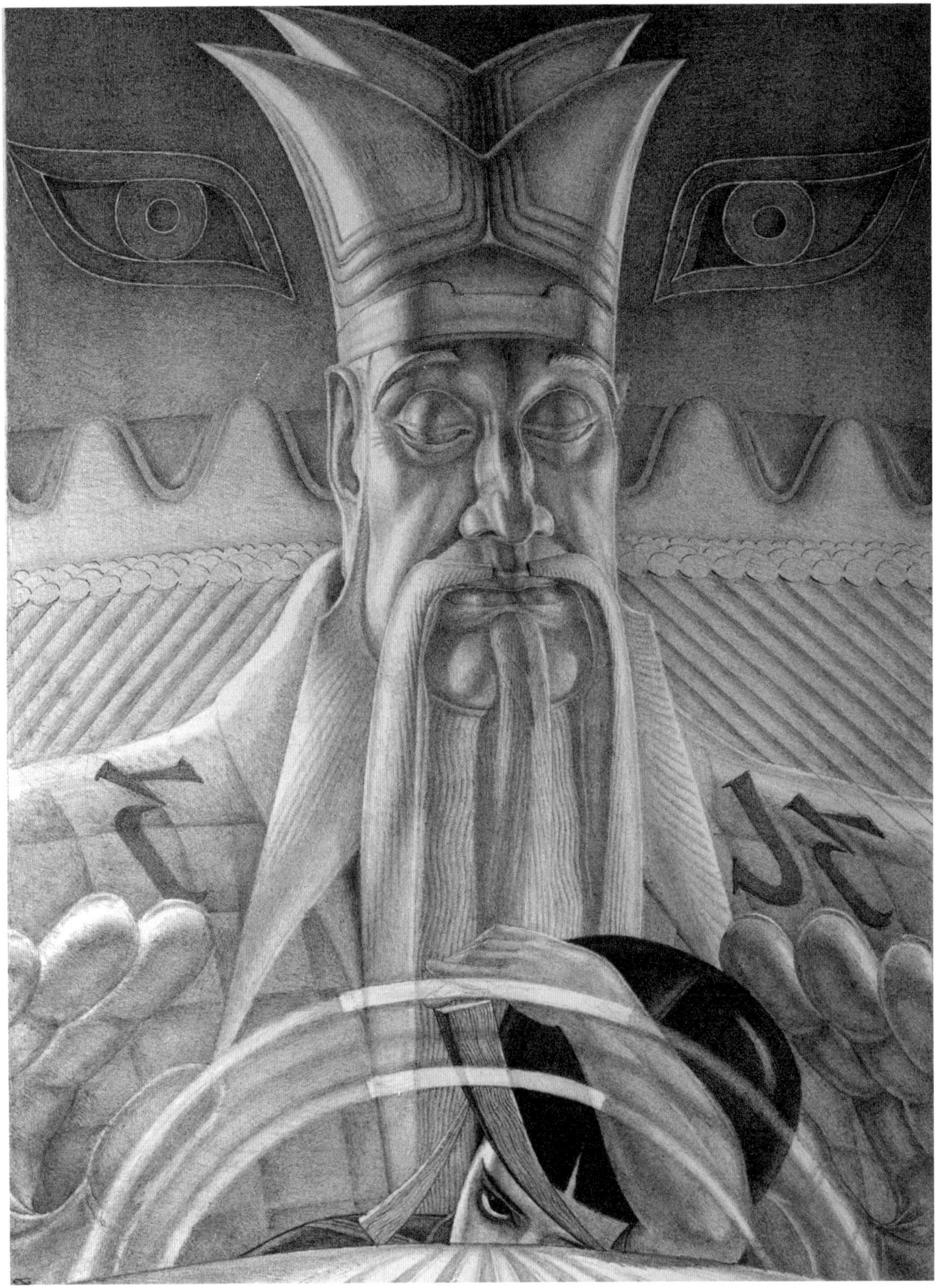

Kungfutse (Confucius)

Confucius was a son of a very wealthy Chinese family. His father was given vast parts of China to oversee and manage, and every year he sent him to different parts of the possessions in order to make some new dispositions. Confucius' concern over human degradation and tragedy brought him many followers, so that wherever he visited he was thronged with troubled people to hear his advice on the dilemmas of life.

Eventually, there were so many people craving to hear his wisdom that Confucius asked some bright youths to come under his tutelage and learn some of his wisdom, that they might teach among the needy when he could not be present. The admonitions that the youths wrote down, formulating his philosophic ideas, became known as the *Confucian Analects.*

He spoke little of God and the Souls of Men but mainly of the relationships between men. In his teachings no angels are flapping their wings, nor Satans roasting sin-possessed humans in hell-fire. In fact, he taught no theology, but good manners and advised his listeners to combat Greed as the Cause of all Evil. He promised no heavenly rewards and never mentioned the need of absolute obedience, but reasoned co-operation between his fellow men.

If I ever hear the sound of water slushing in the enclosed bucket of my head while walking, and crave some kind of religion, I will most certainly stroll to the nearest church. However, I am most content with myself as my own advisor and will never seek organized tutelage for my spirit. I doubt that I have or have need of a soul. My thoughtfulness over my fellow-men takes the place of a rosary-fingered soul. Of all the soul shepherds, I admire Confucius most, for he never gave an excuse to his followers to turn prayers into jingling money. Behind the aim of all religions were only few ideal individuals with the pedagogic intention to guard morally frail mankind and conduct them into a kinder, juster behavior, so that their potential Nobility would hatch out of the originally avaricious mammal.

There is a Chinese character called *T'ien* that looks like a mountaintop with two horizontal lines above it. The Chinese tell us that the word means "heaven," but I tell you that I, the creator of the new science of Pictography, know better. This character is the pictograph of a land that was submerged. Its name derived from the Polish-Protong word "cien" (pron. "tsien") which means "shadow," therefore it represents the land where the spirits of our Ancestors dwell: Easter Island.

Beneath the blessing hands of Confucius bends thoughtfully a child, gazing at us, the contemporaries, but with its mind dwelling on the things ancient that remain beneath the double lines that form the land of the Ancestors (called "Celestials" by the Chinese) and its deluging seas.

Above the shoulders of the great religious reformer of China I placed the Eyes of Oce On ("He of the Fathers"), the submerged continent in the Atlantic region.

Moxo Indian

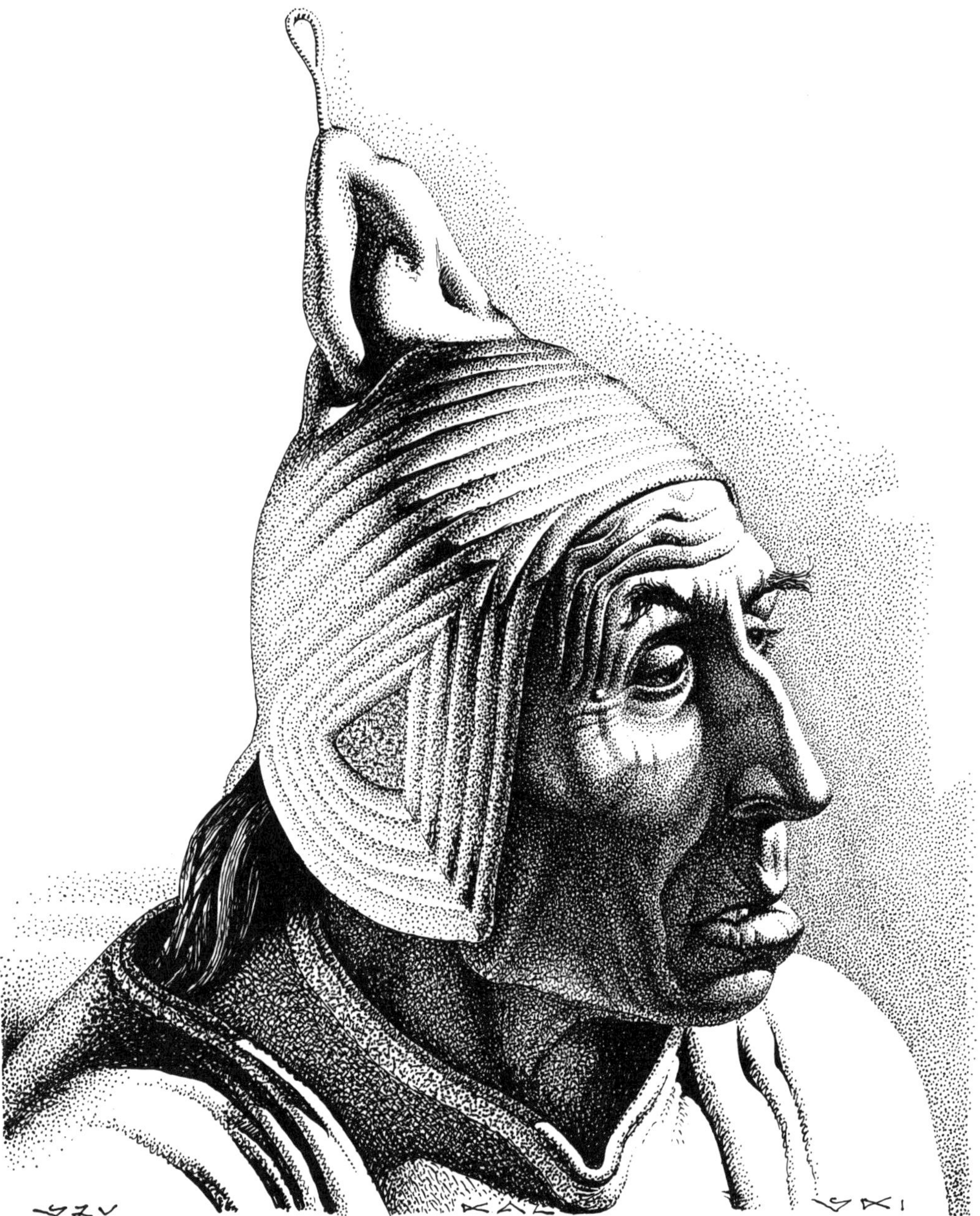

A proboscoid Moxo Indian of Bolivia wearing a "chullo" hat "That Ears" or, in Protong, "Chowa Lu," traditionally harkening to the Farsolar frigid climate which the ancestors survived.

Seminole Priest, 16th Century

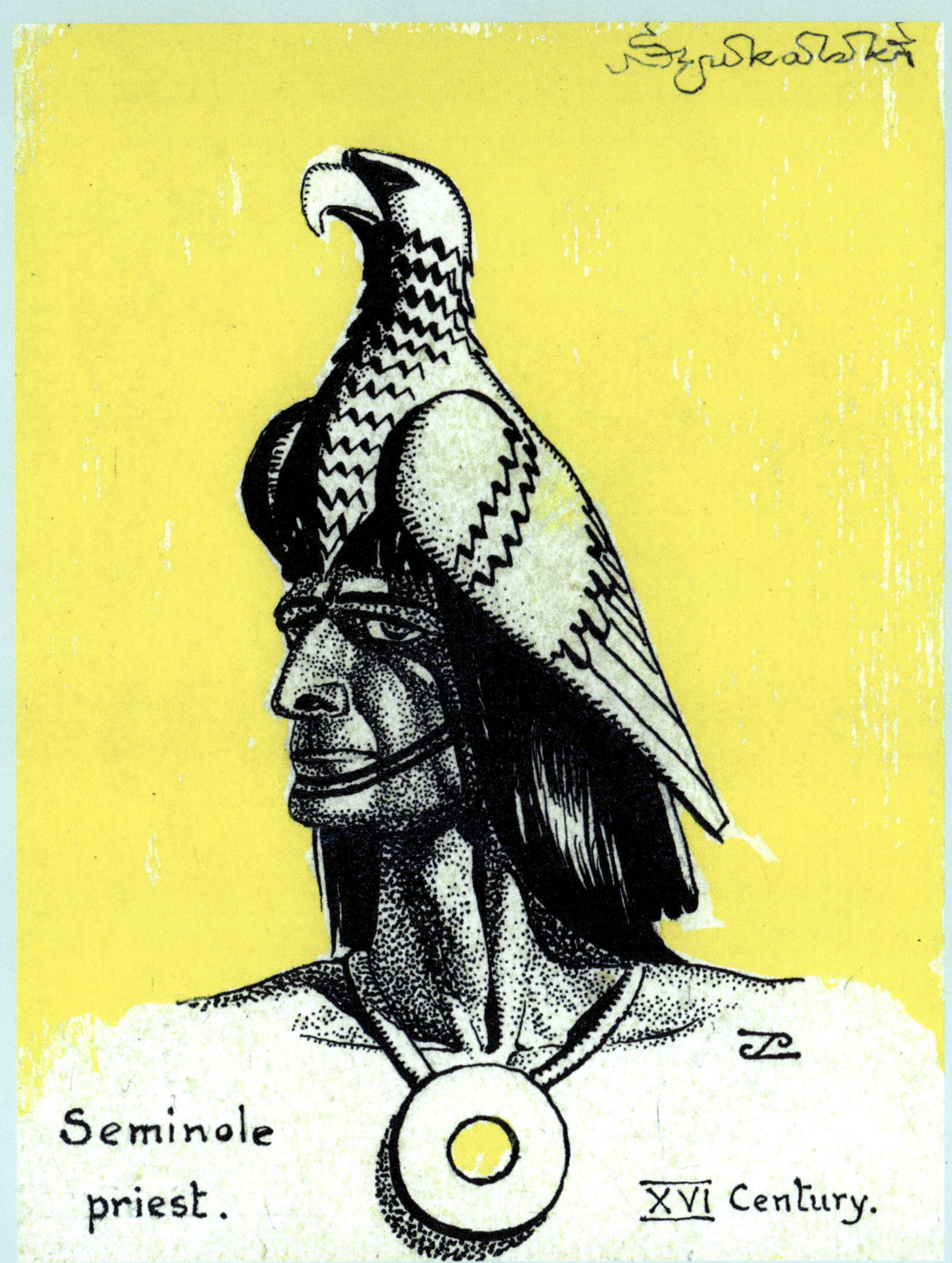

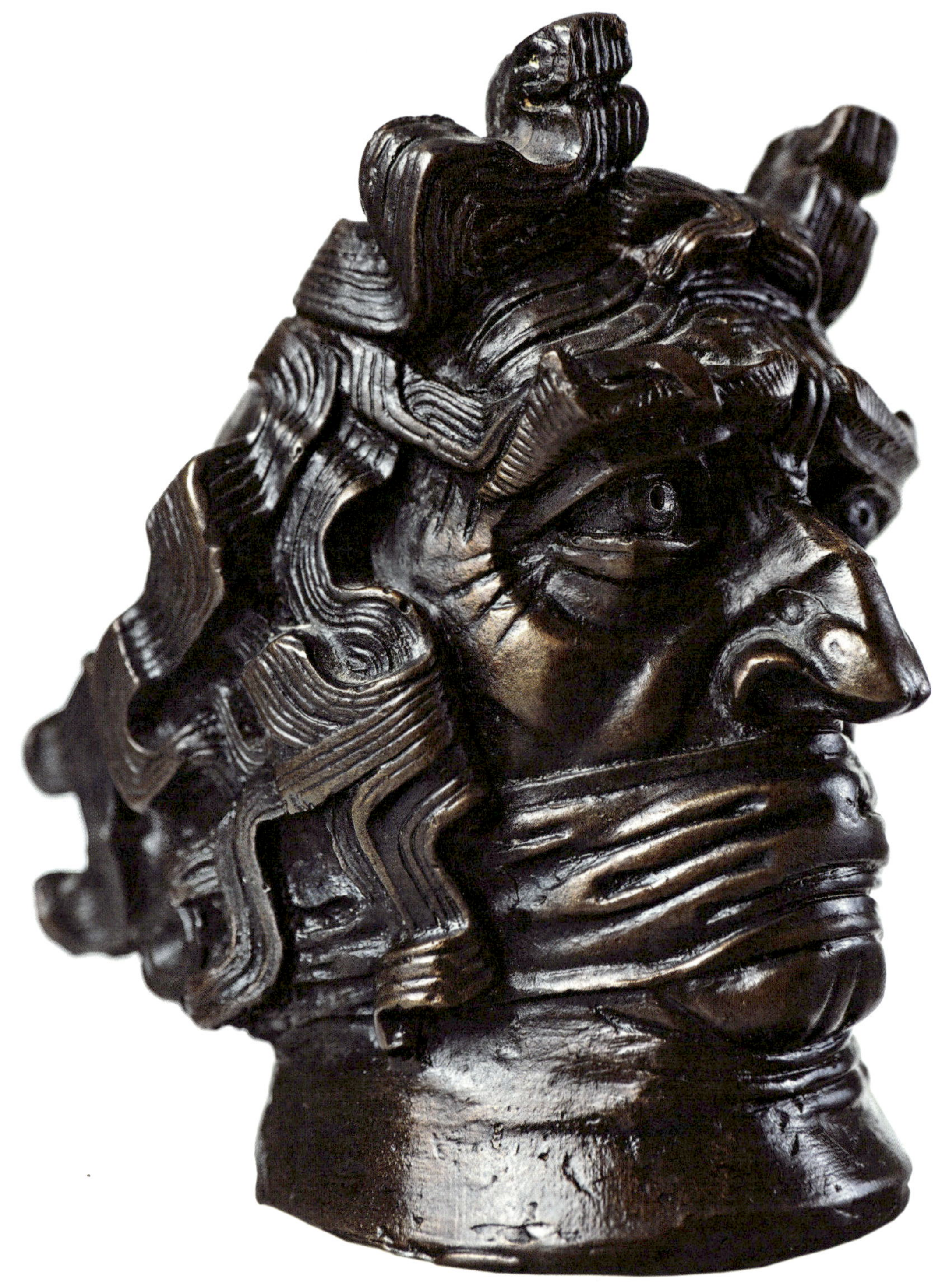

122

Bronze, 4″ tall

Head of Yaltantal

This is the Caucasian Prometheus, called Tantalus, who is a lover of Mankind. In Greek mythology Prometheus was the son of Zeus. For revealing the secrets of the Gods to mankind, he was condemned to stand in cold water, under a tree sagging under the weight of fruits which would vanish before he could grasp them. Even further punishment was inflicted upon him, for when he was thirsty and reached for the water, it would sway away from his cupped hands.

I named my sculpture of the Caucasian parallel version of Prometheus Yaltantal, to commemorate the heinous crime of the betrayal of half of Europe by the Anglomericans, conspiring with the parasitic Moscovites at the Conventicle of Yalta. There, a procession of eleven nations was signed away into Communist slavery, which was ratified by the Anglomerican Senate and Congress.

When nations lose the capacity for Moral Indignation, then they are ready to BETRAY their families, their friends, their allies and their civilization. By diminishing the size of Free Europe, the Anglomericans have added over 260 million humans to the inherently parasitic subhumans, the *Yetinsyny* (Russian for "Sons of the Yeti") who, unlike HUMANS, are totally devoid of human emotions and, therefore, of Honor, Morality, Ethics and Compassion; whose aberration is to exterminate as many Humans as possible under their hateful, formalized Communist "ideology" as was done under the Nazi "ideology" of Hitler and his German Yetinsyny.

He is the image of Mankind Betrayed, suffering the Nightmare of Vanquished Freedoms imposed upon the world by the Yetinsyn fraternity of Roosevelt–Stalin–Churchill. If you have heard about the Fabian Conspiracy, you will understand why Anglomericans are the victims of suicidal psychosis, and why this Wondermerica is being victimized by their Treason.

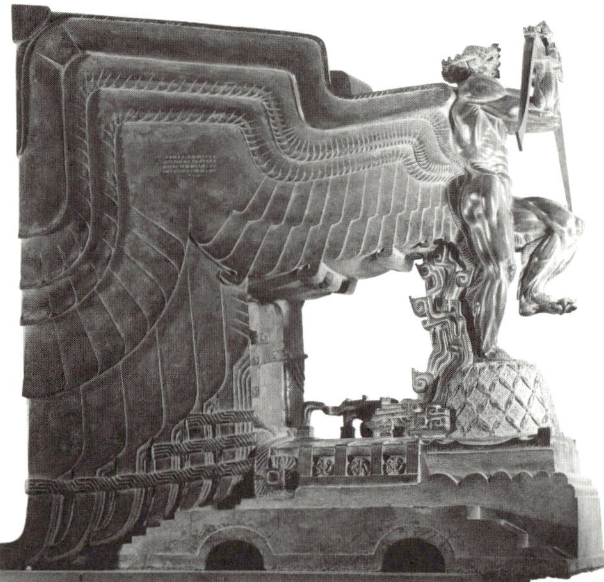

124   *Head of Yaltantal* is a detail of a project for a monument that was to be erected near the buildings of the United Nations in New York. The full sculpture design was flown to New York for an exhibition by the Cultural Clubs of American Poles and never returned to me. They ignored my letters. It was later seen in the Polish Communist Consulate in New York, then transported to either Russia or Poland, after being sold by the Polish writer Yanta, then the president of these Cultural (?) Clubs.

WIDE HEAD OF YALTANTAL
The same head, pulled apart from the back by the artist while the
plaster mold was still moist, resulting in an even more powerful
conveyance of despair.
Bronze, 4" tall, 8" wide

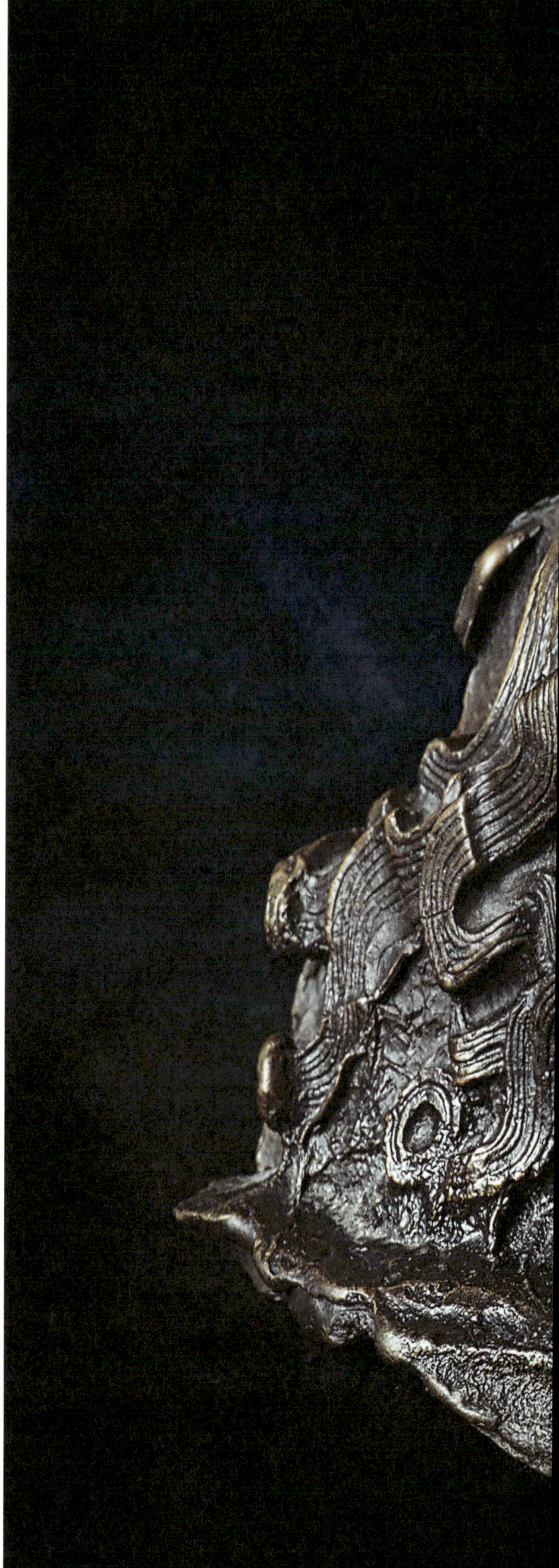

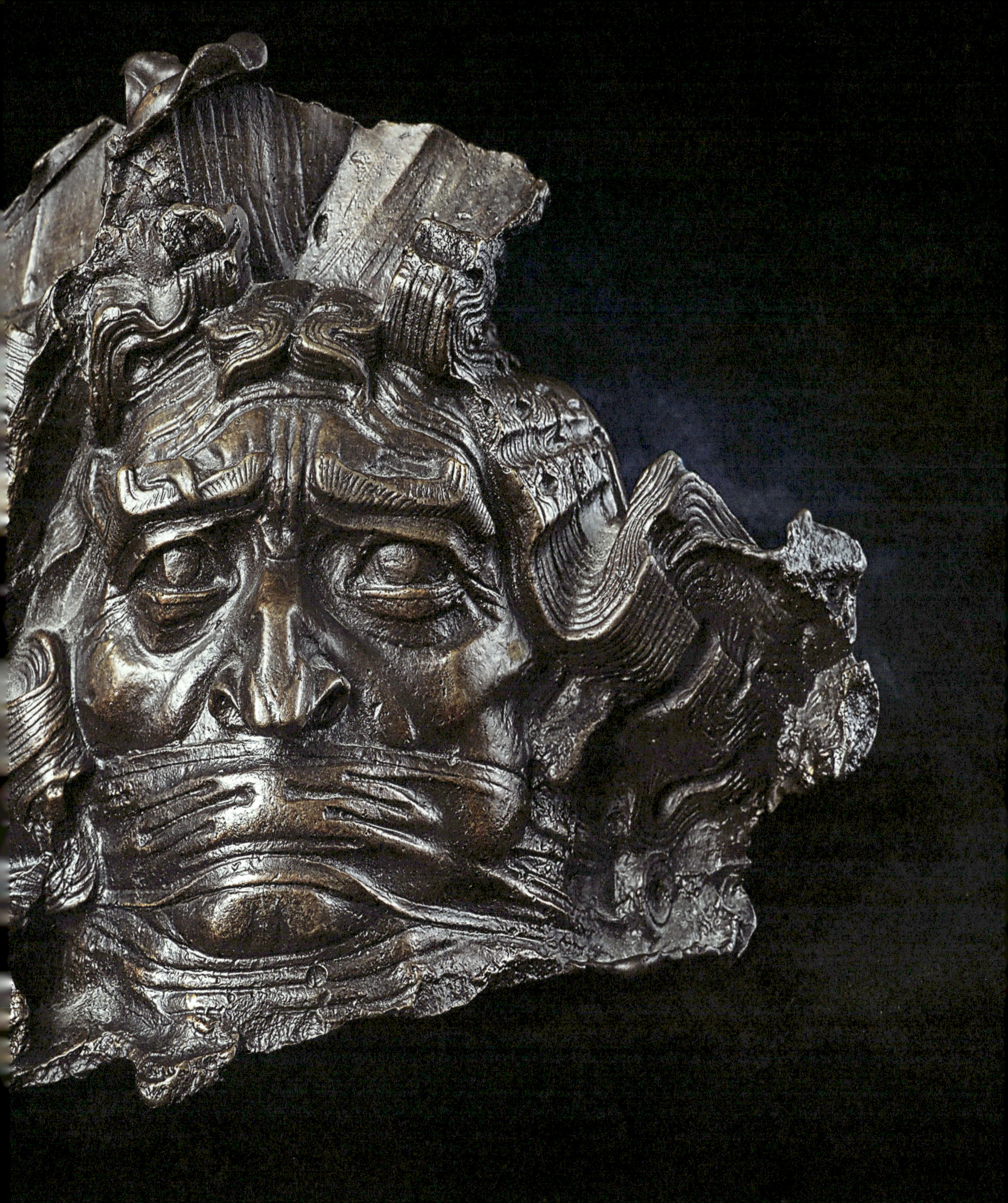

Gazelle Head

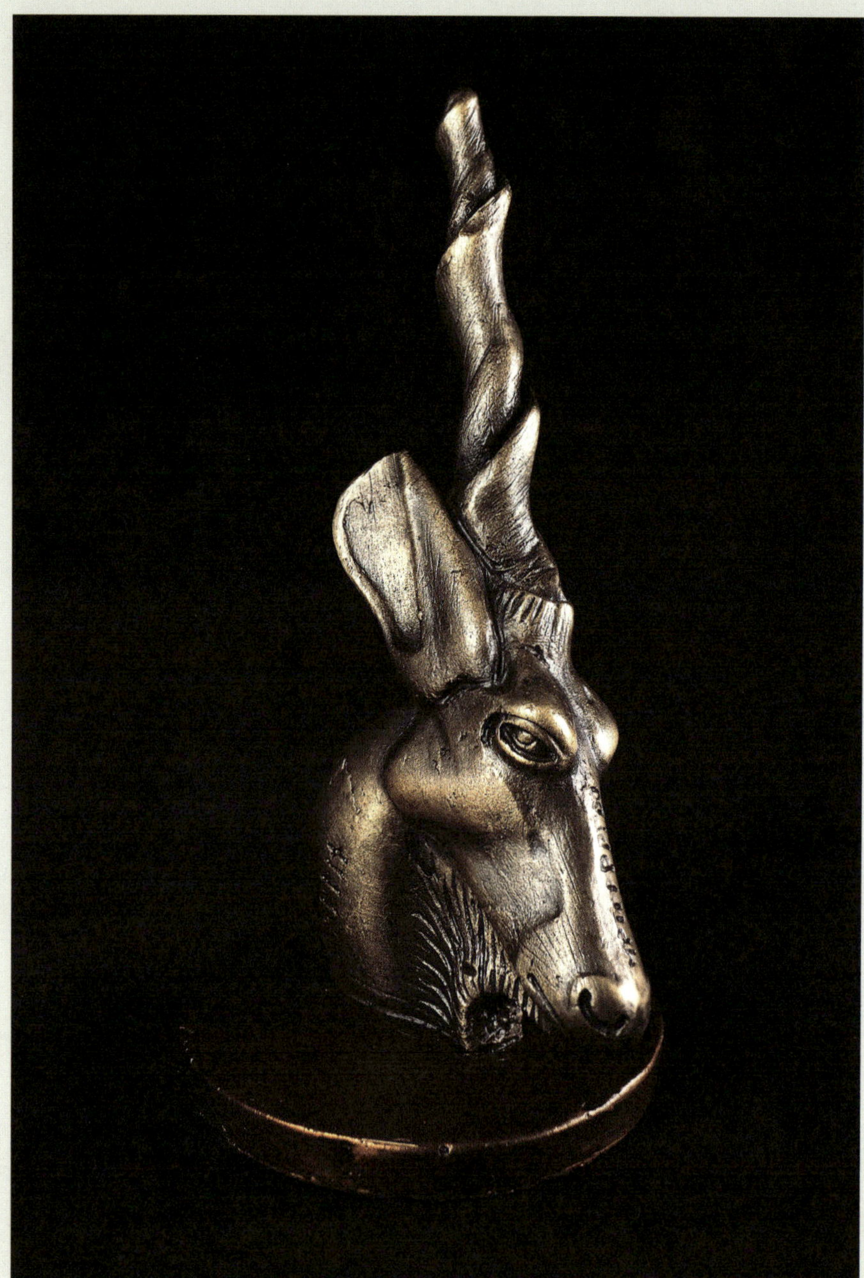

Photo–Bill Debley

Bronze, 4″ tall

A·Human / Human

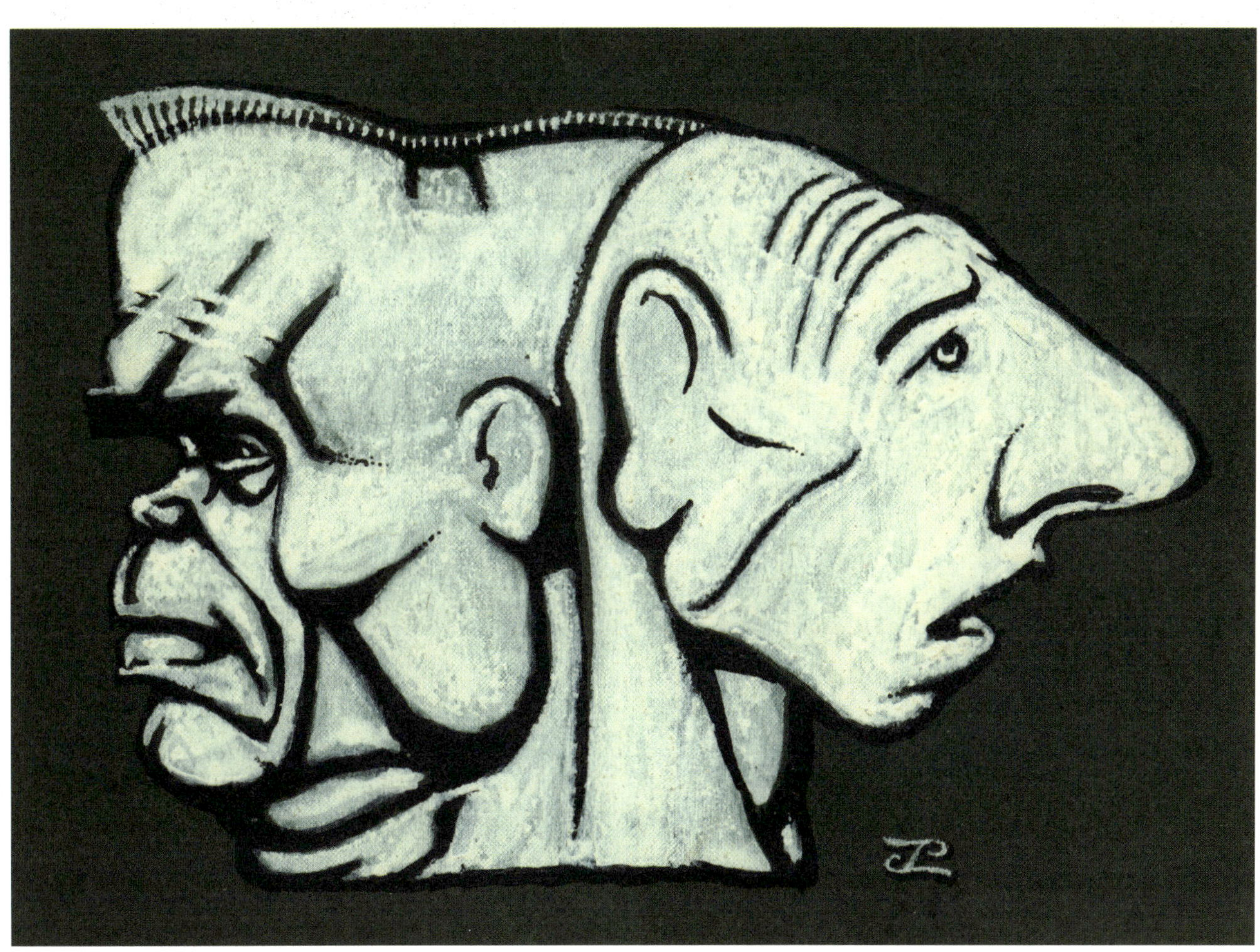

127

Face of a Satyr

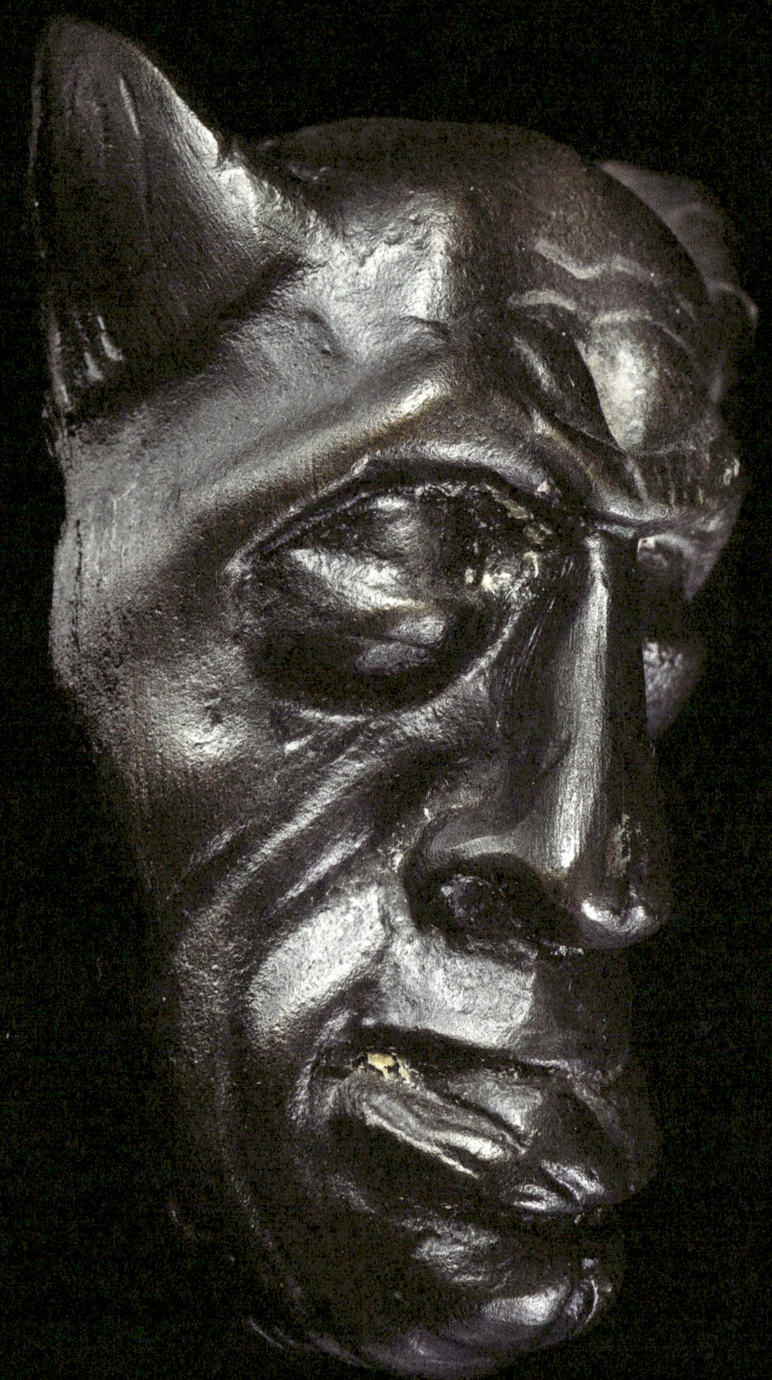

Bronze, 2½" tall
Photo—Bill Debley

"Come On Boys, Let Her Have It!"

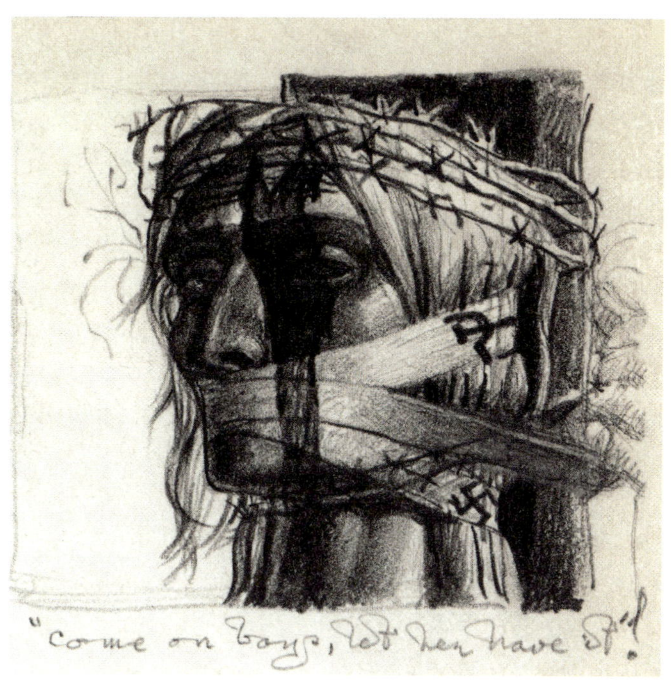

Gregory Peck / Alida Valli

Although he never mentioned it to me, Szukalski apparently did work for the Hollywood studios in the 1940s. According to IMDb (the International Movie Database), *Duel in the Sun* (1946) and *The Paradine Case* (1947), both starring Gregory Peck, were produced by David O. Selznick and both scripts had uncredited assists from Ben Hecht. It is easy to imagine Szukalski, Hecht's close friend, in the mix.

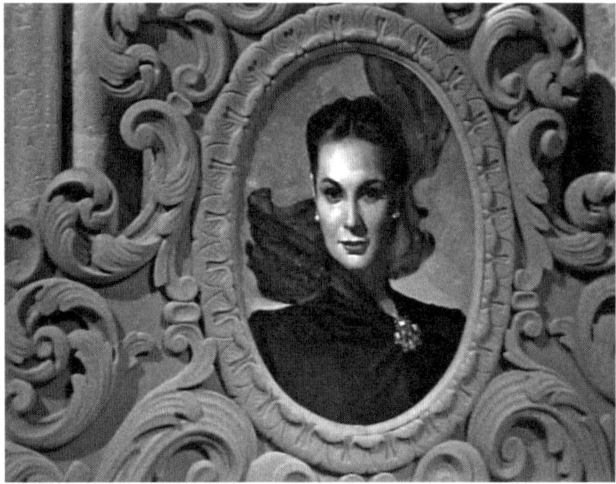

The starring actress in *The Paradine Case* was Alida Valli, whose character's portrait played an important role in the movie. Although Szukalski was not credited in the movie itself, IMDb lists his name under Art Department of this film as "painter: Valli's portrait (uncredited)."

– *Editor*

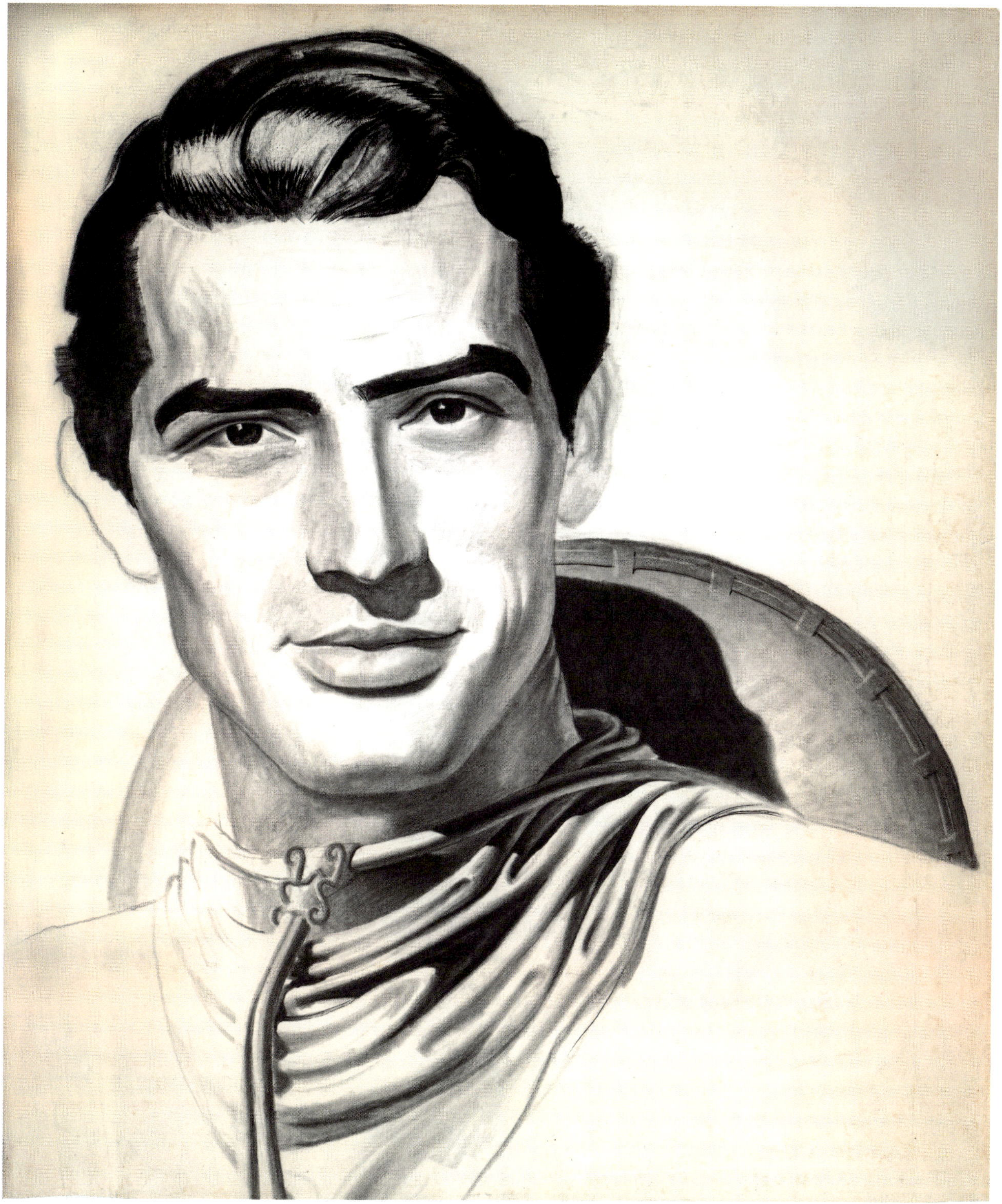

The Astrologer

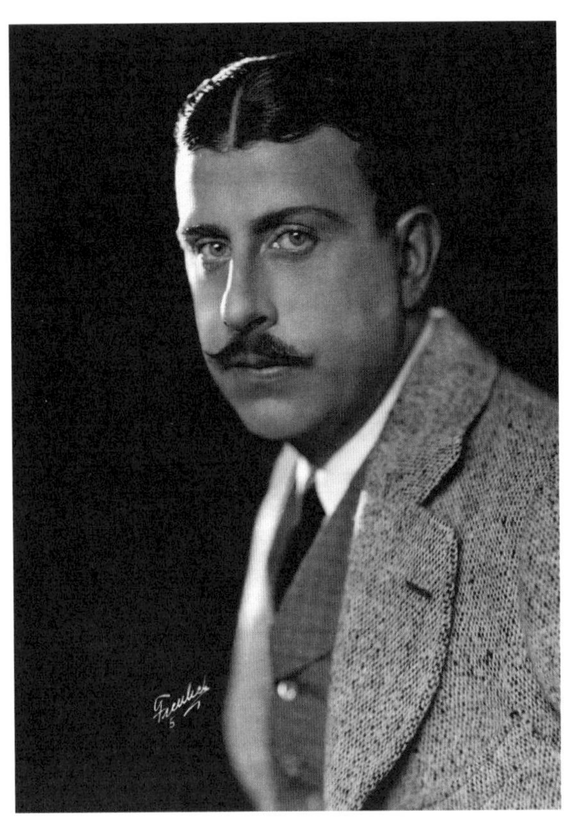

STUART HOLMES

We knew each other for many years while I lived in California. He was an actor who had played in early motion pictures with Pearl White and had gone on to many roles in sound movies. Being of pleasant disposition, he was very companionable, and full of anecdotes. His wife was a well-known astrologer and he too became apt in this pseudo-science.

He stood for me while I began to model him in clay in the outdoors, which was a new experience for me. I found it to be ideal, for the sunlight came from directly above. I needed him to pose for about an hour, then finished the sculpture from memory.

His interest in astrology was one of his special charms. He and his wife Bianca had many extravagant things to tell about me as a Sagittarius. I believed only the things I liked, and what I didn't like I regarded as the "mistakes" that astrologers make. Since he was born under the sign of the Pisces, I gave him two fish at the base of the neck.

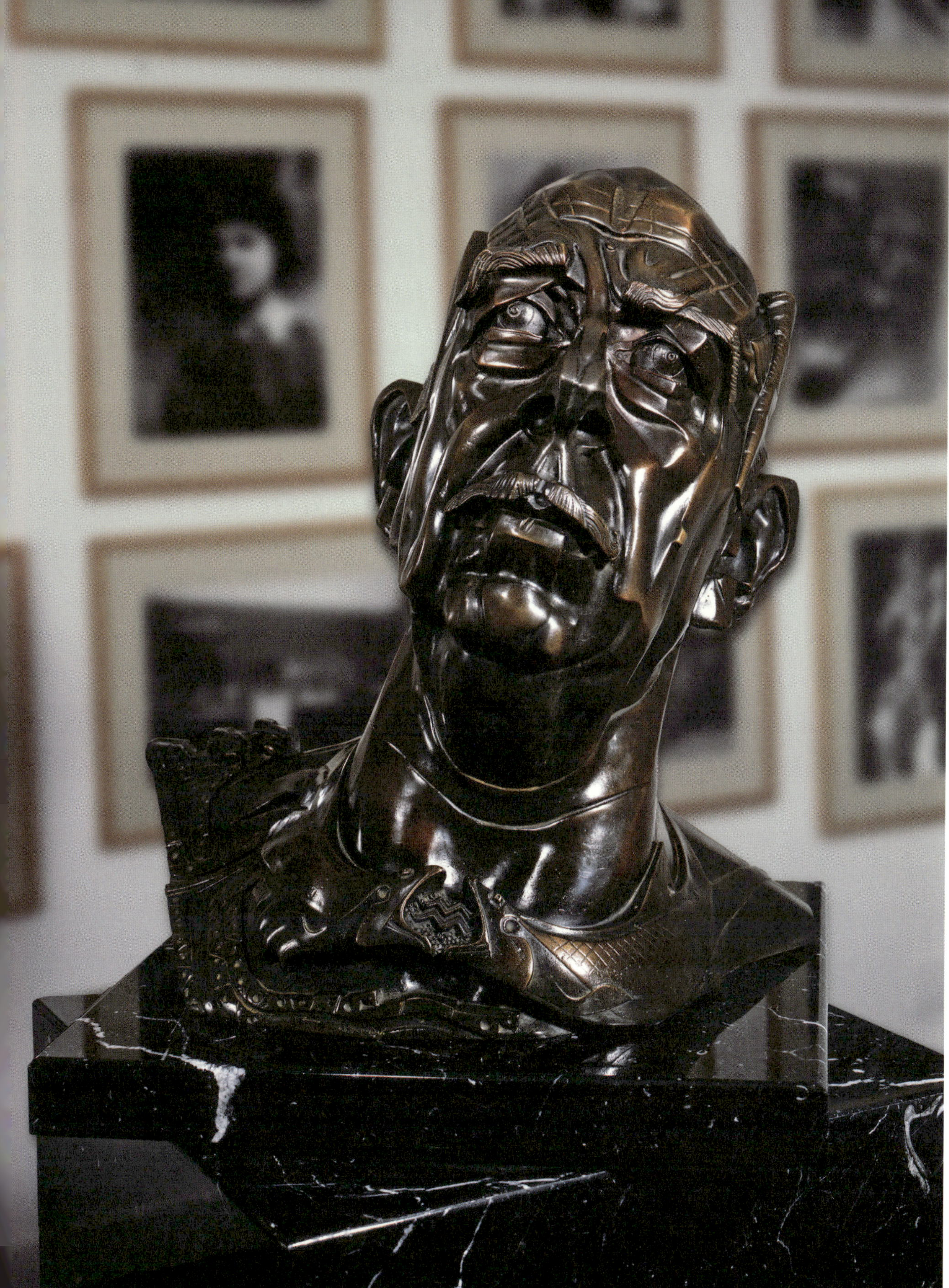

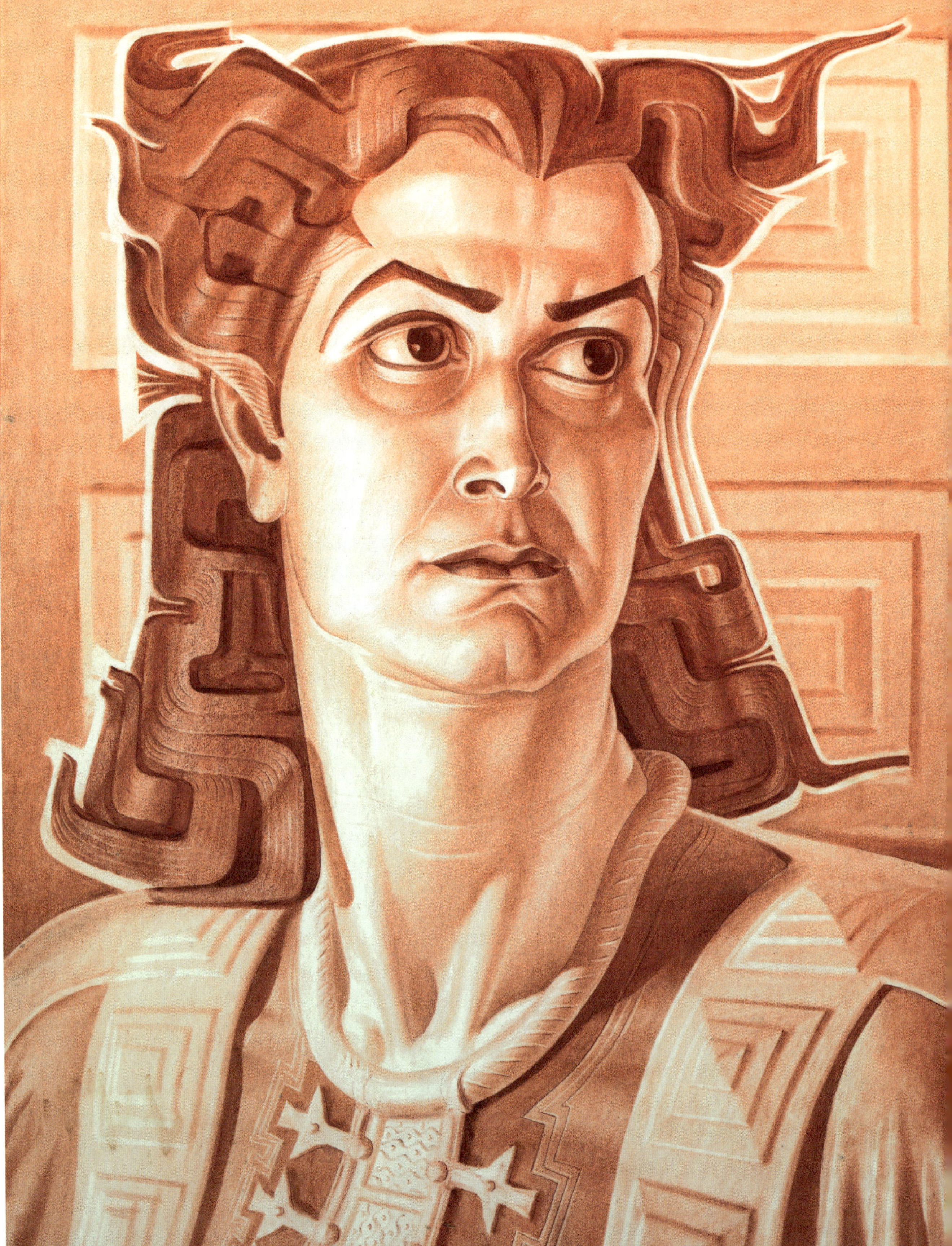

Mrs. Johnson

I have always been in great awe of women, particularly if they are pretty. My sister made me feel uncomfortable when she had girlfriends at our home, and when fourteen, I entered the Art Academy, which had only male students, so my entire youth was without the company of girls.

I am always under awful tension when a lady sits for her portrait. I feel I am imposing too much when I ask her to sit "this way" or "that" in attempting to get a view that would be more picturesque. So I do not ask these things and my portraits of ladies start very badly. However, if the lady has a natural way of sitting interestingly, not merely plopped onto a seat, I am thrilled to draw her. But I fear my enthusiasm, which would exaggerate her features and displease her. My tendency to monumentalize, hence make more masculine, would be a fatal offence to her marvelous femininity. So I usually refrain from using women in my works. While I have always thought mostly of them as a form of escapism from the trivia of daily life and would rather commit suicide than be without their presence in this world, I furthermore exclude them from my creative deeds, because the subjects I carve or paint often deal with Death and Enslavement of Humanity by the Sneak-Predators, and it is too solemn and grievous a world of my mind's preoccupation to have their adorable company so misused and abused.

At any time, I would rather be in a woman's company than a man's. I have been told by women that I should always have their company, for, socially, I am then at my best, purring with happiness and using my clavichord from one end to the other. I dislike to be "charming" in men's company, which would make me appear as if I were afflicted with the Anglosex problem, which makes me cramp my style and appear most unfriendly. But ladies…, they are my element where I straighten my wings and feel my oats.

One of my pleasures is the kissing of ladies' hands, for it comes nearest to " having" them, if only for an instant. Though in America, I do this seldom, since there are not many FEMININE women and I do not kiss women's hands. Women are not ladies. Sex makes women, but GRACIOUSNESS makes ladies. I do not desire women, but I cannot restrain my impulses in the presence of real ladies.

If you backtrack your basic motivation of all your desperate efforts to achieve worthy things, your patriotism, your heroic promptings, ALL, ALL are triggered by the thought of being admired by women, and particularly by that ONE. What is behind the struggle for freedom? The hope of being free to fare well, have one's own home, and the luck to have as patron saint the lady you love.

Portrait of a Wistful Lady

Sometimes it is a difficult task for an artist to make an interesting portrait, however excellent a technician he may be. It is often unfair to him, as well as to the sitter, if the facial features are not markedly… different. A face well-proportioned may become a nondescript model to paint. And the model will say: "But you made the Japanese girl so beautiful, and look at my ponrait," or thinks so without saying. And I lamely must defend myself: "Yes, that Japanese has certain disproportionate features. She has raven-black hair that folds as if glass!" It really is like having sixteen pennies for candy one morning, and the next week only two.

Although we may be the most beautiful people inside, our façade can be unassuming and often overlooked. Some books hide in drab covers, while inside, our heart finds an unforgettable feast of the ages, while other books are empty-paged, yet have covers elaborately promising.

This dear lady, the German-American wife of an American Pole was anaemic, hence prevalently dejected in spirit. The overlapping upper eyelids, denoting kidney malfunction, made her predominant expression that of melancholic sadness. Faces are like lanterns, some of them unlighted by the spark of vivacious life.

I took liberty with her hair, standing on end some seashells.

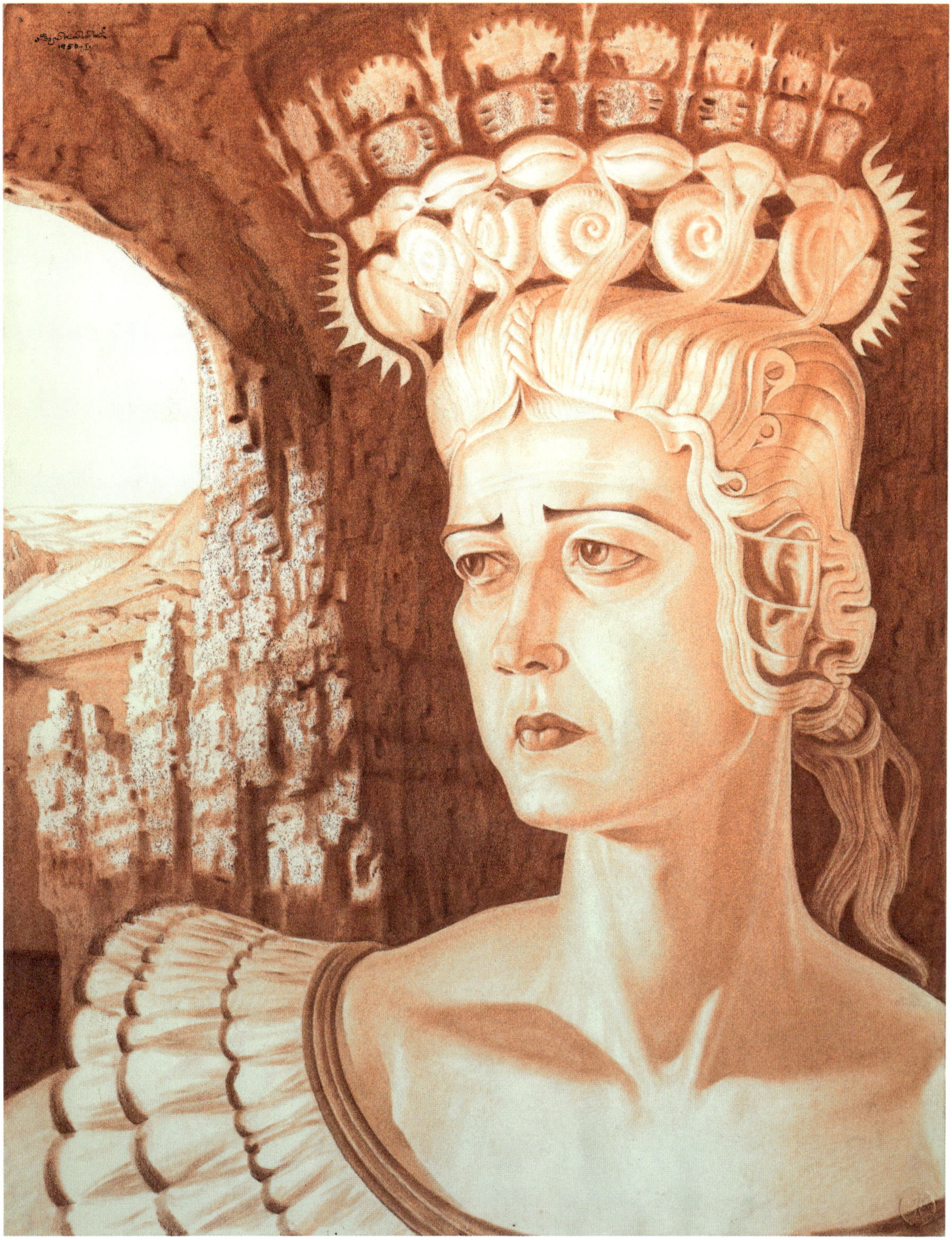

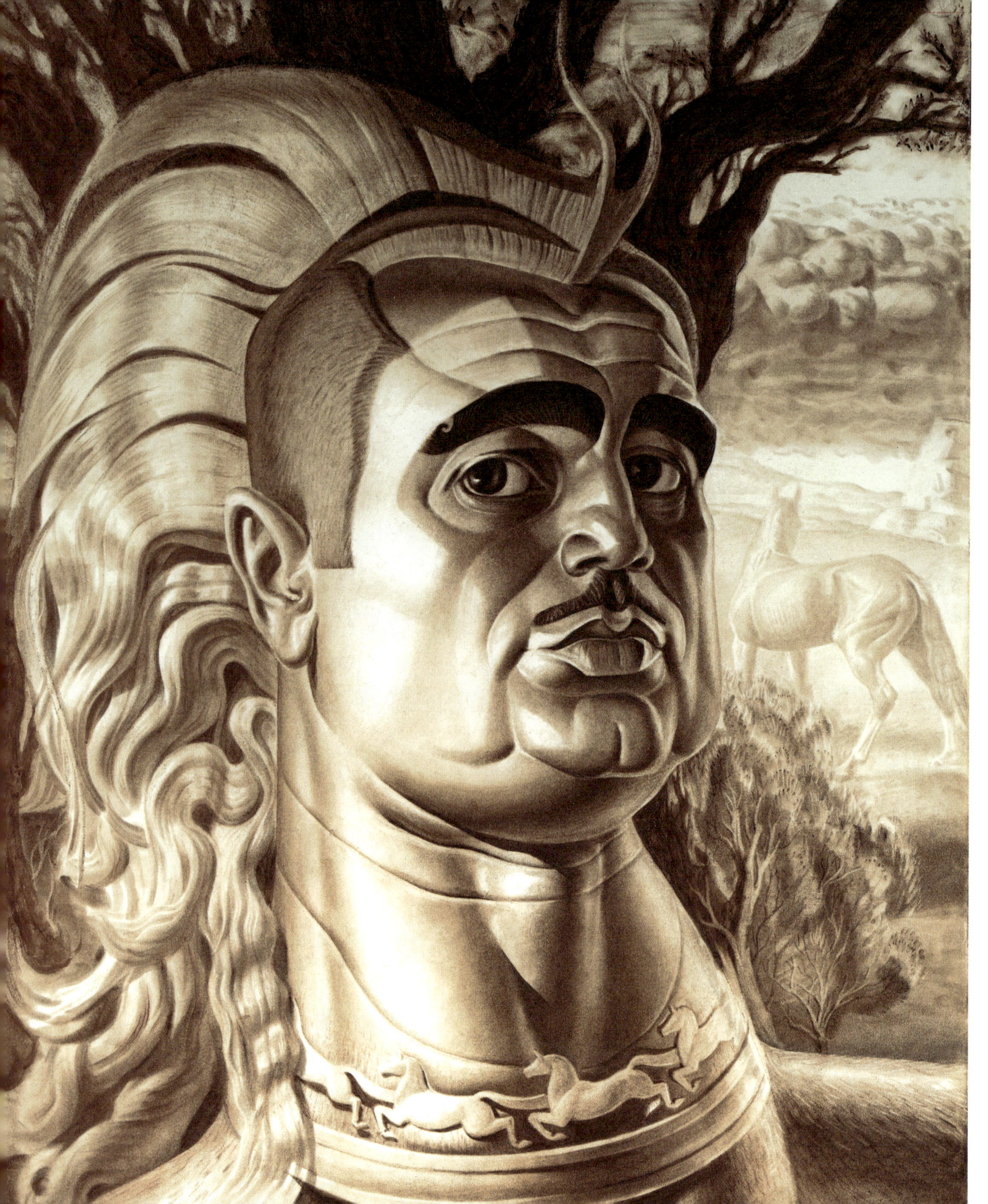

A Centaur

Since this portrait, too, was drawn for posterity, I took liberty with both the background and his image. I thickened the neck, so as to resemble a Centaur's, adding the horse's mane and galloping horses on the golden necklace. All details are imaginary. His right eyebrow has an interesting twirl of hair which I slightly exaggerated.

As I explained earlier, exact likenesses are not enough, as prove plaster masks of Napoleon: we have to be told whom they represent. Portraits should be on the verge of caricature, accentuating or enlarging interesting idiosyncracies and "harping" on them as if making fun of the person. Since a good artist understands physiognomy better than the layman, he should make much ado about this. Thus, the person is revealed wordlessly.

Dr. Lange, professor of veterinary medicine, lives in Santa Barbara, from where he extended his magic to the Arab mares that for some time refused to conceive whatever the stallions imparted to them. They simply began to be less and less susceptible to any intimate conceptions, perhaps dreaming of Pegasus with wings and heaven-to-come, and come, and come, to no avail.

It was Dr. Lange who corrected me that one cannot interbreed chicken with turkey, that they are different species, but I insisted that by artificial insemination we have already gained the smaller cream-colored turkeys from white hens. Hence, could not we artificially inseminate a donkey mare with turkey gobbler's ecstasy and thus gain in such mad-alchemy a Pegasus to fill the California air with "he-haw-he-hawing?" But he was reluctant to experiment. And so the turkey gobbler never had the fun of knowing that he could have become the father of the Pegasus.

Dr. Lange did, however, develop a method of his own, whereby a mare will again become the subject of inspired visits from the stable stork and produce a foal beautiful enough to make the King of Saudi Arabia do a "double take."

Inside Portrait of a Man

Likenesses not necessarily do good portraits make. Often, a lifecast of a person's face will not resemble him. Brunettes will not look as well in sculpture as blondes, for black eyes and hair do not look black in sculpture.

If you are an artist and commissioned to make a portrait of a person on the condition that no words will be exchanged between the two of you for as long as it takes to make it "perfect;" then you are to make another portrait of the same person being permitted to be together for a solid week, eating, discussing, quarreling, and laughing, so you can make ANOTHER judgement of the sitter while painting and both pieces turn out identical… you are a worthless artist. For you absolutely CANNOT paint the portraits identical, once you have "learned" the man sitting in front of you and know that he murdered seven people or saved seven from a band of Communist killers.

We stood in front of the store where this man sold arty objects to the class of people who are so conscious of being the personification of Prosaicism that they often exclaim that they "love Culture and things like that!"

There had been an accident outside the store and people gathered quickly to see what had happened. A customer had banged his head into a board that was dangerously placed head-high. I proposed that the board was useless and should be removed. But the owner insisted that it should remain. His wife grudgingly explained that the man had placed the board there purposely, so that when people bumped their heads on it, he could roar with hysterical laughter.

On another occasion, a stranger entered the store asking directions. My model for this portrait told the man that there were two paths to follow, a short walk or a long walk, that the longer walk was much more scenic and easier to travel. The visitor thanked him and left. My humorous sitter then offered his reason for advising the stranger to take the longer route. In that section of the country there were many poison oak plants, and perhaps the foolish inquisitor would get his hands and face covered with a rash. For some reason my model had a grudge against Humanity, and not being a Kommissar in Russia, he had found his personal way to assuage his craving to inflict suffering.

While I was drawing him before me, he became bored and forgot that he was not alone, falling into his pit of obsessive interests. He did not know how he looked for there was no mirror to reveal the tightening of his tin-can lips, edged like a steel trap. I dressed him into the deceptive vestment of a monk while growing Pan's horns in order to hint at a disguised potential sadist.

On seeing that I had caught him in this secular escapade, he wished to buy the portrait from me, but the drawing was worth more than his money.

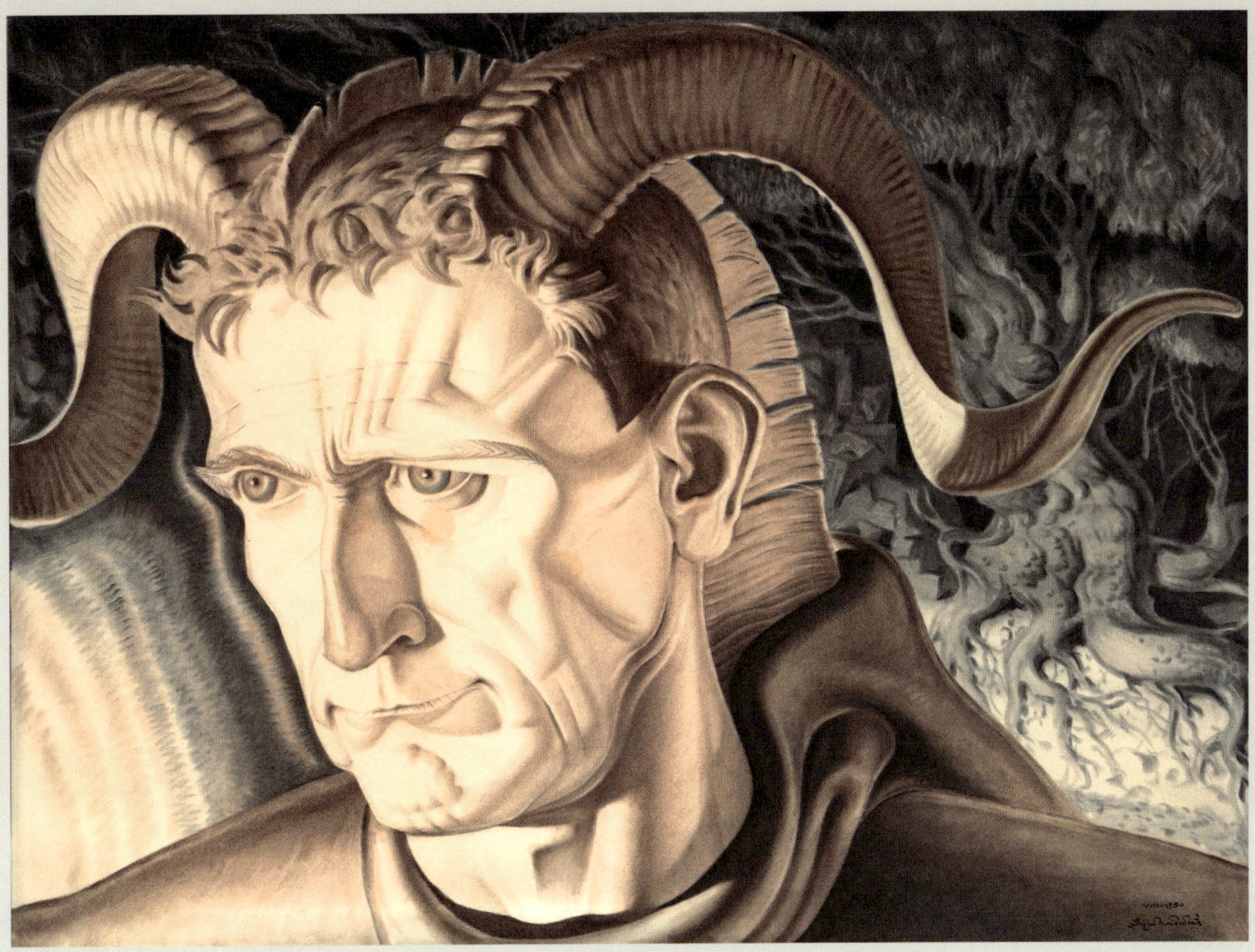

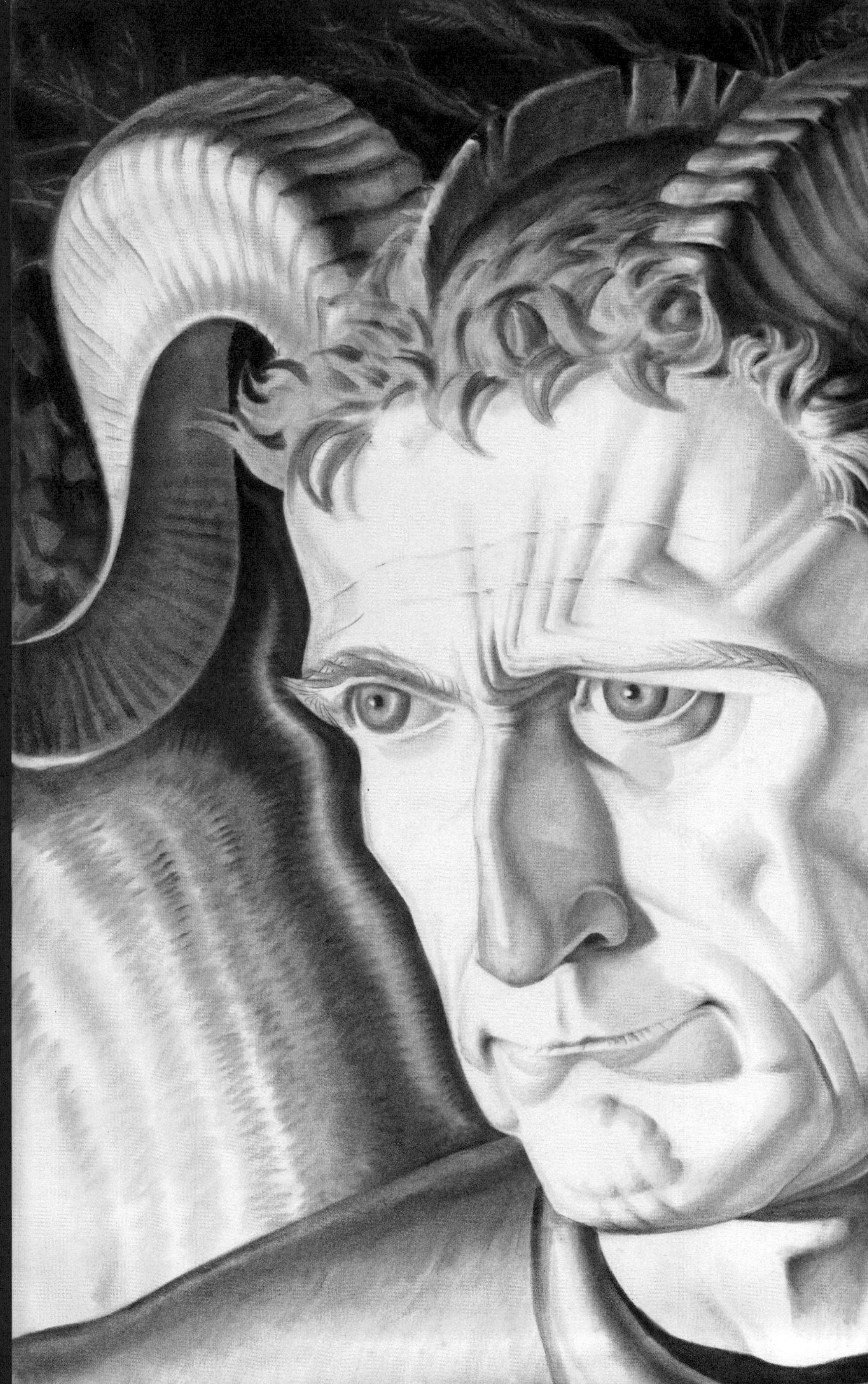

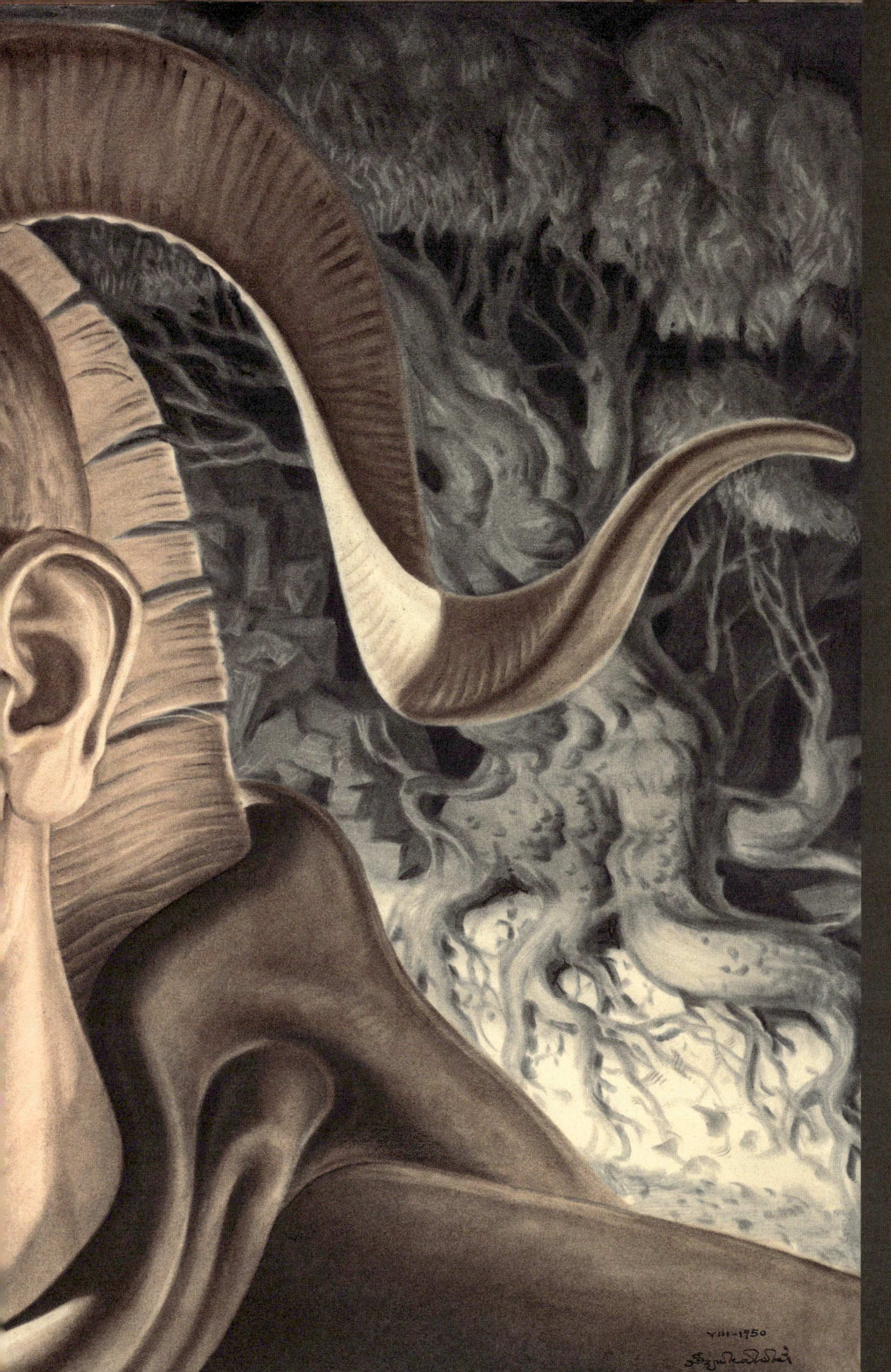
VIII-1950

Ainu Man

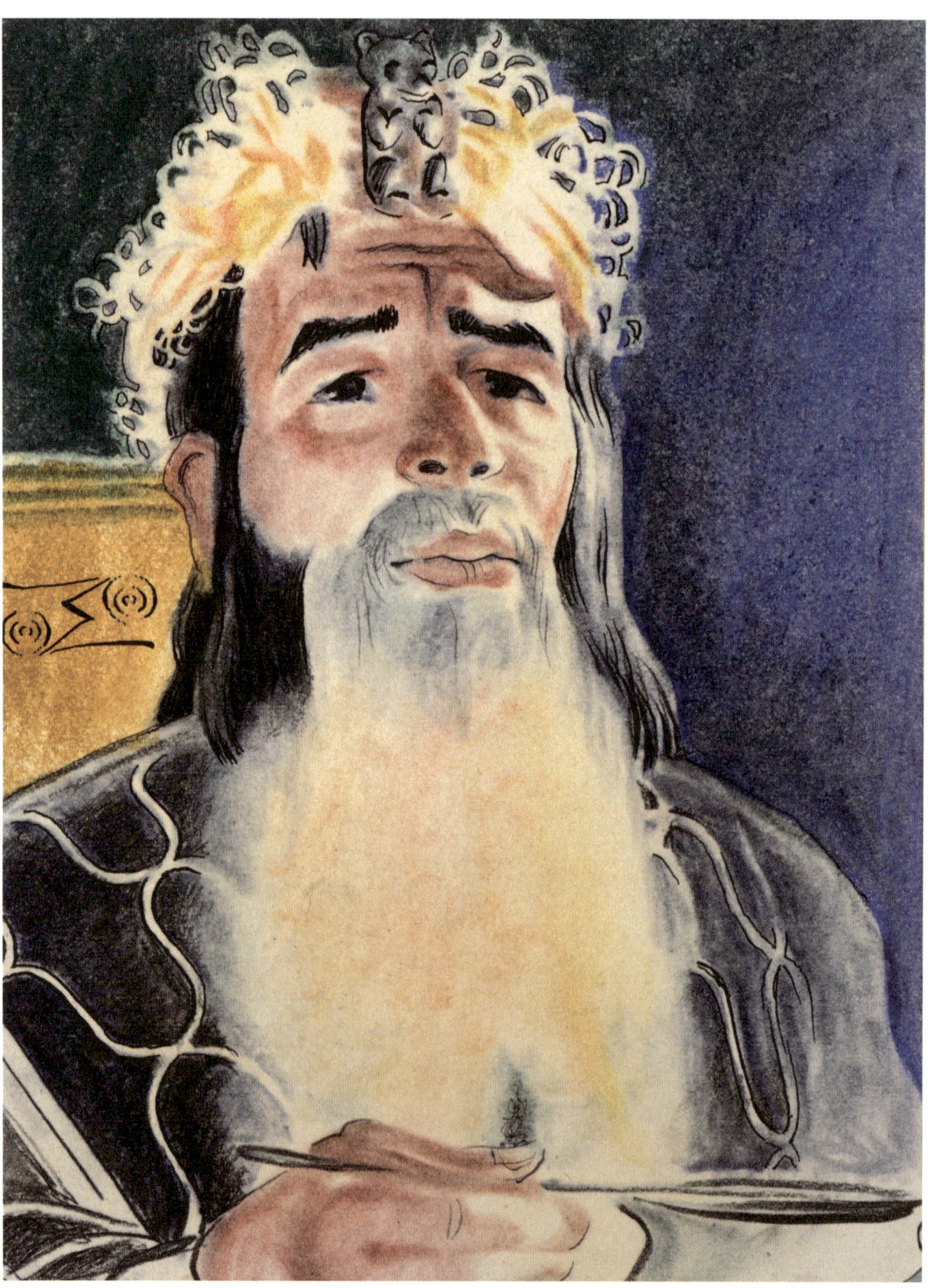

144

Aviation Engineer

■ 1950 ■

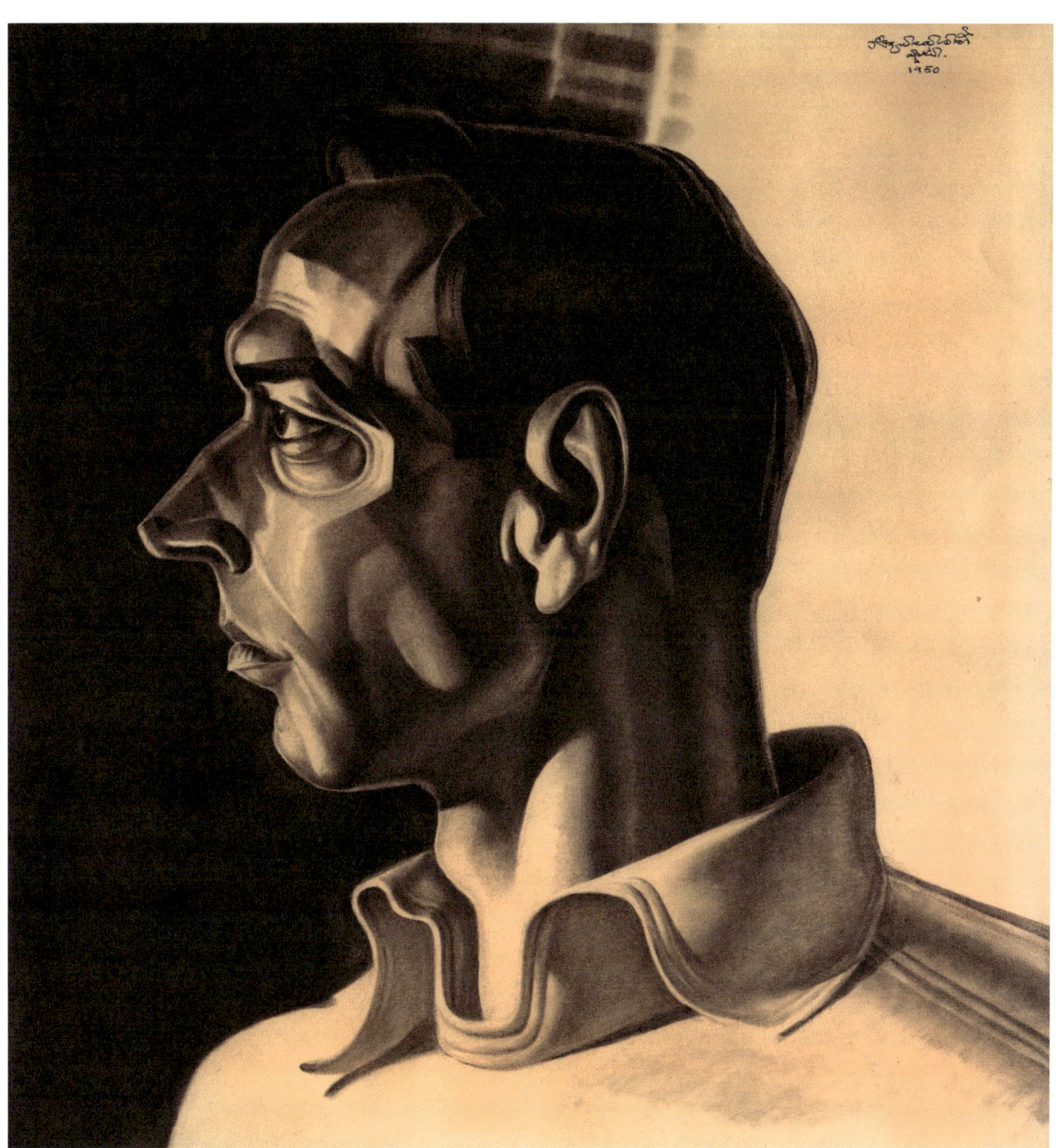

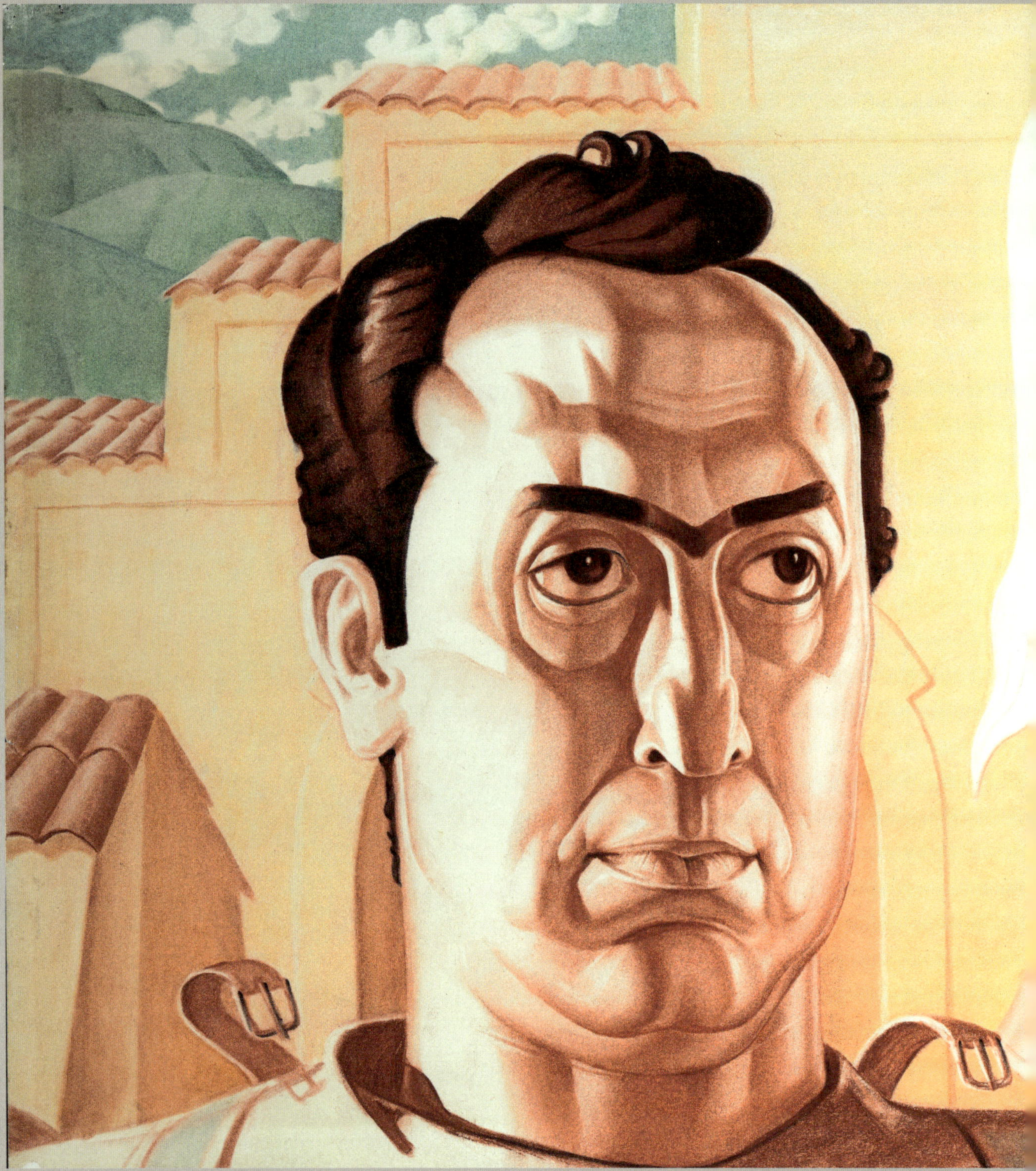

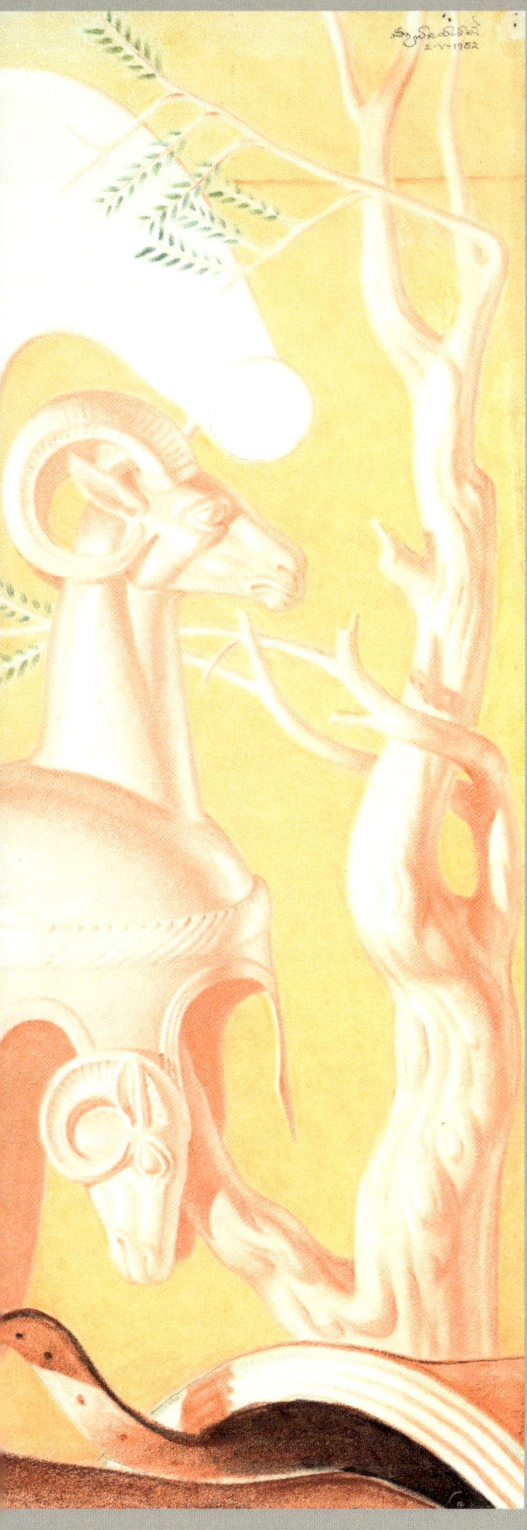

Mr. Saz

I often ask friends or strangers to pose for me if they have unusual types of faces. In this case Mr. Saz attracted my attention because of his gladiator-type features. After sketching his proportions (always over life-size), I finished the portrait from memory, including the armor and helmet which had recently been excavated in Greece. The helmet has a ram's head on it, hence making it a ceremonial object referring to Pallas Athene who – according to my anthropological findings – personified the Mother of the Dawn God. The ram is used as a Rebus for the Protong word "Baran" which means "White Morn."

I combined this portrait with the ancient helmet because Mr. Saz draws his nose in like a ram, and his brow is projected ram-like as if to break down walls. The rippling shadows on his face may make the portrait a subject for a study in physiognomy.

147

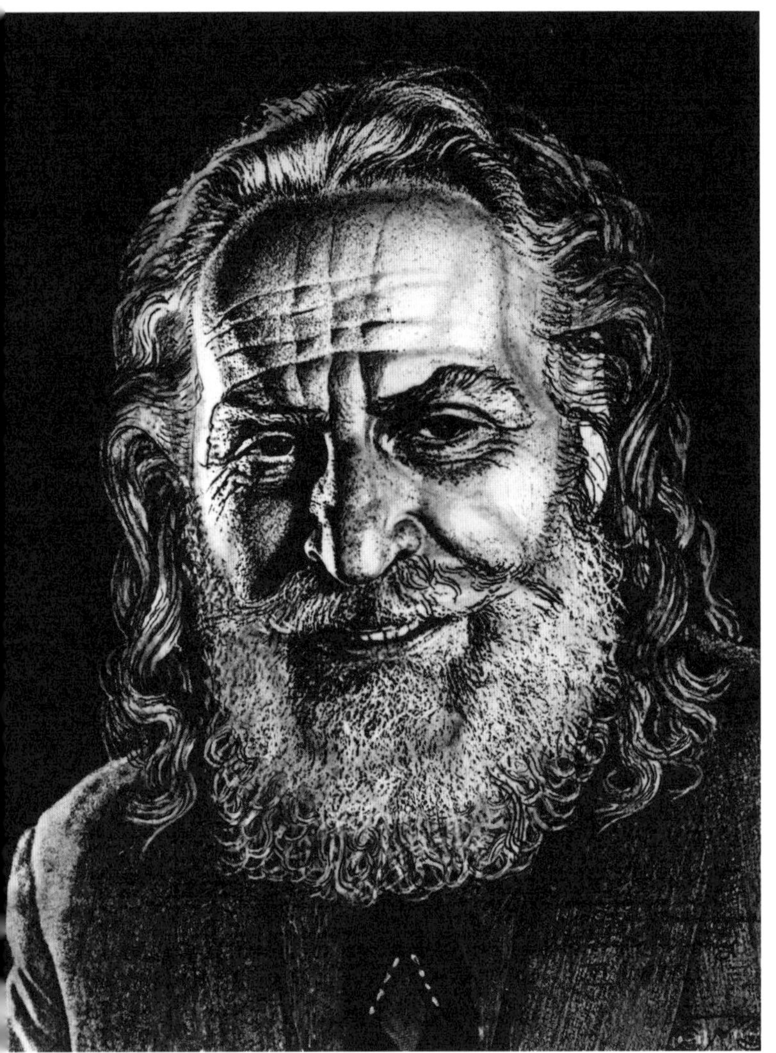

Leonidas Dudarew-Ossetynski

A friend of mine for many years, who lives in the vicinity of Hollywood. An occasional actor, but more interested in teaching acting to youths who somehow journey to California in order to become his pupils. He was born in Wilno, Poland (now Lithuania). Presently, he flourishes an avalanche-of-a-mane which he trims only when it gets under his seat. Otherwise, his pupils use it to hide under during the winter rains. His beard is really very patriarchal.

Whenever we forget the futility of arguments berween actors and sculptors about the fundamentals of the Theatre, we argue. Ossetynski insists that it is the actors who make good theatre, while I persist that it is the AUTHORS who make the institution. When I applaud a fine musician at a concert, it is the composer's piece I cheer, not the virtuoso's acrobatics. I regard actors and all performers at concerts as waiters who merely distribute the dishes, prepared by the invisible cook who has no time to collect the applause he earned in the kitchen. If we like a particular restaurant, it is because of the flavor from the sweat of the cook's brow that has dropped in our soup, the salt of the creative man's birth-giving pains.

Performers are innumerable. If any director whistles with crooked fingers at the corner of Hollywood and Vine, within minutes he will be inundated with hordes of the finest pretenders of Othello and Hamlet.

I still think that Theatre, when worthy of the term, depends on fine literature, unless it is a circus, disguised.

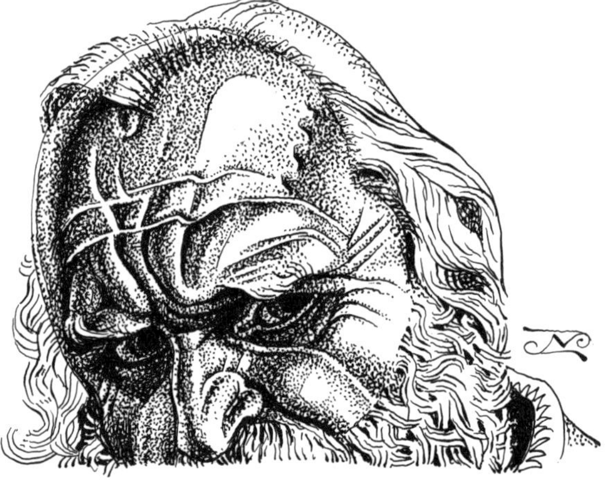

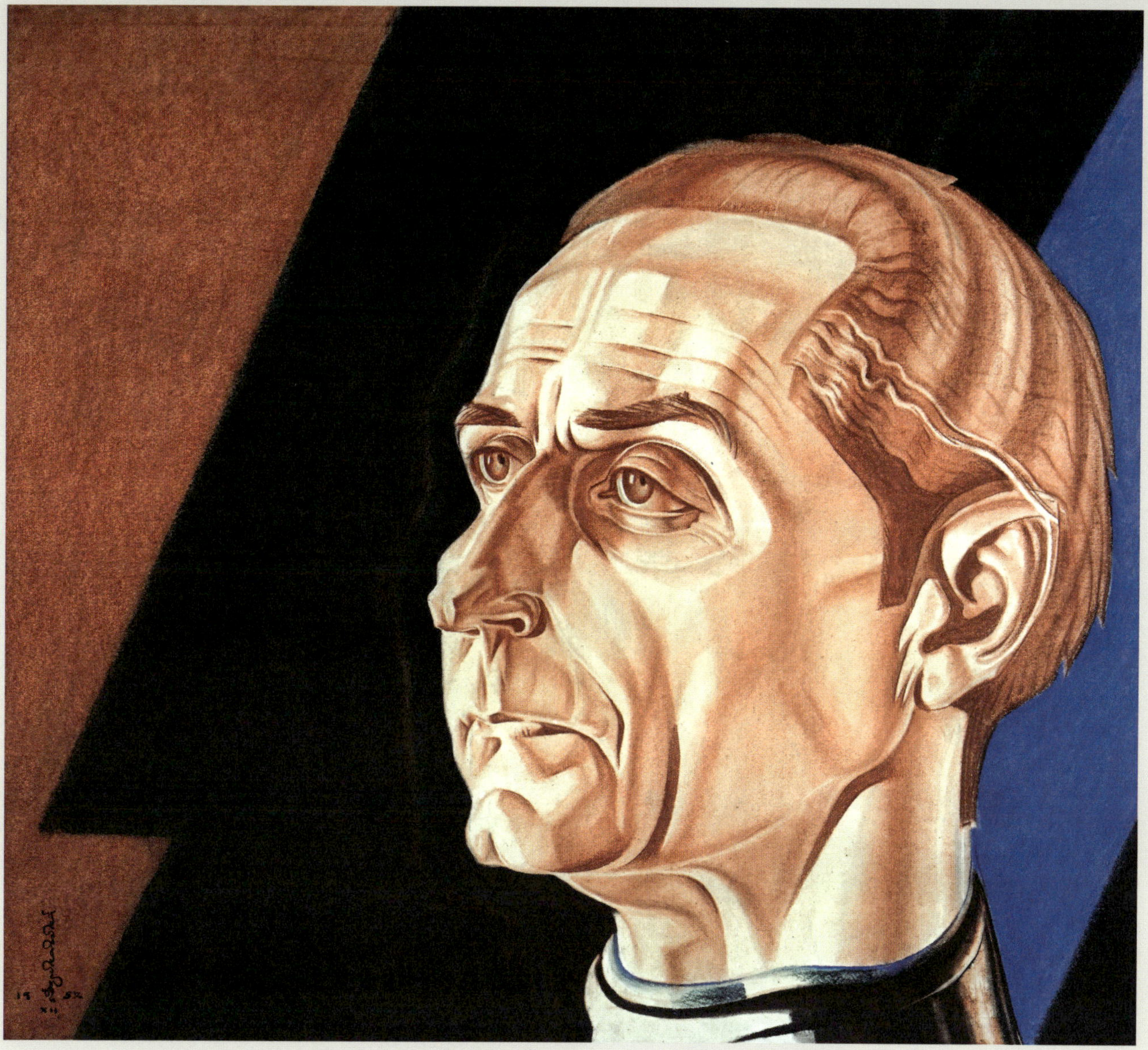

Charles Bounds

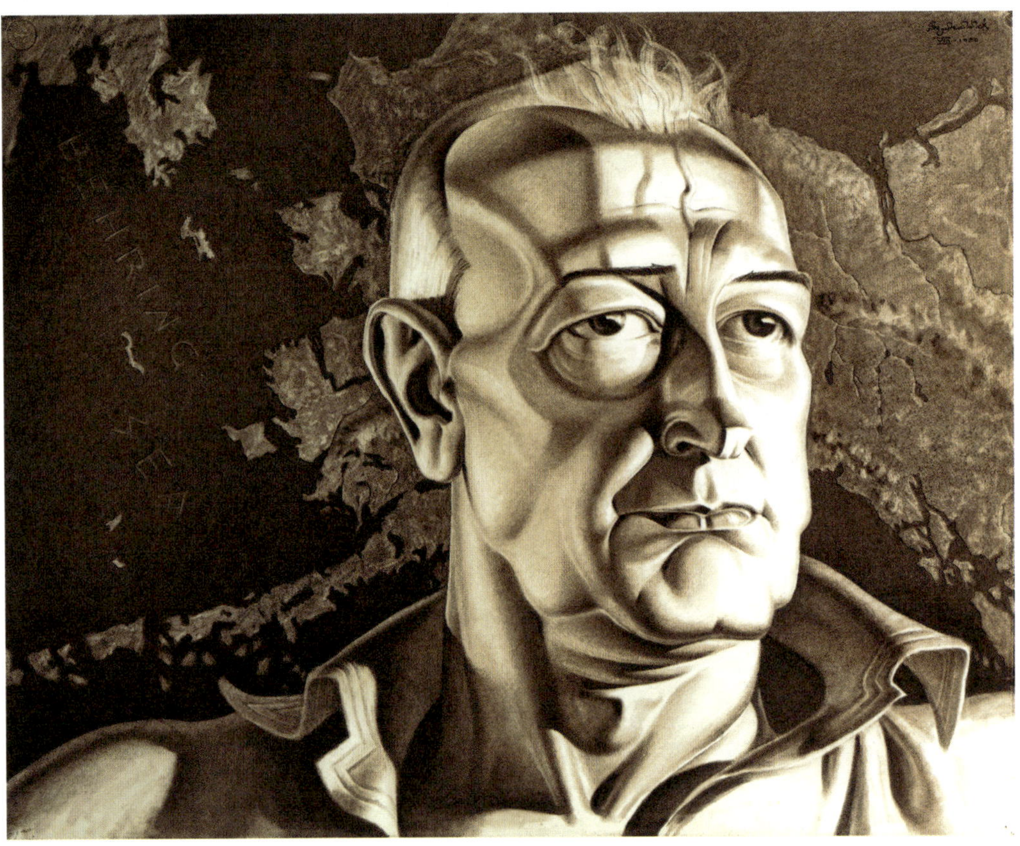

A neighbor who to me represented the real American; and I asked him to pose for me, that I might immortalize him. He, too, was a man who relied on his own opinions. Though innately gentle, he radiated self-assurance and that unbridled American power that made this Civilization. He is of the type of man that created the pre-Roosevelt America, when nobility of motivation and Common Sense stirred citizens to do Errands for Divine Providence, without the need of higher education.

Landscape Painter as Cloud-Picker

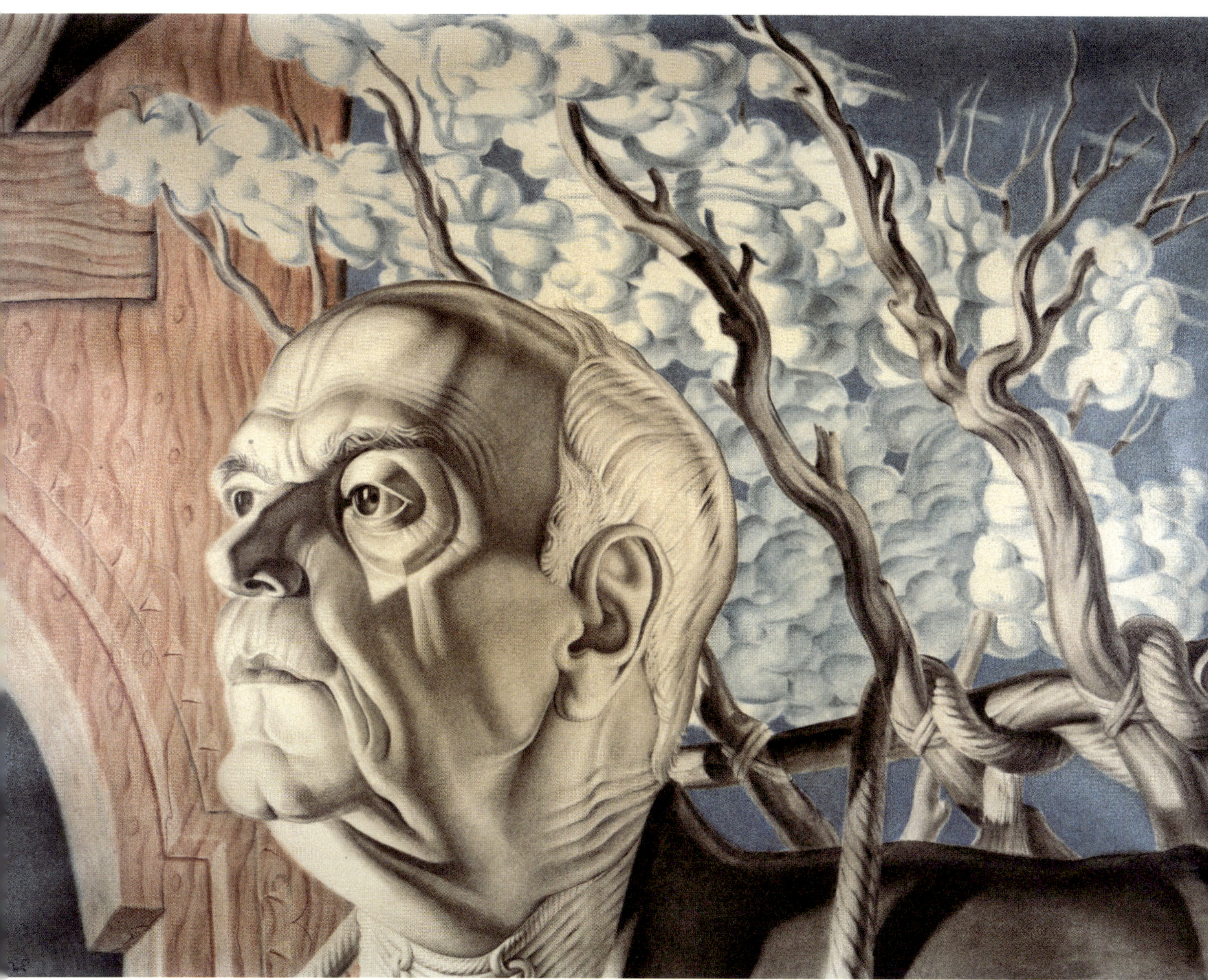

Fantasy Portrait of a Woman

■ 1953 ■

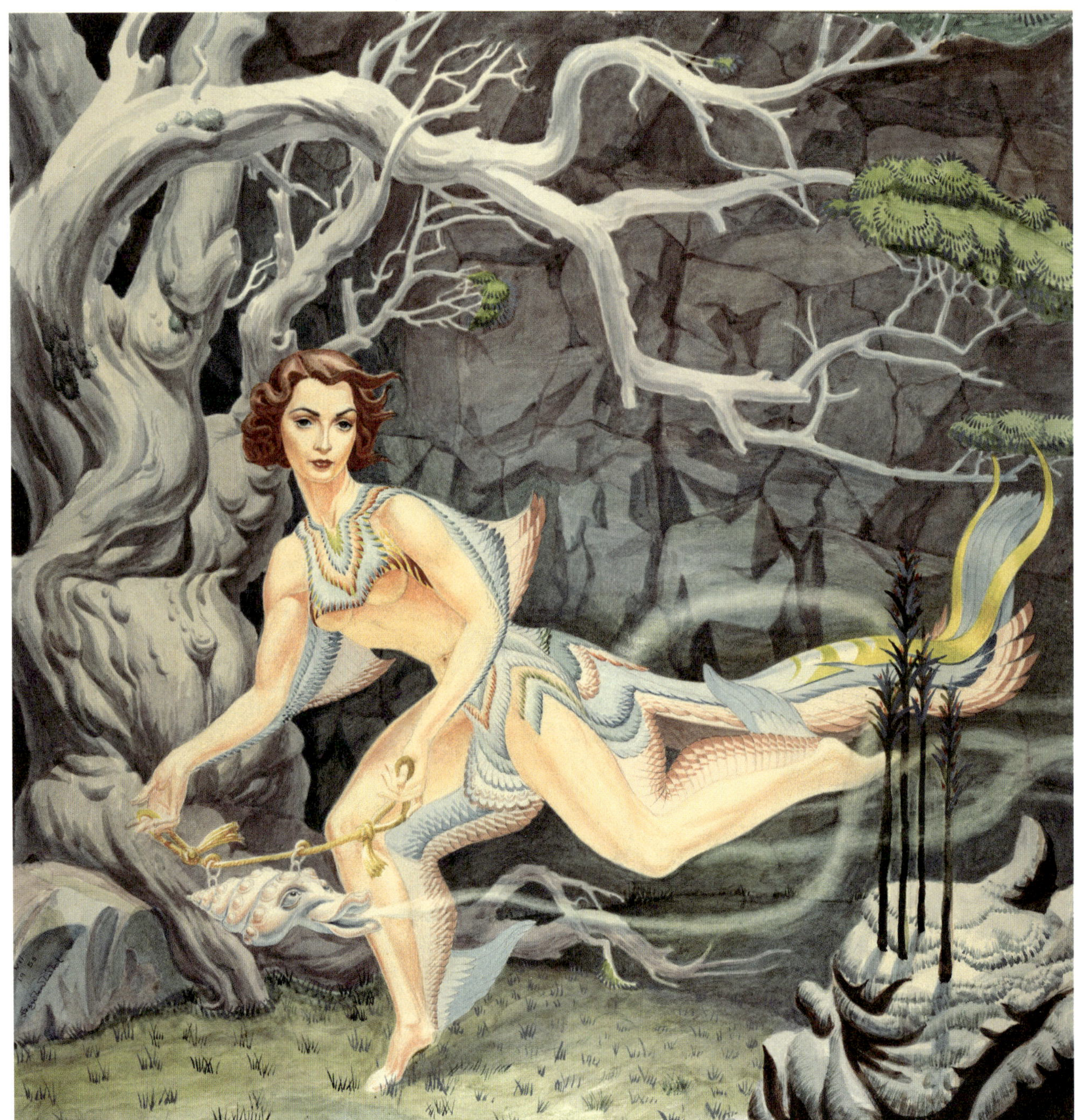

An Art Student

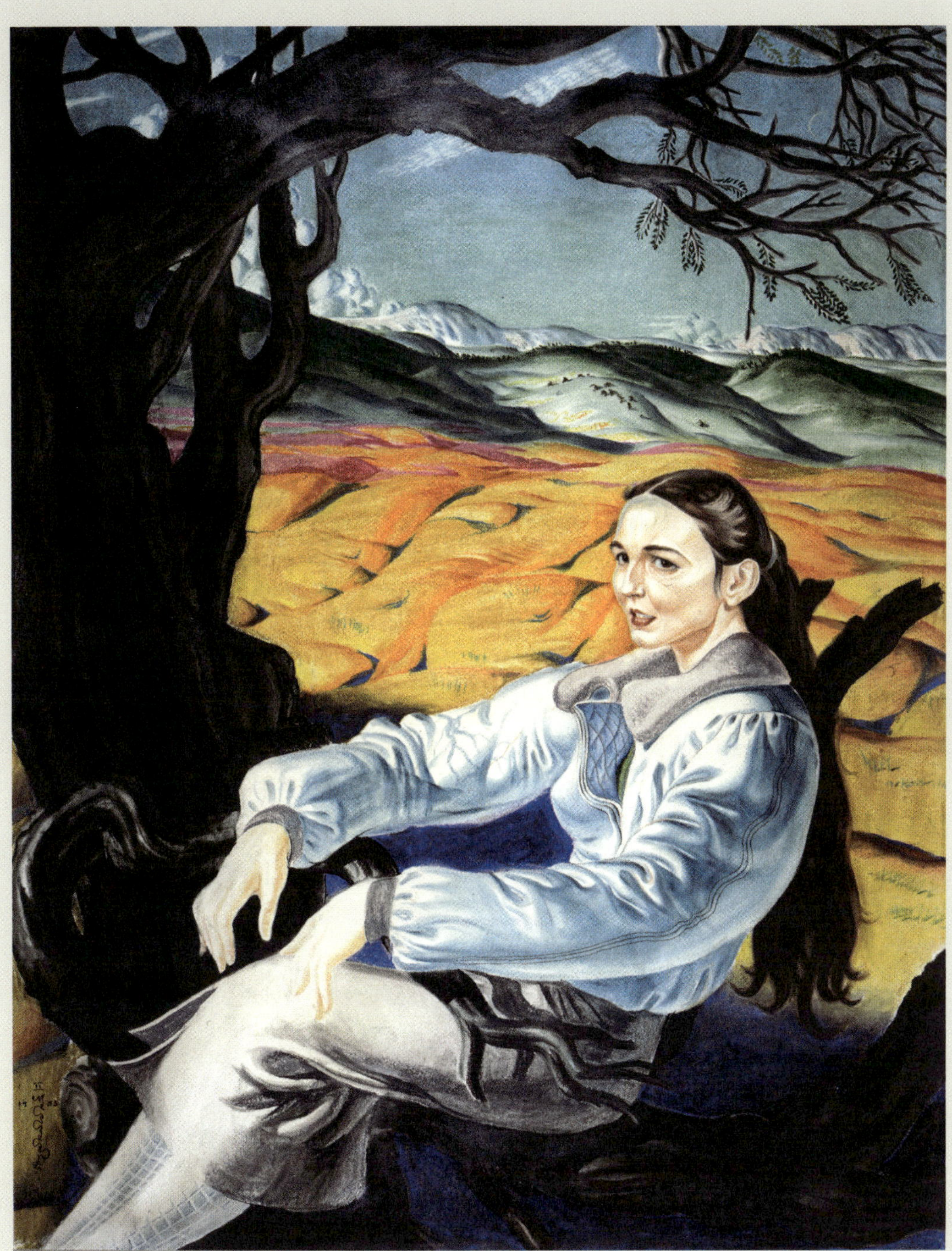

Heir

After returning to California from besieged and leveled Warsaw, carrying two suitcases and everything else gone, I had no studio to work and keep my sculptures in. For fourteen years, with my beloved wife Joan Donovan, I lived and worked in a converted chicken house, in Tarzana, California. Having no place to accumulate new sculptures, I drew this fragment of a larger composition. This is the inheritor of the national Destiny.

Poland's Ministry of Art and Culture, having looted or destroyed all of my life's achievement, deprived me of having exhibitions and reduced me to the status of an unknown man in this land (where Art critics must be paid for publicity, which I refuse to comply with).

The American Poles NEVER printed a word about me or my achievements. They are Americanized peasants who are totally oblivious of Culture, while in Poland the Communist traitors will not tolerate intrinsic Art, for Predatory Russia cannot produce real artists under its tyranny, as Nazi Germany could not, for real Art is the blossoming of Freedom. Though Russia is intolerant of abstract Modernism in her own territories in its futile hope of producing its own Art, it employs Art critics in the enslaved countries like Poland, Hungary and Czechoslovakia, whose function (as in America) is to campaign against serious Art and all creative men by only raving about the Picasso-type of doodlings, so to prevent these nations from having any Art. Particularly any individual or national tendency is blocked in gaining popularity and fame, but every form of modernist doodling is advocated by the Press. (Therefore, there is no American Art.) Lenin, in one of his epistles, advised his subservient Yetinsyn followers: "So to control each nation's society, we first must control Art." Men of my caliber are destroyed and buried alive, being stifled to premature death by the species of prosaic society that condoned enslavement of half of Europe at Yalta.

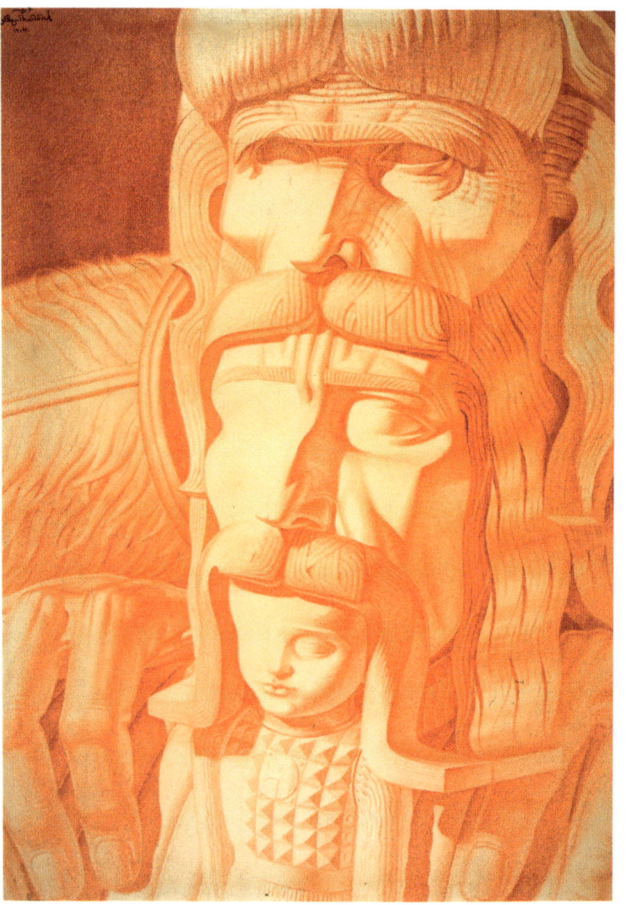

HEIR
1941

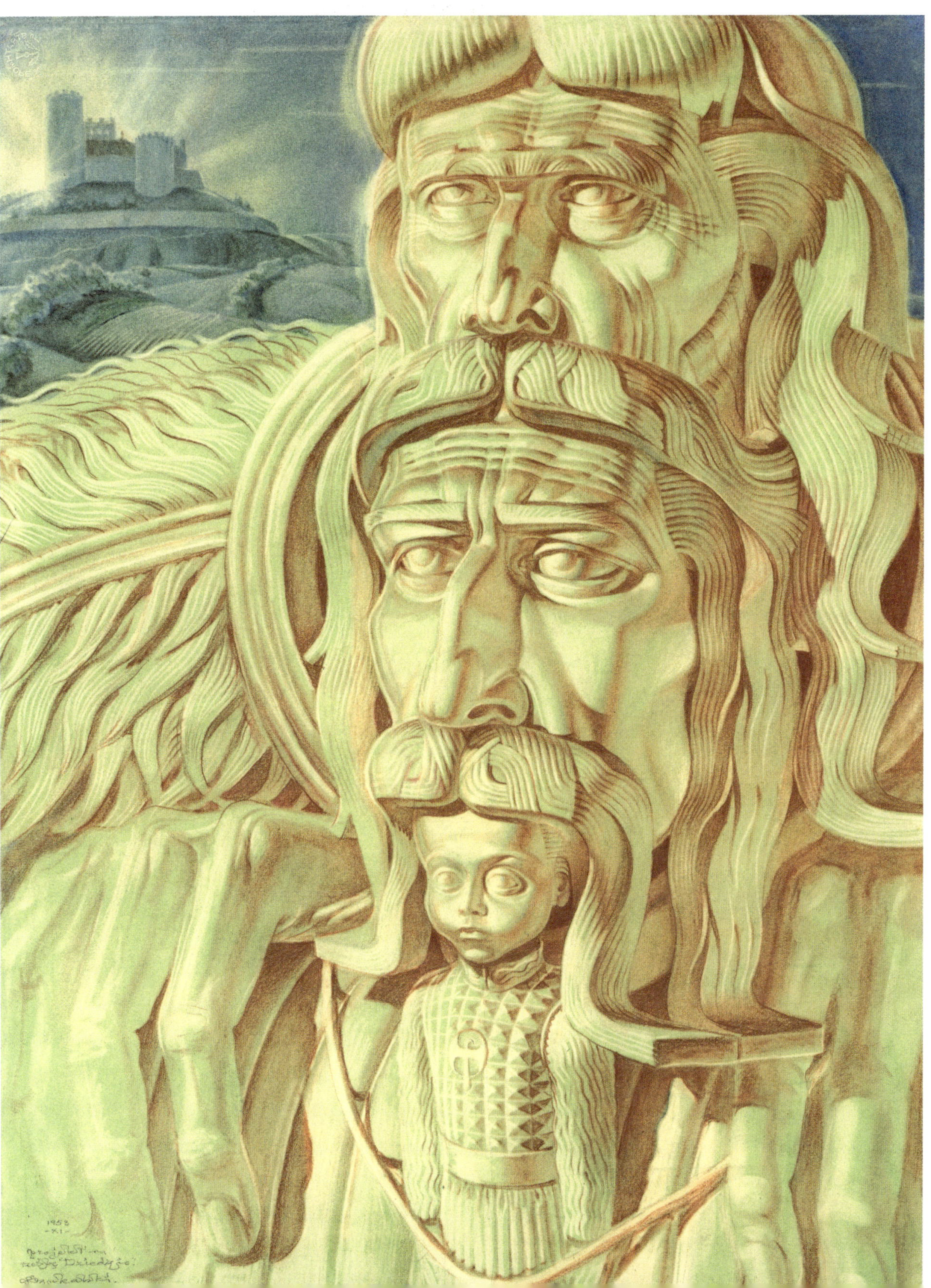

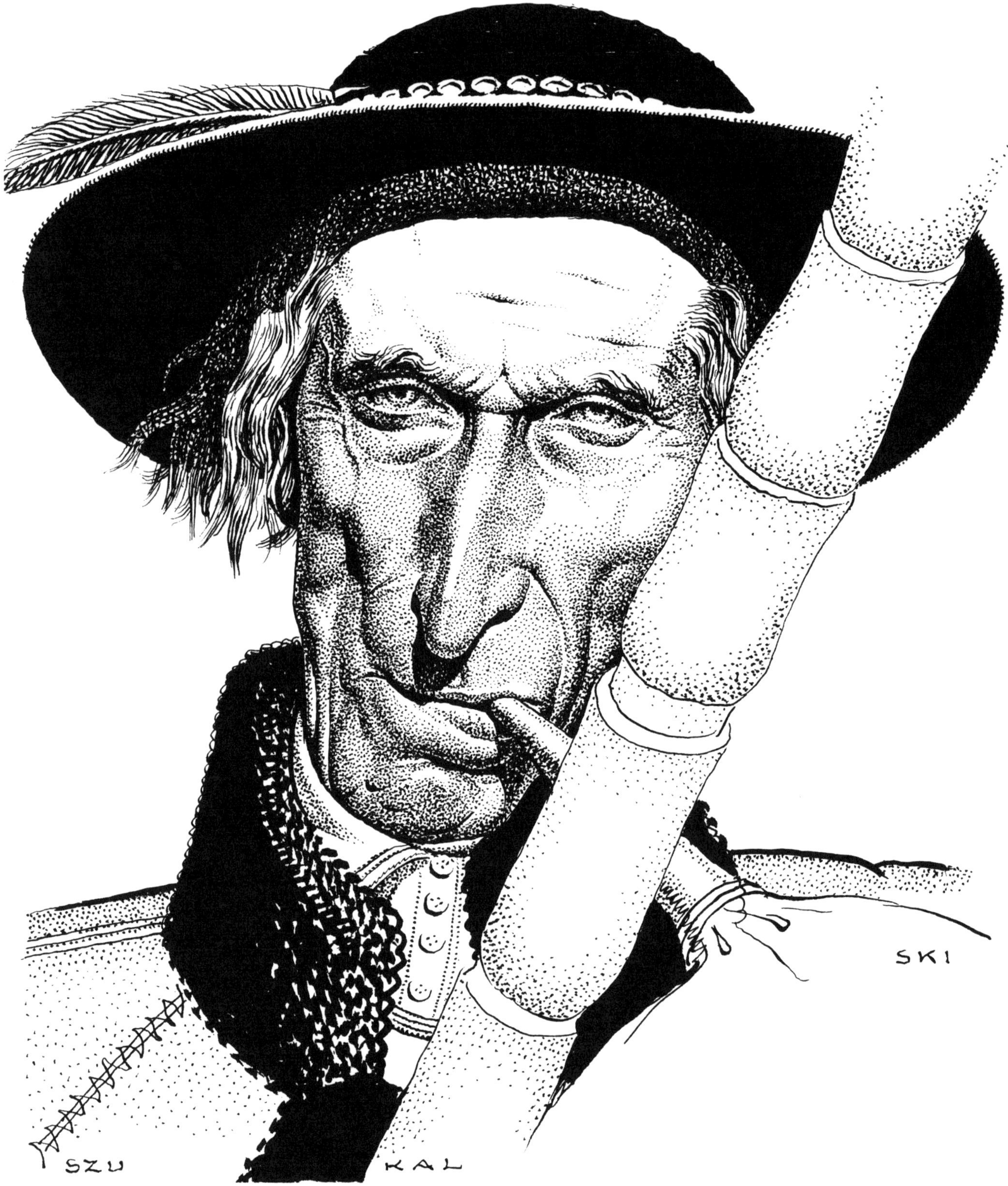

Mroz, the Bagpiper

Look at another face of the Cro-Magnon type of man of total Nobility. When at the Academy of Kraków and on later occasions, I had the opportunity to draw him from life. He was a mountaineer from the Carpatian range, where Hungary and Czechoslovakia meet. Mroz (pron. "mrooz") was a musician in a mountaineers group of a few players on bagpipe, a fiddle called *gesla*, and a few voices. Their music is based on a quarter-tone system similar to the one used in Ancient Greece.

The mountain people of Poland have predominantly aquiline noses, being the descendants of the people who survived the Pacific Deluge and, floating on the newly directed gulf streams, shored on the high parts of Europe which first re-emerged as tiny isles.

Mroz's eyes were so pale blue that from six feet in front of him, you could not discern any color at all in them. He was tall, slim, and exceedingly gentle. The tradition of his people's little hats serves as an attestation to my theories on the Great Deluge. The hats are pictographic of an "island" surrounded by seas, hence the little conch shells that have been placed there since remote ages as to emulate the water surface beneath which live the sea-snails. These shells, called *muszle* in Polish, serve as a rebus for "Mu Z Le," which is a Protong phrase meaning that these high-nosed people came "From Seas Flooding." Here we should compare the "hats" imposed atop the gigantic heads of Easter Island, which are also shaped as pictographs of sinking continents, with these little hats of the Polish mountaineers.

Bertrand Russell

■ 1974 ■

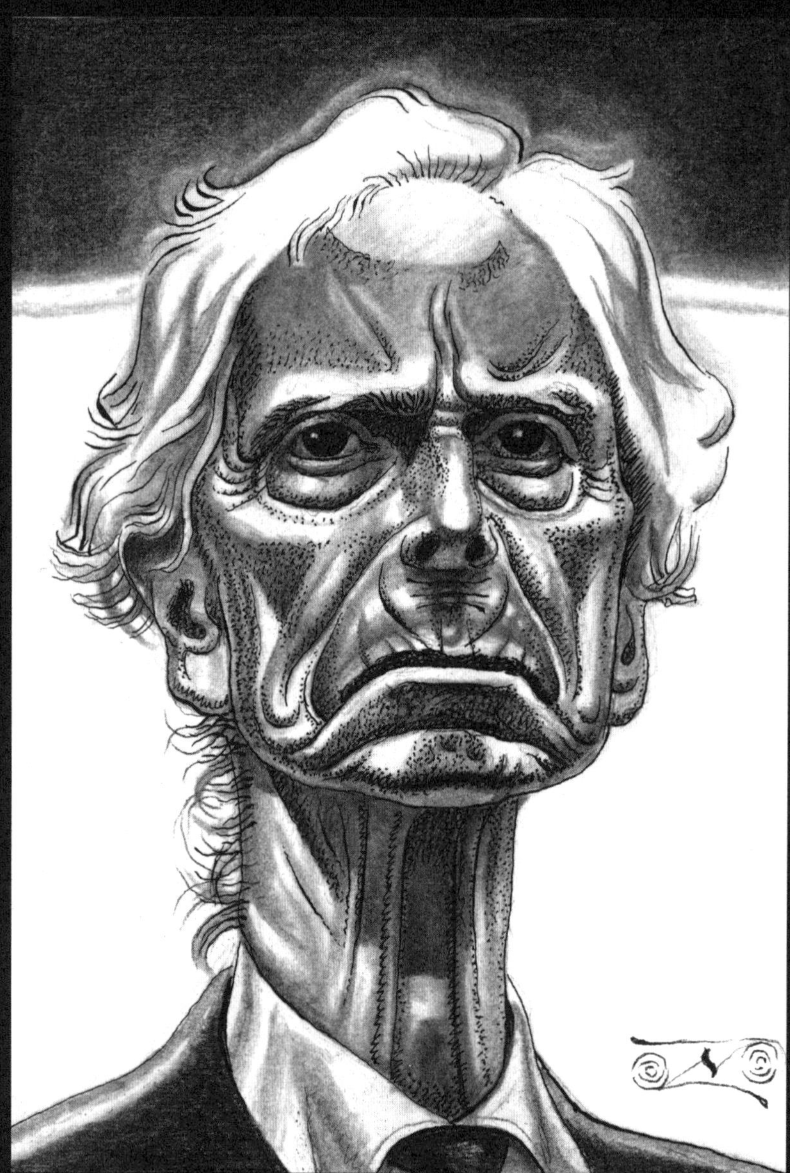

Russell strived to bait Providence by going to Russia and ordering his services. He baited the English nation by urging to give up common sense and emulate Russian ways. Eventually he was such a good Providence-baiter that he became universally regarded as the Master Baiter of the British Empire.

The Face of Communism

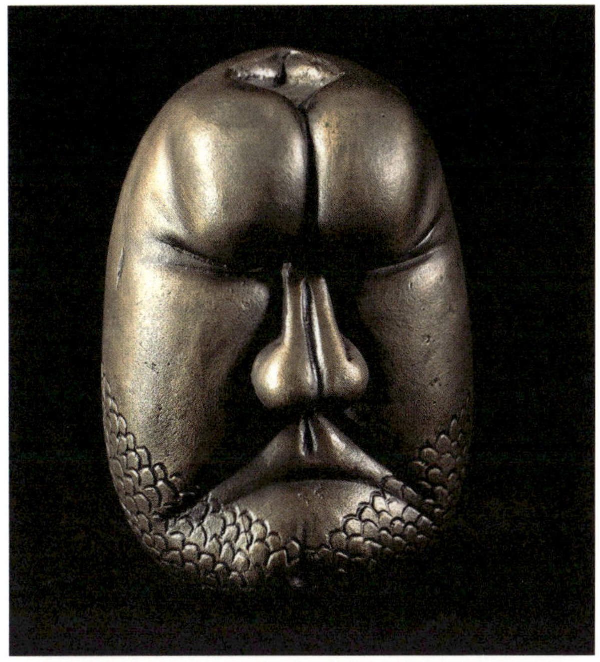

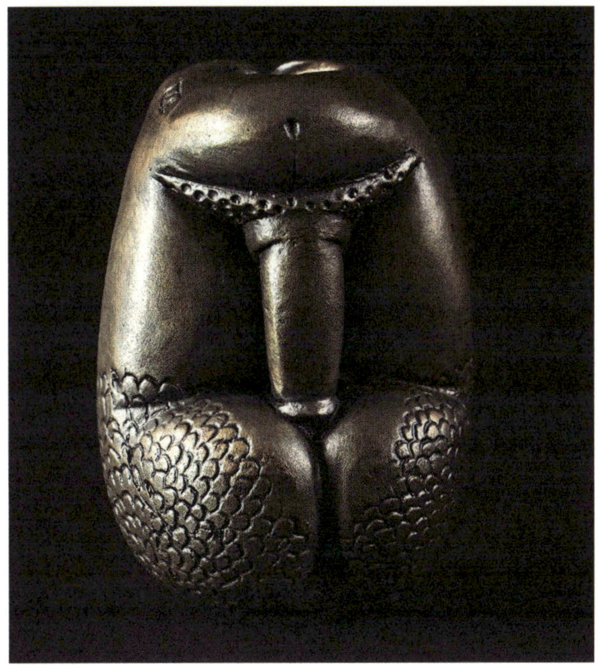

Photo—Bill Debley

Bronze, 3″ tall

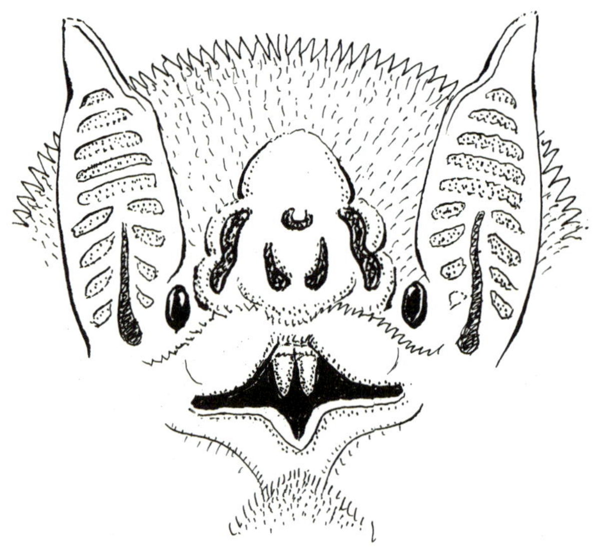

A Vampire Bat

The acme of Parasitism which infects its victims with rabies. His eyes are below the nose.

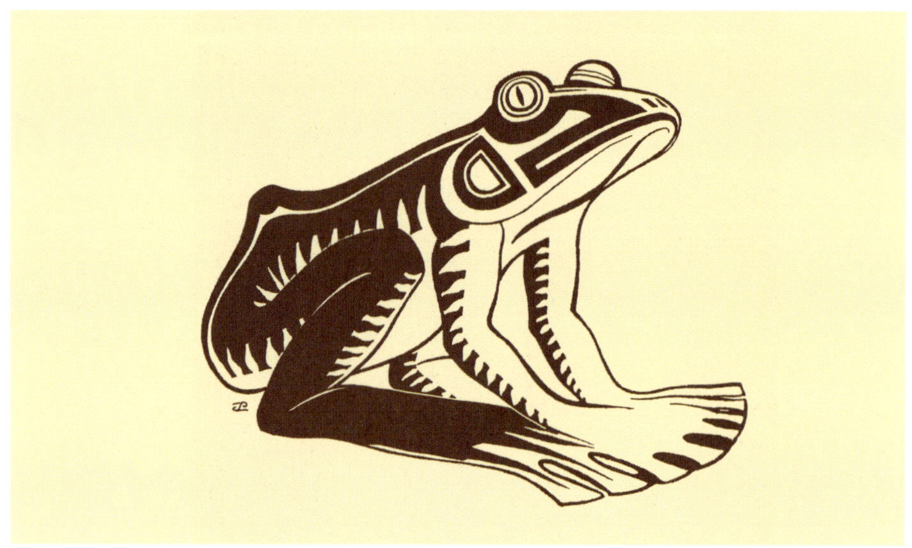

A Frog

From the back cover of *Krak Syn Ludoli* **(1938)**

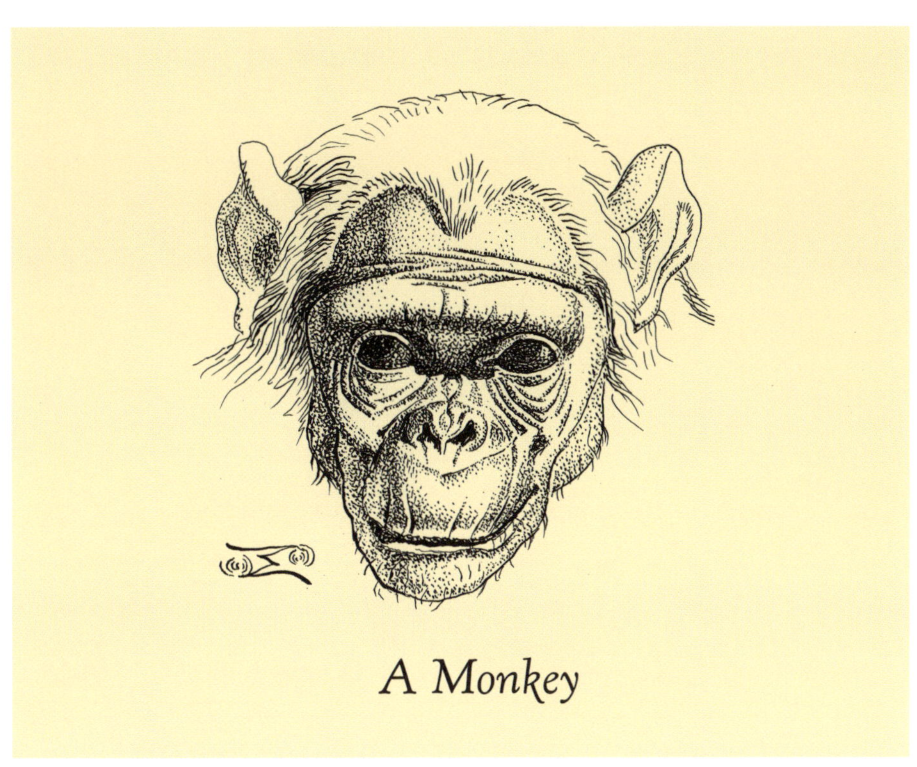

A Monkey

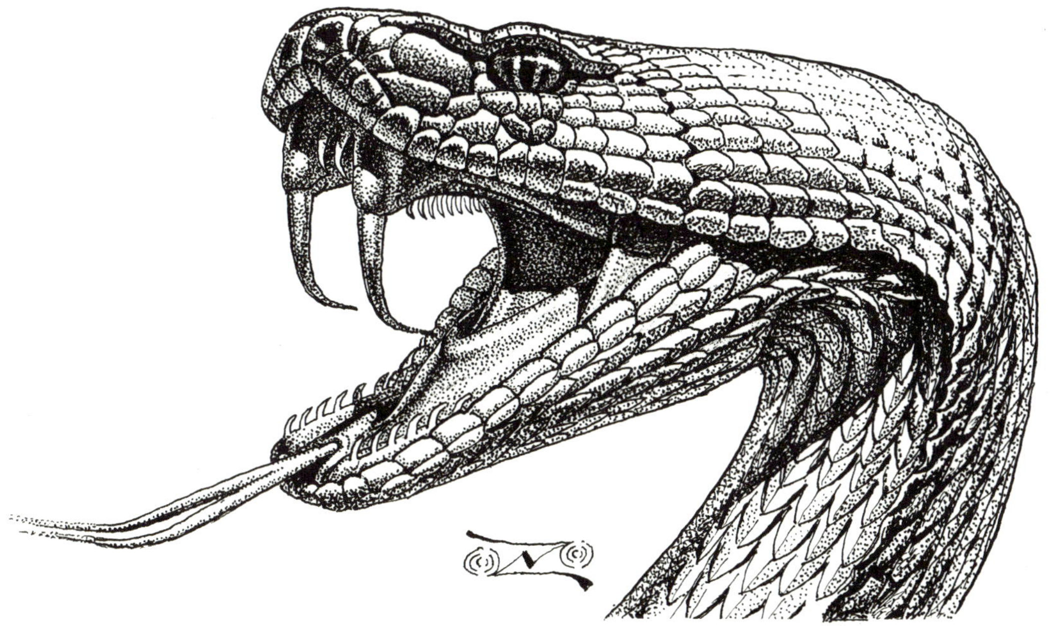

A Snake

Portrait of an Eagle

■ CIRCA 1960 ■

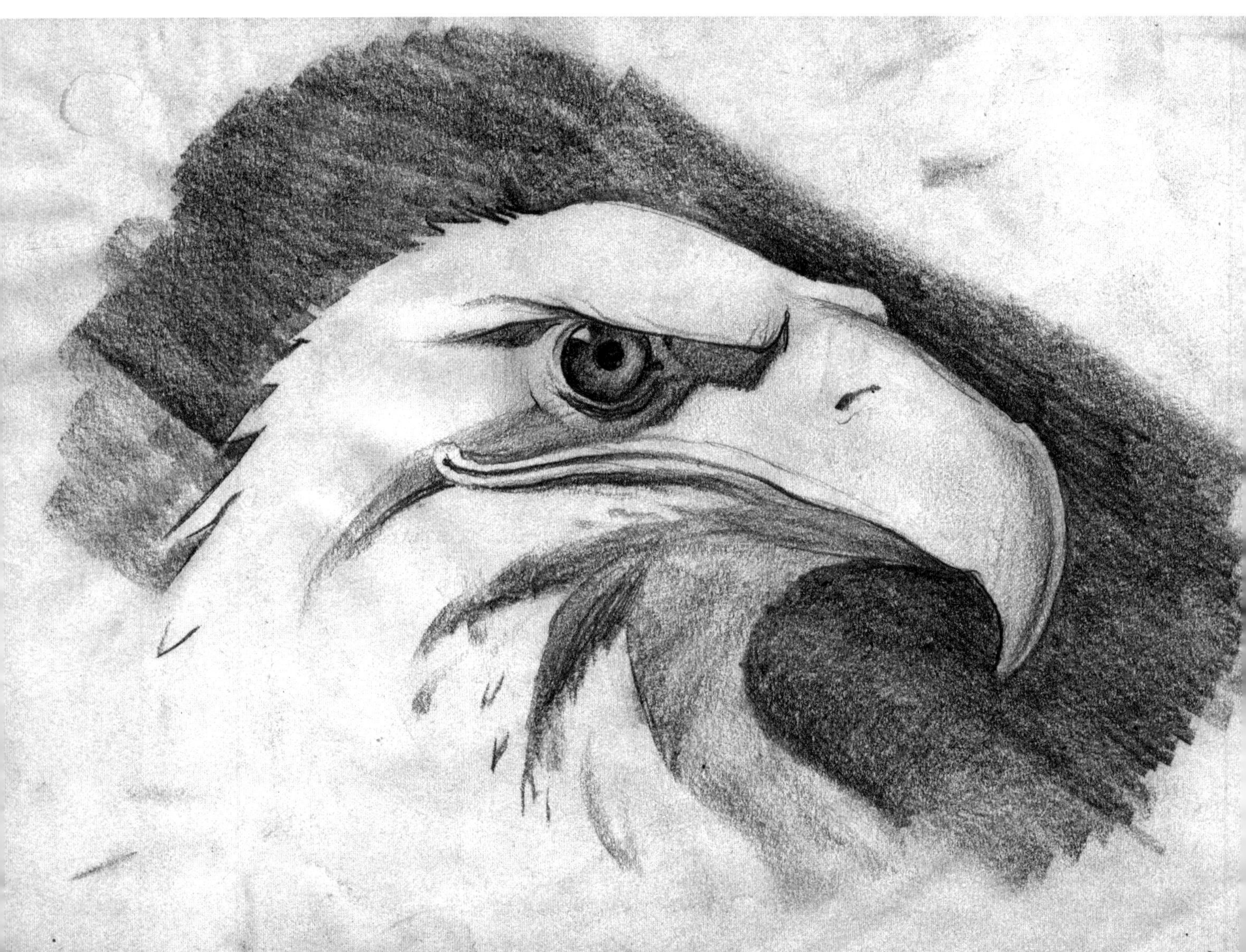

Portrait of a Tortoise

■ CIRCA 1960 ■

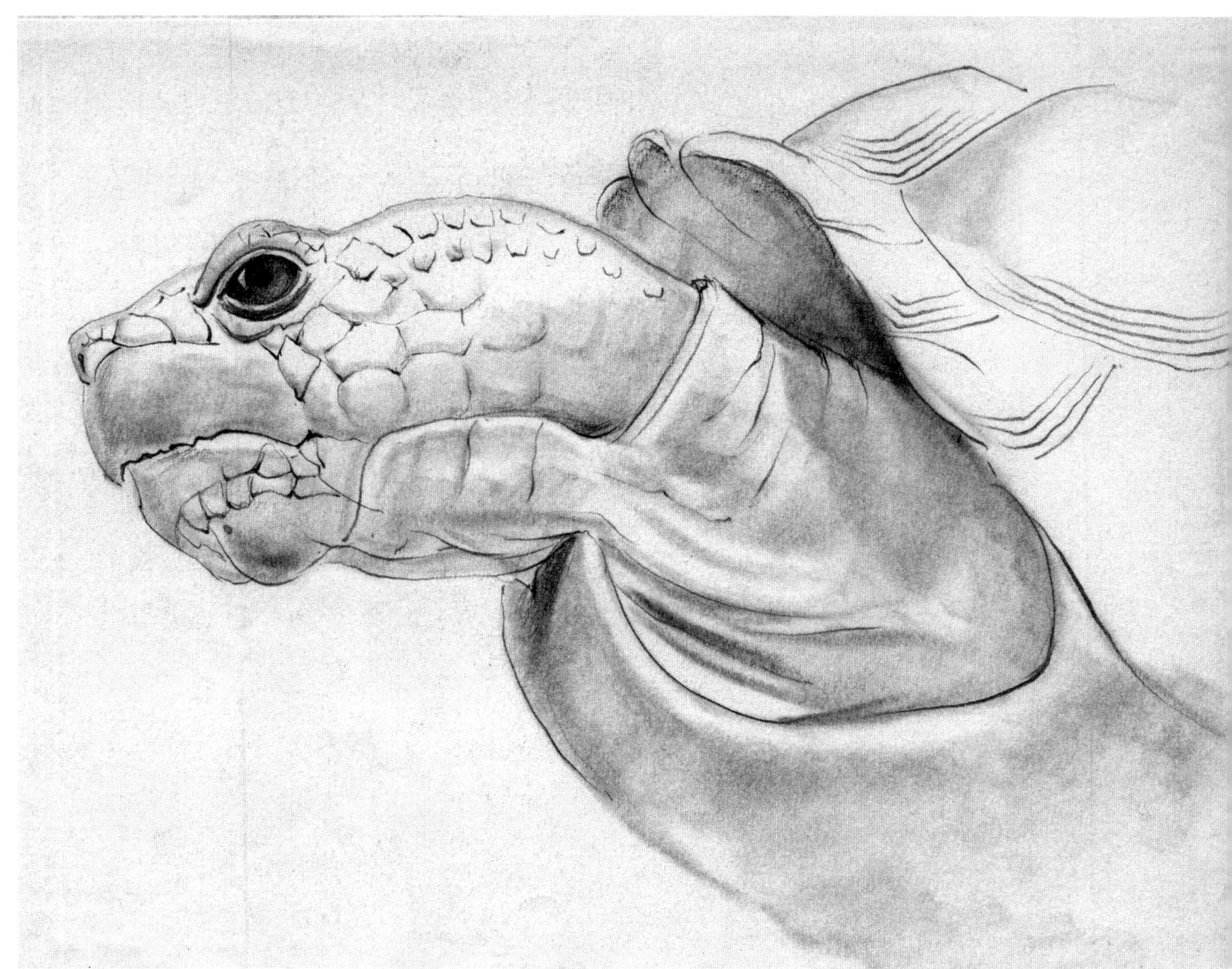

Kuakari (San Diego Zoo)

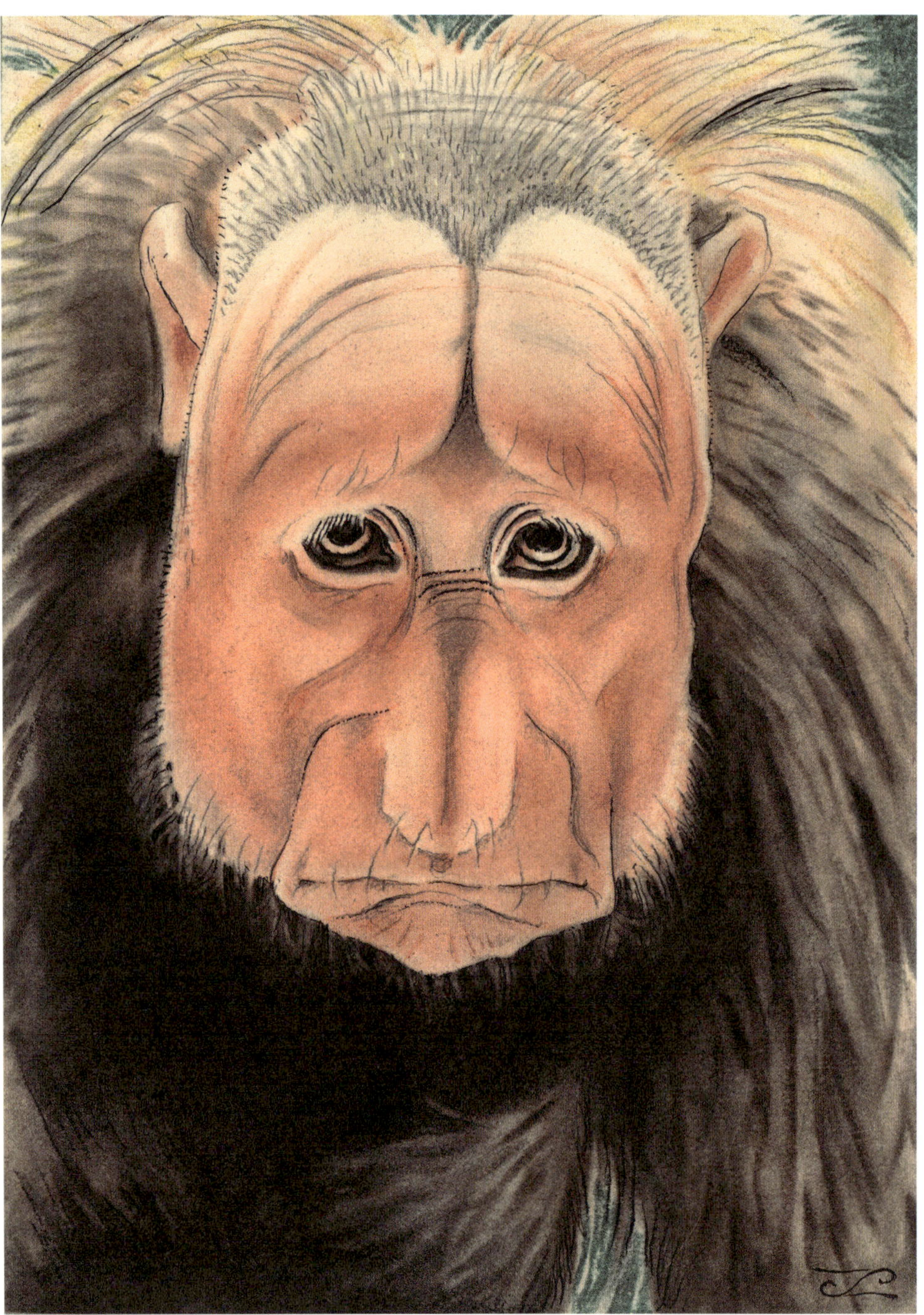

Sloth

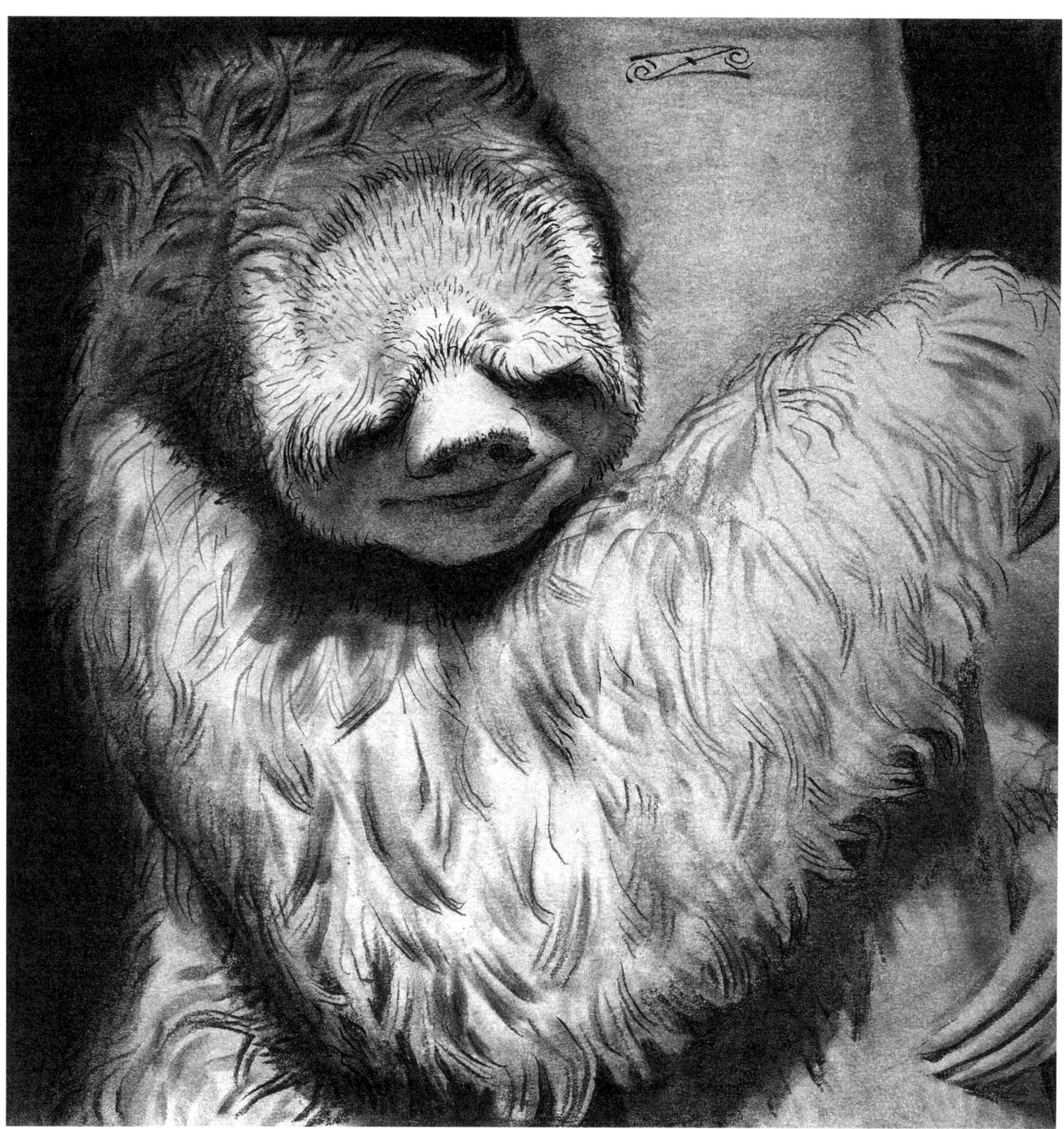

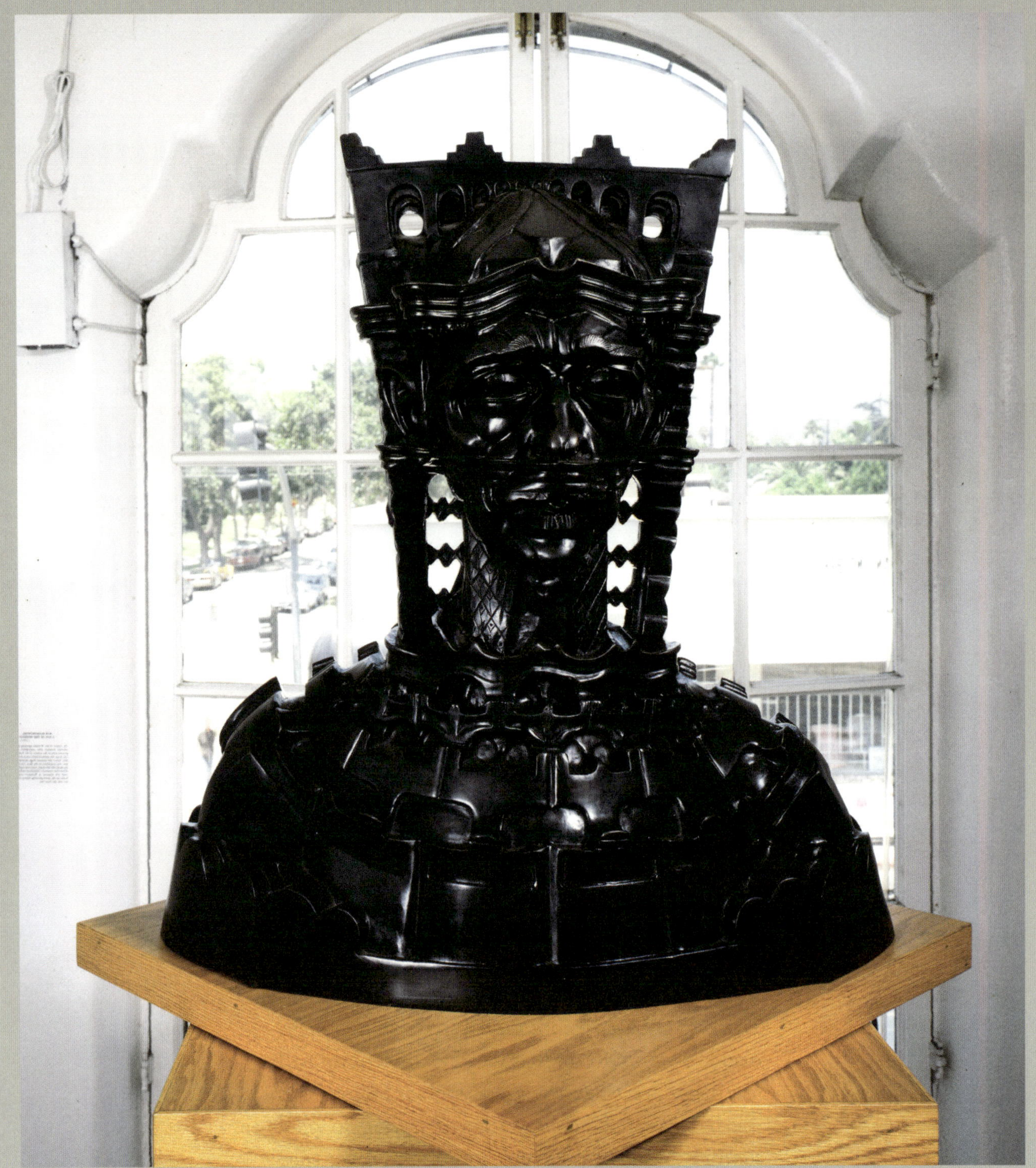

The sculpture on display at the La Luz de Jesus Gallery, 1989

A Son of the Mermaid

■ 1962 ■

This is the portrait of the leader of the Warsaw Uprising against the German destroyers and occupants of the Polish capital. Bór-Komorowski, a very slight man, was a regular military officer and a member of a wealthy family. Before the last war he was renowned for his equestrian championships.

My thirty-eight years dedicated to anthropology, in which archeology plays a vital role, led me to discover that the Mermaid used to be worshipped universally. Christian iconography superimposed itself and erased all prehistoric pictographs, so that mankind forgot her importance and meaning. Only Warsaw has sustained her in its Coat of Arms, not knowing why.

I covered Bór-Komorowski's skin with fish-scales, so as to hint at his descent from the Mermaid.

Since the Poles under his command, mostly students and other young citizens, assembled in the sewers of the city where the stolen machine guns, ammunition and emergency hospitals were hidden, I gave Bór-Komorowski horizontal water waves. Like frogs, the Uprisers had to duck into the sewerage filth; hence, frogs can be seen, in conventionalized form, between the waves of scum below his neck. Filth of the sewer drips from his face. Over the pate of his head flow the Swastika and Hammer and Sickle-marked excrements of the Predators who occupied the capital of Poland.

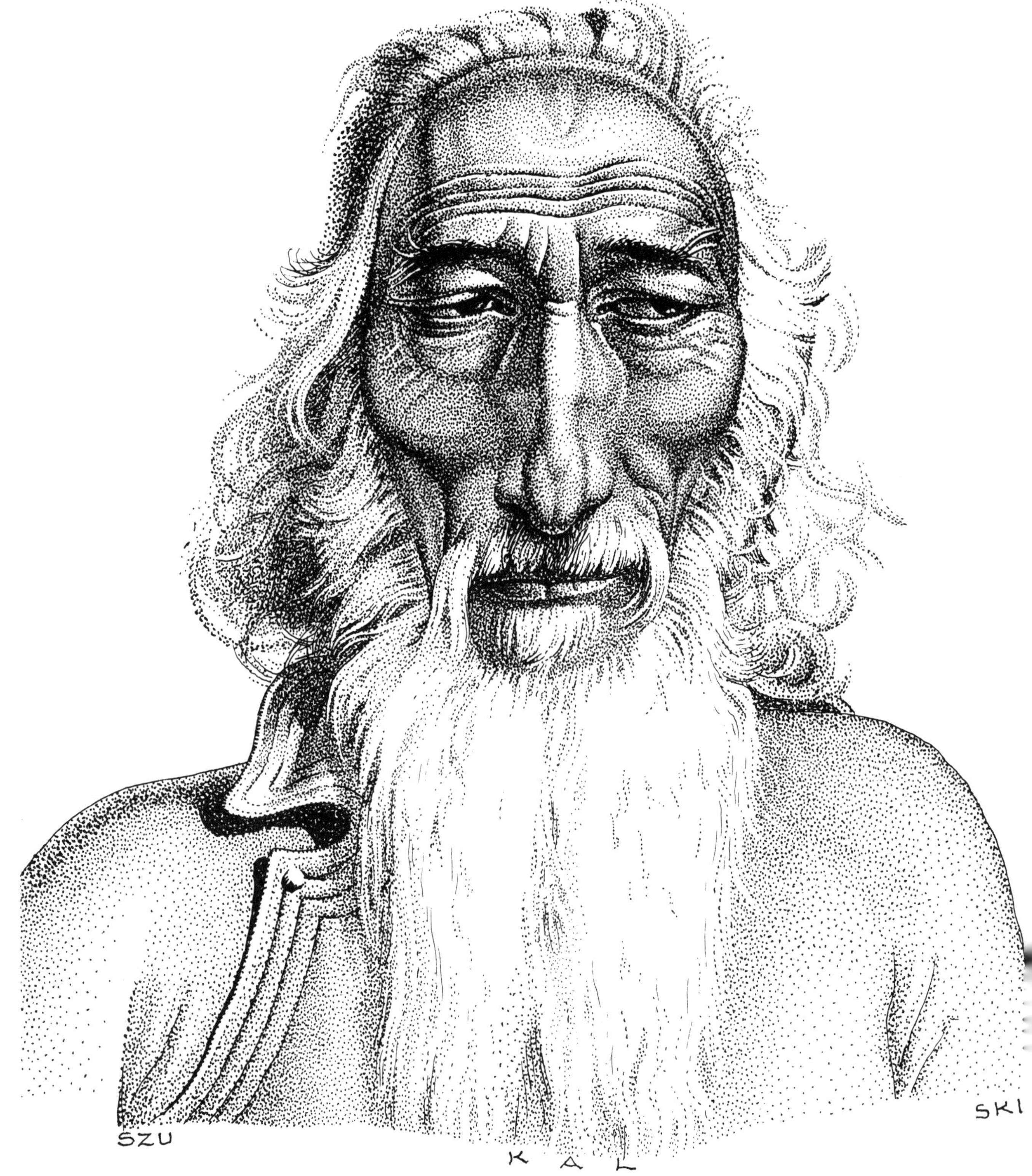

SZU
KAL
SKI

The Celestial Ancestor

■ 1962 ■

In the 1950s I came across this magnificent face in a
book on China. There was no indication of who he
was, or from what part of the country. There was
only mention that he was a merchant.

It is a rule that
if the subject I draw is repulsive to me, I will make
a very bad drawing. If interesting, I will exert all my
efforts to make it as perfect as I am capable of. The
singular meaning of finding this type of face in China thrilled me beyond words and I think this is the
most supreme drawing I have ever made.

This is a
pure Cro-Magnon racial type, having the tremendous nose of the proboscoid Human, which makes a
long distance between the eyes and the mouth (the
Socratic facial proportion) with an extremely short
upper lip.

I place this face as being closely akin to
our original Human ancestors. Through my findings,
I know that our ancestors looked much like what
has been termed microcephalic. Microcephalies (pin-
headed, narrow shouldered) are overtly calm, gently stupid, slow-moving, grinning simpletons. They
were the first to be imprisoned and destroyed by the
future Empire Amassers. But their human memory
helps them to avoid danger, hence to survive. They
are the noblest of beings.

Great Chief Washaki (Sioux)

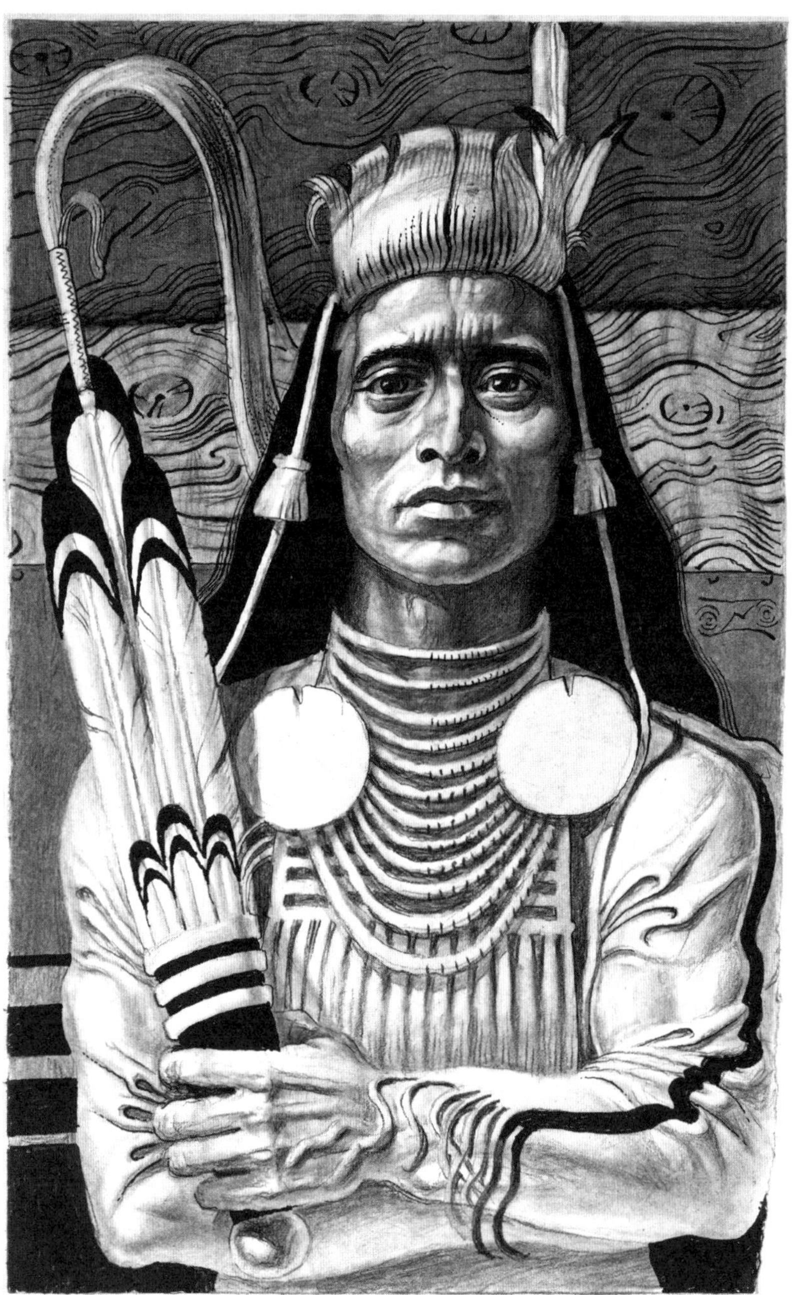

Leader of the Soshone people and a great politician and diplomat whose reputation lives on to this day

A Syrian Dwarf

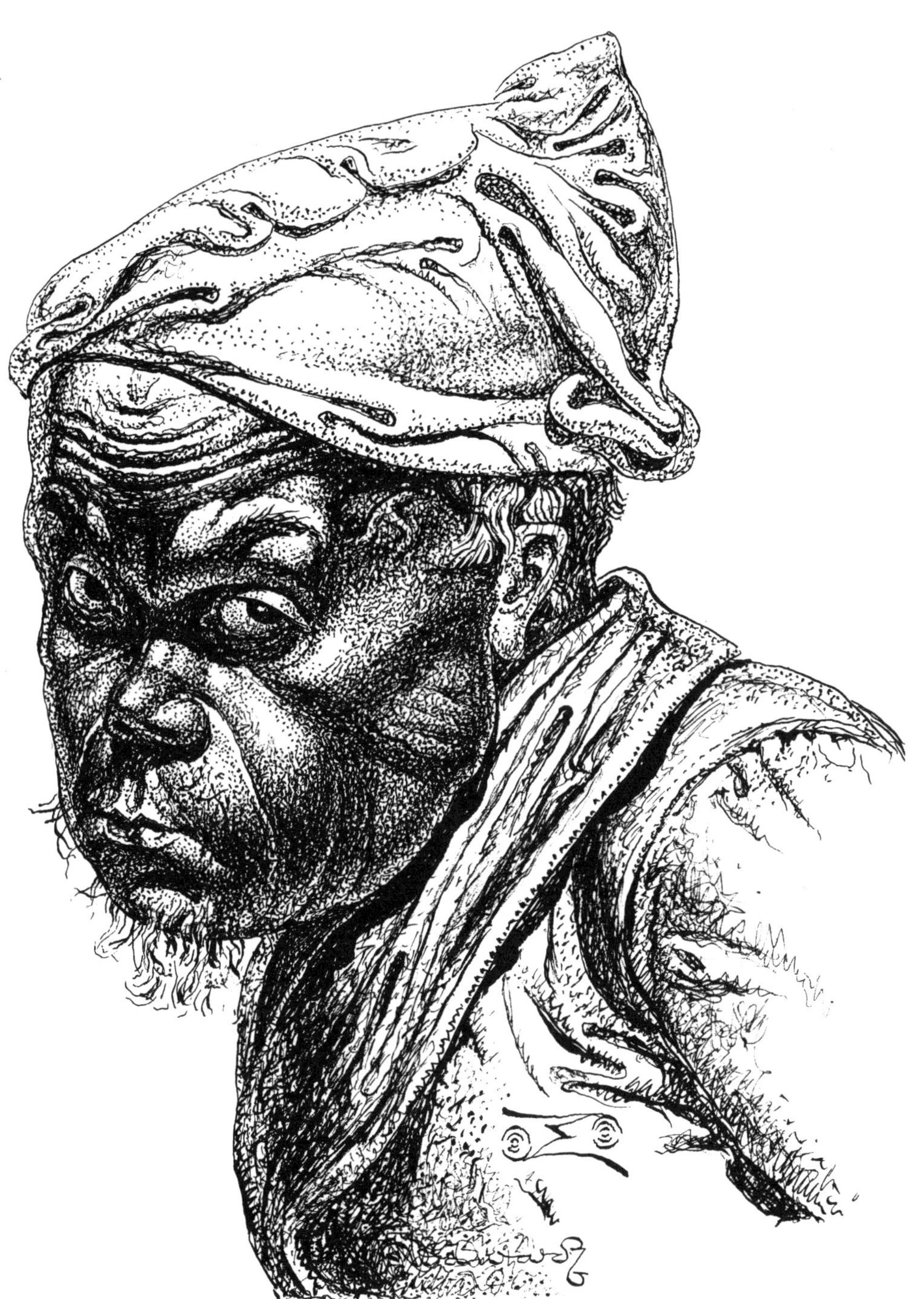

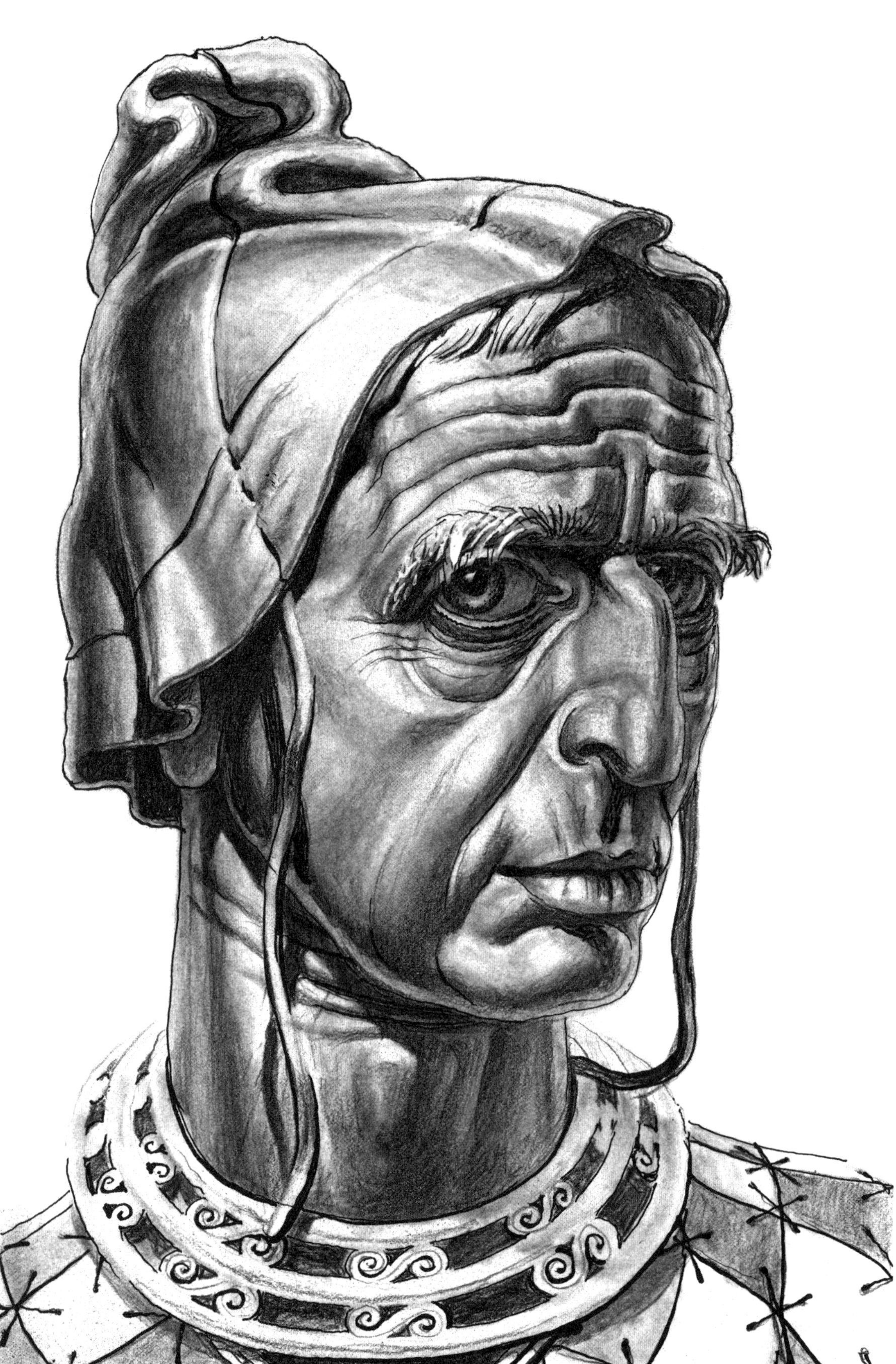

Bulge-Eye, the Tollund Man of Jutland

■ 1965 ■

Wherever there are ancient swamplands where millions of generations of weeds and bulrushes died, the water turns reddish brown from the tannic acid that seeps out of their roots. This incidentally is the best preserver of all things dead, so that they accumulate in bulk and gradually change the water into solid land.

Throughout the centuries in Scandinavian bogs, perfectly preserved bodies have been found of… intentionally drowned men. In most cases they had ropes around their throats, tightened, and sometimes with weights tied to the other end.

Among such victims was this man found in Tollund. I opened his eyes in the drawing, that he may testify to the crime committed.

His stomach contained food, every item he had just chewed perfectly preserved, so that we could still tell what his breakfast had consisted of. I drew him because of his nose: the clue to the species of man he belonged to. The usual profile of his contemporaries shows the forehead overhanging the mask in such a way, that we could tilt the head to the ceiling just by placing our thumb beneath the frowning brow. Not so with this man. Here the line coming down from the top of the head does not go UNDER the forehead, coming back to the tip of the nose, but instead comes forward immediately at the bridge of the nose, making it project directly from the forehead.

This then classes him as a Cro-Magnon human from the pre-Bronze Age who had migrated to Europe from the Pacific region at the onset of the Great Deluge.

Literally hundreds of such mummified men were excavated or dragged out of the swamp vegetation, the preserved witnesses of crimes committed against Humanity. Hundreds more will be discovered in Scandinavia, Lithuania, Estonia, Latvia, as well as in Mexico City's extinct crater that now forms a lake in the city park. (In modern history, during WWI, General von Hindenburg intentionally drowned 41,000 Russian soldiers in Mazurian Lake in Poland.)

Though the archeologists propose that these drowned persons were sacrificial victims, I propose that they were the victims of assassinations by wart-nosed conspirators for being superior personages. In my opinion a *troll* or dwarf-like servant, while traveling on a boat with his master, would suddenly throw a noose around the head of his lord from the rear, stunning him with a rock attached to the other end. Many a rowboat had a large stone on its bottom at the time, tied to a rope, serving as an anchor. Sacrifices were consumed by fire on specifically designated slabs. Drownings with rocks and nooses were assassinations by the species of Yetinsyn, the disproportionate offshoot of the Manape. The Scandinavian scientists should make a count of all the skulls discovered in the swamps and note the percentage of tall people with the proboscis type of face versus the usual contemporary type. If the first prevails, my Anthropolitical Motivations theory is proven correct, and they were the victims of traitorous killings.

Benjamin Thayer

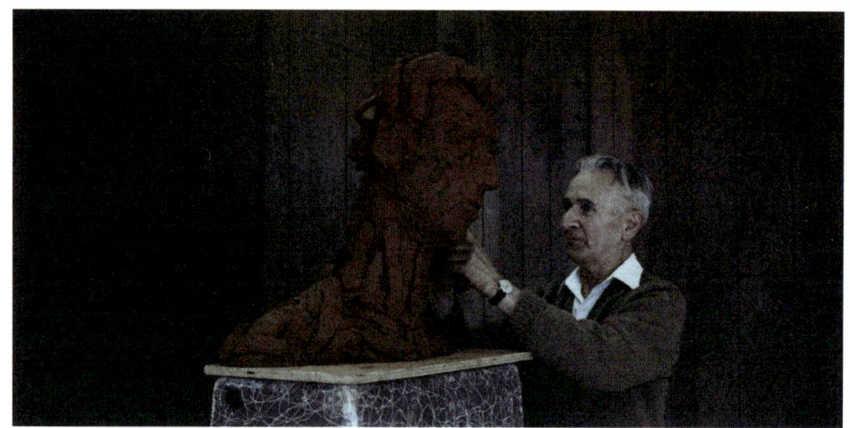

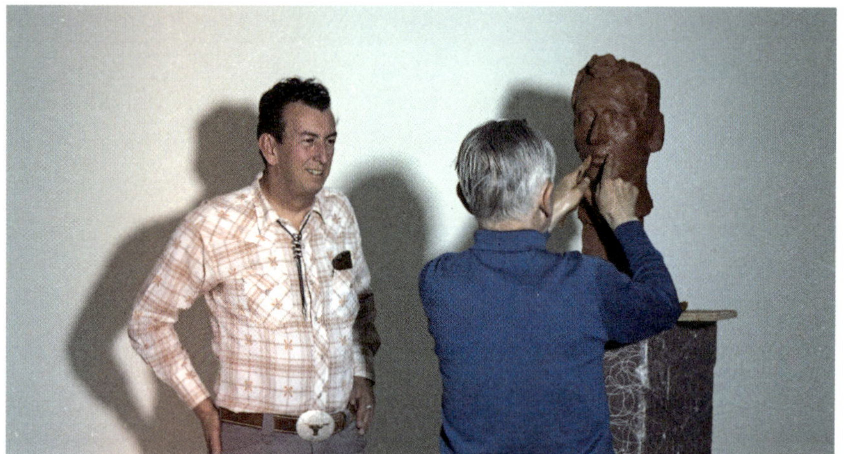

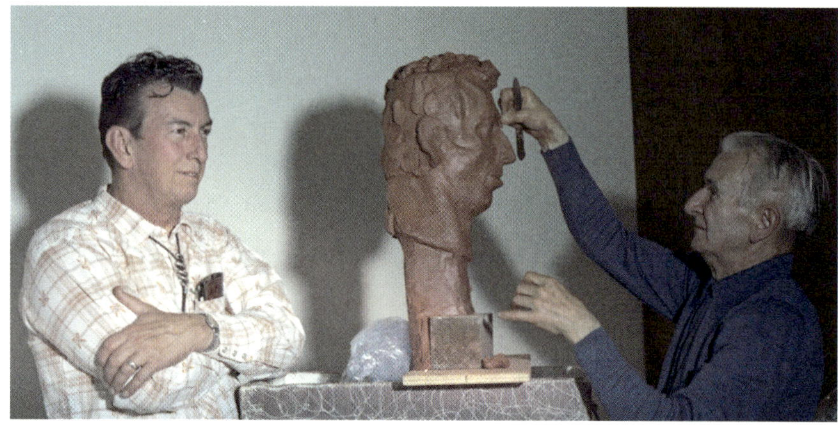

In the 1960s Szukalski was offering sculpture and draw-ing classes at a site he rented in Calabasas, CA. At the same time he accepted a job teach-ing sculpture classes at Pierce College in Woodland Hills, CA.

In very few instances do we have a photo of the artist crafting his work hands-on. For the class, these photos were taken to show the pro-gression of sculpture-making.

One of the students, Benjamin Thayer, was chosen by Szukalski as an example of how to capture a likeness di-rectly, without having it seen photographed. – *Ed.*

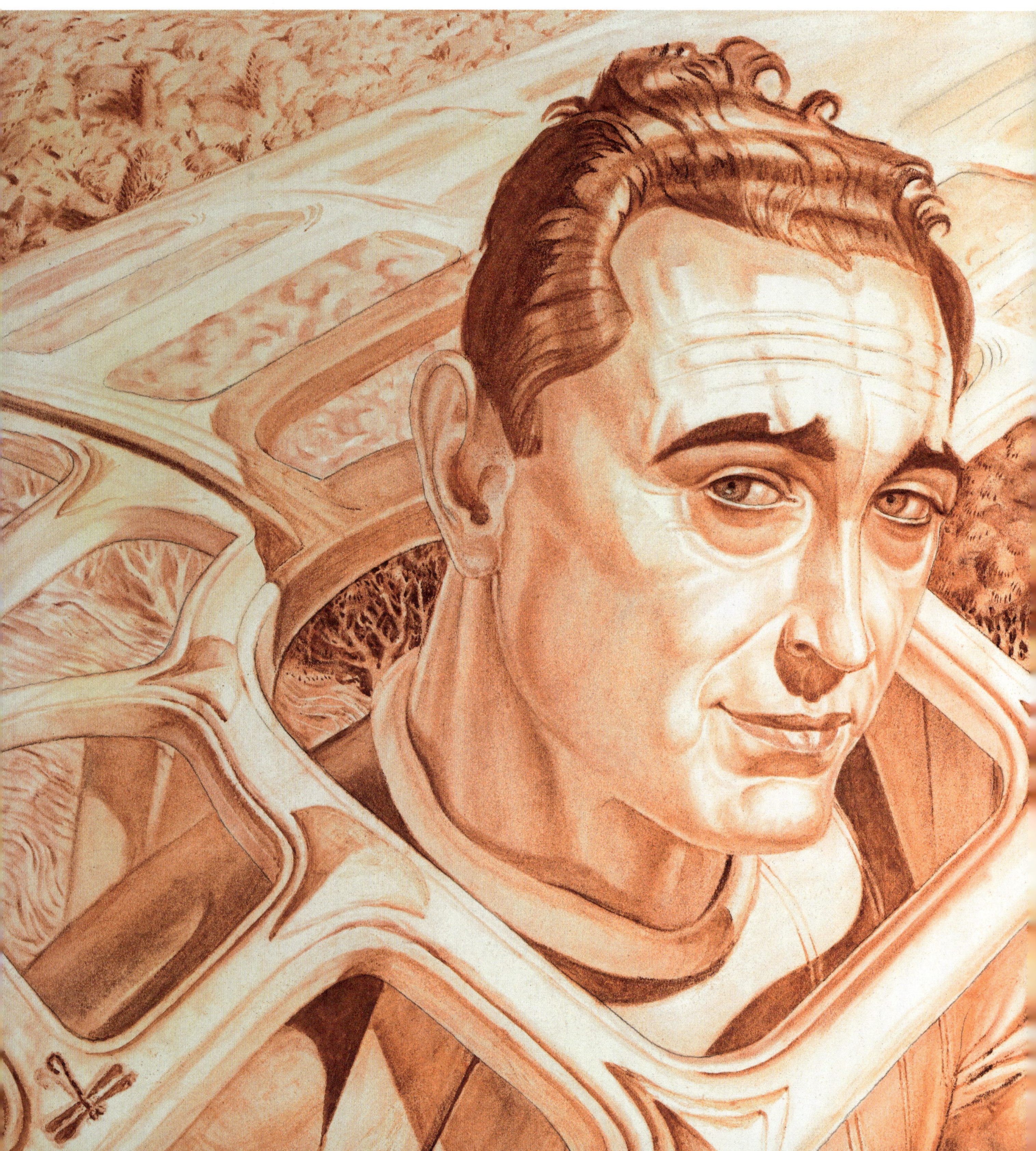

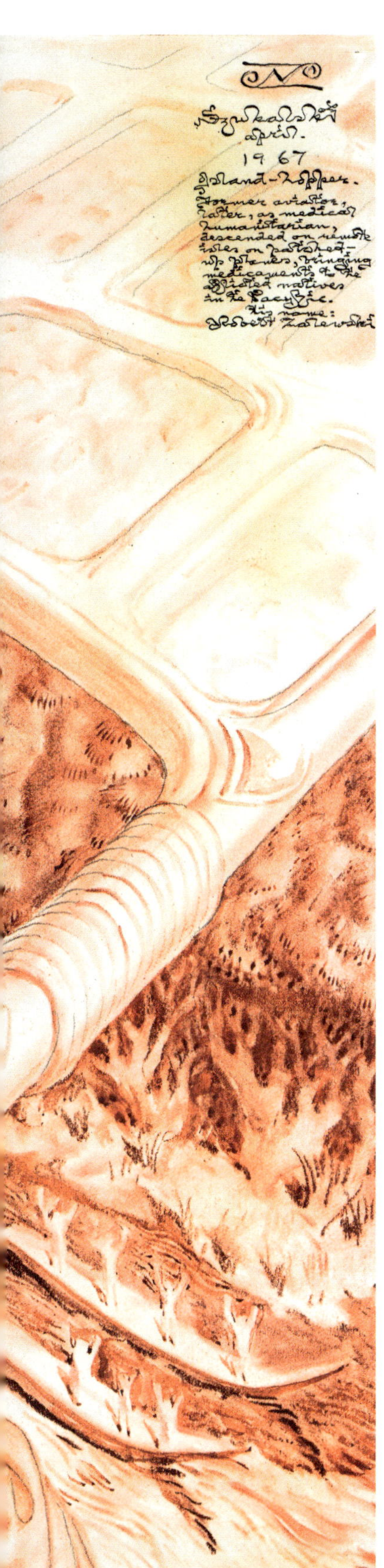

The Aviator Zalewski

■ 1967 ■

There are no meaningless "names." Every family name originally had its meaning. "Zalewski" derived from *Za Lasem* (*-ski* is the Polish possessive form), which means "Beyond Forest." In the United States there are many apparently meaningless names, because, having been brought from non-Anglo countries, the foreign names were gradually misspelled beyond recognition. If we would approach these names in other tongues, we would find that they too were derived from compound-descriptions hence nicknames, like Skinny, Curley, Knock-kneed, Skinflint, or Smith (one of the most ancient that describe professions).

The meaning of its name has a profound influence on the members of a family. For that reason, among the muchly historic Poles, the family name is the most sacred heritage a person will possess. Thus, the Poles never change their names, unless they are peasant immigrants, shamed into assuming English names by the monolingual Anglomericans, who themselves would never stoop to adopt a foreign name. (Yet English names are foreign to foreigners, but the Americans are insensitive to such delicacies of feeling.) Most Poles look with contempt upon "alternames," regarding them as opportunists, which is considered equivalent to betrayal of one's Ancestor's historicity.

Zalewski, until recently, commuted flying between Los Angeles and Japan. After serving his number of years in the American Army during the war, he was discharged, but remained in Indonesia. He proceeded to construct himself a plane of odds and pieces, till it rose and carried him wherever there was need for him. He brought medicine to the afflicted and help to the helpless, flying between godforgotten islands, for he knew God was too busy attending to those who communicated with Him in Latin or Hebrew.

Now! This is a Pole who deserves respect, for he was not educated in Poland, where he would have stunk up the air in ant-hill cafés. Zalewski did all his humanitarian work on his own, without funds or assistance from anywhere. I am proud of his Polish origin and am happy to have known him.

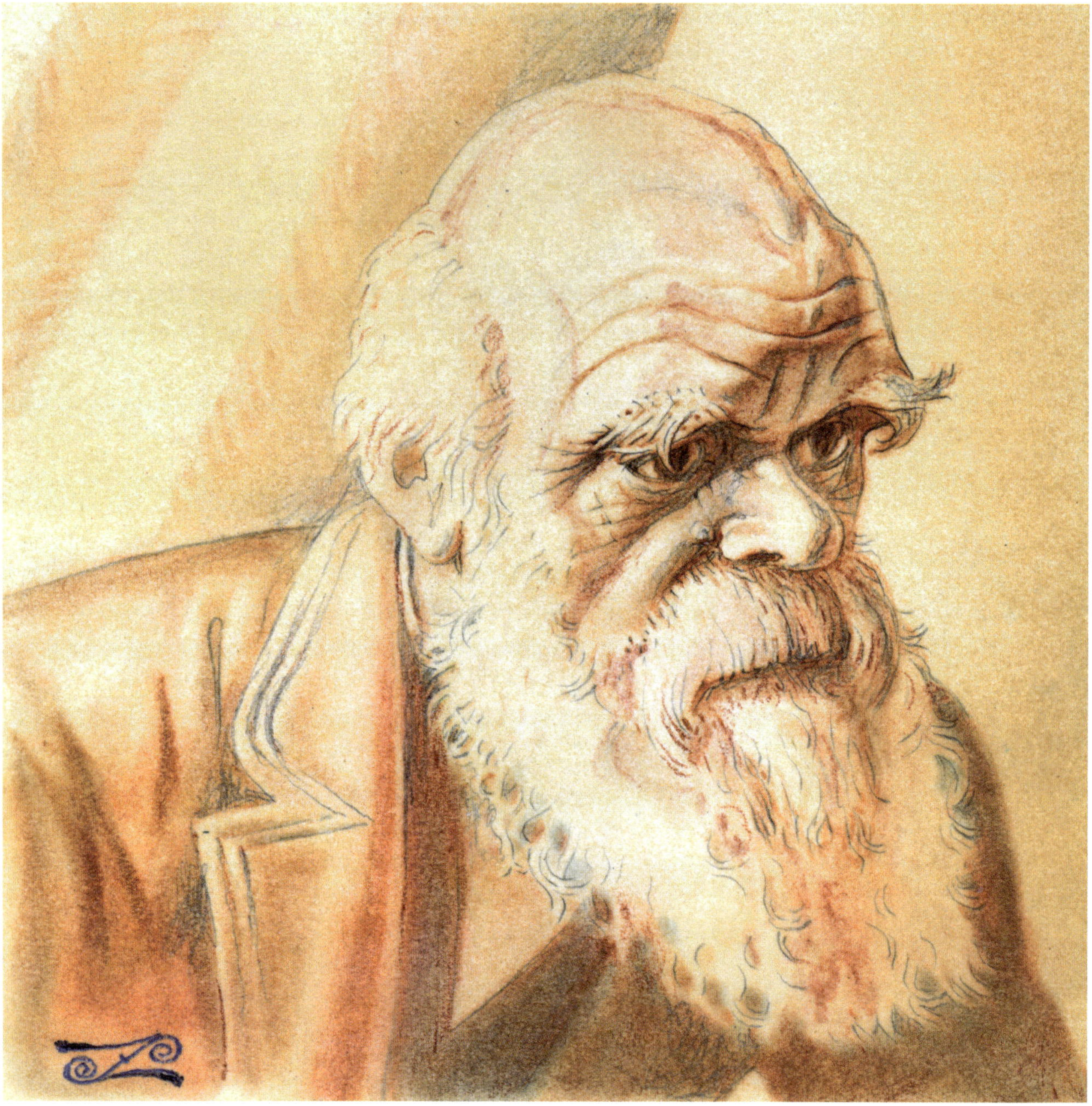

178

Darwin

There is an accumulation of drawings I have made for another book, of famed personalities from classic times to modern, whose names are made of the Protong language informing us of their diluvial origins. Like the names of towns, villages and rivers all over the world, they seem without meaning until I resegment them to their original Protong elements and we learn of their astounding age.

The name of the Darwin family developed from "Dar W In." Interpreted, this little phrase describes the one who was first given this denomination as "Given In Elsewhere," meaning: he came from the Netherworld, beneath the waters of the Great Deluge.

No doubt, Darwin, in his adolescence, was very self-conscious about his overhanging brow, bridgeless nose and very long upper lip, which hindered him in being popular with beautiful girls. However, he had a spark of inquisitiveness and a speculative mind which carried him into daring intellectual enterprise brought about by the notion that his face had the likeness of that of some apes. In consequence of his constant sense of inferiority, he developed the theory of man's evolution or descent from apes.

Had he been carried away in the opposite direction by his self-deprecation, he might have become a philosopher with a grudge against Mankind, whereby he would have picked on Capitalism or another element of Civilization and concocted a "revolutionary" scheme whereby all misfits would choose him as their teacher. Fortunately, despite his Yetinsynism (evidenced also by body proportions) he became a benefactor to mankind, which dismissed his theories when they became to be regarded as imperfect and incomplete. Only in science do we dismiss notions, honored for some time, when we find ones improving them. Only in religion do things never change, for they are based on anti-reason.

Inu

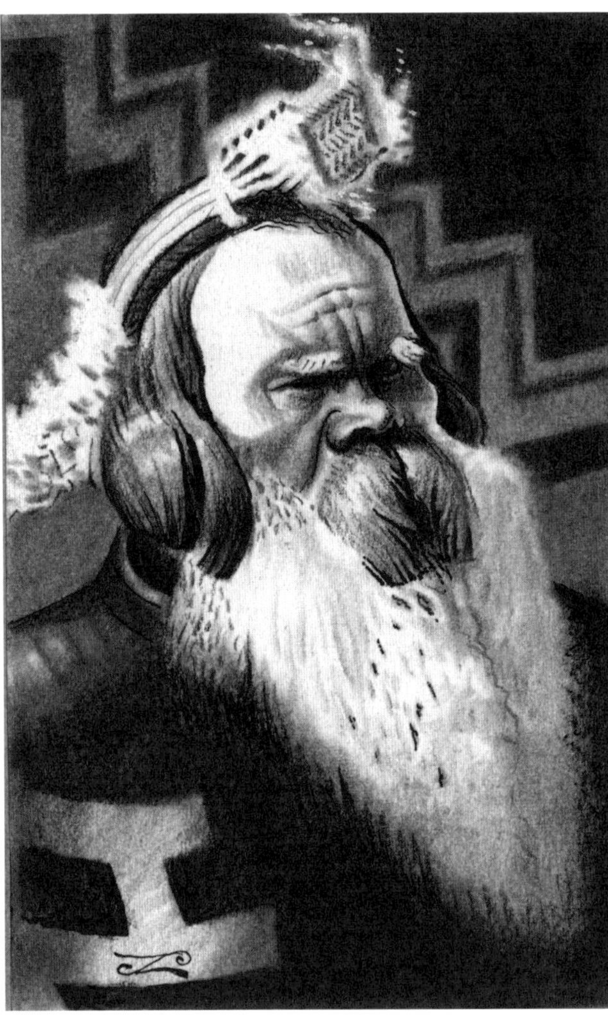

Coming down the map from the north of Sakhalin Island, we next meet Hokkaido Island that parenthesizes the sea of Japan, and then Japan proper. It was anciently inhabited by the Inu (pron. "Eenoo," not "Ainu") people, called the "Hairy Ones" because their bodies were thickly covered with hair.

The term *Inu* evolved, however, from Protong "In U(t)," which means "Elsewhere S(unken)," as a reference to the original homeland which had submerged in the Deluge. The name of the island was anciently "Go Ka Id (J)o,"also remembering the motherland: "Exiled Where Migrated I (from)."

Coincidentally, the Eskimos have another, very similar name for themselves, Inuit, which evolved from "In U(t) Id:" "Elsewhere S(unken) Migrated (from)." Their original homeland, now taken by the sea, is the same as the homeland of the Inus.

To me the Inu faces look most representatively Russian (as a child I have seen Russian soldiers permanently stationed in Polish towns), specifically in the extremely short, bridgeless wart-nose. One often sees Russian subjects, however, who seem mistakenly handsome. The reason is simply that these are no part of the Tataroid Moscovian minority, but of some 60 nations that are permanently parasited on by this minority.

The Inu, however, having lived in the hardships of the sub-Arctic region for multi-millennia, never became parasites of other nations as this facial type so often does.

Inside-Out Portrait of McNamara

Only the artist with a penetrating mind can see certain inside traits of some types of people, which sometimes pass for other characteristics. The artist, like a learned psychiatrist, must "dig deep" to locate the biological mission of the person.

The Anglomerican people, being unhistoric (untried by crushing calamities as in Europe), have exceedingly slow memories. History means REMEMBRANCE. Today, not long after the defeat of the United States armies in Vietnam, we have forgotten the doings of this man and his sinister plan in the struggle against Communism. He is forgotten like Alger Hiss, therefore his subversion has been disregarded, and he became respected as "having done the right things."

Whatever he did, was not because he had a choice to make on his own, but only because he had a preordained mission to fulfill. We do not choose our biological destiny, same as we do not choose our profiles, noses, or beady eyes. By making this portrait in caricature, I have deprived him of his deceptive covering (like combed and divided hair to imply cultivated manners). I have brought him back to the looks of his simian predecessors, the Pans and Egyptian Besses. If he was an uneducated villager, he would have frightened the babies in the neighborhood. Rightly, with his face, he should have been a *chinovnik* (executor of orders) in Tsarist or Communist Russia, since like them he resembles the majority of the anti-Human predatory species. However, he could have become a benefactor of mankind, if during his youth he had been drawn to medicine, electronics, or mechanical engineering.

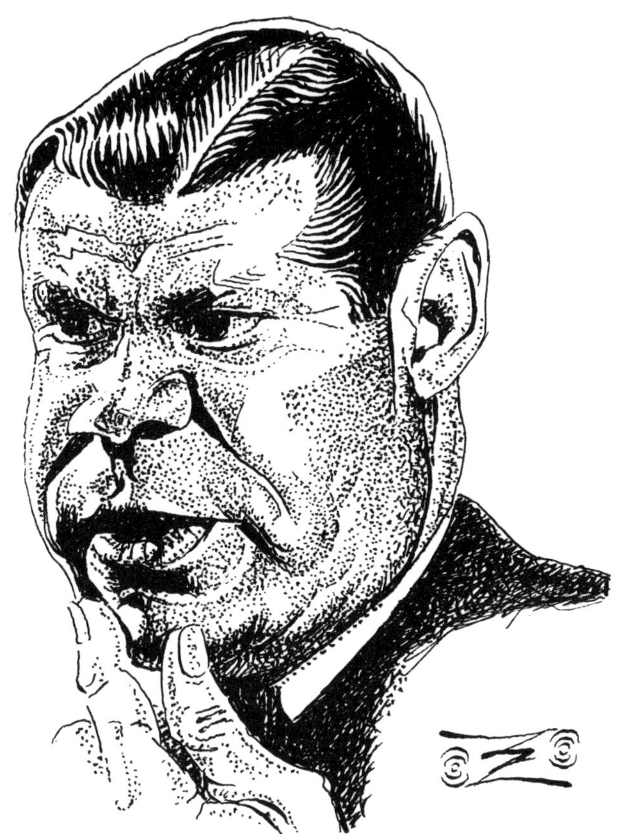

181

Our press is not free. It is "owned," therefore it serves specific conspiracies; but since Anglomericans do not possess a sense of indignation, they do not retain the memory of the misdeeds by various public figures. I used to publish a small periodical in Poland, called *The Krak's Attack*, in Polish, which had the permanently printed motto "WHEN YOU HAVE NO MORE CAPACITY FOR INDIGNATION, THEN YOU WILL BE READY FOR TREASON." Lack of indignation marks this society as depraved and immoral.

Ernest Borgnine

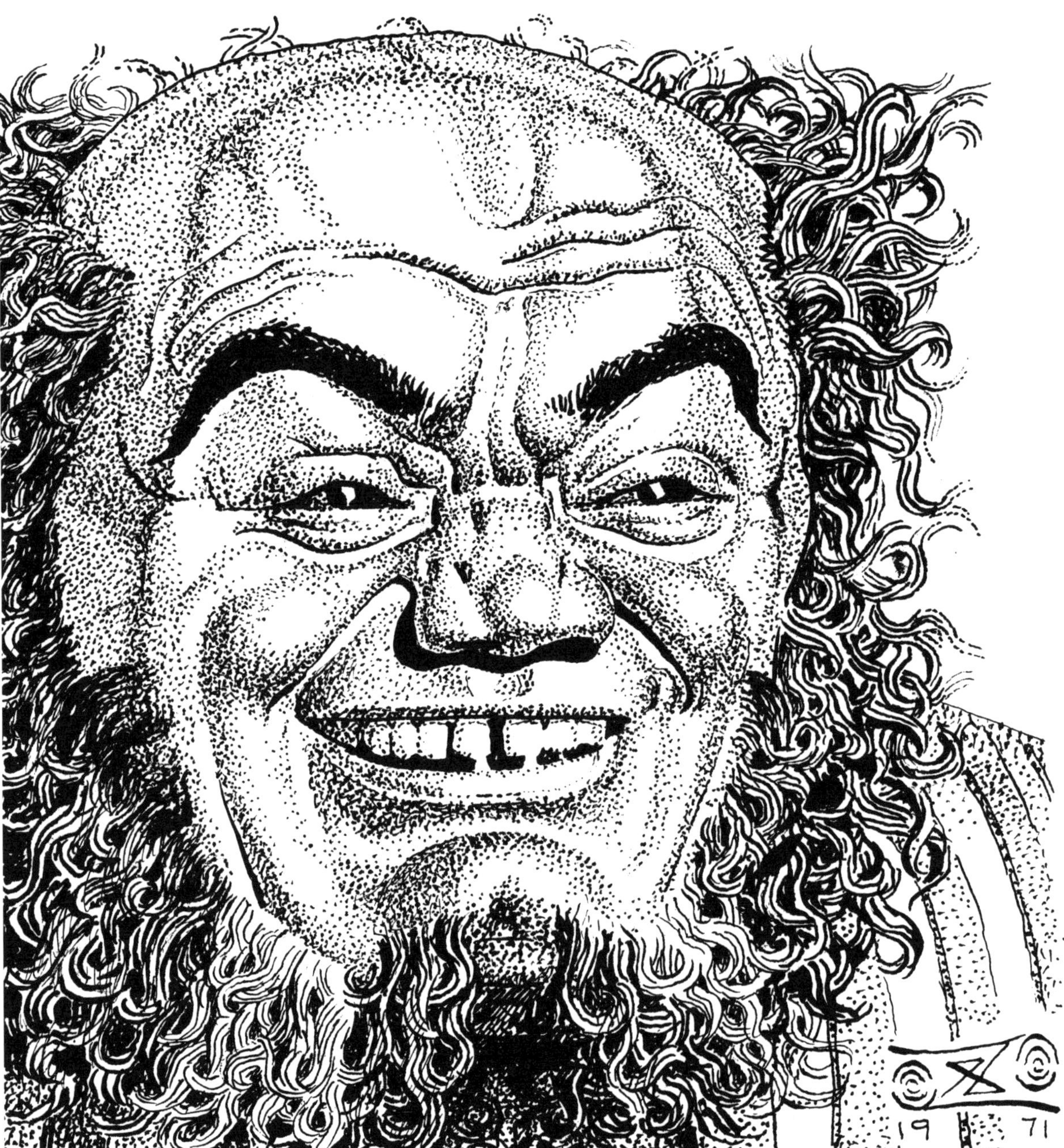

Beloved American actor of the mid-1900s

Gandhi

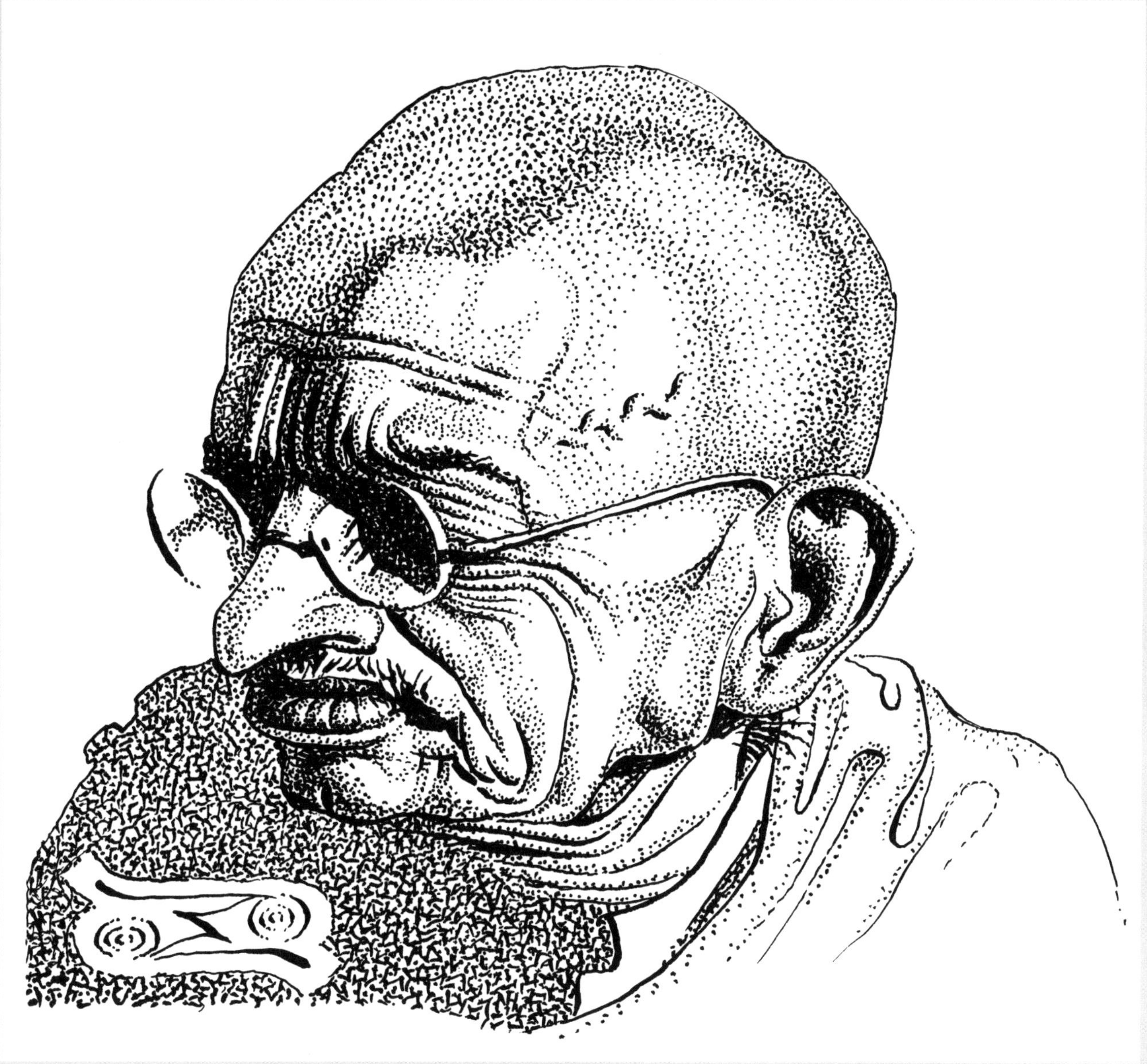

Nonviolent resistance leader in the campaign for India's independence from Great Britain's rule in the early 1900s

Michelangelo di Lodovico Buonarroti Simoni

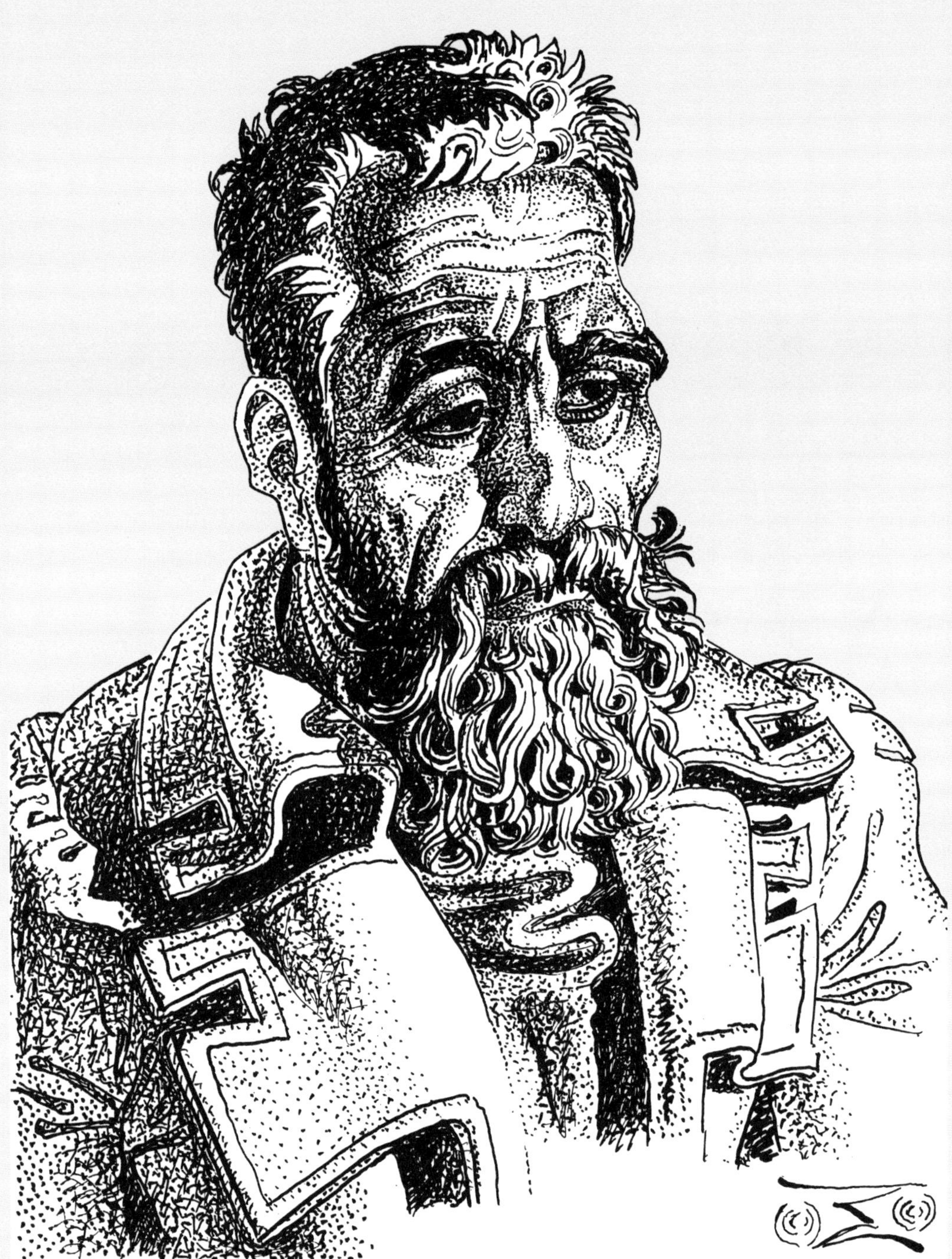

THREEFACED

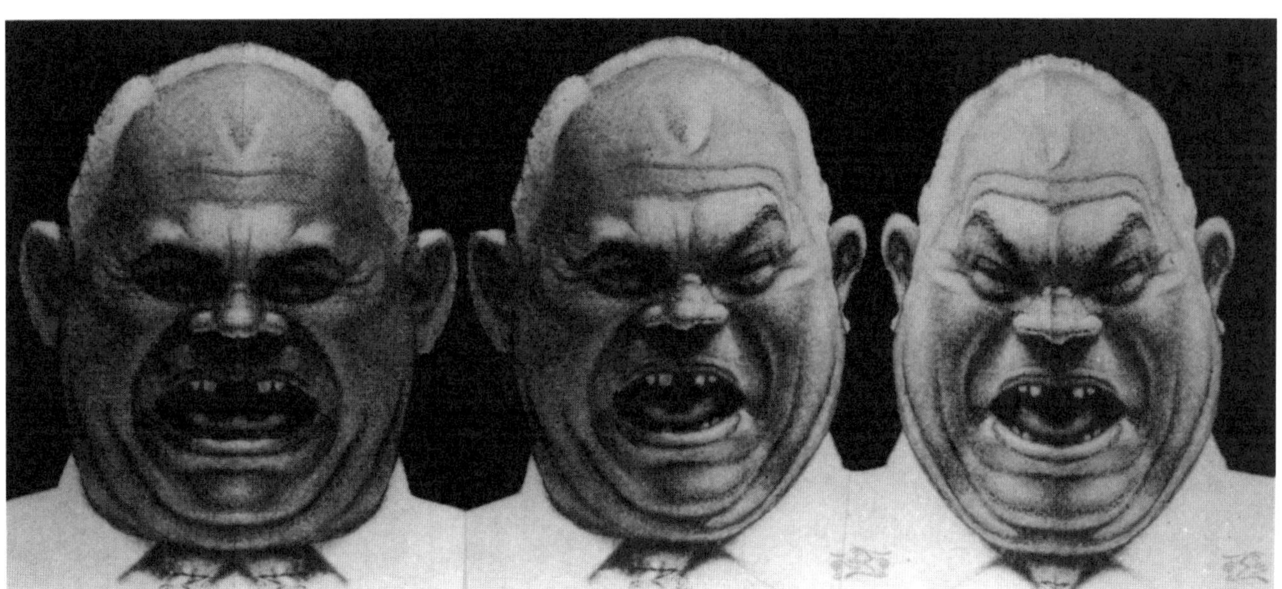

MOSCOVITE HYENAGOG

Nikita Khrushchev was the leader of the Soviet Union during the Cold War years.

Head of Meteorphei

186

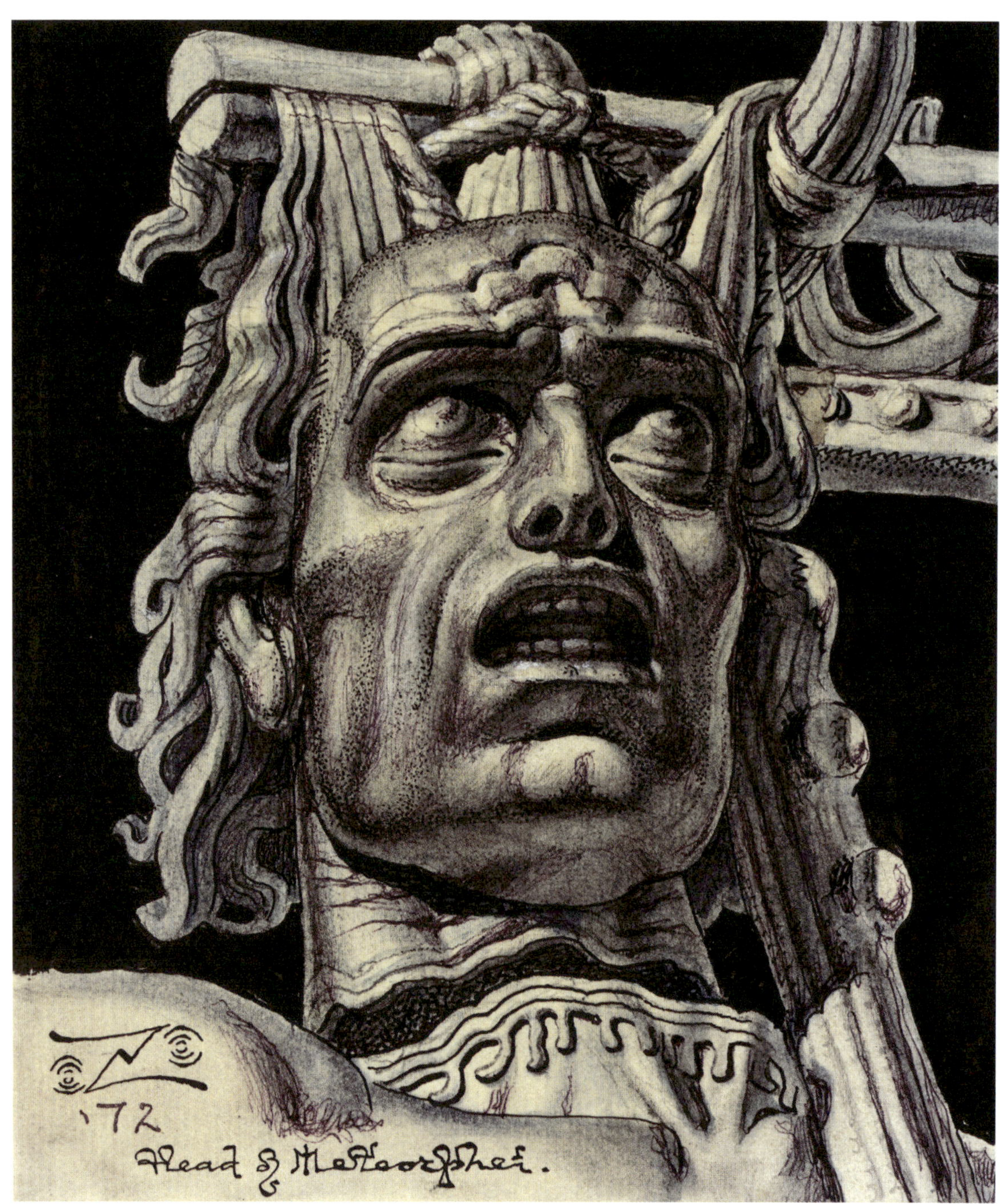

Assiniboin Portrait

■ CIRCA 1970 ■

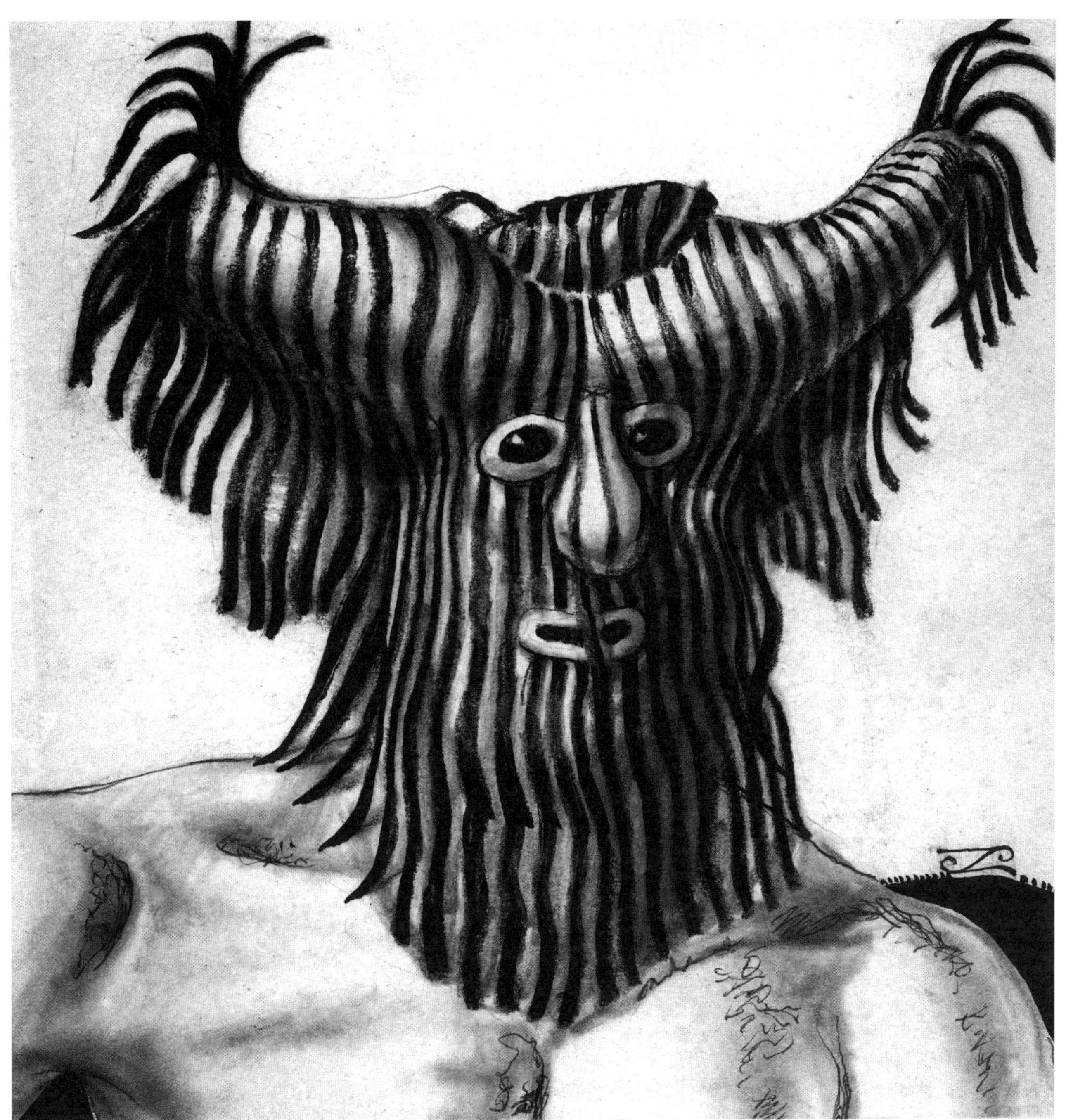

Directress of a Nazi Extermination Camp

■ CIRCA 1970 ■

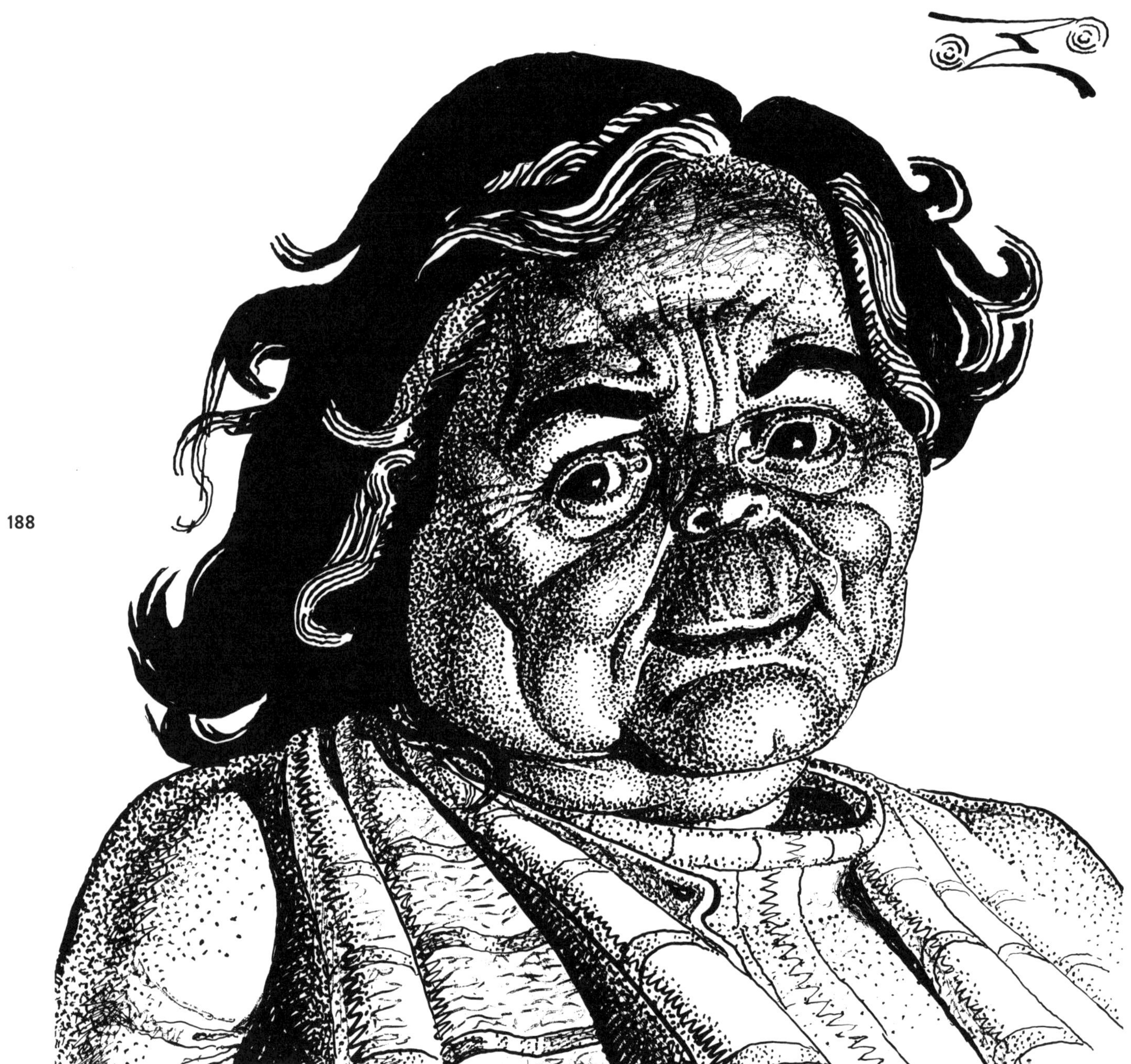

Eisenhower

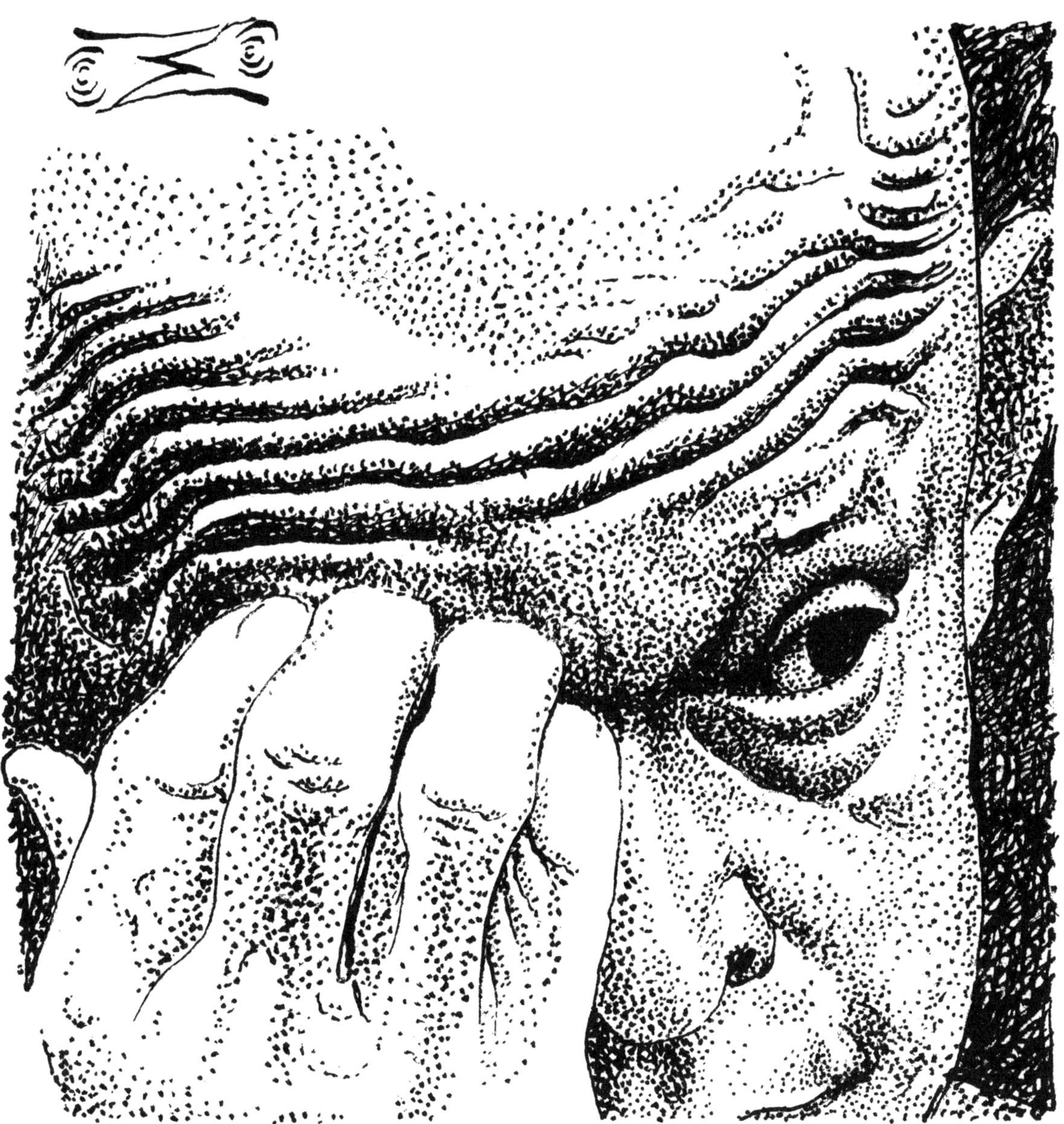

The most perplexed of beings, President Eisenhower prepared every point he made by a phrase that assured everyone how "crystal clear" he would make it.

Rodin

190

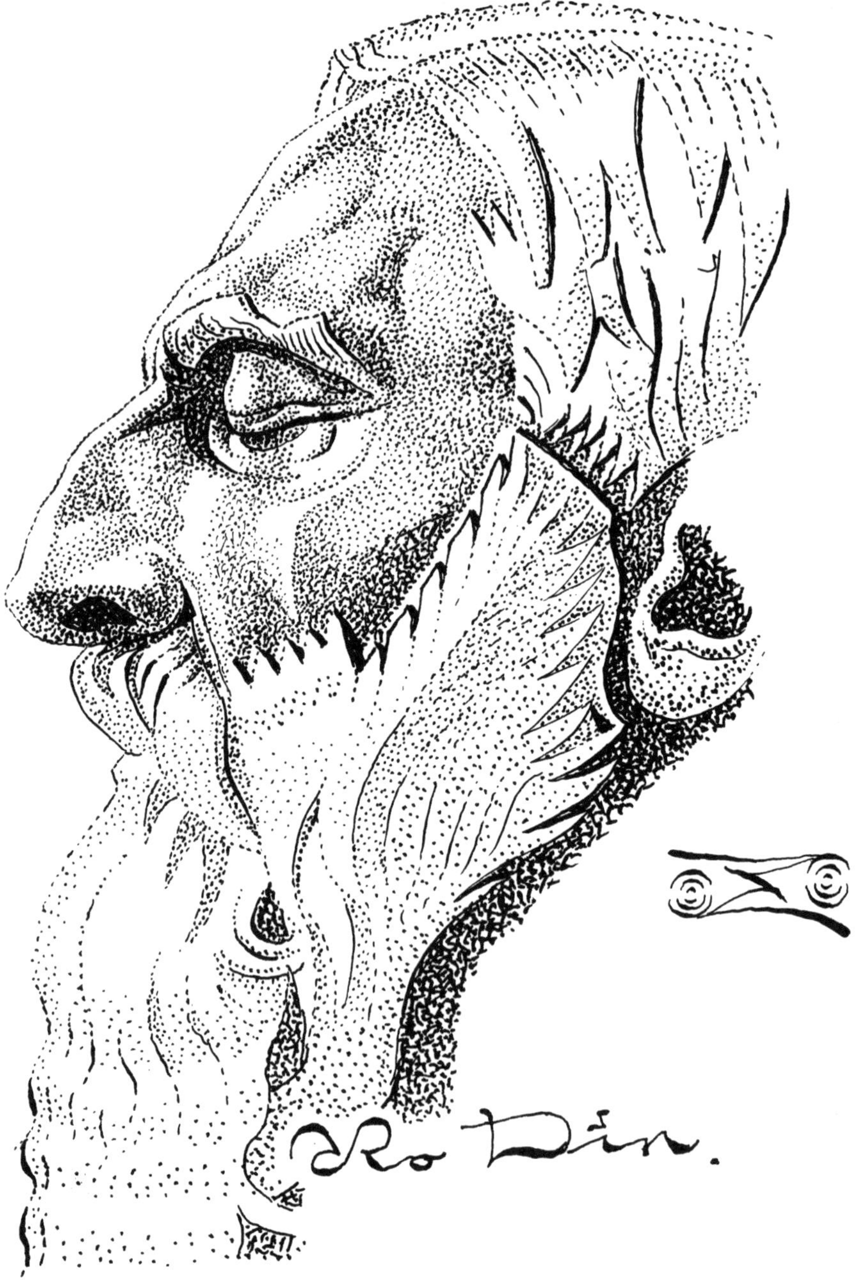

Auguste Rodin, French sculptor from the turn of the last century

Portrait of a Jew

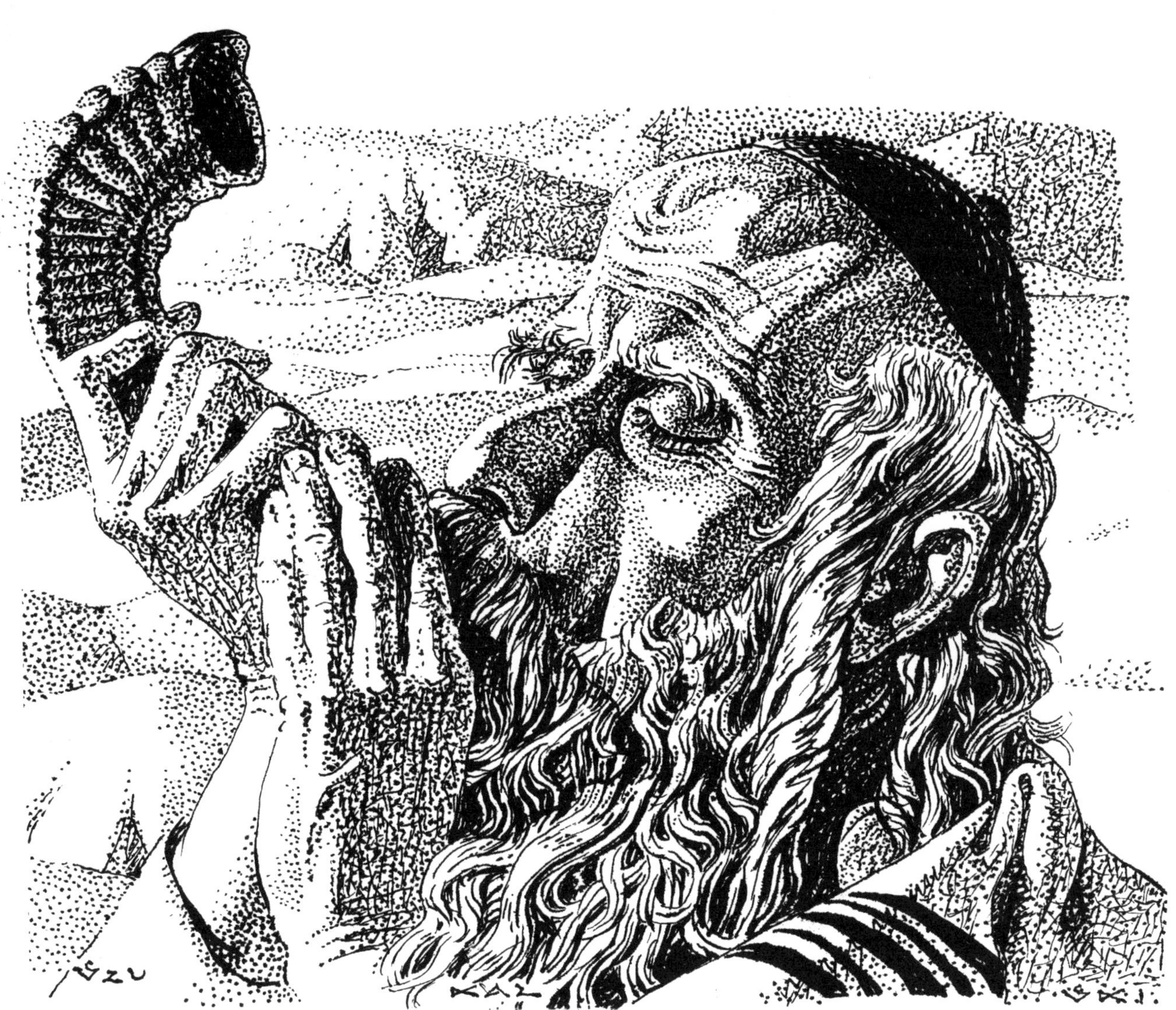

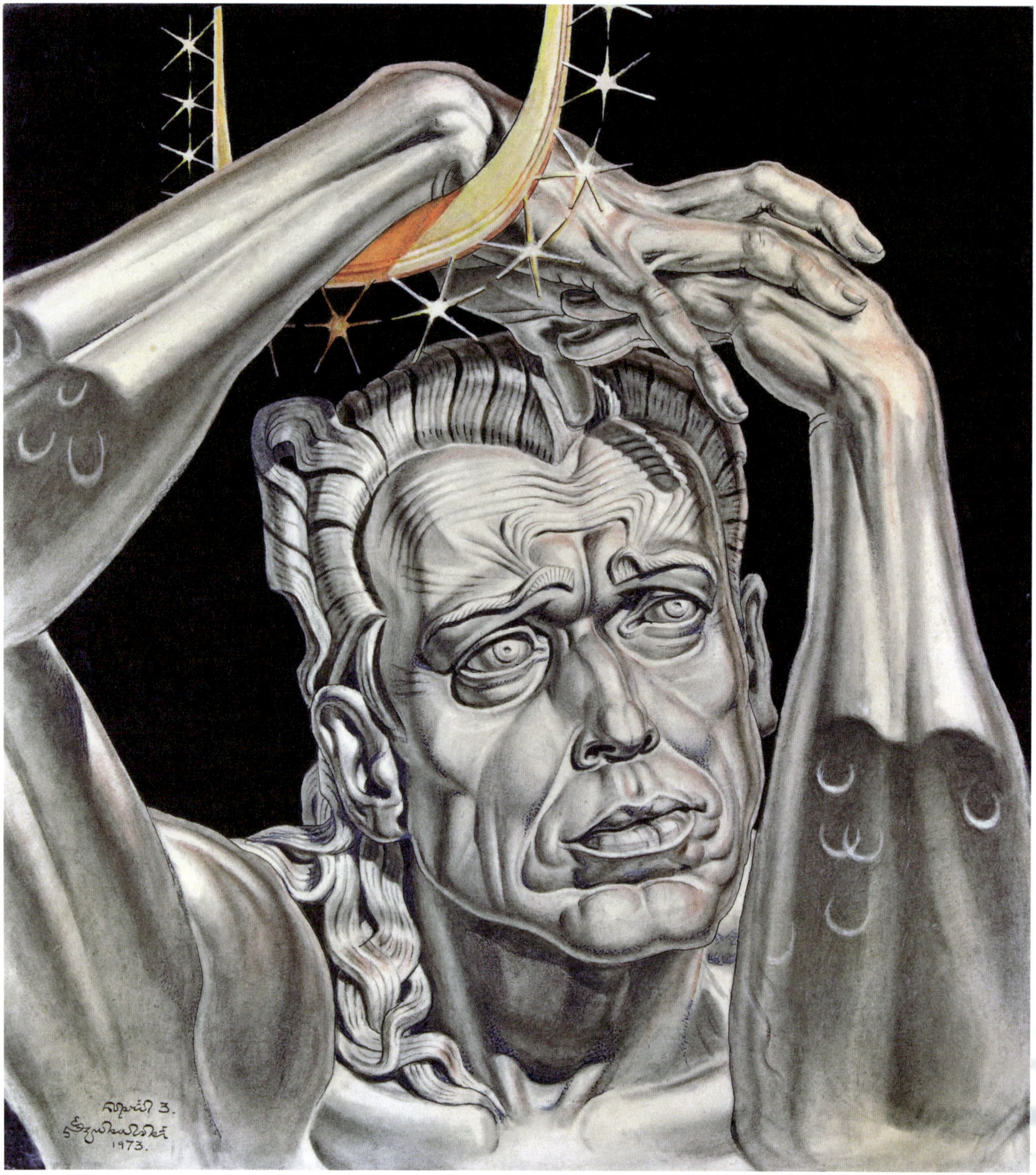

Hipparchus

■ 1973 ■

The first astronomer in history to apply mathematics to astronomy. He counted, located and named 800 stars so that others could follow their positions. He died in 126 B.C.

Since there is no known portrait of him, I invented his likeness, giving him an expression of great consternation, for, being that closely involved with the planetary vastness, he became tremendously concerned with individual destinies. For spending most of his 62 years fraternizing with the planets, I made him lean upon the crescent of the Moon.

It takes creative temerity for astronomers to pry in God's business, to poke in matters celestial, doubting the explanations of the theologians who have decided how things heavenly are to be for all times. Undoubtedly, Hipparchus was branded a heretic for his enlightenment in measuring speed and distance between planets.

This carbon drawing was a project for a sculpture which, like so many – due to the untoward circumstances of my life in this Cultural Siberia of America and Polish Thievery – I was never able to undertake.

A Talk Show Host

■ 1976 ■

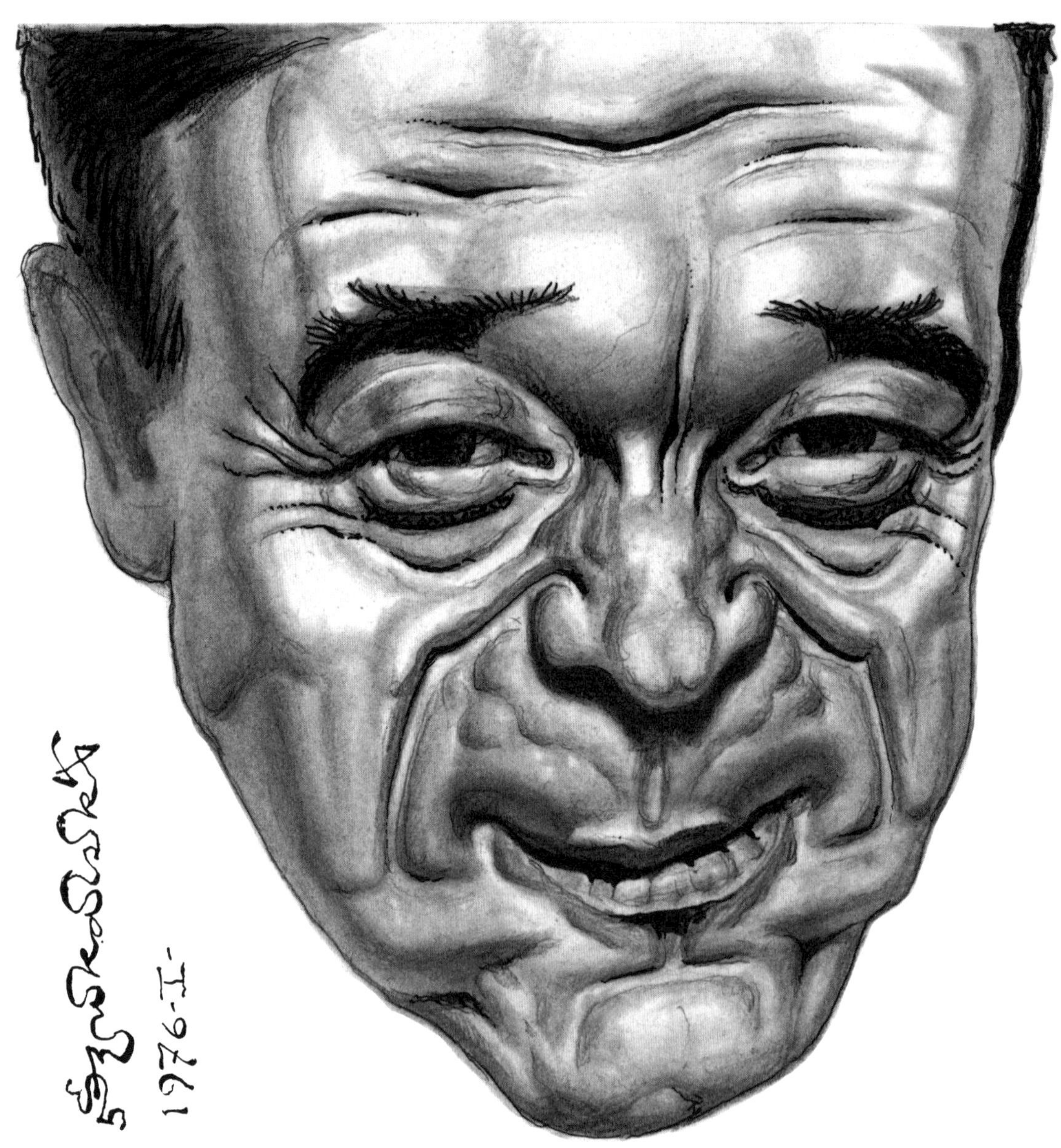

Solzhenitsyn

■ 1975 ■

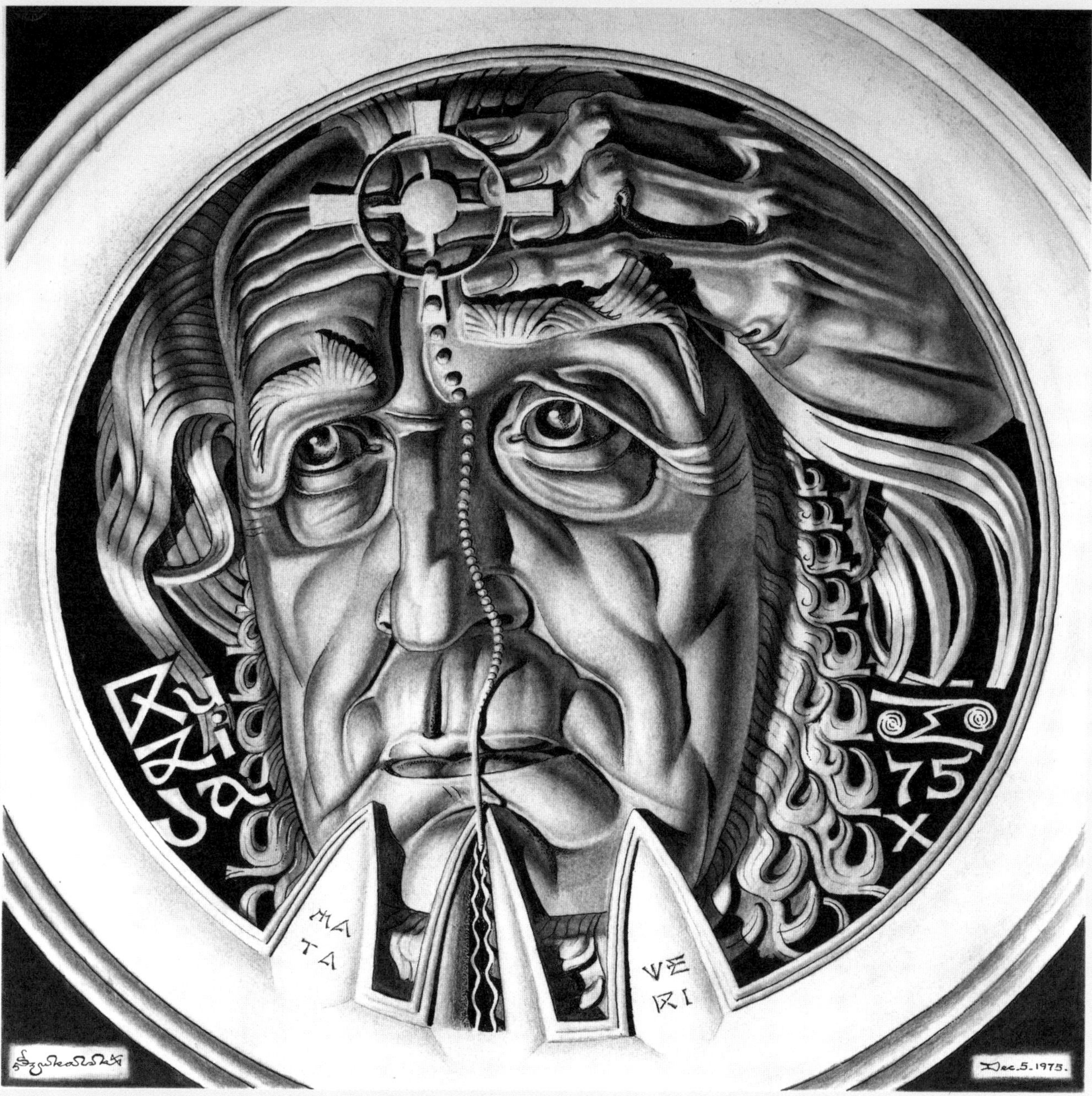

Russian novelist who wrote an exposé of the Gulag labor camps in the 1950s in the Soviet Union, making the Western world aware of the human suffering there

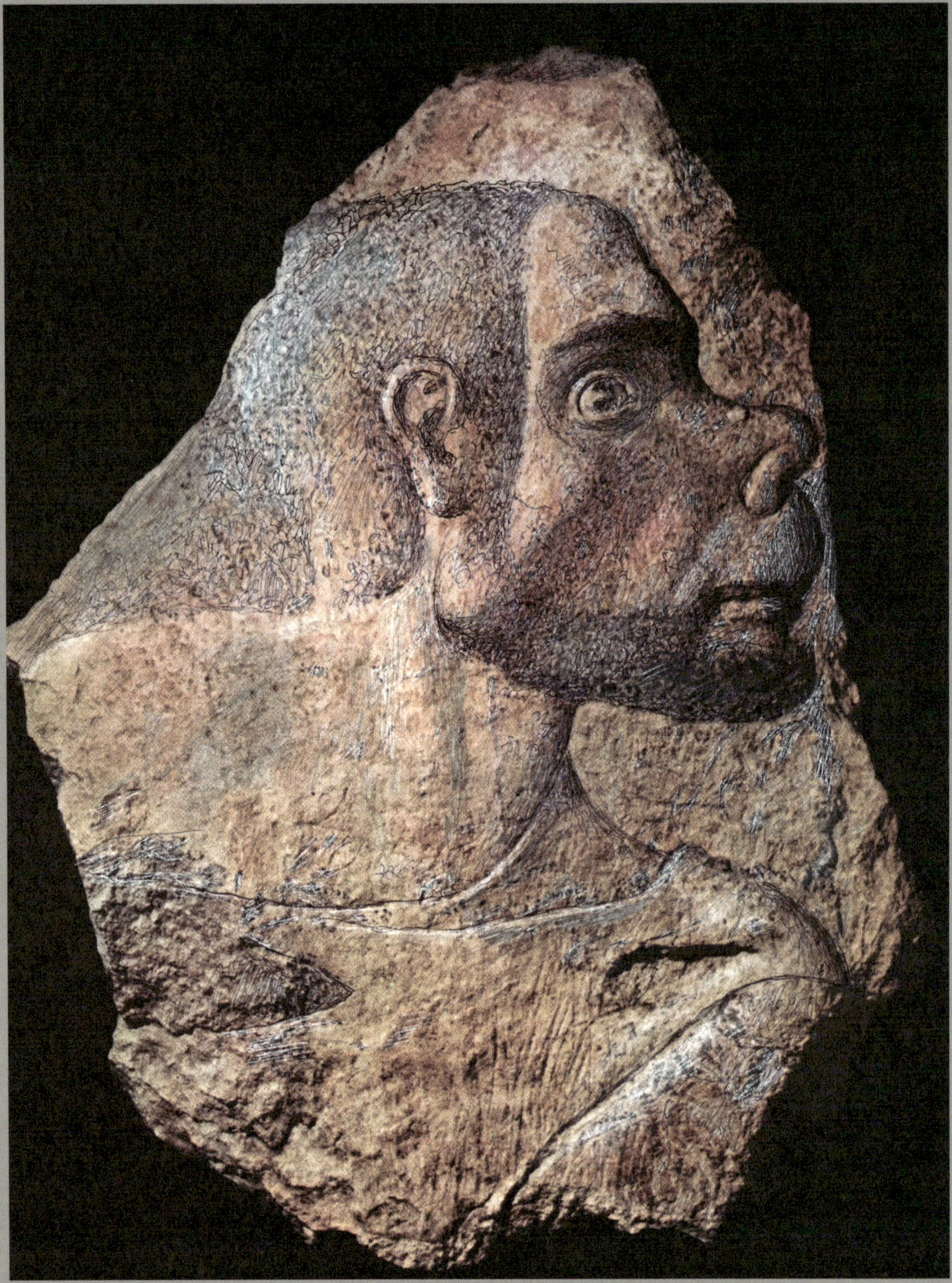

Father of the Predatory Empire-Builders

I have contrived a method with which, from photographs of rust-eaten bronze sculptures or eroded carvings, I can reverse the process of obliteration and bring back almost all vanished details, ornaments and inscriptions.

There is a reproduction of a very early Etruscan mask hammered out of a bronze sheet, that was obliterated in every detail, yet I undertook to re-establish its former shape and brought back half of it, leaving the other half unchanged, just to demonstrate that where previously there had not been any lines, I had been able to "see" and revive them. A naive person may describe my ability to see things that have chemically vanished as a particular genius. However, I think that EVERYTHING that the human mind can dream of, can be done. The term genius, to me, is not a compliment, but a mere classification of a type of mind that makes perfect whatever it concentrates on. The chief ingredient of that genius is… PATIENCE. And with patience, I can return to life things archeological.

My dear friends, the Brays, publishers of the present and future books, brought me a book on prehistoric Art in which this faint relief is reproduced. Instantly, I saw in it the ancestor of Karl Marx, Lenin, Gorky, Malenkow, Yagoda, Brezniev, Tito, Hitler, Mussolini, LaGuardia, John L. Lewis, and Hoffa.

Look at this protruding muzzle of the apeoid and the telltale wart on the nose, an apeoid colony of flesh that is dead because apes live shorter than humans. Only the eyebrows belong to the forehead. What seems the forehead, actually belongs to the top of the head, as is characteristic of primates. The nostrils stand vertically, instead of horizontally as yours and mine, so that through them you can see the inside workings of the Moscovian schemings. Here you have the Commu-Nazi mind that is consumed with the obsessive passion to kill-kill-kill.

The resemblance to the traitors of the world is remarkable. Of course while they were on their way to power, their potato-noses and

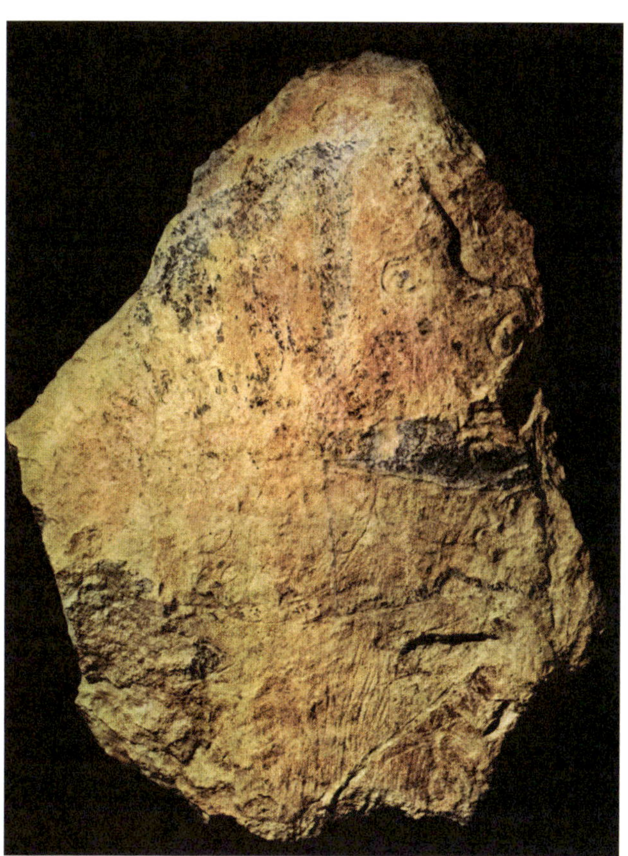

FINDING THE EARLIEST REALISTIC PORTRAIT IN THE HISTORY OF MAN

By Professor Dorothy Garrod, Disney Professor of Archaeology, University of Cambridge

Recent excavations in a prehistoric rock-shelter at Angles-sur-l'Anglin, in the Vienne Department of Central France, have brought to light a remarkable series of limestone blocks, sculptured, engraved and painted by Magdalenian man. These excavations, which are being carried out by Mlle. Suzanne de Saint-Mathurin and myself, with the aid of a grant from the Viking Fund, are still at an early stage, and we have great hope of further discoveries.

The rock-shelter known as Cave à Louis Taillebourg (named from its owner, according to local custom) lies at the foot of limestone cliffs in the thickly-wooded valley of the River Anglin, a mile away from the little mediaeval town of Angles. . . .

By the end of the season it had become clear that the site was not a small cave, as Rousseau had thought, but a great rock-shelter, filled to the roof with earth and stones, extending along the foot of the cliffs to a distance whose limit has not yet been determined. The archaeological horizon, with its charcoal and burnt food remains, was covered by an overburden of fallen rock, due to a partial collapse of the shelter roof which took place after its occupation by Magdalenian man. This made digging a very laborious affair, as a disproportionate amount of time had to be given to removing the rocks in order to uncover even a small area of prehistoric hearth. In spite of this, by the end of September we had obtained a large number of flint tools, together with spearheads fashioned of reindeer antler, pierced shells and teeth, which must have formed part of necklaces, and pendants carved in bone and ivory. . . .

The most astonishing finds, however, were still to come. In the Easter vacation of 1949 we spent a fortnight at Angles carrying out work which was meant to be preparatory to the dig planned for this summer. Our first task was to remove a heap of stones thrown out by M. Rousseau which hampered the approach to the shelter. . . . Within the first half-hour we came upon a magnificent sculptured block showing life-size and in high relief the head and neck of a young ibex, certainly one of the most beautiful and appealing works of this kind yet found in any Palaeolithic site. We were gazing at this with delight when our workman, Edouard Gornay, called out that he had a stone showing traces of paint. This was removed with great precaution, and we saw that under a coating of earth there were not only patches of black paint but an engraved ellipse which looked like an eye; a few seconds later we realised with amazement that a human profile was sculptured on the edge of the block *(Plate 35, p. 224)*. Gornay at once fetched a bucket of water from the river, and we gently washed away the earth until there was revealed the head and shoulders of a Magdalenian hunter, carried out in a combination of painting, engraving and sculpture – the first life-size realistic portrait of a man of the Old Stone Age. After this, a block showing in very high relief the chest and fore-legs of an animal, probably a horse, came as an anti-climax, though it was interesting because made by the same pecking technique as the bison's hoof discovered *in situ* the previous summer. This was the end of sensational discoveries, though the rest of the dump yielded a number of engraved stones of exactly the same type as those already found in the Magdalenian horizon.

Angles-sur-l'Anglin, France, 1949

apron-upperlips could have given their nations the warning hints of things to come. But in America I have methodically been kept speechless by the Anglomerican conspiracy to keep MUTE all those "2nd class citizens" who are of continental derivation, so that their racial genius will become extinct in the presence of the Anglosex dominancy. Thus, the subversives and the traitors could undermine this Amiraculous Civilization and sell it to predatory Russia.

The same pathological ilk has been working in England for generations, against the British State, and is working in Italy as Communists right now. They are everywhere alike, because their bodily misproportions harken to the Yeti and other Manapes who anciently in all countries raped our women, thus producing the bi-species of "ideological" killers.

It were the giant, noble Cro-Magnon men in their cavern-temples who carved and painted these ghouls, so that other Cro-Magnons could see them and get the warning from their looks to guard themselves against sexual mixing. The Greeks later did the same in their morality plays, where actors portrayed Pans (the Feared Ones) who enticed human women in order to rape them.

This Neanderthal was already a mixed specimen, for over his shoulder we see an animal skin that must have been shaved with a flint-chip. Only Humans could have devised and shown how to do this. Also, the Yetinsyn has a chin, small but well indicated. The Manape has no chin.

This sculptured likeness is the most ancient representation of a man known to us. Found at Angles-sur-l'Anglin, Central France.

Galileo Galilei

A physicist and astronomer born in 1564, who finally pleased the Church by dying in 1642. At first he wanted to be a painter, but decided to study medicine instead. As a boy he was already extremely clever in constructing his inventions, and in his nineteenth year, he observed in a local church how the great chandelier, suspended on a very long chain, swung in an extremely slow, almost imperceptible circle once a day, thus discovering the physical law that is named after him and is still demonstrated in every stellar observatory. At twenty-two, he invented the Hydrostatic Balance.

Being poor, he supported himself teaching astrology and astronomy. Indeed, it was the former out of which astronomy evolved, and while the latter became an extraordinarily precise science, astrology remained an almost static system of superstitions.

For generations hence, the learned strata of society in Europe, more out of snobbery than knowledge, had geared their thinking according to Aristotlean teachings. Galileo, however, disagreed with some principles and on one occasion asked his disputants to walk over to the leaning tower of Pisa and wait below, while he climbed it. From the top, he simultaneously dropped two objects, one weighing two pounds, the other ten. Aristotle had claimed that the lighter object would touch the ground a little later than the heavier one, but the two objects traveled the same speed, touching the ground at the same time. Consequently, Galileo was accused of having used some dishonest magical trick, for no one could disprove what the entire world believed. But he always dismissed all authority, trusting only, from the start, his own opinion.

Thus, he also invented the compass, which we still use in our age, unaltered. And, on hearing that somebody in Holland had devised a contraption that made objects across the street look as if they were within touch when you peered through its glass, he proceeded to make four more, each more powerful, till suddenly… he looked at the Moon and saw its mountains. Instantly, he came to the conclusion that the Moon was a planet like ours, which was another unbelievable discovery, for Aristotle had pronounced once and for all, that it was a smoothly polished ball.

Of course, the learned elite of that epoch of backwardness, having been raised to BELIEVE everything that the theologians proclaimed, did not know the term PROGRESS yet. It is now, when no rational mind can accept theological gibberish as KNOWLEDGE, that real progress is made, depending on the very latest scientfic TRUTHS being corrected, footnoted or disproven.

Look at Galileo's eyes! I was able to paint them making him being far, far away from this theology-befuddled world.

If an impertinent fly suddenly sets her rump on my nose, just three inches away from my two eyes, which are 3 and 1/8 inches apart, I will startle you by looking at her, looking horribly cross-eyed. But my eyes return to their normal expression looking at you, across the table,

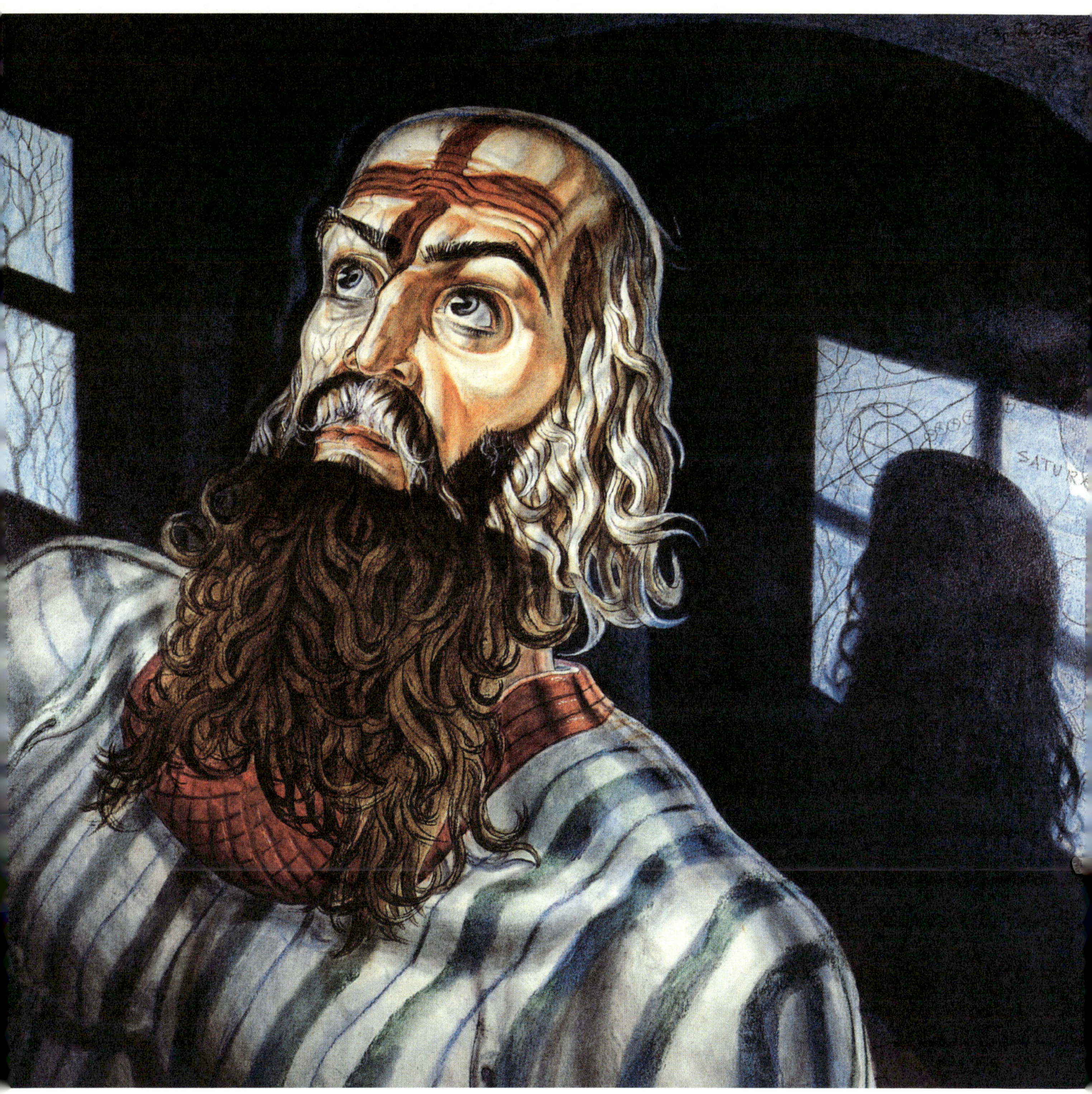

SATUR

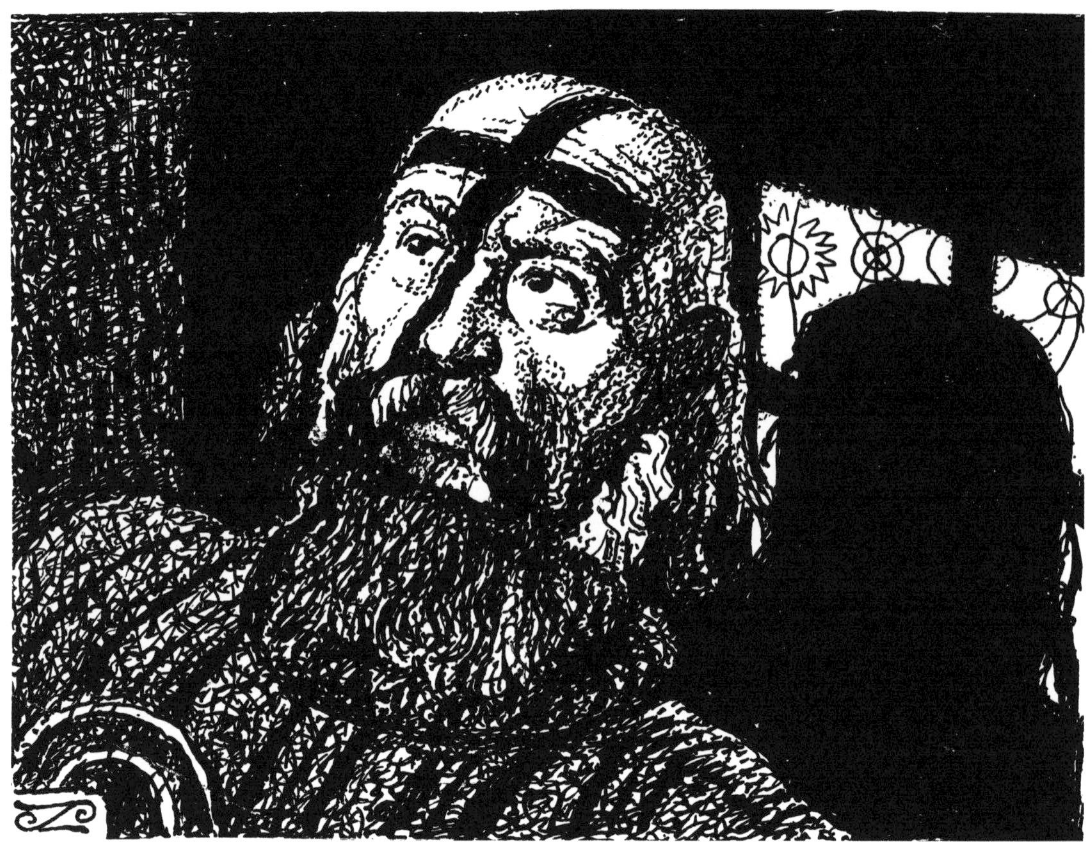

for that distance obliges them to make a "longer" triangle between them and their focal point (since I cannot see both of your eyes at once, the choice comes to one.) The farther you look, let us say to a point on the horizon of a prairie, the more the triangle between the eyes and that point is elongated.

However, when you sit in front of me after speaking with me about my recently departed Joan, my wife, and after saying something meaningless and vanishing behind the curtain of being too far away to still be on this earth, you will notice, without my seeing you, that my eyes, though open, form NO TRIANGLE at all, for their retinas are as far apart as a newborn calf's legs. To convey in sculpture or painting an expression of being lost in thought, perhaps of sobbing before your own grief, on your knees, you must make the eyes look parallel at… nothing.

Galileo, instead of being cherished as mankind's benefactor who gave his Enlightenment when there was none, was packed into prison, where he was torturously kept for many years, to please the Christian God and the Virgin Mary, for to REALLY KNOW was un-Christian.

A Religious Zealot

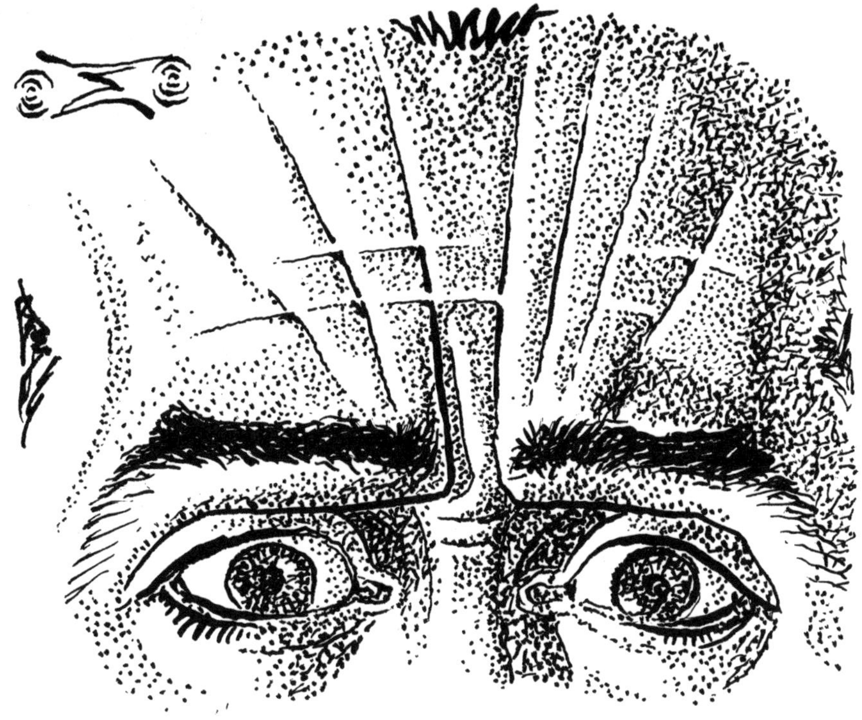

To see is not the same as to comprehend. Though people know that we all wrinkle our brows, no one – despite the passage of a million years – ever pays any attention to these wrinkles, for when talking to one another, we look into each other's eyes.

But I am making a collection of all the unsuspected SYSTEMS of wrinkles, thereby finding a solid base for a new science: EGOGLYPHY.

From the "Zermatism" volume *Egoglyphy*

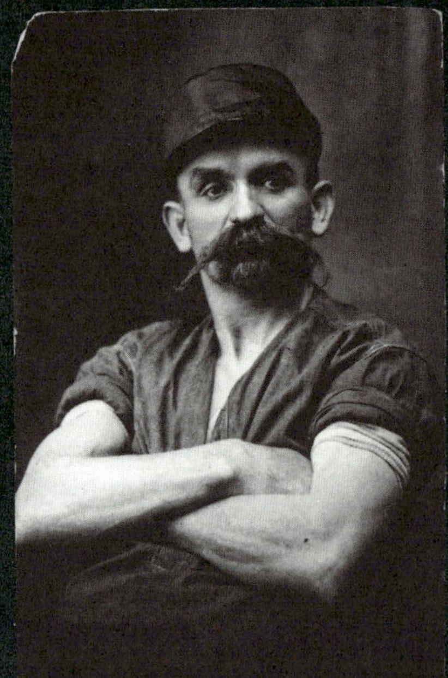

DYONIZY SZUKALSKI
The artist's father, circa 1910

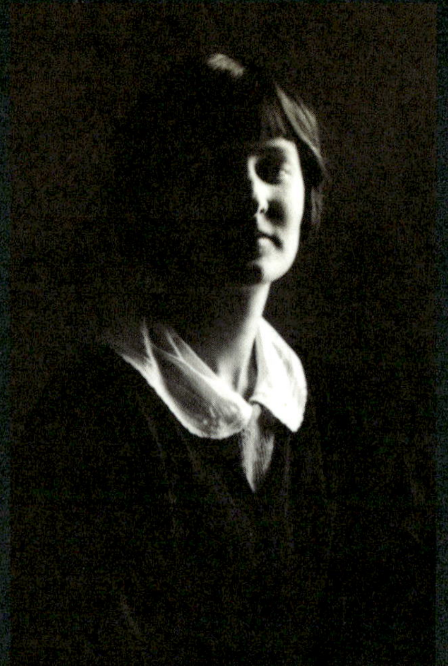

HELEN WALKER
posing for Szukalski, circa 1923

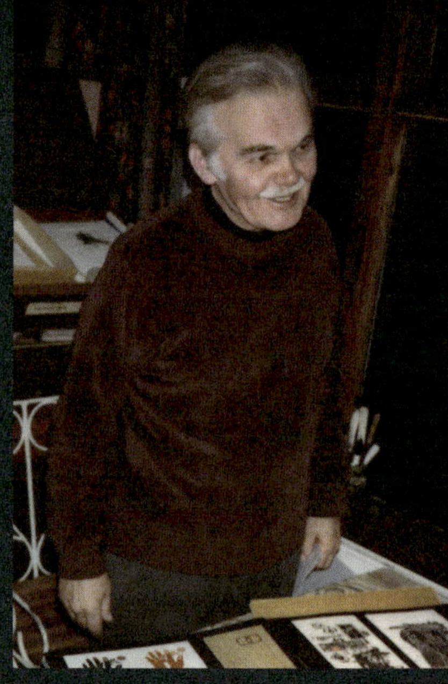

STANISLAW GLIWA
London, 1981

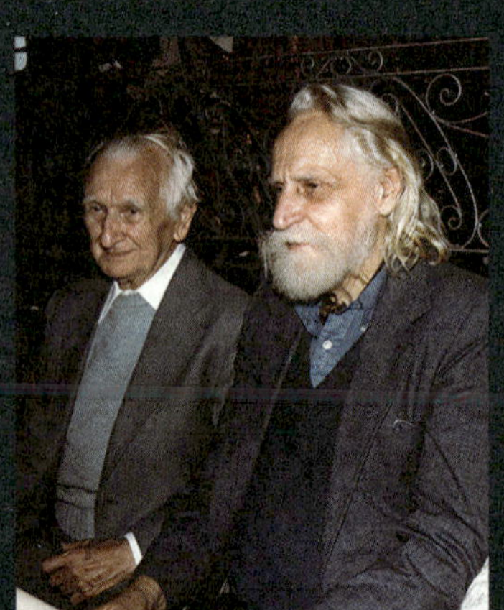

L. DUDAREW-OSSETYNSKI
with the artist, circa 1965

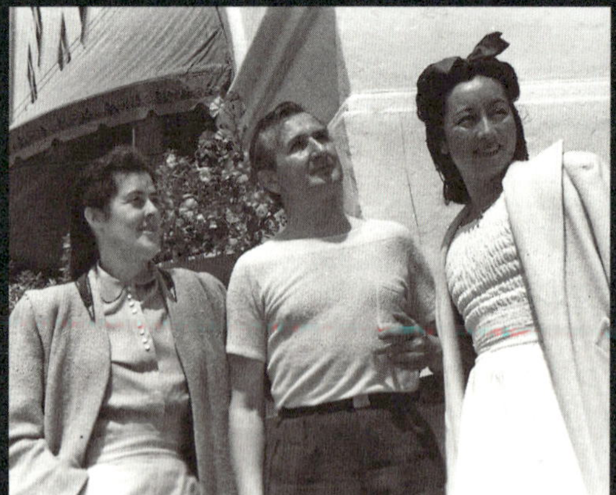

JOAN SZUKALSKI, STANISLAV, AND LOTUS
Laguna Beach, circa 1940

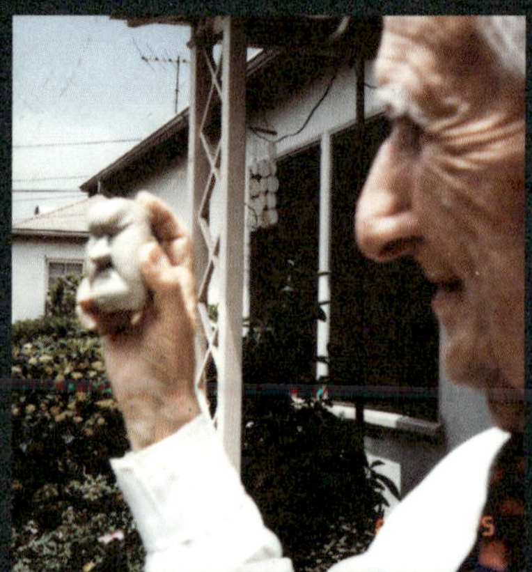

THE FACE OF COMMUNISM
Burbank, California, circa 1982